ACCA

P
R
A
C
T
I
C
E
&
R
E
V
I
S
I
O
N
K
I
T

PAPER F8

AUDIT AND ASSURANCE

FOR EXAMS UP TO JUNE 2015

BPP
LEARNING MEDIA

First edition 2007
Seventh edition January 2013

ISBN 9781 4727 1105 2
(previous ISBN 9781 4453 6649 4)

e-ISBN 9781 4727 1169 4

British Library Cataloguing-in-Publication Data
A catalogue record for this book
is available from the British Library

Published by

BPP Learning Media Ltd
BPP House, Aldine Place
London W12 8AA

www.bpp.com/learningmedia

Printed in the United Kingdom by

Polestar Wheatons
Hennock Road
Marsh Barton
Exeter
EX2 8RP

We are grateful to the Association of Chartered Certified
Accountants for permission to reproduce past
examination questions. The suggested solutions in the
practice answer bank have been prepared by BPP
Learning Media Ltd, except where otherwise stated.

Your learning materials, published by BPP Learning
Media Ltd, are printed on paper obtained from
traceable, sustainable sources.

ii

Contents

A note about copyright

Dear Customer

What does the little © mean and why does it matter?

Your market-leading BPP books, course materials and e-learning materials do not write and update themselves. People write them: on their own behalf or as employees of an organisation that invests in this activity. Copyright law protects their livelihoods. It does so by creating rights over the use of the content.

Breach of copyright is a form of theft – as well as being a criminal offence in some jurisdictions, it is potentially a serious breach of professional ethics.

With current technology, things might seem a bit hazy but, basically, without the express permission of BPP Learning Media:

- Photocopying our materials is a breach of copyright
- Scanning, ripcasting or conversion of our digital materials into different file formats, uploading them to Facebook or emailing them to your friends is a breach of copyright

You can, of course, sell your books, in the form in which you have bought them – once you have finished with them. (Is this fair to your fellow students? We update for a reason.) Please note the e-products are sold on a single user licence basis: we do not supply 'unlock' codes to people who have bought them second-hand.

And what about outside the UK? BPP Learning Media strives to make our materials available at prices students can afford by local printing arrangements, pricing policies and partnerships which are clearly listed on our website. A tiny minority ignore this and indulge in criminal activity by illegally photocopying our material or supporting organisations that do. If they act illegally and unethically in one area, can you really trust them?

Question index

The headings in this checklist/index indicate the main topics of questions, but questions are expected to cover several different topics.

Questions set under the old syllabus *Audit and Internal Review* (AIR) paper are included because their style and content are similar to those which appear in the F8 exam. The questions have been amended to reflect the current exam format.

	Marks	Time allocation Mins	Page number Question	Page number Answer

Part D: Audit evidence

BPP LEARNING MEDIA

Mock exam 1

Mock exam 2

Mock exam 3 (Specimen paper)

Topic index

Listed below are the key Paper F8 syllabus topics and the numbers of the questions in this Kit covering those topics. If you need to concentrate your practice and revision on certain topics or if you want to attempt all available questions that refer to a particular subject, you will find this index useful.

Syllabus topic	Question numbers
Accounting estimates	76, 114, 115, 122
Analytical procedures	42, 47, 67, 79, 80, 95, ME2 Q3
Assurance engagement	3, 4, 7, 23
Audit evidence	46, 67, 85, 98, 102, 106, 107, 114
Audit planning and documentation	28, 30, 32, 35, 38, 42, 44, 47
Audit regulation	2, 3, 4, 9, 25
Audit reporting	112, 119, 121, 122, 123, 124, 125, 126
Audit risk	28, 31, 34, 37, 41, 45, 46, 47, 48, 49, 80, 96, 103
Audit sampling	73, ME2 Q3, 88, 97
CAATs	ME2 Q3, 74, 84, 86, 96, 105
Cash and bank	52, 58, 61, 75, 101
Corporate governance	5, 8, 10, 11, 18, 19, 64
Engagement letters	39
Ethics	3, 6, 12, 13, 14, 16, 19, 107, 118
Experts	72, 94
External audit	7, 21, 23, 24, 25
External confirmations	75
Fraud, laws and regulations	19, 51, 68
Going concern	111, 112, 113, 118, 120, 126
Interim audit	26, 29, 36, 69, 70
Internal audit	11, 12, 17, 20,21, 22, 23, 26, 49, 54, 62, 66, 86, 90
Internal controls	45, 51, 52, 53, 55, 58, 62, 63, 65, 66, 67, 68, 69, 70, 89, 103
Inventory	34, 38, 48, 49, 56, 57, 70, 78, 82, 85, 92, 114, 117
Materiality and misstatements	7, 35, 97, 110, 119
Negative assurance	26, 46
Non-current assets	63, 69, 72, 78, 88, 89, 99
Not-for-profit organisations	45, 60, 104
Payables and accruals	66, 83, 102, 107, 108
Provisions and contingencies	34, 90, 102, 103, 107, 114, 123
Purchases systems	55, 66, 83, 108
Receivables and revenue	68, 75, 76, 107, 114
Sales systems	52, 64
Subsequent events	95, 116, 117, 124, 125
Wages systems	53, 59, 63, 65, 105
Written representations	110, 111, 112, 114

BPP
LEARNING MEDIA

Helping you with your revision

BPP Learning Media – Approved Learning Partner – content

As ACCA's **Approved Learning Partner – content**, BPP Learning Media gives you the **opportunity** to use **exam team reviewed** revision materials. By incorporating the examination team's comments and suggestions regarding syllabus coverage, the BPP Learning Media Practice and Revision Kit provides excellent, **ACCA-approved** support for your revision.

Tackling revision and the exam

Using feedback obtained from ACCA exam team review:

- We look at the dos and don'ts of revising for, and taking, ACCA exams

- We focus on Paper F8; we discuss revising the syllabus, what to do (and what not to do) in the exam, how to approach different types of question and ways of obtaining easy marks

Selecting questions

We provide signposts to help you plan your revision.

- A full **question index**

- A **topic index** listing all the questions that cover key topics, so that you can locate the questions that provide practice on these topics, and see the different ways in which they might be examined

Making the most of question practice

At BPP Learning Media we realise that you need more than just questions and model answers to get the most from your question practice.

- Our **top tips** included for certain questions provide essential advice on tackling questions, presenting answers and the key points that answers need to include

- We show you how you can pick up **easy marks** on some questions, as we know that picking up all readily available marks often can make the difference between passing and failing

- We include **marking guides** to show you what the examiner rewards

- We include **comments from the examiners** to show you where students struggled or performed well in the actual exam

- We refer to the **2014 BPP Study Text** (for exams up to June 2015) for detailed coverage of the topics covered in questions

- In a bank at the end of this Kit we include the **official ACCA answers** to the Specimen paper. Used in conjunction with our answers they provide an indication of all possible points that could be made, issues that could be covered and approaches to adopt.

Attempting mock exams

There are three mock exams that provide practice at coping with the pressures of the exam day. We strongly recommend that you attempt them under exam conditions. **Mock exams 1 and 2** reflect the question styles and syllabus coverage of the exam, and **Mock exam 3** is the Specimen paper.

Revising F8

The F8 paper assumes knowledge of Paper F3 *Financial Accounting*. It is important, therefore, that candidates can apply the knowledge they have gained in this paper to the audit and assurance context of Paper F8.

All questions are compulsory so you must revise the **whole** syllabus. Since the exam includes 12 multiple choice questions in Section A, you should expect questions to cover a large part of the syllabus. Selective revision **will limit** the number of questions you can answer and hence reduce your chances of passing. It is better to go into the exam knowing a reasonable amount about most of the syllabus rather than concentrating on a few topics to the exclusion of the rest.

In Section B, all questions will require a written response but there may be questions requiring the calculation and interpretation of some basic ratios in the context of audit planning or review.

In short, remember that **all** the questions in this paper are compulsory. Therefore, we **strongly advise** that you do not selectively revise certain topics – any topic from the syllabus could be examined. Selective revision will limit the number of questions you can answer and hence reduce your chances of passing this paper.

Question practice

Practising as many exam-style questions as possible will be the key to passing this exam. You must do questions under **timed conditions** and ensure you write full answers to the discussion parts as well as doing the calculations.

Avoid looking at the answer until you have finished a question. Your biggest problem with F8 questions may be knowing how to start, and this needs practice.

Also ensure that you attempt all three mock exams under exam conditions.

Passing the F8 exam

Displaying the right qualities and avoiding weaknesses

In order to pass this paper it is important that you get some of the basics right. These include the following:

Read the question

Again this sounds obvious but is absolutely critical. When you are reading the question think about the following:

- Which technical area is being tested?

  This should let you identify the relevant areas of technical knowledge to draw on.

- What am I being asked to do?

  (We will take a more detailed look at the wording of requirements later.)

- Are there any key dates?

  This is important in questions on inventory. If the inventory count takes place at a time other than the year-end you need to be aware of this.

- What is the status of your client?

  For example is it large or small, is it a new or existing client? This might affect issues such as risk.

- What is the nature of the business?

  This is particularly relevant in planning questions as it will have an impact on risk areas.

- How many marks are allocated to each part of the question so approximately how many points do I need to make?

  When you think about the number of points you need to achieve you need to consider this in relation to the requirement. If you are asked for explanation it is likely that you will score more marks per point than if you are simply asked for a list of points.

You also need to think about the order in which you read information in the question. If the question is scenario based it is important that you read the requirement first so that as you read through the rest of the information you are aware of the key matters/issues which you are looking out for. For example if you are asked for risks in a scenario you can try to identify as many risk factors as possible as you read the detailed information.

You should also try to read the question as 'actively' as possible. Underline key words, annotate the question and link related points together. These points can often serve as the basis for an outline plan.

Understand the requirements

It is important that you can understand and differentiate between the requirements and terms that the examiner typically uses. Here are some examples:

Requirement	Meaning
Explain	Make a point clear, justify a point of view
Describe	Give an account of something, including the key features
Define	Give the meaning of
Recommend	Advise the appropriate actions to pursue in terms the recipient will understand
Discuss	Critically examine an issue
List	Normally punchier points than 'explain' or 'discuss'
Illustrate	Explain by using examples
Audit procedures/audit tests	Actions
Enquiries	Questions
Evidence	Source (eg document) and what it proves

Think and plan

No matter how well prepared you are you are going to have to do some thinking in the exam. Obviously you will be under time pressure, but if used effectively thinking and planning time should not be seen as a waste of time.

Generating ideas can often be a problem at this stage. Remember that your knowledge of key ISAs can serve as a good starting point.

In audit evidence questions you may think about the financial statement assertions (completeness, accuracy, valuation etc). You could also think about the different types of procedures (inspection, observation, inquiry, confirmation, recalculation/reperformance and analytical procedures).

In risk questions it might be helpful to think about the different elements of risk (inherent risk, control risk, detection risk).

Repeating this knowledge will not be sufficient in most cases to pass the question but these ideas can form a very sound basis for developing a good answer.

Keep going back to the requirement and make sure that you really are answering the question. One of the most common errors in auditing papers is identifying the correct point but using it in the wrong way. Make sure that your answer is focused on the requirements. It may be tempting to write everything you know about a particular point but this will not help you to pass the exam. This 'scattergun' approach will attract few, if any, marks.

Producing your answer

Although much of the hard work has been done by the time you get to this stage you need to think carefully about how you put down each point on paper. The way you make the point can make a difference to the number of marks scored. You need to make sure your answers do not suffer from a lack of clarity and precision. This is particularly the case regarding questions on audit evidence. For example lists of tests stating 'check this' and 'check that' without explaining what is being checked and why is likely to score few marks. If you find it difficult to gauge the right level of detail try to imagine that you are explaining the procedure to a junior member of staff. Would they be able to perform the procedure based on your description?

Think about your style. A well structured answer with clearly identifiable points is generally preferable to long paragraphs of text. However, do not fall into the trap of producing note-form answers. This is rarely sufficiently detailed to score marks.

Using the reading time

- Speed read through the question paper, jotting down any ideas that come to you about any of the questions.

- Decide the order in which you are likely to tackle questions (possibly the multiple choice questions first, but possibly last). Decide the order in which you will tackle the longer questions (probably easiest questions first, most difficult questions last).

- Spend the remainder of the reading time looking at the questions in detail analysing scenarios, jotting down answer plans to longer questions. (Any plans written on the question paper should be reproduced in the answer booklet).

- When you can start writing get straight on with the questions you have planned to tackle first. One approach may be to answer first of all the multiple choice questions you think you can answer, and leave those you are less certain about until later. You can return to these after you have answered the longer questions in Section B of the paper.

Gaining the easy marks

Easy marks in this paper tend to fall into three categories.

Multiple choice questions

Some MCQs are easier than others. Answer those that you feel fairly confident about as quickly as you can. Come back later to those you find more difficult. This could be a way of making use of the time in the examination most efficiently and effectively.

Many MCQs will not involve calculations. Make sure that you understand the wording of 'written' MCQs before selecting your answer.

Discussions in Section B questions

A Section B question may separate discussion requirements from calculations, so that you do not need to do the calculations first in order to answer the discussion part. This means that you should be able to gain marks from making sensible, practical comments without having to complete the calculations.

Discussions that are focused on the specific organisation in the question will gain more marks than regurgitation of knowledge. Read the question carefully and more than once, to ensure you are actually answering the specific requirements.

Pick out key words such as 'describe', 'evaluate' and 'discuss'. These all mean something specific.

- 'Describe' means to communicate the key features of
- 'Evaluate' means to assess the value of
- 'Discuss' means to examine in detail by argument

Clearly label the points you make in discussions so that the marker can identify them all rather than getting lost in the detail.

Provide answers in the form requested. Use a report format if asked for and give recommendations if required.

Tackling questions

In summary, you'll improve your chances by following a step-by-step approach along the following lines.

Step 1 **Read the requirement**

Identify the knowledge areas being tested and see precisely what the examiner wants you to do. This will help you focus on what's important in the scenario.

Step 2 **Check the mark allocation**

This shows the depth of answer anticipated and helps you allocate time.

Step 3 **Read the scenario/preamble**

Identify which information is relevant to which part. There are lots of clues in the scenario so make sure you identify those that you should use in your answer.

Step 4 **Plan your answer**

Consider the formats you'll use and discussion points you'll make.

Step 5 **Write your answer**

BPP
LEARNING MEDIA

Exam information

The F8 examiner

The examiner's approach article to F8 was published in 2010. You must make sure you read this article on the ACCA's website as it provides useful information about the F8 exam from the examiner's perspective. It includes a description of the format and style of each question in the exam, along with some indication of how different areas might be examined.

An examiner's approach interview is also available on the F8 area of the ACCA website along with an examiner's analysis interview looking at student performance in various exam sittings, which highlights how students can improve their performance.

The exam paper

The F8 exam is a three-hour paper with 15 minutes of reading time and consists of two sections.

Section A of the exam will consist of multiple choice questions. These questions can cover any part of the syllabus, so it is important to gain a precise knowledge of each of the syllabus areas.

Section B of the exam will comprise four 10-mark written questions and two 20-mark questions. The 10-mark questions will each test a single syllabus area, and may comprise of pure knowledge-based requirements or a short scenario. The 20-mark questions will involve a scenario and will focus predominantly on audit planning, internal control and audit evidence, but other syllabus areas could also be examined.

The pass mark is 50%.

Additional information

The Study Guide provides more detailed guidance on the syllabus.

Useful websites

The websites below provide additional sources of information of relevance to your studies for *Audit and Assurance*.

- www.accaglobal.com

  ACCA's website. The students' section of the website is invaluable for detailed information about the qualification, past issues of *Student Accountant* (including technical articles) and a free downloadable Student Planner App.

- www.bpp.com

  Our website provides information about BPP products and services, with a link to the ACCA website.

- www.ifac.org

  This website provides information on international accounting and auditing issues.

- www.ft.com

  This website provides information about current international business. You can search for information and articles on specific industry groups as well as individual companies.

Questions

AUDIT FRAMEWORK AND REGULATION

Questions 1 – 26 cover Audit framework and regulation, the subject of Part A of the BPP Study Text for F8.

1 Multiple choice questions

85 mins

1   Is the following statement regarding stewardship true or false?

Directors are stewards of the investment made by shareholders in a company.

A   True
B   False

(1 mark)

2   Which **two** of the following are elements of an assurance engagement?

(1)   A three-party relationship
(2)   Suitable criteria
(3)   Determination of materiality
(4)   An engagement letter

A   (1) and (2) only
B   (1) and (3) only
C   (2) and (3) only
D   (1), (2) and (3)

(2 marks)

3   What is the correct order of the following stages involved in the development of an ISA?

(1)   Distribution of exposure draft for public comment
(2)   Consideration of comments received as a result of the exposure draft
(3)   Approval by IAASB members
(4)   Establishment of task force to develop draft standard
(5)   Discussion of proposed standard at a public meeting

A   (1), (5), (4), (3), (2)
B   (3), (4), (1), (2), (5)
C   (4), (5), (1), (2), (3)
D   (5), (4), (2), (1), (3)

(2 marks)

4   Who normally appoints the external auditors of a company?

A   Directors
B   Shareholders
C   Audit committee
D   Senior management

(1 mark)

5   Which of the following is the most appropriate definition of the external audit?

A   The external audit is an exercise carried out by auditors in order to give an opinion on whether the financial statements of a company are materially misstated.

B   The external audit is an exercise carried out in order to give an opinion on the effectiveness of a company's internal control system.

C   The external audit is performed by management to identify areas of deficiency within a company and to make recommendations to mitigate those deficiencies.

D   The external audit provides negative assurance on the truth and fairness of a company's financial statements.

(2 marks)

6   The level of assurance provided by an external audit is absolute.

Is this statement true or false?

A   True
B   False

(1 mark)

7   Which of the following is/are **not** a statutory right of the auditors of a limited liability company?

(1)   A right to attend all directors' meetings and receive all notices and communications relating to such meetings.

(2)   A right to speak at general meetings on any part of the business that concerns them as auditors.

(3)   A right to attend any general meeting and receive all notices and communications relating to such meetings.

A   (1) only
B   (1) and (3)
C   (2) only
D   (2) and (3)

(2 marks)

8   Is the following statement true or false?

In an effective system of corporate governance the directors take responsibility for risk management strategies within the business.

A   True
B   False

(1 mark)

9   Which of the following are recognised threats to independence and objectivity as identified in ACCA's *Code of Ethics and Conduct*?

(1)   Familiarity
(2)   Self-interest
(3)   Integrity
(4)   Advocacy

A   (1), (2), (3) and (4)
B   (1), (2) and (4)
C   (2), (3) and (4)
D   (2) and (4) only

(2 marks)

10   In which of the following situations would the auditor be able to disclose confidential information about a client?

(1)   Disclosure is required by law.
(2)   Disclosure is permitted by law but the auditor has not requested the client's permission.
(3)   The auditor suspects that the client has committed money-laundering offences.

A   (1) and (2) only
B   (1) and (3) only
C   (2) and (3) only
D   (1), (2) and (3)

(2 marks)

11   Andrew Jones has been the key audit partner of X Co, a public interest entity, for seven years. For how long must he be rotated off the audit as a minimum to comply with ACCA's *Code of Ethics and Conduct*?

      A   1 year
      B   2 years
      C   3 years
      D   4 years   **(2 marks)**

12   AAB & Co is the statutory auditor of Y Co, a public interest entity.

      Which of the following services is AAB & Co prohibited from providing to Y Co under any circumstances?

      A   Provision of bookkeeping services
      B   Assistance in the resolution of tax disputes
      C   Internal audit services
      D   Valuation services where the valuation will have a material effect on the financial statements
                                                                                                     (2 marks)

13   Who is ultimately responsible for a company's system of internal controls?

      A   External auditors
      B   Board of directors
      C   Internal auditors
      D   Audit committee   **(2 marks)**

14   Every company must have an audit committee.

      Is this statement true or false?

      A   True
      B   False   **(1 mark)**

15   Which of the following statements is true regarding the audit committee?

      A   An audit committee must comprise at least four independent non-executive directors.

      B   Where there is no internal audit function the audit committee should consider the need for one on an annual basis.

      C   The role and responsibilities of the audit committee are set out in statute.   **(1 mark)**

16   Which of the following are valid disadvantages of having an audit committee?

      A   It can undermine the authority of the board of directors.

      B   The internal audit function may communicate directly with the audit committee rather than with management.

      C   It may be difficult to find non-executive directors with the relevant experience.   **(1 mark)**

17   AB & Co audits DEF Co. In accordance with ACCA *Code of Ethics and Conduct* which **two** of the following circumstances would constitute a threat to objectivity?

      (1)   An employee of AB & Co owns shares in DEF Co but is not part of the audit team
      (2)   The best friend of the engagement partner owns a significant indirect financial interest in DEF Co
      (3)   The audit manager of DEF Co owns a small number of shares in DEF Co
      (4)   The husband of the audit partner owns shares in DEF Co

      A   (1) and (2)
      B   (1) and (4)
      C   (2) and (3)
      D   (3) and (4)   **(2 marks)**

18   Which of the following internal audit assignments is described below?

The examination of the economy, efficiency and effectiveness of activities and processes.

    A   Regulatory compliance audit
    B   Value for money audit
    C   Financial audit
    D   IT audit

(2 marks)

19   Which **two** of the following characteristics apply to internal audit?

    (1)   The purpose is to improve the company's operations.
    (2)   Reports to shareholders on whether the financial statements give a true and fair view of affairs.
    (3)   Auditors may be employees of the company.
    (4)   Evidence is collected in accordance with relevant ISAs.

    A   (1) and (3)
    B   (2) and (4)
    C   (1) and (4)
    D   (2) and (3)

(2 marks)

20   Which type of risk is the internal auditor normally responsible for monitoring?

    A   Audit risk
    B   Business risk
    C   Audit risk and business risk
    D   Neither audit risk nor business risk

(2 marks)

21   Which of the following internal audit assignments aims to monitor management's performance and ensure that company policy is followed?

    A   Value for money
    B   Fraud investigation
    C   Financial
    D   Operational

(2 marks)

22   The format of the internal audit report is governed by statute.

Is this statement true or false?

    A   True
    B   False

(1 mark)

23   Which of the following is a limitation of the internal audit function?

    A   The internal audit report is not circulated to the members.
    B   Internal audit assignments are designed to meet the needs of the business.
    C   Internal auditors may be employees of the company.
    D   Internal auditors may report to an audit committee.

(2 marks)

24   Is the following statement about outsourcing the internal audit function true or false?

One of the advantages of outsourcing the internal audit function is that the company will not need to exercise any controls over the outsourced department.

    A   True
    B   False

(1 mark)

25   Which of the following activities should the internal audit function **not** be involved in?

    A   Monitoring of management's performance
    B   Reviewing adequacy of management information for decision-making purposes
    C   Taking responsibility for the implementation of a new sales ledger system
    D   Assessing compliance with regulation relevant to the business   **(2 marks)**

---

26   The role of the internal audit function in risk management is to identify risk and implement strategies to minimise risks.

Is this statement true or false?

    A   True
    B   False   **(1 mark)**

---

27   Which of the following is **not** a benefit of establishing an audit committee?

    A   Reduced opportunity of fraud, as the audit committee can advise the executive directors on managing the risks in the financial reporting process.

    B   Greater external audit independence, as the audit committee can be responsible for appointing the external auditors

    C   Reduced external audit fees, as the presence of the audit committee reduces audit risk and consequently, the amount of audit procedures required.   **(1 mark)**

---

28   A private company has requested that its auditor prepare a valuation report on a prospective acquisition target in order to help it obtain finance for the acquisition from its bank.

Which **two** of the following threats may arise if the auditor agrees to take on this assignment?

    A   Self-review threat
    B   Familiarity threat
    C   Advocacy threat
    D   Self-interest threat   **(2 marks)**

---

29   Which of the following statements best reflects the auditor's duty of confidentiality?

    A   Auditors must never, under any circumstances, disclose any matters of which they become aware during the course of the audit to third parties, without the permission of the client.

    B   Auditors may disclose any matters in relation to criminal activities to the police or taxation authorities, if requested to do so by the police or a tax inspector.

    C   Auditors may disclose matters to third parties without their client's consent if it is in the public interest, and they must do so if there is a statutory duty to do so.

    D   Auditors may only disclose matters to third parties without their client's consent if the public interest or national security is involved.   **(2 marks)**

---

2 Audit regulation   18 mins

(a)   Explain how ISAs are developed by the International Auditing and Assurance Standards Board (IAASB).
    (5 marks)

(b)   Explain the role of the professional bodies in the regulation of auditors.   **(5 marks)**

    (Total = 10 marks)

3 Regulation and ethics

18 mins

(a) Auditors are regulated by professional bodies and should follow recognised auditing standards such as International Standards on Auditing (ISAs).

Required

Explain why it is important for audits to be conducted in accordance with auditing standards that are common to all audits. **(3 marks)**

(b) The ACCA *Code of Ethics and Conduct* highlights a number of areas in which threats might arise to independence and objectivity.

Required

(i) Explain what is meant by an advocacy threat and give an example of a situation which may create an advocacy threat.

(ii) State the category of threat that arises from an inappropriately close business relationship with a client and give **two** examples of close business relationships that would cause such a threat.

(5 marks)

(c) An audit is one type of assurance engagement, but practitioners may carry out other assurance engagements, such as review engagements.

Required

Describe a review engagement and explain the level of assurance given in such an engagement.   **(2 marks)**

(Total = 10 marks)

4 Assurance and regulation

18 mins

(a) Explain the terms 'accountability', 'stewardship' and 'agency' and explain how they can be applied to the relationship between directors and shareholders. **(3 marks)**

(b) (i) State the objective of:

- A review engagement
- An audit engagement

(ii) Explain how the differing objectives of the two engagements affects the level of assurance given.

(4 marks)

(c) Briefly explain the relationship between International Standards on Auditing set by the IAASB and national standards and regulations applicable to auditing. **(3 marks)**

(Total = 10 marks)

5 Corporate governance

18 mins

(a) The UK Corporate Governance Code is an established code of best practice and applies to all companies with Premium Listing of equity shares in the UK.

Required

List the advantages and disadvantages of voluntary codes of corporate governance. **(3 marks)**

(b) List four main principles relating to board effectiveness as recommended by the UK Corporate Governance Code. **(4 marks)**

(c) Briefly explain the function of an audit committee. **(3 marks)**

(Total = 10 marks)

6 Ethical issues

(a) List and briefly explain the main threats to independence and objectivity as identified in the ACCA's *Code of Ethics and Conduct*. For each threat you should give an example. **(5 marks)**

(b) Briefly explain the fundamental principle of confidentiality and list the circumstances in which obligatory and voluntary disclosure of information may be applicable. **(5 marks)**

(Total = 10 marks)

7 True and fair, ISAs and assurance engagements (6/10) (amended)
18 mins

Professional accountants are often involved in many different types of work ranging from performing the external audit to providing wider assurance services.

Where an external audit is carried out the auditor is required to give an opinion as to whether the financial statements present fairly the activities of the business over a period of time.

(a) Explain the concept of **true** and **fair** presentation. **(3 marks)**
(b) Explain the status of International Standards on Auditing. **(2 marks)**
(c) Describe the elements of an assurance engagement. **(5 marks)**

(Total = 10 marks)

8 NorthCee (Pilot Paper) (amended)
18 mins

You are the audit manager in the audit firm of Dark & Co. One of your audit clients is NorthCee Co, a company specialising in the manufacture and supply of sporting equipment.

You are now planning the audit for the year ending 31 December 20X7. Following an initial meeting with the directors of NorthCee, you have established that NorthCee plans to obtain a listing on a recognised stock exchange. The directors have established an audit committee, as required by corporate governance regulations, although no further action has been taken in this respect. Information on the listing is not yet public knowledge.

Required

(a) Explain the actions that the board of directors of NorthCee Co must take in order to meet corporate governance requirements for the listing of NorthCee Co. **(6 marks)**

(b) Explain why your audit firm will need to communicate with NorthCee Co's audit committee for this and future audits. **(4 marks)**

(Total = 10 marks)

9 International Standards on Auditing (AIR 6/06) (amended)
18 mins

International Standards on Auditing (ISAs) are produced by the International Auditing and Assurance Standards Board (IAASB), which is a technical committee of the International Federation of Accountants (IFAC). In recent years, there has been a trend for more countries to implement the ISAs rather than produce their own auditing standards.

A friend is considering joining ACCA as a trainee accountant however, she is concerned about the extent of regulations which auditors have to follow and does not understand why ISAs have to be used in your country.

Required

Explain the regulatory framework which applies to auditors.

You should cover the following points:

(a)	Describe the role of the IAASB.	**(2 marks)**
(b)	Explain the process involved in issuing an ISA.	**(4 marks)**
(c)	Explain the extent to which an auditor must follow ISAs.	**(4 marks)**

(Total = 10 marks)

10 Jumper (AIR 6/06) (amended)   18 mins

You are the audit manager of Tela & Co, a medium sized firm of accountants. Your firm has just been asked for assistance from Jumper & Co, a firm of accountants in an adjacent country. This country has just introduced a requirement for entities to conform to the internationally recognised codes on corporate governance and Jumper & Co has a number of clients where the codes are not being followed. One example of this, from SGCC, a listed company, is shown below. As your country already has appropriate corporate governance codes in place, Jumper & Co have asked for your advice regarding the changes necessary in SGCC to achieve appropriate compliance with corporate governance codes.

Extract from financial statements regarding corporate governance

Mr Sheppard is the Chief Executive Officer and board chairman of SGCC. He appoints and maintains a board of five executive and two non-executive directors. While the board sets performance targets for the senior managers in the company, no formal targets are set and no review of board policies is carried out. Board salaries are therefore set and paid by Mr Sheppard based on his assessment of all the board members, including himself, and not their actual performance.

Internal controls in the company are monitored by the senior accountant, although detailed review is assumed to be carried out by the external auditors; SGCC does not have an internal audit department.

Annual financial statements are produced, providing detailed information on past performance.

Required

Describe **five** corporate governance weaknesses faced by SGCC and provide recommendations to address each weakness, to ensure compliance with corporate governance principles.   **(10 marks)**

11 Conoy (6/09) (amended)   18 mins

Conoy Co designs and manufactures luxury motor vehicles. The company employs 2,500 staff and consistently makes a net profit of between 10% and 15% of sales. Conoy Co is not listed; its shares are held by 15 individuals, most of them from the same family. The maximum shareholding is 15% of the share capital.

The executive directors are drawn mainly from the shareholders. There are no non-executive directors because the company legislation in Conoy Co's jurisdiction does not require any. The executive directors are very successful in running Conoy Co, partly from their training in production and management techniques, and partly from their 'hands-on' approach providing motivation to employees.

The board are considering a significant expansion of the company. However, the company's bankers are concerned with the standard of financial reporting as the financial director (FD) has recently left Conoy Co. The board are delaying provision of additional financial information until a new FD is appointed.

Conoy Co does have an internal audit department, although the chief internal auditor frequently comments that the board of Conoy Co do not understand his reports or provide sufficient support for his department or the internal control systems within Conoy Co. The board of Conoy Co concur with this view. Anders & Co, the external auditors have also expressed concern in this area and the fact that the internal audit department focuses work on control systems, not financial reporting. Anders & Co are appointed by and report to the board of Conoy Co.

The board of Conoy Co are considering a proposal from the chief internal auditor to establish an audit committee. The committee would consist of one executive director, the chief internal auditor as well as three new appointees. One appointee would have a non-executive seat on the board of directors.

Required

Describe **five** roles of the audit committee and explain how Conoy Co would benefit from each of these roles.

(10 marks)

12 Goofy (6/11) (amended)   18 mins

You are an audit manager in NAB & Co, a large audit firm which specialises in the audit of retailers. The firm currently audits Goofy Co, a food retailer, but Goofy Co's main competitor, Mickey Co, has approached the audit firm to act as auditors. Both companies are highly competitive and Goofy Co is concerned that if NAB & Co audits both companies then confidential information could pass across to Mickey Co.

Required

(a)   Explain the safeguards that your firm should implement to ensure that this conflict of interest is properly managed. **(4 marks)**

Goofy Co's year end is 31 December, which is traditionally a busy time for NAB & Co. Goofy Co currently has an internal audit department of five employees but they have struggled to undertake the variety and extent of work required by the company, hence Goofy Co is considering whether to recruit to expand the department or to outsource the internal audit department. If outsourced, Goofy Co would require a team to undertake monthly visits to test controls at the various shops across the country, and to perform ad hoc operational reviews at shops and head office.

Goofy Co is considering using NAB & Co to provide the internal audit services as well as remain as external auditors.

Required

(b)   Discuss the advantages and disadvantages to both Goofy Co and NAB & Co of outsourcing their internal audit department. **(6 marks)**

(Total = 10 marks)

13 L V Fones (6/10) (amended)   18 mins

You are the audit manager of Jones & Co and you are planning the audit of LV Fones Co, a listed company, which has been an audit client for four years and specialises in manufacturing luxury mobile phones.

During the planning stage of the audit you have obtained the following information. The employees of LV Fones Co are entitled to purchase mobile phones at a discount of 10%. The audit team has in previous years been offered the same level of staff discount.

During the year the financial controller of LV Fones was ill and hence unable to work. The company had no spare staff able to fulfil the role and hence a qualified audit senior of Jones & Co was seconded to the client for three months. The audit partner has recommended that the audit senior work on the audit as he has good knowledge of the client. The fee income derived from LV Fones was boosted by this engagement and along with the audit and tax fee, now accounts for 16% of the firm's total fees.

From a review of the correspondence files you note that the partner and the finance director have known each other socially for many years and in fact went on holiday together last summer with their families. As a result of this friendship the partner has not yet spoken to the client about the fee for last year's audit, 20% of which is still outstanding.

Required

(a)   Explain the ethical threats which may affect the independence of Jones & Co's audit of LV Fones Co.

(5 marks)

(b)   For each threat explain how it might be avoided. **(5 marks)**

(Total = 10 marks)

14 Ethics

In order for the public to have confidence in the work performed by professional accountants it is essential to have a system of regulation. Regulation can take the form of both ethical and statutory guidance.

(a) State the **five** threats contained within ACCA's *Code of Ethics and Conduct* and for each threat list **one** example of a circumstance that might create the threat.   (5 marks)

(b) Explain the auditor's ethical responsibilities with regard to client confidentiality and when they have:

   (i)   An obligatory responsibility
   (ii) A voluntary responsibility

   To disclose client information.   (5 marks)

                                                                                  (Total = 10 marks)

15 Code of Ethics and Conduct   18 mins

(a) Explain each of the five fundamental principles of ACCA's *Code of Ethics and Conduct*.   (5 marks)

Compliance with the fundamental principles in ACCA's *Code of Ethics and Conduct* can be threatened in a number of ways.

Required

(b) List the **five** ethical threats to independence and objectivity and for **each** threat identify **one** example of a circumstance that may create the threat.   (5 marks)

                                                                                  (Total = 10 marks)

16 Stark (12/08) (amended)   18 mins

You are a manager in the audit firm of Ali & Co; and this is your first time you have worked on one of the firm's established clients, Stark Co. The main activity of Stark Co is providing investment advice to individuals regarding saving for retirement, purchase of shares and securities and investing in tax efficient savings schemes. Stark is regulated by the relevant financial services authority.

You have been asked to start the audit planning for Stark Co, by Mr Son, a partner in Ali & Co. Mr Son has been the engagement partner for Stark Co, for the previous nine years and so has excellent knowledge of the client. Mr Son has informed you that he would like his daughter Zoe to be part of the audit team this year; Zoe is currently studying for her first set of fundamentals papers for her ACCA qualification. Mr Son also informs you that Mr Far, the audit senior, received investment advice from Stark Co during the year and intends to do the same next year.

In an initial meeting with the finance director of Stark Co, you learn that the audit team will not be entertained on Stark Co's yacht this year as this could appear to be an attempt to influence the opinion of the audit. Instead, he has arranged a balloon flight costing less than one-tenth of the expense of using the yacht and hopes this will be acceptable. The director also states that the fee for taxation services this year should be based on a percentage of tax saved and trusts that your firm will accept a fixed fee for representing Stark Co in a dispute regarding the amount of sales tax payable to the taxation authorities.

Required

(a) Explain the ethical threats which may affect the auditor of Stark Co.   (5 marks)
(b) For each ethical threat, discuss how the effect of the threat can be mitigated.   (5 marks)

                                                                                  (Total = 10 marks)

17 Governance

18 mins

SPD Co has been trading for 10 years and provides advice on pensions and other financial products to its clients. SPD Co is not listed on a stock exchange but is regulated by a government body which aims to ensure that financial advice is always provided in the best interests of the customer.

SPD Co has seen rapid growth in its revenue over the last 12 months and expects this trend to continue. In order to meet client demand and offer new products, SPD Co is now offering more complex financial products than it has ever done before.

SPD Co is also in need of additional funding to support its anticipated growth and will shortly need to approach its bank to determine whether additional funding might be available. The Board of Directors is also considering whether or not SPD Co should obtain a listing on a stock exchange as an alternative way of raising finance.

(a)	Explain what is meant by 'corporate governance' and explain why it is important.	**(3 marks)**
(b)	Discuss the benefits to SPD Co of establishing an internal audit department.	**(7 marks)**

(Total = 10 marks)

18 Serena (12/11) (amended)

18 mins

Serena VDW Co has been trading for over 20 years and obtained a listing on a stock exchange five years ago. It provides specialist training in accounting and finance.

The listing rules of the stock exchange require compliance with corporate governance principles, and the directors are fairly confident that they are following best practice in relation to this. However, they have recently received an email from a significant shareholder, who is concerned that Serena VDW Co does not comply with corporate governance principles.

Serena VDW Co's board is comprised of six directors; there are four executives who originally set up the company and two non-executive directors who joined Serena VDW Co just prior to the listing. Each director has a specific area of responsibility and only the finance director reviews the financial statements and budgets.

The chief executive officer, Daniel Brown, set up the audit committee and he sits on this sub-committee along with the finance director and the non-executive directors. As the board is relatively small, and to save costs, Daniel Brown has recently taken on the role of chairman of the board. It is the finance director and the chairman who make decisions on the appointment and remuneration of the external auditors. Again, to save costs, no internal audit function has been set up to monitor internal controls.

The executive directors' remuneration is proposed by the finance director and approved by the chairman. They are paid an annual salary as well as a generous annual revenue related bonus.

Since the company listed, the directors have remained unchanged and none have been subject to re-election by shareholders.

Required

Describe **five** corporate governance weaknesses faced by Serena VDW Co and provide recommendations to address each weakness, to ensure compliance with corporate governance principles. **(10 marks)**

19 Orange (6/12) (amended)

18 mins

You are the audit manager of Currant & Co and you are planning the audit of Orange Financials Co (Orange), who specialise in the provision of loans and financial advice to individuals and companies. Currant & Co has audited Orange for many years.

The directors are planning to list Orange on a stock exchange within the next few months and have asked if the engagement partner can attend the meetings with potential investors. In addition, as the finance director of Orange is likely to be quite busy with the listing, he has asked if Currant & Co can produce the financial statements for the current year.

During the year, the assistant finance director of Orange left and joined Currant & Co as a partner. It has been suggested that due to his familiarity with Orange, he should be appointed to provide an independent partner review for the audit.

Once Orange obtains its stock exchange listing it will require several assignments to be undertaken, for example, obtaining advice about corporate governance best practice. Currant & Co is very keen to be appointed to these engagements, however, Orange has implied that in order to gain this work Currant & Co needs to complete the external audit quickly and with minimal questions/issues.

The finance director has informed you that once the stock exchange listing has been completed, he would like the engagement team to attend a weekend away at a luxury hotel with his team, as a thank you for all their hard work. In addition, he has offered a senior member of the engagement team a short-term loan at a significantly reduced interest rate.

Required

(a) Explain **five** ethical threats which may affect the independence of Currant & Co's audit of Orange Financials Co. **(5 marks)**

(b) For each threat explain how it might be reduced to an acceptable level. **(5 marks)**

(Total = 10 marks)

20 Internal audit function   18 mins

(a) List the types of activity normally carried out by internal audit departments. **(3 marks)**

(b) Briefly explain the main differences between internal and external auditors in respect of objectives, scope of work and reporting responsibilities. **(3 marks)**

(c) Explain the term 'outsourcing' and list **three** advantages and **three** disadvantages of outsourcing an internal audit department. **(4 marks)**

(Total = 10 marks)

21 Internal audit responsibilities   18 mins

(a) There are similarities and differences between the responsibilities of internal and external auditors. Both internal and external auditors have responsibilities relating to the prevention, detection and reporting of fraud, for example, but their responsibilities are not the same.

Required

Explain the difference between the responsibilities of internal auditors and external auditors for the prevention, detection and reporting of fraud and error. **(6 marks)**

(b) ISA 610 *Using the work of internal auditors* provides guidance to external auditors on the use of internal audit work.

Required

List and explain the various criteria that should be considered by external auditors when assessing whether to place reliance on work performed by internal audit. **(4 marks)**

(Total = 10 marks)

22 MonteHodge (6/08) (amended)   18 mins

MonteHodge Co has total revenue of $253 million and employs 1,200 people in 15 different locations. The company provides various financial services, from giving pension and investment advice to individuals, to maintaining cash books and cash forecasting in small to medium-sized companies. It is owned by six shareholders, who belong to the same family; it is not listed on any stock exchange and the shareholders have no intention of applying for a listing. However, an annual audit is required by statute and additional regulation of the financial services sector is expected in the near future.

Most employees are provided with online, real-time computer systems, which present financial and stock market information to enable the employees to provide up-to-date advice to their clients. Accounting systems record income, which is based on fees generated from investment advice. Expenditure is mainly fixed, being salaries, office rent, lighting and heating, etc. Internal control systems are limited; the directors tending to trust staff and being more concerned with making profits than implementing detailed controls.

Four of the shareholders are board members, with one member being the chairman and chief executive officer. The financial accountant is not qualified, although has many years experience in preparing financial statements.

Required

Discuss the arguments for and against having an internal audit department in MonteHodge Co. **(10 marks)**

23 Avocado (6/12) (amended) 18 mins

Avocado International Co (Avocado) is a manufacturer of African-inspired wooden toys. You are an audit manager of Lime & Co, Avocado's external auditor.

(a) Avocado's finance director has expressed an interest in Lime & Co performing other review engagements in addition to the external audit. However, he is unsure how much assurance would be gained via these engagements and how this differs to the assurance provided by an external audit.

Required

Identify and explain the level of assurance provided by an external audit and other review engagements.

(2 marks)

Avocado's directors are considering establishing an internal audit department next year, and the finance director has asked about the differences between internal audit and external audit and what impact, if any, establishing an internal audit department would have on future external audits performed by Lime & Co.

Required

(b) Distinguish between internal audit and external audit. **(4 marks)**

(c) Explain the potential impact on the work performed by Lime & Co during the interim and final audits, if Avocado International Co was to establish an internal audit department. **(4 marks)**

(Total = 10 marks)

24 Wood Industries (AIR 6/05) (amended) 18 mins

You are the audit manager of Wood Industries Co (Wood), a limited liability company. The company's annual revenue is over $10 million.

Required

(a) Compare the responsibilities of the directors and auditors regarding the published financial statements of Wood. **(6 marks)**

(b) The directors of Wood have prepared a cash flow forecast for submission to the bank. They have asked you as the auditor to provide a limited assurance report on this forecast.

Required

Briefly explain the difference between reasonable and limited assurance, outlining the advantages to the directors of providing limited assurance on their cash flow forecast. **(4 marks)**

(Total = 10 marks)

25 Regulation and limitations (12/12) (amended)

18 mins

(a) In order for auditors to operate effectively and to provide an opinion on an entity's financial statements, they are given certain rights.

Required

State **three** rights of an auditor, excluding those related to resignation and removal. **(3 marks)**

(b) Explain the overall authority of International Standards on Auditing (ISAs) and how they are applied in individual countries. **(4 marks)**

(c) Describe **three** limitations of external audits. **(3 marks)**

(Total = 10 marks)

26 Brampton (12/09)

18 mins

You are the senior in charge of the audit of Brampton Co for the year ending 31 January 2010 and are currently planning the year-end audit. Brampton specialises in the production of high quality bread of various kinds.

During the interim audit you noted that, in the present economic downturn, the company has suffered as its costs are increasing and its prices have been higher than its competitors because of lower production runs. One indicator of the problems facing the company is that it has consistently used a bank overdraft facility to finance its activities.

At the time of the interim audit you had discussed with company management what actions were being taken to improve the liquidity of the company and you were informed that the company plans to expand its facilities for producing white bread as this line had maintained its market share. The company has asked its bank for a loan to finance the expansion and also to maintain its working capital generally.

To support its request for a loan, the company has prepared a cash flow forecast for the two years from the end of the reporting period and the internal audit department has reported on the forecast to the board of directors. However, the bank has said it would like a report from the external auditors to confirm the accuracy of the forecast. Following this request the company has asked you to examine the cash flow forecast and then to report to the bank.

Required

(a) Explain whether you would be able to rely on the work of the internal auditors. **(5 marks)**

(b) Describe **three** procedures you would adopt in your examination of the cash flow forecast. **(3 marks)**

(c) Explain the kind of assurance you could give in the context of the request by the bank. **(2 marks)**

(Total = 10 marks)

PLANNING AND RISK ASSESSMENT

Questions 27 – 49 cover Planning and risk assessment, the subject of Part B of the BPP Study Text for F8.

27 Multiple choice questions

74 mins

1   When gaining an understanding of the specific business operations of an audit client which of the following matters would an auditor need to consider?

   A   Accounting principles and industry specific practices relevant to the client's business
   B   Acquisitions or disposals of the client's business activities
   C   Leasing of property, plant or equipment for use in the client's business
   D   Products or services and markets of the client's business   **(2 marks)**

2   Which of the following statements about materiality are correct?

   (1)   Information is material if its omission or misstatement could influence the economic decisions of users of the financial statements.

   (2)   Materiality is based on the auditor's experience and judgement.

   (3)   Materiality is always based on revenue.

   (4)   Materiality should only be calculated at the planning stage of the audit.

   A   (1), (2) and (3)
   B   (1), (3) and (4)
   C   (1) and (2)
   D   (2) and (4)   **(2 marks)**

3   Which of the following procedures must the auditor use to obtain an understanding of the entity and its environment in accordance with ISA 315 *Identifying and assessing the risks of material misstatement through understanding the entity and its environment*?

   (1)   Analytical procedures
   (2)   Inquiry
   (3)   Confirmation
   (4)   Reperformance

   A   (1), (2) and (3)
   B   (1) and (2)
   C   (2), (3) and (4)
   D   (1) and (4)   **(2 marks)**

4   What are the two elements of the risk of material misstatement at the assertion level?

   A   Inherent risk and detection risk
   B   Audit risk and detection risk
   C   Inherent risk and control risk
   D   Detection risk and control risk   **(2 marks)**

5   What are the purposes of planning the audit?

   (1)   To ensure appropriate attention is devoted to different areas of the audit
   (2)   To identify potential problem areas
   (3)   To facilitate delegation of work to audit team members
   (4)   To ensure the audit is completed within budget and time restraints

   A   (1), (2), (3) and (4)
   B   (1), (3) and (4)
   C   (1), (2) and (3)
   D   (2) and (3)   **(2 marks)**

6 Which of the following factors influence the form and content of audit working papers?

    (1)   Risks of material misstatement
    (2)   Exceptions identified
    (3)   Nature of the package used for documentation
    (4)   Cost to the audit

    A   (1), (2) and (4)
    B   (1), (3) and (4)
    C   (1) and (2)
    D   (2) and (4)   (2 marks)

7 Performance materiality levels are higher than the materiality for the financial statements as a whole.

Is this statement true or false?

    A   True
    B   False   (1 mark)

8 'Audit risk' represents the risk that the auditor will give an inappropriate opinion on the financial statements when the financial statements are materially misstated. Which of the following categories of risk can be controlled by the auditor?

Category of risk:

    (1)   Control risk
    (2)   Detection risk
    (3)   Sampling risk

    A   (1) and (2)
    B   (2) only
    C   (1) and (3)
    D   (2) and (3)   (2 marks)

9 Which of the following statements are **correct** with regard to the relationship between the audit plan and the audit strategy for an external audit engagement?

    (1)   The audit plan should be developed before the audit strategy is established.
    (2)   The audit plan and the audit strategy should be established and developed at the same time.
    (3)   The overall audit strategy should be more detailed than the audit plan.
    (4)   The audit strategy should be established before the audit plan is developed.

    A   (1) and (3)
    B   (2) only
    C   (3) and (4)
    D   (4) only   (2 marks)

10 The definition of the risk of material misstatement is 'Inherent Risk × Control Risk × Detection Risk'.

Is this statement true or false?

    A   True
    B   False   (1 mark)

11 Which of the following would normally be included in the audit plan?

    A   Reporting objectives
    B   Industry-specific financial reporting requirements
    C   Nature, timing, and the extent of planned risk assessment procedures   (1 mark)

12   Is the following statement regarding the interim audit true or false?

The higher the risk of material misstatement the more likely it is that the auditor will decide to perform substantive procedures during the interim audit rather than at the period end.

A   True
B   False   **(1 mark)**

13   The auditor of Z Co has set performance materiality at $100,000. Which of the following could be the materiality level set for the financial statements as a whole for Z Co?

A $80,000
B $95,000
C $100,000
D $120,000   **(2 marks)**

14   Which of the following statements is/are true with respect to analytical procedures?

(1)   Analytical procedures can be used throughout the audit.
(2)   Analytical procedures must be used as risk assessment procedures.

A   (1) only
B   (2) only
C   (1) and (2)
D   Neither (1) nor (2)   **(2 marks)**

15   Who is responsible for the prevention and detection of fraud?

A   Internal auditors
B   External auditors
C   Those charged with governance and management
D   The audit committee   **(2 marks)**

16   Which of the following is an appropriate response to the risks of material misstatement at the assertion level?

A   Emphasising the need to maintain professional scepticism
B   Increasing supervision on the audit
C   Increasing sample sizes for inspecting recorded assets where assets are more susceptible to theft
D   Making changes to the nature of the audit procedures   **(2 marks)**

17   The auditor of A Co wishes to reduce audit risk. Which of the following actions could the auditor take to achieve this?

(1)   Increase sample sizes
(2)   Reduce control risk
(3)   Assign more experienced staff to the engagement team

A   (1) only
B   (2) only
C   (1) and (3)
D   (2) and (3)   **(2 marks)**

18   Which of the following correctly describes the auditors' responsibilities in accordance with ISA 240 *The auditor's responsibilities relating to fraud in an audit of financial statements*?

   A   The auditor is responsible for the prevention and detection of fraud and error.

   B   The auditor is not responsible for the prevention of fraud and error but is responsible for detection.

   C   The auditor is responsible for obtaining reasonable assurance that the financial statements are free from material misstatement whether caused by fraud or error.

   D   The auditor is responsible for detecting all errors and should attempt to detect fraud where information comes to light as a result of standard audit procedures.   **(2 marks)**

19   Is the following statement true or false regarding the retention of working papers?

   ACCA recommends that working papers should be retained for a minimum period of five years.

   A   True
   B   False   **(1 mark)**

20   When determining whether the preconditions for an audit are present the auditor obtains management's agreement that it acknowledges and understands its responsibilities. Which of the following is **not** included in the agreement obtained by the auditor?

   A   Management's responsibility for preparing the financial statements

   B   Management's responsibility for internal control to enable the preparation of financial statements which are free from material misstatement

   C   Management's responsibility to provide the auditor with all information relevant to the preparation of the financial statements

   D   Management's responsibility to prevent and detect fraud   **(2 marks)**

21   Which of the following **must** be included in an audit engagement letter?

   A   Arrangements concerning the use of experts
   B   Obligations to make audit working papers available to other parties
   C   Expected form and content of any reports
   D   Basis on which fees are computed   **(2 marks)**

22   It is not the auditor's responsibility to ensure that the entity complies with relevant laws and regulations.

   Is this statement true or false?

   A   True
   B   False   **(1 mark)**

23   F Co owns a chain of four restaurants, and is subject to national regulation concerning hygiene in the food preparation process. Non-compliance can result in a large fine, or closure of the restaurant concerned.

   As F Co's external auditor, what is your responsibility regarding the company's compliance with the hygiene regulations?

   A   Actively prevent and detect non-compliance with the regulations
   B   Perform specific audit procedures to identify possible non-compliance
   C   Obtain sufficient appropriate audit evidence about F Co's compliance with the regulations
   D   Nothing – the food hygiene regulations do not have a direct effect on the financial statements

   (1 mark)

24   In accordance with ISA 250 *Consideration of laws and regulations in an audit of financial statements* what are the responsibilities of the external auditor?

A   To obtain sufficient appropriate evidence regarding compliance with laws and regulations that have both a direct and indirect effect on the financial statements

B   To obtain sufficient appropriate evidence regarding compliance with laws and regulations that have a direct effect on the financial statements only

C   To obtain sufficient appropriate evidence regarding compliance with laws and regulations that have an indirect effect on the financial statements only

D   To prevent and detect all non-compliance with laws and regulations which affect the business

(2 marks)

28 Audit risk and planning   18 mins

(a)   State the objective of the statutory audit and explain how carrying out the audit in accordance with ISAs helps the auditor to achieve that objective.   **(4 marks)**

(b)   ISA 315 *Identifying and assessing the risks of material misstatement through understanding the entity and its environment* sets out matters that should be documented during the planning stage of an audit.
Required

List **six** matters that should be documented during audit planning.   **(3 marks)**

(c)   ISA 230 *Audit documentation* provides guidance to auditors in respect of audit working papers.

Required

List **six** factors which affect the form and content of audit working papers.   **(3 marks)**

(Total = 10 marks)

29 Interim audit   18 mins

An audit is often carried out in more than one sitting, especially when there are tight reporting deadlines. The auditors will carry out an interim audit during the period under review followed by a final audit shortly after the year end.

Required

(a)   Explain the types of audit procedures which are likely to be carried out during an interim audit.   **(4 marks)**

(b)   Describe the impact of the work done at the interim audit on the final audit.   **(2 marks)**

(c)   Assuming an interim audit has taken place and work on internal controls was carried out, list the factors the auditor should consider when deciding how much more work is needed at the final audit in relation to internal controls.   **(4 marks)**

(Total = 10 marks)

30 Audit planning   18 mins

During the planning process, the auditor will develop an audit strategy and also produce a detailed audit plan. They will also make an assessment of the level of materiality to be used during the audit.

Required

(a)   State the purpose of the 'audit strategy' and describe **two** areas that would be covered by the audit strategy.

(3 marks)

(b)   Explain what an 'audit plan' is and give **two** examples of items that would ordinarily be included in the audit plan.   **(3 marks)**

(c)   Define the term 'performance materiality' and explain how it is determined.   **(4 marks)**

    (Total = 10 marks)

31 Mason Air Services   18 mins

Mason Air Services is a company that provides specialist helicopter support to the emergency services and the coastguard. Two owner managers (directors) set up the company nine years ago.

You are the audit senior and you are planning the audit for the year ended 31 December 20X0. Following a recent visit to the client you have ascertained the following information.

The company maintains a helicopter fleet comprising a range of aircraft types and carrying specialist equipment. The company also trains and provides specialist pilots.

Under the terms of a five year contract, they charge an annual fee to their customers to cover the maintenance, storage and testing of the aircraft and equipment. The annual fee is payable in advance each year with the first annual payment being paid on the date the contract commences.

Customers are then also charged an additional fee per 'flying hour' based on the usage of an aircraft. This charge per flying hour is also set out in the contract. However, when preparing sales invoices, rather than going back to the contract the financial controller said they use the last invoice to pick up the hourly charge.

Their customers comprise solely of the police, the ambulance service, the fire service and the coastguard. The contracts in place are all of a similar value and are considered by management to be very profitable. The company has always made a healthy profit before interest and tax.

However, Mason Air Services owns the helicopters and funded the original purchase of each aircraft with a secured loan carrying substantial interest charges. As a result the anticipated draft profits for 20X0 after interest and tax are relatively modest at around $500,000 for the year when compared with the expected revenue of $45m.

The contract with the police force expires in March 20X1 and the police are trying to substantially reduce the amount they pay annually and per flying hour in the wake of government cuts. It is thought that the contract will be put out to tender, and another aircraft provider may also bid for the contract. A new contract for the provision of air ambulances was signed during the year with increased flying hour charges.

Although no new helicopters have been purchased during the year to 31 December 20X0 there has been a lot of re-fitting, replacement and adding of specialist equipment to some of the aircraft. This has been necessary to keep up with the latest developments in search and rescue, and to maintain the aircraft to the high standard required under the contracts in place.

The company maintains around $2m of aircraft spares which are included within inventory. Approximately a quarter of this value is made up of specialist equipment taken out of aircraft when it was replaced by newer or more advanced equipment. The directors have estimated the value of this equipment and have included it within inventory as they say it still works as well as it did when it was installed.

Required

Using the information provided, describe **five** audit risks and explain the auditor's response to each risk in planning the audit of Mason Air Services.   **(10 marks)**

32 Bingsby   18 mins

You are an audit senior working for Sams Co and are now commencing the planning of the annual audit of Bingsby Co (Bingsby), which owns and runs a chain of gastro pubs in the southwest of England. The date is 4 December 20X9 and Bingsby's year end is 31 December 20X9.

Bingsby has proved to be very popular in recent years. This year, it saw its revenue from sales of food and drink increase by 15% compared to the previous year. In view of its success, the directors are considering plans to expand the business by acquiring other pubs in the region. 70% of Bingsby's takings are paid in cash, with the remainder being paid by credit card.

For the first time this year, Bingsby has outsourced its payroll function to a firm of accountants called Ricks & Co. Payroll costs form a substantial cost in Bingsby's statement of profit or loss. Ricks & Co prepare the payroll records and update it for starters and leavers based on information provided by Bingsby.

A series of payroll reports are securely e-mailed to Bingsby each month and reviewed by the appropriate management. Payments are made to employees on the basis of a net pay report provided and journals are put through to reflect the wages costs and related liabilities.

Required

(a) List and explain the purpose of **three** of the main sections of an audit strategy document and for each section, provide an example relevant to Bingsby. **(6 marks)**

(b) Describe the audit team's responsibilities in relation to obtaining an understanding of the services provided by Ricks & Co when planning the audit of Bingsby. **(4 marks)**

(Total = 10 marks)

33 Risks and professional scepticism   18 mins

Auditors are required to plan and perform an audit with professional scepticism, to exercise professional judgement and to comply with ethical standards.

Required

(a) Explain what is meant by 'professional scepticism' and why it is so important that the auditor maintains professional scepticism throughout the audit. **(3 marks)**

(b) Define 'professional judgement' and describe two areas where professional judgement is applied when planning an audit of financial statements. **(3 marks)**

(c) Discuss the importance of assessing risks at the planning stage of an audit. **(4 marks)**

(Total = 10 marks)

34 Sleeptight   18 mins

You are an audit senior for Mills & Co and are in the process of planning the audit of Sleeptight Co, which has been an audit client of Mills & Co for several years.

Sleeptight's principal activity is the manufacture and sale of expensive high quality beds. Each bed is crafted by hand in the company's workshop, and personalised in accordance with each customer's specific requirements.

The shares in Sleeptight are owned by the two joint Managing Directors who are sisters, Anna and Sophie Jones. Both have a number of other business interests. As a result, they only spend a few days a week working at the company and rely on the small accounts department to keep the finances in order and to keep them informed. There is no finance director but the financial controller is a qualified accountant.

Sleeptight requires customers who place an order to pay a deposit of 40% of the total order value at the time the order is placed. The beds will take 4 to 8 weeks to build, and the remaining 60% of the order value is due within a week of the final delivery. Risks and rewards of ownership of the beds do not pass to the customer until the beds are delivered and signed for. Beds also come with a two year guarantee and the financial controller has made a provision in respect of the expected costs to be incurred in relation to beds still under guarantee.

The company undertakes a full count of raw materials at the year end. The quantities are recorded on inventory sheets and the financial controller assigns the costs based on the cost assigned in the previous year or, if there was no cost last year, using the latest invoice. Most beds are made of oak or other durable woods and the cost of these raw materials is known to fluctuate considerably.

It is expected that work in progress will be insignificant this year, but there will be a material amount of finished goods awaiting dispatch. Anna Jones will estimate the value of these finished goods and has said she will take into account the order value when doing so.

Required

Using the information provided, describe **five** audit risks and explain the auditor's response to each risk in planning the audit of Sleeptight Co. **(10 marks)**

35 Materiality and documentation (12/10) (amended)   18 mins

(a) ISA 320 *Materiality in Planning and Performing an Audit* provides guidance on the concept of materiality in planning and performing an audit.

Required

Define materiality and explain how the level of materiality is assessed. **(5 marks)**

(b) ISA 230 *Audit Documentation* deals with the auditor's responsibility to prepare audit documentation for an audit of financial statements.

Required

Explain **five** benefits of documenting audit work. **(5 marks)**

(Total = 10 marks)

36 Interim v final audit (AIR 12/04) (amended)   18 mins

The external audit process for the audit of large entities generally involves two or more recognisable stages. One stage involves understanding the business and risk assessment, determining the response to assessed risk, testing of controls and a limited amount of substantive procedures. This stage is sometimes known as the interim audit. Another stage involves further tests of controls and substantive procedures and audit finalisation procedures. This stage is sometimes known as the final audit.

Required

Describe and explain the main audit procedures and processes that take place during the interim and final audits of a large entity. **(10 marks)**

37 Donald (6/11) (amended)   18 mins

Donald Co operates an airline business. The company's year end is 31 July 20X1.

You are the audit senior and you have started planning the audit. Your manager has asked you to have a meeting with the client and to identify any relevant audit risks so that the audit plan can be completed. From your meeting you ascertain the following:

In order to expand their flight network, Donald Co will need to acquire more airplanes; they have placed orders for another six planes at an estimated total cost of $20m and the company is not sure whether these planes will be received by the year end. In addition the company has spent an estimated $15m on refurbishing their existing planes. In order to fund the expansion Donald Co has applied for a loan of $25m. It has yet to hear from the bank as to whether it will lend them the money.

The company receives bookings from travel agents as well as directly via their website. The travel agents are given a 90-day credit period to pay Donald Co, however, due to difficult trading conditions a number of the receivables are struggling to pay. The website was launched in 20X0 and has consistently encountered difficulties with customer complaints that tickets have been booked and paid for online but Donald Co has no record of them and hence has sold the seat to another customer.

Donald Co used to sell tickets via a large call centre located near to their head office. However, in May they closed it down and made the large workforce redundant.

Required

Using the information provided, describe **five** audit risks and explain the auditor's response to each risk in planning the audit of Donald Co. **(10 marks)**

38 Bridgford Products

18 mins

Your firm, Ovette & Co, has been appointed as the auditor of Bridgford Products, a large company. The company sells televisions, DVD players and Blu-ray Disc players to electrical retailers.

You are planning the audit for the year ended 31 January 20X9. The audit for the year ended 31 January 20X8 was carried out by another firm of auditors.

Information obtained from a client visit

During a recent visit to the company you obtained the following information.

(i)   The company installed a new computerised inventory control system which has operated from 1 June 20X8. As the inventory control system records inventory movements and current inventory quantities, the company is proposing:

  •   To use the inventory quantities on the computer to value the inventory at the year-end
  •   Not to carry out an inventory count at the year-end

(ii)   You are aware there have been reliability problems with the company's products, which have resulted in legal claims being brought against the company by customers, and customers refusing to pay for the products.

(iii)   Sales have increased during the year ended 31 January 20X9 by attracting new customers and offering extended credit. The new credit arrangements allow customers three months credit before their debt becomes overdue, rather than the one month credit period allowed previously. As a result of this change, trade receivables age has increased from 1.6 to 4.1 months.

Required

(a)   Explain why it is important for auditors to plan their audit work.   **(4 marks)**

(b)   Describe **three** matters you will consider in planning the audit and explain the further action you will take concerning the information you obtained during your recent visit to the company.   **(6 marks)**

(Total = 10 marks)

39 Cinnamon

18 mins

Curcuma & Co, a firm of Chartered Certified Accountants, has recently obtained a new audit client, Cinnamon Brothers Co (Cinnamon), whose year end is 31 December. Cinnamon requires its audit to be completed by the end of February; however, this is a very busy time for Curcuma and so it intends to use more junior staff as they are available. Additionally, in order to save time and cost, Curcuma has not contacted Cinnamon's previous auditors.

Required

(a)   Describe the steps that Curcuma & Co should take in relation to Cinnamon:

  (i)   Prior to accepting the audit   **(5 marks)**
  (ii)   To confirm whether the preconditions for the audit are in place   **(3 marks)**

(b)   State **four** matters that should be included within an audit engagement letter.   **(2 marks)**

(Total = 10 marks)

40 Cardamom

(a)   ISA 260 *Communication with Those Charged with Governance* deals with the auditor's responsibility to communicate with those charged with governance in relation to an audit of financial statements.

Required

Describe **two** specific responsibilities of those charged with governance.   **(2 marks)**

(b)   Cardamom Co (Cardamom) operates from 20 different locations in one country. The accounting systems are designed and implemented from the company's head office by the internal audit department.

Cardamom has an internal audit department of six staff, all of whom have been employed at the company for a minimum of five years and some for as long as 15 years. In the past, the chief internal auditor appoints staff within the internal audit department, although the chief executive officer (CEO) is responsible for appointing the chief internal auditor. The chief internal auditor reports directly to the finance director. The finance director also assists the chief internal auditor in deciding on the scope of work of the internal audit department.

Required

Explain the issues which limit the independence of the internal audit department in Cardamom Co. Recommend a way of overcoming each issue.   **(8 marks)**

(Total = 10 marks)

41 South

ISA 315 *Identifying and Assessing the Risks of Material Misstatement Through Understanding the Entity and Its Environment* requires auditors to obtain an understanding of the entity and its environment, including its internal control.

Required

(a)   Explain why obtaining an understanding of the entity and its environment is important for the auditor.

(4 marks)

(b)   Your firm has recently been appointed as the auditor to South, a private company that runs seven supermarkets situated in the southern area of the UK. You are currently planning your firm's first audit of South and are now aware of the following information after a preliminary visit to South's head office.

The company installed a new till system in all supermarkets four months before the year end. The new till system is linked to the accounting system at head office and automatically posts transactions to the accounting system. Previously journals were made manually based on totals on till rolls.

After a number of people living close to one of South's stores became seriously ill, the source of the illness was traced back to meat the customers had purchased from South. Legal proceedings were commenced against South by a number of customers during the financial year. However the outcome of the legal proceedings is uncertain, as it is unclear whether the fault lies with South for incorrectly storing the meat or with the local farmer who may have contaminated the meat prior to it being supplied to South.

Required

Using the information provided, describe **three** audit risks and explain the auditor's response to each risk in planning the audit of South.   **(6 marks)**

(Total = 10 marks)

42 Planning, analytical procedures and interim audit   18 mins

(a)   ISA 300 *Planning an Audit of Financial Statements* provides guidance to assist auditors in planning an audit.

Required

Explain the benefits of audit planning.   **(4 marks)**

(b)   ISA 520 *Analytical procedures* provides guidance on the use of analytical procedures during the course of the external audit. Analytical procedures can be used as substantive audit procedures during audit fieldwork, as well as during planning and review.

Required

Identify **four** factors to consider when using analytical procedures at the planning stage of the audit.
                                                                                            (2 marks)

(c)   Explain the difference between the interim audit and the final audit.   **(4 marks)**

                                                                                      (Total = 10 marks)

43 Specs4You (AIR 6/07)   36 mins

ISA 230 *Audit documentation* establishes standards and provides guidance regarding documentation in the context of the audit of financial statements.

Required

(a)   List the purposes of audit working papers.   **(3 marks)**

(b)   You have recently been promoted to audit manager in the audit firm of Trums & Co. As part of your new responsibilities, you have been placed in charge of the audit of Specs4You Co, a long established audit client of Trums & Co. Specs4You Co sells spectacles; the company owns 42 stores where customers can have their eyes tested and choose from a range of frames.

Required

List the documentation that should be of assistance to you in familiarising yourself with Specs4You Co. Describe the information you should expect to obtain from each document.   **(8 marks)**

(c)   The time is now towards the end of the audit, and you are reviewing working papers produced by the audit team. An example of a working paper you have just reviewed is shown below.

Client Name **Specs4You Co**   Year end **30 April**   Page **xxxxx**

Working paper **Payables transaction testing**

                                                        Prepared by   Date
                                                        Reviewed by **CW**   Date **12 June 20X7**

Audit assertion: To make sure that the purchases day book is correct.

Method: Select a sample of 15 purchase orders recorded in the purchase order system. Trace details to the goods received note (GRN), purchase invoice (PI) and the purchase day book (PDB) ensuring that the quantities and prices recorded on the purchase order match those on the GRN, PI and PDB.

Test details: In accordance with audit risk, a sample of purchase orders were selected from a numerically sequenced purchase order system and details traced as stated in the method. Details of items tested can be found on another working paper.

Results: Details of purchase orders were normally correctly recorded through the system. Five purchase orders did not have any associated GRN, PI and were not recorded in the PDB. Further investigation showed that these orders had been cancelled due to a change in spectacle specification. However, this does not appear to be a system weakness as the internal controls do not allow for changes in specification.

Conclusion: Purchase orders are completed recorded in the purchase day book.

Required

Explain why the working paper shown above does not meet the standards normally expected of a working paper.

Note. You are not required to reproduce the working paper.

(9 marks)

(Total = 20 marks)

44 Tempest (AIR 12/05)   36 mins

(a) ISA 300 *Planning an audit of financial statements* states that an auditor must plan the audit.

   Explain why it is important to plan an audit.   **(5 marks)**

(b) You are the audit manager in charge of the audit of Tempest, a limited liability company. The company's year end is 31 December, and Tempest has been a client for seven years. The company purchases and resells fittings for ships including anchors, compasses, rudders, sails etc. Clients vary in size from small businesses making yachts to large companies maintaining large luxury cruise ships. No manufacturing takes place in Tempest.

   Information on the company's financial performance is available as follows:

	20X7 Forecast	20X6 Actual
	$'000	$'000
Revenue	45,928	40,825
Cost of sales	(37,998)	(31,874)
Gross profit	7,930	8,951
Administration costs	(4,994)	(4,758)
Distribution costs	(2,500)	(2,500)
Net profit	436	1,693
Non-current assets (at carrying amount)	3,600	4,500
Current assets		
Inventory	200	1,278
Receivables	6,000	4,052
Cash and bank	500	1,590
Total assets	10,300	11,420
Capital and reserves		
Share capital	1,000	1,000
Accumulated profits	5,300	5,764
Total shareholders' funds	6,300	6,764
Non-current liabilities	1,000	2,058
Current liabilities	3,000	2,598
	10,300	11,420

Other information

The industry that Tempest trades in has seen moderate growth of 7% over the last year.

- Non-current assets mainly relate to company premises for storing inventory. Ten delivery vehicles are owned with a carrying amount of $300,000.

- One of the directors purchased a yacht during the year.

- Inventory is stored in ten different locations across the country, with your firm again having offices close to seven of those locations.

- A computerised inventory control system was introduced in August 20X7. Inventory balances are now obtainable directly from the computer system. The client does not intend to count inventory at the year-end but rely instead on the computerised inventory control system.

Required

Using the information provided above, prepare the audit strategy for Tempest for the year ending 31 December 20X7. **(15 marks)**

(Total = 20 marks)

45 EuKaRe (12/08)   36 mins

(a)   Explain the term 'audit risk' and the three elements of risk that contribute to total audit risk.   **(4 marks)**

The EuKaRe charity was established in 1960. The charity's aim is to provide support to children from disadvantaged backgrounds who wish to take part in sports such as tennis, badminton and football.

EuKaRe has a detailed constitution which explains how the charity's income can be spent. The constitution also notes that administration expenditure cannot exceed 10% of income in any year.

The charity's income is derived wholly from voluntary donations. Sources of donations include:

(i)   Cash collected by volunteers asking the public for donations in shopping areas

(ii)   Cheques sent to the charity's head office

(iii)   Donations from generous individuals. Some of these donations have specific clauses attached to them indicating that the initial amount donated (capital) cannot be spent and that the income (interest) from the donation must be spent on specific activities, for example, provision of sports equipment.

The rules regarding the taxation of charities in the country EuKaRe is based are complicated, with only certain expenditure being allowable for taxation purposes and donations of capital being treated as income in some situations.

Required

(b)   Identify areas of inherent risk in the EuKaRe charity and explain the effect of each of these risks on the audit approach.   **(12 marks)**

(c)   Explain why the control environment may be weak at the charity EuKaRe.   **(4 marks)**

(Total = 20 marks)

46 Serenity (AIR 12/06) (amended)   36 mins

(a)   ISA 315 *Identifying and assessing the risks of material misstatement through understanding the entity and its environment* requires the auditor to perform risk assessment procedures which include obtaining an understanding of the entity and its environment, including its internal control.

Required

(i)   Explain the purpose of risk assessment procedures.   **(3 marks)**

(ii)   Outline the sources of audit evidence the auditor can use as part of risk assessment procedures.   **(3 marks)**

(b)   Mal & Co, an audit firm, has seven partners. The firm has a number of audit clients in different industrial sectors, with a wide range of fee income.

An audit partner of Mal & Co has just delegated to you the planning work for the audit of Serenity Co. This company provides a range of mobile communication facilities and this will be the second year your firm has provided audit services.

You have just met with the financial controller of Serenity prior to agreeing the engagement letter for this year. The controller has informed you that Serenity has continued to grow quickly, with financial accounting systems changing rapidly and appropriate control systems being difficult to maintain. Additional services in terms of review and implementation of control systems have been requested. An internal audit department

has recently been established and the controller wants you to ensure that external audit work is limited by using this department.

You have also learnt that Serenity is to market a new type of mobile telephone, which is able to intercept messages from law enforcement agencies. The legal status of this telephone is unclear at present and development is not being publicised.

The granting of the licence to market the mobile telephone is dependent on the financial stability of Serenity. The financial controller has indicated that Mal & Co may be asked to provide a report to the mobile telephone licensing authority regarding Serenity's cash flow forecast for the year ending December 20X7 to support the licence application.

Required

As part of your risk assessment procedures for the audit of Serenity Co for the year ending 31 December 20X6, identify and describe the issues to be considered when providing services to this client.　**(10 marks)**

(c)　Explain the term 'negative assurance' and why this is used when reporting on a cash flow forecast.

(4 marks)

(Total = 20 marks)

47 Redsmith (12/10)　　　　　　　　　　　　　　　　　　　　**36 mins**

(a)　In agreeing the terms of an audit engagement, the auditor is required to agree the basis on which the audit is to be carried out. This involves establishing whether the preconditions for an audit are present and confirming that there is a common understanding between the auditor and management of the terms of the engagement.

Required

Describe the process the auditor should undertake to assess whether the **preconditions** for an audit are present.　**(3 marks)**

(b)　List **four** examples of matters the auditor may consider when obtaining an understanding of the entity.

(2 marks)

(c)　You are the audit senior of White & Co and are planning the audit of Redsmith Co for the year ended 30 September 2010. The company produces printers and has been a client of your firm for two years; your audit manager has already had a planning meeting with the finance director. He has provided you with the following notes of his meeting and financial statement extracts.

Redsmith's management were disappointed with the 2009 results and so in 2010 undertook a number of strategies to improve the trading results. This included the introduction of a generous sales-related bonus scheme for their salesmen and a high profile advertising campaign. In addition, as market conditions are difficult for their customers, they have extended the credit period given to them.

The finance director of Redsmith has reviewed the inventory valuation policy and has included additional overheads incurred this year as he considers them to be production related. He is happy with the 2010 results and feels that they are a good reflection of the improved trading levels.

Financial statement extracts for the year ended 30 September

	DRAFT 2010 $m	ACTUAL 2009 $m
Revenue	23.0	18.0
Cost of sales	(11.0)	(10.0)
Gross Profit	12.0	8.0
Operating expenses	(7.5)	(4.0)
Profit before interest and taxation	4.5	4.0
Inventory	2.1	1.6
Receivables	4.5	3.0
Cash	–	2.3
Trade payables	1.6	1.2
Overdraft	0.9	–

Required

Using the information above:

(i) Calculate **five** ratios, for **both** years, which would assist the audit senior in planning the audit.

(5 marks)

(ii) From a review of the above information and the ratios calculated, explain the audit risks and describe the appropriate responses to these risks. **(10 marks)**

(Total = 20 marks)

48 Abrahams (12/11)   36 mins

(a) Explain the components of audit risk and, for each component, state an example of a factor which can result in increased audit risk. **(6 marks)**

Abrahams Co develops, manufactures and sells a range of pharmaceuticals and has a wide customer base across Europe and Asia. You are the audit manager of Nate & Co and you are planning the audit of Abrahams Co whose financial year end is 31 January. You attended a planning meeting with the finance director and engagement partner and are now reviewing the meeting notes in order to produce the audit strategy and plan. Revenue for the year is forecast at $25 million.

During the year the company has spent $2.2 million on developing several new products. Some of these are in the early stages of development whilst others are nearing completion. The finance director has confirmed that all projects are likely to be successful and so he is intending to capitalise the full $2.2 million.

Once products have completed the development stage, Abrahams begins manufacturing them. At the year end it is anticipated that there will be significant levels of work in progress. In addition the company uses a standard costing method to value inventory; the standard costs are set when a product is first manufactured and are not usually updated. In order to fulfil customer orders promptly, Abrahams Co has warehouses for finished goods located across Europe and Asia; approximately one third of these are third party warehouses where Abrahams just rents space.

In September a new accounting package was introduced. This is a bespoke system developed by the information technology (IT) manager. The old and new packages were not run in parallel as it was felt that this would be too onerous for the accounting team. Two months after the system changeover the IT manager left the company; a new manager has been recruited but is not due to start work until January.

In order to fund the development of new products, Abrahams has restructured its finance and raised $1 million through issuing shares at a premium and $2.5 million through a long-term loan. There are bank covenants attached to the loan, the main one relating to a minimum level of total assets. If these covenants are breached then the loan becomes immediately repayable. The company has a policy of revaluing land and buildings, and the finance director has announced that all land and buildings will be revalued as at the year end.

The reporting timetable for audit completion of Abrahams Co is quite short, and the finance director would like to report results even earlier this year.

Required

(b)   Using the information provided, identify and describe **five** audit risks and explain the auditor's response to each risk in planning the audit of Abrahams Co.   **(10 marks)**

(c)   Describe substantive procedures you should perform to obtain sufficient appropriate evidence in relation to:

      (i)   Inventory held at the third party warehouses
      (ii)   Use of standard costs for inventory valuation   **(4 marks)**

                                                                                                   (Total = 20 marks)

49 Sunflower (12/12)   36 mins

Sunflower Stores Co (Sunflower) operates 25 food supermarkets. The company's year end is 31 December 2012. The audit manager and partner recently attended a planning meeting with the finance director and have provided you with the planning notes below.

You are the audit senior, and this is your first year on this audit. In order to familiarise yourself with Sunflower, the audit manager has asked you to undertake some research in order to gain an understanding of Sunflower, so that you are able to assist in the planning process. He has then asked that you identify relevant audit risks from the notes below and also consider how the team should respond to these risks.

Sunflower has spent $1.6 million in refurbishing all of its supermarkets; as part of this refurbishment programme their central warehouse has been extended and a smaller warehouse, which was only occasionally used, has been disposed of at a profit. In order to finance this refurbishment, a sum of $1.5 million was borrowed from the bank. This is due to be repaid over five years.

The company will be performing a year-end inventory count at the central warehouse as well as at all 25 supermarkets on 31 December. Inventory is valued at selling price less an average profit margin as the finance director believes that this is a close approximation to cost.

Prior to 2012, each of the supermarkets maintained their own financial records and submitted returns monthly to head office. During 2012 all accounting records have been centralised within head office. Therefore at the beginning of the year, each supermarket's opening balances were transferred into head office's accounting records. The increased workload at head office has led to some changes in the finance department and in November 2012 the financial controller left. His replacement will start in late December.

Required

(a)   List **five** sources of information that would be of use in gaining an understanding of Sunflower Stores Co, and for each source describe what you would expect to obtain.   **(5 marks)**

(b)   Using the information provided, describe **five** audit risks and explain the auditor's response to each risk in planning the audit of Sunflower Stores Co.   **(10 marks)**

(c)   The finance director of Sunflower Stores Co is considering establishing an internal audit department.

      Required

      Describe the factors the finance director should consider before establishing an internal audit department.
                                                                                                   (5 marks)

                                                                                                   (Total = 20 marks)

INTERNAL CONTROL

Questions 50 – 70 cover Internal control, the subject of Part C of the BPP Study Text for F8.

50 Multiple choice questions
65 mins

1   Is the following statement regarding the assurance provided by an internal control system true or false?

An effective internal control system provides the auditor with absolute assurance that control objectives have been achieved.

    A   True

    B   False   **(1 mark)**

2   Which of the following methods of recording an accounting and controls system is a series of questions used to determine whether controls exist which meet specific control objectives?

    A   Internal control questionnaire

    B   Internal control evaluation questionnaire

    C   Flowchart   **(1 mark)**

3   Application controls relate to procedures used to initiate, record, process and report transactions and other financial data.

Which **two** of the following are application controls?

    (1)   Records of program changes

    (2)   Virus checks

    (3)   Batch reconciliations

    (4)   Document counts

    A   (1) and (2)

    B   (1) and (4)

    C   (2) and (3)

    D   (3) and (4)   **(2 marks)**

4   General IT controls are policies and procedures that relate to many applications and support the effective functioning of application controls.

Which **two** of the following are general IT controls?

    (1)   Testing procedures using test data

    (2)   One for one checking

    (3)   Disaster recovery procedures

    (4)   Hash totals

    A   (1) and (3)

    B   (1) and (4)

    C   (2) and (3)

    D   (2) and (4)   **(2 marks)**

5   One of the control objectives of the sales system of B Co is to ensure that goods and services are sold to credit-worthy customers.

Which of the following control activities would assist B Co in achieving this objective?

    A   All sales orders are based on authorised price lists.

    B   Credit limits are checked before sales orders are accepted.

    C   Overdue debts are chased each month by the credit controller.

    D   The aged-debt listing is reviewed by the finance director on a monthly basis.   **(2 marks)**

6   A control objective of the purchases system of D Co is to ensure that all liabilities for purchases are valid obligations of the company.

Which of the following control activities would help to ensure that this objective is achieved?

A   Reconciliation of the payables control account to the purchase ledger
B   Matching of suppliers' invoices to purchase orders and goods received notes
C   Checking of the mathematical accuracy of the supplier invoice
D   Sequential numbering of goods received notes   (2 marks)

7   Which of the following controls helps to ensure that payroll payments are only made to bona fide employees?

(1)   Personnel records maintained for all employees
(2)   Comparison of bank transfer listing with payroll
(3)   Segregation of duties between staff involved in human resources and payroll functions
(4)   Reperformance of the calculation of a sample of payroll deductions

A   (1) and (2)
B   (1) and (3)
C   (2) and (4)
D   (3) and (4)   (2 marks)

8   B Co maintains perpetual inventory records.

Which of the following control activities would contribute to the auditor's confidence that inventory recorded in the financial statements exists?

(1)   Procedures to identify obsolete and damaged inventory
(2)   Physical safeguards to protect inventory from theft
(3)   Sequential numbering of goods dispatched notes
(4)   Reconciliation of inventory records to results of inventory counts

A   (1) and (2)
B   (1) and (3)
C   (2) and (3)
D   (2) and (4)   (2 marks)

9   C Co ensures that two individuals are always present when the post is opened. Which control objective does this help to achieve?

A   That cash is banked on a regular basis.
B   That cash and cheques are accurately recorded in the general ledger.
C   That cash and cheques are not misappropriated.   (1 mark)

10   Which control objective would be satisfied by the authorisation of capital expenditure by the board?

A   To ensure that investment in non-current assets is made for valid business purposes
B   To ensure that expenditure is correctly classified as capital expenditure
C   To ensure that all non-current assets are recognised in the non-current asset register
D   To ensure that non-current assets are valued correctly   (2 marks)

11   Is the following statement regarding tests of control true or false?

Tests of control are designed to detect material misstatements in the financial statements.

A   True
B   False   (1 mark)

12   Which of the following is **not** a test of control?

   A   Inspection of purchase order documentation to confirm that it has been authorised
   B   Review of monthly bank reconciliations performed by the audit client
   C   Examination of purchase invoices for evidence of mathematical accuracy checks
   D   Agreement of the cost of non-current asset additions to purchase documentation   **(2 marks)**

13   S Co ensures that all goods received are valid business purchases by matching all deliveries to an authorised order before issuing a goods received note.

   Which of the following would be an appropriate test of control to confirm that the control is operating effectively?

   A   For a sample of orders check that there is a matching goods received note
   B   Check that the numerical sequence of purchase orders is complete
   C   For a sample of goods received notes check that there is an authorised purchase order
   D   Check that the numerical sequence of goods received notes is complete   **(2 marks)**

14   The sales invoices of Z Co are matched to dispatch notes with any mismatched items investigated before they are recorded in the sales day book.

   Which of the following control objectives does this help to achieve?

   A   It ensures that sales and receivables are valid and accurate.
   B   It ensures that all goods dispatched are recognised as sales and receivables.
   C   It ensures that all goods ordered by customers are dispatched.
   D   It ensures that customers do not exceed their credit limits.   **(2 marks)**

15   Which of the following controls would be designed to ensure accuracy over input of data?

   A   A range check
   B   A sequence check
   C   Password protection
   D   Authorisation   **(2 marks)**

16   The auditor of Q Co has identified that Q Co does not match dispatch notes to sales invoices as part of the controls in the sales system.

   What is the potential consequence of this deficiency?

   A   Customer orders may not be fulfilled accurately.
   B   Sales and trade receivables may be overstated.
   C   Sales and trade receivables may be understated.
   D   Sales invoices may be posted inaccurately in the receivables control account.   **(2 marks)**

17   The external auditor has identified a deficiency in the internal controls of S Co.

   Which of the following factors would indicate that the deficiency is a significant deficiency in accordance with ISA 265 *Communicating Deficiencies in Internal Control to those Charged with Governance and Management*?

   (1)   The likelihood of the deficiency leading to material misstatement is low
   (2)   There is a risk of fraud
   (3)   The number of transactions affected by the deficiency is low
   (4)   The deficiency interacts with other deficiencies identified

   A   (1) and (2)
   B   (1) and (3)
   C   (2) and (4)
   D   (3) and (4)   **(2 marks)**

18   Which of the following statements is **true** regarding the controls in a small company?

(1)   The external auditor will never be able to rely on the controls in a small company.
(2)   Segregation of duties may be inadequate due to staff numbers.
(3)   Evidence of the operation of controls is more likely to be available in documentary form.
(4)   The external auditor will assess the attitudes, awareness and actions of management.

A   (1) and (3)
B   (1) and (4)
C   (2) and (3)
D   (2) and (4)   (2 marks)

19   Is the following statement regarding internal control questionnaires true or false?

Internal control questionnaires are used to determine whether there are controls which prevent or detect specified errors or omissions.

A   True
B   False   (1 mark)

20   During the course of the audit the auditor may identify deficiencies in internal control which must be reported to management.

Which of the following statements is correct regarding the report to management sent by the auditor?

(1)   The report must include a description of the deficiencies and an explanation of their potential effects.

(2)   The report includes an explanation of the purpose of the audit.

(3)   The report states that the results of the audit work have enabled the auditor to express an opinion on the operating effectiveness of internal control.

A   (1) and (2) only
B   (1) and (3) only
C   (2) and (3) only
D   (1), (2) and (3)   (2 marks)

21   Is the following statement regarding the auditor's responsibility to report deficiencies in internal controls true or false?

All deficiencies in internal controls which the auditor judges should be reported to management must be reported in writing.

A   True
B   False   (1 mark)

51 Documenting internal controls (6/11) (amended) 18 mins

(a) Auditors are required to document their understanding of the client's internal controls. There are various options available for recording the internal control system. Two of these options are narrative notes and internal control questionnaires.

Required

Describe the advantages and disadvantages to the auditor of narrative notes and internal control questionnaires as methods for documenting the system. **(6 marks)**

(b) ISA 315 *Identifying and assessing the risks of material misstatement through understanding the entity and its environment* requires auditors to obtain an understanding of control activities relevant to the audit.

Control activities are the policies and procedures that help ensure that management directives are carried out; and which are designed to prevent and detect fraud and error occurring. An example of a control activity is the maintenance of a control account.

Required

Apart from maintenance of a control account, explain **four** control activities a company may undertake to prevent and detect fraud and error. **(4 marks)**

(Total = 10 marks)

52 Flowers Anytime (AIR 12/02) (amended) 18 mins

Flowers Anytime sells flowers wholesale. Customers telephone the company and their orders are taken by clerks who take details of the flowers to be delivered, the address to which they are to be delivered, and account details of the customer. The clerks input these details into the company's computer system (whilst the order is being taken) which is integrated with the company's inventory control system. The company's standard credit terms are payment one month from the order (all orders are dispatched within 48 hours) and most customers pay by bank transfer. An accounts receivable ledger is maintained and statements are sent to customers once a month. Credit limits are set by the credit controller according to a standard formula and are automatically applied by the computer system, as are the prices of flowers.

Required

Describe and explain the purpose of the internal controls you might expect to see in the sales system at Flowers Anytime over the:

(a) Receipt, processing and recording of orders **(6 marks)**
(b) Collection of cash **(4 marks)**

(Total = 10 marks)

53 North 18 mins

Your firm acts as the auditor to North, a private company that runs seven supermarkets situated in the north of England. You are currently planning the audit for the year ended 31 March 20X3.

During your visit to North, you obtained some information on the company's wages system.

Supermarket employees are paid weekly by direct transfer into their bank accounts. Employees record their hours worked on timesheets which are reviewed by the relevant supermarket supervisor. The supervisor then signs them, scans them in to a computer, and e-mails them to the payroll clerk at the company's head office. The payroll clerk checks the timesheets to ensure they are all there, and to ensure that they have been signed by the appropriate supervisor. She does not enter them onto the payroll system until she has obtained a valid signature.

The payroll clerk enters the hours worked into the payroll system which automatically calculates the gross and net pay, and the deductions. A printout of the current period's payroll is generated, showing the employee hours, gross pay, deductions and net pay, including totals for each. The printout is passed to the chief accountant who checks the hours paid on the computer printout to the scanned timesheets before running a final set of reports.

The final reports include a payroll journals report which the chief accountant uses to update the general ledger, plus an employee payments list showing employee reference and the amount to be paid to each employee.

The employee payments list is e-mailed to the finance director, who reviews the payments list before signing in to North's online business banking facility using his password and transferring the details to the company's bank. The bank already has the employee references and employee bank details and makes the relevant payments before providing North with a confirmation listing.

Required

Recommend **five** tests of controls the auditor could carry out on the wages system of North, and explain the reason for each test. **(10 marks)**

54 Value for money audit (AIR 12/06) (amended)   18 mins

You are an audit manager in the internal audit department of KLE Co. The internal audit department is auditing the company's procurement system in the company. Extracts from your system notes, which are correct and contain no errors, are provided below.

Details on ordering department:

- Six members of staff – one buyer and five purchasing clerks.

- Receives about 75 orders each day, many orders for duplicate items come from different departments in the organisation.

- Initial evaluation of internal controls is high.

Procurement systems

Ordering department

All orders are raised on pre-numbered purchase requisitions and sent to the ordering department.

In the ordering department, each requisition is signed by the chief buyer. A purchasing clerk transfers the order information onto an order form and identifies the appropriate supplier for the goods.

Part one of the two part order form is sent to the supplier and part two to the accounts department. The requisition is thrown away.

Goods inwards department

All goods received are checked for damage. Damaged items are returned to the supplier and a damaged goods note completed.

For undamaged items a two-part pre-numbered Goods Received Note (GRN) is raised.

- Part one is sent to the ordering department with the damaged goods notes.

- Part two is filed in order of the reference number for the goods being ordered (obtained from the supplier's goods dispatched documentation), in the goods inwards department.

Ordering department

GRNs are separated from damaged goods notes, which are filed. The GRN is forwarded to the accounts department.

Accounts department

GRNs matched with the order awaiting the receipt of the invoice.

Required

In respect of the internal control of KLE Co:

(i)   Identify and explain **five** deficiencies.
(ii)   Provide a recommendation to alleviate each deficiency.   **(10 marks)**

55 ICQs and ICEQs   18 mins

ISA 315 *Identifying and assessing the risks of material misstatement through understanding the entity and its environment* details the auditor's responsibilities in relation to an entity's system of internal controls.

Required

(a)   Explain the auditor's responsibilities in relation to an entity's system of internal controls.   **(3 marks)**

(b)   Other than internal control questionnaires and internal control evaluation questionnaires state **two** methods which an auditor may use to document an entity's internal controls.   **(1 mark)**

(c)   Explain what is meant by 'internal control questionnaires' and 'internal control evaluation questionnaires'. For each type of questionnaire, give **one** example of a question that might be included in respect of the purchases cycle.   **(6 marks)**

                                                                                    (Total = 10 marks)

56 Smoothbrush (6/10) (amended)   18 mins

Smoothbrush Paints Co is a paint manufacturer and has been trading for over 50 years. It operates from one central site, which includes the production facility, warehouse and administration offices.

In recent years, Smoothbrush has reduced the level of goods directly manufactured and instead started to import paint from South Asia. Approximately 60% is imported and 40% manufactured. Within the production facility is a large amount of old plant and equipment that is now redundant and has minimal scrap value. Purchase orders for overseas paint are made six months in advance and goods can be in transit for up to two months. Smoothbrush accounts for the inventory when it receives the goods.

To avoid the disruption of a year end inventory count, Smoothbrush has this year introduced a continuous/ perpetual inventory counting system. The warehouse has been divided into 12 areas and these are each to be counted once over the year. The counting team includes a member of the internal audit department and a warehouse staff member. The following procedures have been adopted.

1   The team prints the inventory quantities and descriptions from the system and these records are then compared to the inventory physically present.

2   Any discrepancies in relation to quantities are noted on the inventory sheets (which are printed including the expected quantities), including any items not listed on the sheets but present in the warehouse area.

3   Any damaged or old items are noted and they are removed from the inventory sheets.

4   The sheets are then passed to the finance department for adjustments to be made to the records when the count has finished.

5   During the counts there will continue to be inventory movements with goods arriving and leaving the warehouse.

At the year end it is proposed that the inventory will be based on the underlying records.

Required

Identify and explain suitable controls that should operate over the continuous/perpetual inventory counting system, to ensure the completeness and accuracy of the existing inventory records at Smoothbrush Paints Co.   **(10 marks)**

57 Lily (12/12) (amended)

Lily Window Glass Co (Lily) is a glass manufacturer, which operates from a large production facility, where it undertakes continuous production 24 hours a day, seven days a week. Also on this site are two warehouses, where the company's raw materials and finished goods are stored. Lily's year end is 31 December.

Lily is finalising the arrangements for the year-end inventory count, which is to be undertaken on 31 December 20X2. The finished windows are stored within 20 aisles of the first warehouse. The second warehouse is for large piles of raw materials, such as sand, used in the manufacture of glass. The following arrangements have been made for the inventory count:

The warehouse manager will supervise the count as he is most familiar with the inventory. There will be ten teams of counters and each team will contain two members of staff, one from the finance and one from the manufacturing department. None of the warehouse staff, other than the manager, will be involved in the count.

Each team will count an aisle of finished goods by counting up and then down each aisle. As this process is systematic, it is not felt that the team will need to flag areas once counted. Once the team has finished counting an aisle, they will hand in their sheets and be given a set for another aisle of the warehouse. In addition to the above, to assist with the inventory counting, there will be two teams of counters from the internal audit department and they will perform inventory counts.

The count sheets are sequentially numbered, and the product codes and descriptions are printed on them but no quantities. If the counters identify any inventory which is not on their sheets, then they are to enter the item on a separate sheet, which is not numbered. Once all counting is complete, the sequence of the sheets is checked and any additional sheets are also handed in at this stage. All sheets are completed in ink.

Any damaged goods identified by the counters will be too heavy to move to a central location, hence they are to be left where they are but the counter is to make a note on the inventory sheets detailing the level of damage.

As Lily undertakes continuous production, there will continue to be movements of raw materials and finished goods in and out of the warehouse during the count. These will be kept to a minimum where possible.

The level of work-in-progress in the manufacturing plant is to be assessed by the warehouse manager. It is likely that this will be an immaterial balance. In addition, the raw materials quantities are to be approximated by measuring the height and width of the raw material piles. In the past this task has been undertaken by a specialist; however, the warehouse manager feels confident that he can perform this task.

Required

For the inventory count arrangements of Lily Window Glass Co:

(i)   Identify and explain **five** deficiencies.
(ii)   Provide a recommendation to address each deficiency.

The total marks will be split equally between each part.   **(10 marks)**

58 Shiny Happy Windows (6/10)

(a)   Explain the matters which the auditor should consider in determining whether or not each of the internal control deficiencies identified during an audit should be reported to those charged with governance.

                                                                                        (4 marks)

(b)   Shiny Happy Windows Co (SHW) is a window cleaning company. Customers' windows are cleaned monthly, the window cleaner then posts a stamped addressed envelope for payment through the customer's front door.

        SHW has a large number of receivable balances and these customers pay by cheque or cash, which is received in the stamped addressed envelopes in the post. The following procedures are applied to the cash received cycle:

        1   A junior clerk from the accounts department opens the post and if any cheques or cash have been sent, she records the receipts in the cash received log and then places all the monies into the locked small cash box.

2   The contents of the cash box are counted each day and every few days these sums are banked by which ever member of the finance team is available.

3   The cashier records the details of the cash received log into the cash receipts day book and also updates the sales ledger.

4   Usually on a monthly basis the cashier performs a bank reconciliation, which he then files, if he misses a month then he catches this up in the following month's reconciliation.

Required

For the cash cycle of SHW:

(i)   Identify and explain **two** deficiencies in the system.   **(2 marks)**

(ii)   Suggest controls to address each of these deficiencies.   **(2 marks)**

(iii)   List tests of controls the auditor of SHW would perform to assess if the controls are operating effectively.   **(2 marks)**

(Total = 10 marks)

59 SouthLea (Pilot Paper) (amended)   18 mins

SouthLea Co is a construction company (building houses, offices and hotels) employing a large number of workers on various construction sites. The internal audit department of SouthLea Co is currently reviewing cash wages systems within the company.

The following information is available concerning the wages systems:

(i)   Hours worked are recorded using a clocking in/out system. On arriving for work and at the end of each days work, each worker enters their unique employee number on a keypad.

(ii)   Workers on each site are controlled by a foreman. The foreman has a record of all employee numbers and can issue temporary numbers for new employees.

(iii)   Any overtime is calculated by the computerised wages system and added to the standard pay.

(iv)   The two staff in the wages department make amendments to the computerised wages system in respect of employee holidays, illness, as well as setting up and maintaining all employee records.

(v)   The computerised wages system calculates deductions from gross pay, such as employee taxes, and net pay. Finally a list of net cash payments for each employee is produced.

(vi)   Cash is delivered to the wages office by secure courier.

(vii)   The two staff place cash into wages packets for each employee along with a handwritten note of gross pay, deductions and net pay. The packets are given to the foreman for distribution to the individual employees.

Required

(i)   Identify and explain deficiencies in SouthLea Co's system of internal control over the wages system that could lead to misstatements in the financial statements.

(ii)   For each deficiency, suggest an internal control to overcome that deficiency.   **(10 marks)**

60 Burton Housing   18 mins

Your firm is the auditor of Burton Housing, which is a small charity and housing association. Its principal asset is a large freehold building which contains a restaurant, accommodation for 50 young people, and recreational facilities.

The charity is controlled by a management committee which comprises the voluntary chairman and treasurer, and other voluntary members elected annually. However, day-to-day management is by a chief executive who manages the full-time staff who perform accounting, cleaning, maintenance, housing management and other functions.

You are auditing the company's financial statements for the year ended 31 October 20X5. Draft accounts have been prepared by the treasurer from accounting records kept on a laptop computer by the bookkeeper. The partner in

charge of the audit has asked you to consider the audit work you would perform on income from rents, and the income and expenditure account of the restaurant.

For income from rents:

(i)   The housing manager allocates rooms to individuals, and this information is sent to the bookkeeper.

(ii)   Each week the bookkeeper posts the rents to each resident's account on the sales ledger. All rooms are let at the same rent.

(iii)   Rents are received from residents by reception staff who are independent of the housing manager and bookkeeper. Reception staff give the rents to the bookkeeper.

(iv)   The bookkeeper posts cash received for rents to the sales ledger, enters them in the cash book and pays them into the bank.

(v)   The housing manager reports voids (that is, rooms unlet) to the management committee.

The restaurant comprises the manager and four staff, who prepare and sell food to residents and other individuals.

Cash takings from the restaurant are recorded on a till and each day's takings are given to the bookkeeper who records and pays them into the bank. Details of cash takings are recorded on the till roll.

The system for purchasing food comprises the following:

(i)   The restaurant manager orders the food by sending an order to the supplier.

(ii)   Food received is checked by the restaurant manager.

(iii)   The restaurant manager authorises purchase invoices, confirming the food has been received.

(iv)   The bookkeeper posts the purchase invoices to the payables ledger.

(v)   The bookkeeper makes out the cheques to pay the suppliers, which the chief executive signs. The cheques are posted to the payables ledger and cash book.

The bookkeeper is responsible for paying the wages of staff in the restaurant. The restaurant manager notifies the bookkeeper of any absences of staff.

You should assume that the income and expenditure account of the restaurant includes only:

(i)   Income from customers who purchase food
(ii)   Expenditure on purchasing food and wages of restaurant staff

Required

For rents received, consider the control activities which should be in operation and the audit procedures you will carry out to verify:

(i)	Recording of rental income on the sales ledger	**(3 marks)**
(ii)	Receipt and recording of rents received from residents	**(3 marks)**
(iii)	Posting of adjustments, credit notes and write off of bad debts on the sales ledger	**(4 marks)**

(Total = 10 marks)

61 Matalas (12/07) (amended)   18 mins

Matalas Co sells cars, car parts and petrol from 25 different locations in one country. Each branch has up to 20 staff working there, although most of the accounting systems are designed and implemented from the company's head office. All accounting systems, apart from petty cash, are computerised.

You are an audit manager in the internal audit department of Matalas. You are currently auditing the petty cash systems at the different branches. Your initial systems notes on petty cash contain the following information:

1   The average petty cash balance at each branch is $5,000.
2   Average monthly expenditure is $1,538, with amounts ranging from $1 to $500.
3   Petty cash is kept in a lockable box on a bookcase in the accounts office.

4   Vouchers for expenditure are signed by the person incurring that expenditure to confirm they have received re-imbursement from petty cash.

5   Vouchers are recorded in the petty cash book by the accounts clerk; each voucher records the date, reason for the expenditure, amount of expenditure and person incurring that expenditure.

6   Petty cash is counted every month by the accounts clerk, who is in charge of the cash. The petty cash balance is then reimbursed using the 'imprest' system and the journal entry produced to record expenditure in the general ledger.

7   The cheque to reimburse petty cash is signed by the accountant at the branch at the same time as the journal entry to the general ledger is reviewed.

Required

Explain **five** internal control deficiencies in the petty cash system at Matalas Co. For each deficiency, recommend a control to overcome that deficiency.   **(10 marks)**

62 Bluesberry (12/10) (amended)   18 mins

Bluesberry hospital is located in a country where healthcare is free, as the taxpayers fund the hospitals which are owned by the government. Two years ago management reviewed all aspects of hospital operations and instigated a number of measures aimed at improving overall 'value for money' for the local community. Management have asked that you, an audit manager in the hospital's internal audit department, perform a review over the measures which have been implemented.

Bluesberry has one centralised buying department and all purchase requisition forms for medical supplies must be forwarded here. Upon receipt the buying team will research the lowest price from suppliers and a purchase order is raised. This is then passed to the purchasing director, who authorises all orders. The small buying team receive in excess of 200 forms a day.

The human resources department has had difficulties with recruiting suitably trained staff. Overtime rates have been increased to incentivise permanent staff to fill staffing gaps, this has been popular, and reliance on expensive temporary staff has been reduced. Monitoring of staff hours had been difficult but the hospital has implemented time card clocking in and out procedures and these hours are used for overtime payments as well.

The hospital has invested heavily in new surgical equipment, which although very expensive, has meant that more operations could be performed and patient recovery rates are faster. However, currently there is a shortage of appropriately trained medical staff. A capital expenditure committee has been established, made up of senior managers, and they plan and authorise any significant capital expenditure items.

Required

(a)   Identify and explain **four** strengths within Bluesberry's operating environment.   **(6 marks)**

(b)   For each strength identified, describe how Bluesberry might make further improvements to provide best value for money.   **(4 marks)**

(Total = 10 marks)

63 Chuck (12/11) (amended)   18 mins

Introduction and client background

You are the audit senior of Blair & Co and your team has just completed the interim audit of Chuck Industries Co, whose year end is 31 January 20X2. You are in the process of reviewing the systems testing completed on the payroll cycle, as well as preparing the audit programmes for the final audit.

Chuck Industries Co manufactures lights and the manufacturing process is predominantly automated; however there is a workforce of 85 employees, who monitor the machines, as well as approximately 50 employees who work in sales and administration. The company manufactures twenty-four hours a day, seven days a week.

Below is a description of the payroll system along with deficiencies identified by the audit team:

Factory workforce

The company operates three shifts every day with employees working eight hours each. They are required to clock in and out using an employee swipe card, which identifies the employee number and links into the hours worked report produced by the computerised payroll system. Employees are paid on an hourly basis for each hour worked. There is no monitoring/supervision of the clocking in/out process and an employee was witnessed clocking in several employees using their employee swipe cards.

The payroll department calculates on a weekly basis the cash wages to be paid to the workforce, based on the hours worked report multiplied by the hourly wage rate, with appropriate tax deductions. These calculations are not checked by anyone as they are generated by the payroll system.

Each Friday, the payroll department prepares the pay packets and physically hands these out to the workforce, who operate the morning and late afternoon shifts, upon production of identification. However, for the night shift workers, the pay packets are given to the factory supervisor to distribute. If any night shift employees are absent on pay day then the factory supervisor keeps these wages and returns them to the payroll department on Monday.

Sales and administration staff

The sales and administration staff are paid monthly by bank transfer. Employee numbers do fluctuate and during July two administration staff joined; however, due to staff holidays in the HR department, they delayed informing the payroll department, resulting in incorrect salaries being paid out.

Required

For the deficiencies already identified in the payroll system of Chuck Industries Co:

(i)   Explain the possible implications of these.
(ii)   Suggest a recommendation to address each deficiency.   **(10 marks)**

64 Rhapsody (AIR 6/07) (amended)   36 mins

Rhapsody Co supplies a wide range of garden and agricultural products to trade and domestic customers. The company has 11 divisions, with each division specialising in the sale of specific products, for example, seeds, garden furniture, agricultural fertilizers. The company has an internal audit department which provides audit reports to the audit committee on each division on a rotational basis.

Products in the seed division are offered for sale to domestic customers via an internet site. Customers review the product list on the internet and place orders for packets of seeds using specific product codes, along with their credit card details, onto Rhapsody Co's secure server. Order quantities are normally between one and three packets for each type of seed. Order details are transferred manually onto the company's internal inventory control and sales system, and a two part packing list is printed in the seed warehouse. Each order and packing list is given a random alphabetical code based on the name of the employee inputting the order, the date, and the products being ordered.

In the seed warehouse, the packages of seeds for each order are taken from specific bins and dispatched to the customer with one copy of the packing list. The second copy of the packing list is sent to the accounts department where the inventory and sales computer is updated to show that the order has been dispatched. The customer's credit card is then charged by the inventory control and sales computer. Bad debts in Rhapsody are currently 3% of total sales.

Finally, the computer system checks that for each charge made to a customer's credit card account, the order details are on file to prove that the charge was made correctly. The order file is marked as completed confirming that the order has been dispatched and payment obtained.

Required

(a)   In respect of sales in the seeds division of Rhapsody Co, prepare a report to be sent to the audit committee of Rhapsody Co which:

    (i)   Identifies and explains **five** deficiencies in that sales system
    (ii)   Explains the possible effect of each deficiency
    (iii)   Provides a recommendation to alleviate each deficiency

    (**Note**. Up to 2 marks will be awarded for presentation.)   **(17 marks)**

(b)   Explain the advantages to Rhapsody Co of having an audit committee.   **(3 marks)**

                                      (Total = 20 marks)

65 Fitta

36 mins

You are an employee of an audit firm, Mason & Co. Mason & Co are the auditors of Fitta Co, an owner managed company whose principal activity is fitting out shops, hotels and restaurants. Fitta employs 180 weekly-paid employees and all employees are paid by direct transfer into their bank accounts.

Hours worked are recorded on timesheets which are completed by the site and workshop supervisors and submitted to Michelle, the payroll clerk, in the personnel department. Michelle checks the timesheets for completeness and to satisfy herself that they have been signed by the appropriate supervisor.

Michelle accesses the payroll system using a password which is known only to her and Carla, an accounts clerk, who covers for leave of absence. She then enters the hours worked, split between basic and overtime, into a computer and the program calculates the gross and net pay.

A printout of the current period's payroll is generated, detailing for each employee, hours paid, split between basic and overtime, gross pay, deductions, net pay, employer's tax and totals thereof. Michelle checks the hours paid on the computer printout to the timesheets and, if necessary, re-runs the payroll incorporating any amendments, and a printout of the revised payroll is obtained. The following reports are then generated:

Summary: Cumulative details to date per employee
Payslips: Details of gross pay, deductions and net pay
Autopay list: Bank sort code, account number and net pay per employee, and total net pay.

The managing director, Mr Grimshaw, reviews the autopay list before Michelle uses a different password to transmit the details via direct transfer to the company's bank. Two days later a printout, listing bank and net pay details per employee together with the net pay total, is received from the bank and Michelle files it in date order.

On completion of payroll processing Michelle copies the payroll details onto a CD which is stored in the fireproof safe in Mr Grimshaw's office.

Details of starters, leavers and amendments to employee details are recorded on standard forms by the site and workshop supervisors and passed to Michelle for input to the system. After updating the standing data, she obtains a printout and checks the details to the standard form which is filed with the personnel record of the respective employee.

Each month Michelle posts the weekly summaries to the nominal ledger accounts. She also extracts the tax details from the weekly payroll summaries and records the monthly figures on the taxation authority's payslip. The finance director, Mrs Duckworth, reviews the monthly figures for tax and prepares a cheque for the appropriate amount.

Required

(a) Identify the objectives of exercising internal controls in a wages system and discuss the extent to which the procedures exercised by Fitta achieve these objectives. **(10 marks)**

(b) Describe the additional procedures which would strengthen the controls over Fitta's wages system.

(10 marks)

(Total = 20 marks)

66 Greystone (12/10) (amended)

36 mins

Greystone Co is a retailer of ladies clothing and accessories. It operates in many countries around the world and has expanded steadily from its base in Europe. Its main market is aimed at 15 to 35 year olds and its prices are mid to low range. The company's year end was 30 September 20X0.

In the past the company has bulk ordered its clothing and accessories twice a year. However, if their goods failed to meet the key fashion trends then this resulted in significant inventory write downs. As a result of this, the company has recently introduced a just in time ordering system. The fashion buyers make an assessment nine months in advance as to what the key trends are likely to be, these goods are sourced from their suppliers but only limited numbers are initially ordered.

Greystone Co has an internal audit department but at present their only role is to perform regular inventory counts at the stores.

Ordering process

Each country has a purchasing manager who decides on the initial inventory levels for each store, this is not done in conjunction with store or sales managers. These quantities are communicated to the central buying department at the head office in Europe. An ordering clerk amalgamates all country orders by specified regions of countries, such as Central Europe and North America, and passes them to the purchasing director to review and authorise.

As the goods are sold, it is the store manager's responsibility to re-order the goods through the purchasing manager; they are prompted weekly to review inventory levels as although the goods are just in time, it can still take up to four weeks for goods to be received in store.

It is not possible to order goods from other branches of stores as all ordering must be undertaken through the purchasing manager. If a customer requests an item of clothing, which is unavailable in a particular store, then the customer is provided with other branch telephone numbers or recommended to try the company website.

Goods received and invoicing

To speed up the ordering to receipt of goods cycle, the goods are delivered directly from the suppliers to the individual stores. On receipt of goods the quantities received are checked by a sales assistant against the supplier's delivery note, and then the assistant produces a goods received note (GRN). This is done at quiet times of the day so as to maximise sales. The checked GRNs are sent to head office for matching with purchase invoices.

As purchase invoices are received they are manually matched to GRNs from the stores, this can be a very time consuming process as some suppliers may have delivered to over 500 stores. Once the invoice has been agreed then it is sent to the purchasing director for authorisation. It is at this stage that the invoice is entered onto the purchase ledger.

Required

(a)   As the external auditors of Greystone Co, write a report to management in respect of the purchasing system which:

   (i)   Identifies and explains **five** deficiencies in that system.
   (ii)   Explains the possible implication of each deficiency.
   (iii)   Provides a recommendation to address each deficiency.

   A covering letter is required.

   Note: Up to two marks will be awarded within this requirement for presentation.   **(17 marks)**

(b)   Describe additional assignments that the internal audit department of Greystone Co could be asked to perform by those charged with governance.   **(3 marks)**

                                                                                             (Total = 20 marks)

67 Blake (12/08) (amended)   36 mins

Introduction

Blake Co assembles specialist motor vehicles such as lorries, buses and trucks. The company owns four assembly plants to which parts are delivered and assembled into the motor vehicles.

Wages system – shift workers

Shift-workers arrive for work at about 7.00 am and 'clock in' using an electronic identification card. The card is scanned by the time recording system and each production shift-worker's identification number is read from their card by the scanner. Shift-workers are paid from the time of logging in. The logging in process is not monitored as it is assumed that shift-workers would not work without first logging in on the time recording system.

At least 400 vehicles have to be manufactured each day by each work group. The workers normally work a standard eight hour day, but if necessary, overtime is worked to complete the day's quota of vehicles. The shift foreman is not required to monitor the extent of any overtime working although the foreman does ensure workers are not taking unnecessary or prolonged breaks which would automatically increase the amount of overtime worked. Shift-workers log off at the end of each shift by re-scanning their identification card.

Payment of wages

Details of hours worked each week are sent electronically to the payroll department, where hours worked are allocated by the computerised wages system to each employee's wages records. Staff in the payroll department compare hours worked from the time recording system to the computerised wages system, and enter a code word to confirm the accuracy of transfer. The code word also acts as authorisation to calculate net wages. The code word is the name of a domestic cat belonging to the department head and is therefore generally known around the department.

Each week the computerised wages system calculates:

(i)   Gross wages, using the standard rate and overtime rates per hour for each employee
(ii)   Statutory deductions from wages
(iii)   Net pay

The list of net pay for each employee is sent over Blake's internal network to the accounts department. In the accounts department, an accounts clerk ensures that employee bank details are on file. The clerk then authorises and makes payment to those employees using Blake's online banking systems. Every few weeks, the financial accountant reviews the total amount of wages made to ensure that the management accounts are accurate.

Salaries system – shift managers

All shift managers are paid an annual salary; there are no overtime payments.

Salaries were increased in July by 3% and an annual bonus of 5% of salary was paid in November.

Required

(a)   As the external auditors of Blake Co, write a management letter to the directors in respect of the shift-workers wages recording and payment systems which:

(i)   Identifies and explains **five** deficiencies in that system.
(ii)   Explains the possible effect of each deficiency.
(iii)   Provides a recommendation to alleviate each deficiency.

Note up to two marks will be awarded within this requirement for presentation.   **(17 marks)**

(b)   Describe **three** substantive analytical procedures you should perform on the shift managers' salary system.

(3 marks)

(Total = 20 marks)

68 Tinkerbell (6/11) (amended)   36 mins

Introduction

Tinkerbell Toys Co (Tinkerbell) is a manufacturer of children's building block toys; they have been trading for over 35 years and they sell to a wide variety of customers including large and small toy retailers across the country. The company's year end is 31 May 20X1.

The company has a large manufacturing plant, four large warehouses and a head office. Upon manufacture, the toys are stored in one of the warehouses until they are dispatched to customers. The company does not have an internal audit department.

Sales ordering, goods dispatched and invoicing

Each customer has a unique customer account number and this is used to enter sales orders when they are received in writing from customers. The orders are entered by an order clerk and the system automatically checks that the goods are available and that the order will not take the customer over their credit limit. For new customers, a sales manager completes a credit application; this is checked through a credit agency and a credit limit entered into the system by the credit controller. The company has a price list, which is updated twice a year. Larger customers are entitled to a discount; this is agreed by the sales director and set up within the customer master file.

Once the order is entered an acceptance is automatically sent to the customer by mail/email confirming the goods ordered and a likely dispatch date. The order is then sorted by address of customer. The warehouse closest to the customer receives the order electronically and a dispatch list and sequentially numbered goods dispatch notes (GDNs) are automatically generated. The warehouse team pack the goods from the dispatch list and, before they are sent out, a second member of the team double checks the dispatch list to the GDN, which accompanies the goods.

Once dispatched, a copy of the GDN is sent to the accounts team at head office and a sequentially numbered sales invoice is raised and checked to the GDN. Periodically a computer sequence check is performed for any missing sales invoice numbers.

Fraud

During the year a material fraud was uncovered. It involved cash/cheque receipts from customers being diverted into employees' personal accounts. In order to cover up the fraud, receipts from subsequent unrelated customers would then be recorded against the earlier outstanding receivable balances and this cycle of fraud would continue.

The fraud occurred because two members of staff 'who were related' colluded. One processed cash receipts and prepared the weekly bank reconciliation; the other employee recorded customer receipts in the sales ledger. An unrelated sales ledger clerk was supposed to send out monthly customer statements but this was not performed. The bank reconciliations each had a small unreconciled amount but no-one reviewed the reconciliations after they were prepared. The fraud was only uncovered when the two employees went on holiday at the same time and it was discovered that cash receipts from different customers were being applied to older receivable balances to hide the earlier sums stolen.

Required

(a) Recommend **five** tests of controls the auditor would normally carry out on the sales system of Tinkerbell, and explain the objective for each test. **(10 marks)**

(b) Describe substantive procedures the auditor should perform to confirm Tinkerbell's year-end receivables balance. **(3 marks)**

(c) Identify and explain controls Tinkerbell should implement to reduce the risk of fraud occurring again and, for each control, describe how it would mitigate the risk. **(4 marks)**

(d) Describe substantive procedures the auditor should perform to confirm Tinkerbell's revenue. **(3 marks)**

(Total = 20 marks)

69 Pear (6/12) (amended) 36 mins

Pear International Co (Pear) is a manufacturer of electrical equipment. It has factories across the country and its customer base includes retailers as well as individuals, to whom direct sales are made through their website. The company's year end is 30 September 20X2. You are an audit supervisor of Apple & Co and are currently reviewing documentation of Pear's internal control in preparation for the interim audit.

Pear's website allows individuals to order goods directly, and full payment is taken in advance. Currently the website is not integrated into the inventory system and inventory levels are not checked at the time when orders are placed.

Goods are dispatched via local couriers; however, they do not always record customer signatures as proof that the customer has received the goods. Over the past 12 months there have been customer complaints about the delay between sales orders and receipt of goods. Pear has investigated these and found that, in each case, the sales order had been entered into the sales system correctly but was not forwarded to the dispatch department for fulfilling.

Pear's retail customers undergo credit checks prior to being accepted and credit limits are set accordingly by sales ledger clerks. These customers place their orders through one of the sales team, who decides on sales discount levels.

Raw materials used in the manufacturing process are purchased from a wide range of suppliers. As a result of staff changes in the purchase ledger department, supplier statement reconciliations are no longer performed.

Additionally, changes to supplier details in the purchase ledger master file can be undertaken by purchase ledger clerks as well as supervisors.

In the past six months Pear has changed part of its manufacturing process and as a result some new equipment has been purchased, however, there are considerable levels of plant and equipment which are now surplus to requirement. Purchase requisitions for all new equipment have been authorised by production supervisors and little has been done to reduce the surplus of old equipment.

Required

(a)   In respect of the internal control of Pear International Co:

(i)   Identify and explain **five** deficiencies.

(ii)   Recommend a control to address each of these deficiencies.

(iii)   Describe a test of control Apple & Co would perform to assess if each of these controls is operating effectively.   **(15 marks)**

(b)   Describe substantive procedures you should perform at the year end to confirm each of the following for plant and equipment:

(i)   Additions

(ii)   Disposals   **(5 marks)**

(Total = 20 marks)

70 DinZee (12/07) (amended)   36 mins

DinZee Co assembles fridges, microwaves, washing machines and other similar domestic appliances. As part of the interim audit work two weeks prior to the company year-end, you are preparing to attend the inventory count.

Required

(a)   Explain **two** audit procedures that an auditor will normally perform prior to attending the client's premises on the day of the inventory count.   **(2 marks)**

(b)   On the day of the inventory count, you attended depot nine at DinZee. You observed the following activities:

1.   Pre-numbered count sheets were being issued to client's staff carrying out the count. The count sheets showed the inventory ledger balances for checking against physical inventory.

2.   All count staff were drawn from the inventory warehouse and were counting in teams of two.

3.   Three counting teams were allocated to each area of the stores to count, although the teams were allowed to decide which pair of staff counted which inventory within each area. Staff were warned that they had to remember which inventory had been counted.

4.   Information was recorded on the count sheets in pencil so amendments could be made easily as required.

5.   Any inventory not located on the pre-numbered inventory sheets was recorded on separate inventory sheets – which were numbered by staff as they were used.

6.   At the end of the count, all count sheets were collected and the numeric sequence of the sheets checked; the sheets were not signed.

Required

(i)   Identify and explain **five** deficiencies in the control system for counting inventory at depot nine.

(ii)   Explain the possible effect of each deficiency.

(iii)   Provide a recommendation to alleviate each deficiency.   **(15 marks)**

(c)   (i)   State the aim of a test of control and the aim of a substantive procedure.

(ii)   In respect of your attendance at DinZee Co's inventory count, state one test of control and one substantive procedure that you should perform.   **(3 marks)**

(Total = 20 marks)

AUDIT EVIDENCE

Questions 71 – 108 cover Audit evidence, the subject of Part D of the BPP Study Text for F8.

71 Multiple choice questions

83 mins

1   Which **two** of the following would be classified as substantive procedures?

    (1)   Tests of control
    (2)   Walk-through tests
    (3)   Analytical procedures
    (4)   Tests of details

    A   (1) and (2)
    B   (1) and (4)
    C   (2) and (3)
    D   (3) and (4)   **(2 marks)**

2   Is the following statement true or false regarding directional testing?

Directional testing involves the testing of assets and expenditure for overstatement.

    A   True
    B   False

(1 mark)

3   The draft financial statements of T Co show the following information:

	$'000
Revenue	420
Cost of sales	270
Gross profit	150
Trade receivables	160
Trade payables	130

What is the receivables collection period?

    A   139 days
    B   175 days
    C   758 days
    D   958 days   **(2 marks)**

4   Is the following statement regarding audit sampling true or false?

Audit sampling is the application of audit procedures to less than 100% of items within a population of audit relevance such that all sampling units have a chance of selection.

    A   True
    B   False   **(1 mark)**

5 The auditor of L Co has identified an unexpectedly high deviation rate when carrying out tests of control on a sample of sales invoices.

Which **two** of the following would be a satisfactory course of action?

(1) Extend the sample size
(2) Replace the sample
(3) Ignore the deviations as they only affect some of the items tested
(4) Perform alternative substantive procedures

A (1) and (3)
B (1) and (4)
C (2) and (3)
D (2) and (4)   **(2 marks)**

6 The auditor of P Co is planning the audit work on trade receivables.

Which of the following procedures could **not** be performed by using computer-assisted audit techniques?

A Selection of a sample of receivables for confirmation
B Calculation of receivables days
C Production of receivables' confirmation letters
D Evaluation of the adequacy of the allowance for irrecoverable receivables   **(2 marks)**

7 Computer assisted audit techniques include test data and audit software.

In respect of which of the following activities would the use of audit software be most relevant?

A Tests of online passwords
B Testing of computerised in-put controls on sales invoices
C Totalling of the purchase ledger
D Testing controls over computerised credit-limits   **(2 marks)**

8 Is the following statement regarding audit software true or false?

Audit software is used to assist with substantive procedures.

A True
B False   **(1 mark)**

9 Which of the following statements is true regarding an auditor's expert?

(1) The expert must be a partner or member of staff of the audit firm.
(2) Provided that the auditor has assessed the expert to be competent audit evidence provided by the expert can be relied upon.
(3) Unless required to do so by law or regulation the auditor must not refer to the expert in an auditor's report which contains an unmodified opinion.

A (1) only
B (2) only
C (3) only
D (1), (2) and (3)   **(2 marks)**

10   X Co has an internal audit function. The external auditor has concluded that the internal audit function does not apply a systematic and disciplined approach to its work.

How does this affect the extent to which the external auditor can rely on the work of the internal audit function?

A   The external auditor must not use the work of the internal audit function.
B   The external auditor can use the work of the internal audit function provided the individuals have been assessed as competent.
C   The external auditor can use the work of the internal audit function provided the organisational status of the function supports its objectivity.
D   The external auditor can use work performed by the internal audit function which relates to low risk areas of the external audit only.   (2 marks)

11   Is the following statement regarding the use of internal audit work by the external auditor true or false?

The external auditor must reperform some of the work carried out by the internal audit function if the work of the internal auditor is to be relied on.

A   True
B   False   (1 mark)

12   The auditor of G Co is performing audit procedures to confirm the company's ownership of motor vehicles.

Which of the following would provide the most persuasive evidence of this?

A   Physical inspection of the motor vehicles
B   Inspection of vehicle registration documents
C   Checking that the motor vehicles are recorded in the non-current asset register
D   Review of vehicle insurance documentation   (2 marks)

13   Which of the following audit procedures would provide the auditor with evidence of completeness of inventory?

A   Tracing test counts performed at the inventory count to the detailed inventory listing
B   Reviewing the physical condition of inventory when attending the inventory count
C   Casting the inventory listing
D   Vouching the cost of a sample of inventory items to suppliers' invoices   (2 marks)

14   Which **two** of the following statements are true regarding the auditor's attendance at the inventory count?

(1)   It is the auditor's responsibility to organise the inventory count.
(2)   The auditor observes client staff to determine whether inventory count procedures are being followed.
(3)   The auditor reviews procedures for identifying damaged, obsolete and slow-moving inventory.
(4)   If the results of the auditors' test counts are not satisfactory the auditor can insist that inventory is recounted.

A   (1) and (2)
B   (1) and (4)
C   (2) and (3)
D   (3) and (4)   (2 marks)

15   The auditor of Q Co has performed purchases cut-off procedures and has identified that in two material instances goods received prior to the inventory count have not been included on the schedule of 'goods received not invoiced'. At the period end purchase invoices have not been received. What is the auditor's conclusion based on this evidence?

A   Inventory is overstated.
B   Trade payables are understated.
C   Inventory is understated.
D   Trade payables are overstated.   (2 marks)

16 Which of the following statements is/are true regarding direct confirmation of accounts receivable?

    (1)   Responses from the customer must be returned directly to the client.

    (2)   Under the positive method the customer only replies if the amount stated is agrees with the customer's records.

    A   (1) only
    B   (2) only
    C   (1) and (2)
    D   Neither (1) nor (2)   **(2 marks)**

---

17 The key audit risk associated with trade payables is understatement.

Which of the following procedures would provide the most reliable evidence of the completeness of amounts due?

    A   Tracing of amounts due per the payables ledger to purchase invoices
    B   Matching of purchase invoices to goods received notes
    C   Reconciliation of year-end supplier statements
    D   Reconciliation of the payables ledger with the payables ledger control account   **(2 marks)**

---

18 Is the following statement true or false in respect of litigation and claims?

When the auditor believes that litigation or claims may exist the auditor seeks to communicate directly with the client's legal advisers through a letter of inquiry.

    A   True
    B   False   **(1 mark)**

---

19 The auditor of Z Co is auditing share capital. Z Co employs an independent registrar to deal with its share registration work.

Which of the following is the most reliable evidence of the validity of the issued share capital stated in the financial statements?

    A   The balance on the share capital account in the general ledger
    B   A certificate of share capital in issue from the registrar
    C   Z Co's incorporation documentation
    D   Details of share capital recorded on the previous year's audit file   **(2 marks)**

---

20 The auditor of F Co is auditing bank and cash at 31 December 20X4 and has identified a significant number of remittances recorded in the cash book on the last day of the year which do not appear on the bank statement until late January 20X5.

Which of the following steps would the auditor take to help determine whether F Co is involved in window dressing?

    A   Request copies of the cheques from the bank and agree the amounts of the cheques to the entries in the cash book

    B   Agree the bank statement balance to the balance according to the bank confirmation letter

    C   Examine the paying-in slips for the remittances to determine the date that they were actually paid in to the bank   **(1 mark)**

21   The auditor is performing the audit of a charity whose main source of income is derived from street collections.

Which of the following controls would provide the auditor with evidence of completeness of income?

(1)   Numerical controls over collection boxes
(2)   Sealing of collection boxes at the end of each shift
(3)   Matching of paying-in slip details to the bank statement

A   (1) and (2)
B   (1) and (3)
C   (2) and (3)   **(1 mark)**

22   Is the following statement regarding audit considerations when the entity has used a service organisation true or false?

The user auditor may request a report from the service auditor which includes a description of the system at the service organisation and details the design of the controls.

A   True
B   False   **(1 mark)**

23   The auditor of M Co has agreed a sample of non-current assets selected by physical inspection back to the non-current asset register.

For which of the following assertions does this test provide assurance?

A   Completeness
B   Existence
C   Rights and obligations
D   Accuracy and valuation   **(2 marks)**

24   Which of the following techniques is generally accepted to be the most efficient to obtain evidence regarding the existence of bank balances?

A   Reperformance
B   Confirmation
C   Analytical procedures
D   Observation   **(2 marks)**

25   Which of the following assertions about classes of transactions and events for the period under audit is defined below:

'Amounts and other data relating to recorded transactions and events have been recorded appropriately'.

A   Cut-off
B   Accuracy
C   Occurrence
D   Classification   **(2 marks)**

26   Is the following statement regarding audit evidence true or false?

Appropriateness is the measure of the quality of audit evidence.

A   True
B   False   **(1 mark)**

27   As the audit senior on the year end audit of Z Co, you have instructed the audit junior to obtain and inspect supporting sales contracts for large sales transactions.

Which of the following assertions are you seeking to test with this audit procedure?

A   Cut-off
B   Accuracy
C   Occurrence
D   Completeness   **(2 marks)**

28   Is the following statement regarding direct confirmation of accounts receivable true or false?

The verification of trade receivables by direct confirmation provides evidence that the debts are recoverable.

A   True
B   False   (1 mark)

72 Expert (12/08) (amended)   18 mins

You are the audit manager in the firm of WSD & Co, an audit firm with twelve national offices. You are planning the audit of Truse Co, one of your clients which operates as a high street retailer and has 15 shops.

All of the shops are owned by Truse Co and have always been included in the financial statements at cost less depreciation (the shops are depreciated over 50 years). However, you know from discussions with management that this year the company intends to include the largest of its four shops at valuation rather than cost. The revalued amount will be materially above the carrying value of the shop.

Management at Truse Co has explained the reason for the revaluation is because the shop is in an area where property prices are much higher when compared to prices for the areas the other stores are in. They consider the flagship store to be significantly undervalued on the statement of financial position.

They have also said they will not depreciate the revalued amount allocated to the store's building because they maintain the building to a high standard. The valuation will be carried out by an independent valuer.

Required:

(a)   Explain the audit issues arising from management's decision to:

(i)   Revalue the shop
(ii)   Cease to depreciate the revalued shop   (7 marks)

(**Note**: you should refer to the relevant requirements of IAS 16 *Property, plant and equipment* in your answer)

(b)   Explain **three** factors that the external auditor should consider when assessing the competence and objectivity of the auditor's expert.   (3 marks)

(Total = 10 marks)

73 Audit techniques   18 mins

ISA 530 *Audit sampling* states that the objective of the auditor, when using audit sampling, is to provide a reasonable basis for the auditor to draw conclusions about the population from which the sample is selected.

Required

(a)   Explain the difference between statistical and non-statistical sampling and describe four methods of sample selection.   (6 marks)

(b)   Describe the procedures the auditor would perform where errors have been identified in a sample. (4 marks)

(Total = 10 marks)

74 Evidence and assertions (12/09) (amended)   18 mins

(a)   ISA 500 *Audit Evidence* requires audit evidence to be sufficient and appropriate. Evidence is appropriate if it is both relevant and reliable.

Required

Explain **six** factors that influence the sufficiency and reliability of audit evidence.   (6 marks)

(b)   List and explain **four** assertions from ISA 315 *Identifying and assessing the risks of material misstatement through understanding the entity and its environment* that relate to classes of transactions and events.

(4 marks)

(Total = 10 marks)

75 External confirmations   18 mins

(a)   ISA 505 *External confirmations* considers a number of different types of external confirmations including accounts receivables' confirmations.

Required

Explain the difference between a positive and negative confirmation.   **(4 marks)**

(b)   List **six** examples, other than the confirmation of receivables, of situations where external confirmations may be used by the auditor to obtain audit evidence.   **(3 marks)**

(c)   List **six** items of information that could be requested in a bank confirmation letter.   **(3 marks)**

(Total = 10 marks)

76 Accounting estimates   18 mins

ISA 540 *Audit of accounting estimates, including fair value accounting estimates, and related disclosures* provides guidance to auditors on obtaining evidence over accounting estimates..

Required

(a)   Explain the approaches adopted by auditors in obtaining sufficient appropriate audit evidence regarding accounting estimates.   **(3 marks)**

(b)   Describe the procedures you would apply in verifying a receivables allowance consisting of a number of doubtful (potentially irrecoverable) debts.   **(7 marks)**

(Total = 10 marks)

77 Porthos (AIR 12/05) (amended)   18 mins

(a)   Computer-Assisted Audit Techniques (CAATs) are used to assist an auditor in the collection of audit evidence from computerised systems.

Required

List and explain **four** advantages of CAATs.   **(4 marks)**

(b)   Porthos, a limited liability company, is a reseller of sports equipment, specialising in racquet sports such as tennis, squash and badminton. The company purchases equipment from a variety of different suppliers and then resells this using the Internet as the only selling media. The company has over 150 different types of racquets available in inventory, each identified via a unique product code.

Customers place their orders directly on the internet site. Most orders are for one or two racquets only. The ordering/sales software automatically verifies the order details, customer address and credit card information prior to orders being verified and goods being dispatched. The integrity of the ordering system is checked regularly by ArcherWeb, an independent internet service company.

You are the audit manager working for the external auditors of Porthos, and you have just started planning the audit of the sales system of the company. You have decided to use test data to check the input of details into the sales system. This will involve entering dummy orders into the Porthos system from an online terminal.

Required

List the test data you will use in your audit of the financial statements of Porthos to confirm the completeness and accuracy of input into the sales system, clearly explaining the reason for each item of data. **(6 marks)**

(Total = 10 marks)

78 Newthorpe
18 mins

You are auditing the financial statements of Newthorpe Engineering Co, a listed company, for the year ended 30 April 20X7.

In March 20X7 the Board decided to close one of the company's factories on 30 April 20X7. The plant and equipment and inventories will be sold. The employees will either be transferred to another factory or made redundant.

At the time of your audit in June 20X7, you are aware that:

(i) Some of the plant and equipment has been sold
(ii) Most of the inventories have been sold
(iii) All the employees have either been made redundant or transferred to another factory

The company has provided you with a schedule of the closure costs, the realisable values of the assets in (i) and (ii) above and the redundancy cost.

Details of the plant and machinery are maintained in a non-current asset register.

A full inventory count was carried out at 30 April 20X7. Audit tests have confirmed that the inventory counts are accurate and there are no purchases or sales cut-off errors.

You are aware the redundancy payments are based on the number of years service of the employee and their annual salary (or wage). Most employees were given redundancy of one week's pay for each year's service. A few employees have a service contract with the company and were paid the amount stated in their service contract which will be more than the redundancy pay offered to other employees. Employees who are transferred to another factory were not paid any redundancy.

As part of the audit of the closure cost, you have been asked to carry out the audit work described below.

Required

For the factory being closed, describe the audit procedures you will carry out to verify the company's estimates of:

(a) The net realisable value of plant and equipment **(3 marks)**
(b) The inventories **(3 marks)**
(c) The redundancy cost **(4 marks)**

Notes

(1) In auditing inventories, you are required only to verify that the price per unit is correctly determined.

(2) For the redundancy cost, you should ignore any national statutory rules for determining redundancy procedures and minimum redundancy pay. **(Total = 10 marks)**

79 Analytical procedures and bank confirmations (6/08) (amended)
18 mins

(a) With reference to ISA 520 *Analytical Procedures* and ISA 315 *Identifying and assessing the risks of material misstatement through understanding the entity and its environment* explain:

(i) What is meant by the term 'analytical procedures' **(2 marks)**
(ii) The different types of analytical procedures available to the auditor **(3 marks)**
(iii) The situations in the audit when analytical procedures can be used **(2 marks)**

Confirmation of the end of year bank balances is an important audit procedure.

Required

(b)   Explain the procedures necessary to obtain a bank confirmation letter from an audit client's bank. **(3 marks)**

(Total = 10 marks)

80 Zak (6/08) (amended)   18 mins

Zak Co sells garden sheds and furniture from 15 retail outlets. Sales are made to individuals, with income being in the form of cash and debit cards. All items purchased are delivered to the customer using Zak's own delivery vans; most sheds are too big for individuals to transport in their own motor vehicles. The directors of Zak indicate that the company has had a difficult year, but are pleased to present some acceptable results to the members.

The statements of profit or loss for the last two financial years are shown below:

Statements of profit or loss

	31 March 2008	31 March 2007
	$'000	$'000
Revenue	7,482	6,364
Cost of sales	(3,520)	(4,253)
Gross profit	3,962	2,111
Operating expenses		
Administration	(1,235)	(1,320)
Selling and distribution	(981)	(689)
Interest payable	(101)	(105)
Investment income	145	–
Profit/(loss) before tax	1,790	(3)
Financial statement extract		
Cash and bank	253	(950)

Required

As part of your risk assessment procedures for Zak Co, identify and provide a possible explanation for unusual changes in the statement of profit or loss.   **(10 marks)**

81 Perpetual inventory system   18 mins

Plush Toys Co (Plush), a private company that manufactures toys, has been an audit client of your firm for several years. As an audit senior, you are involved in the Plush audit for the first time.

The company operates a perpetual inventory counting system. While looking at the prior year audit files, you note that numerous misstatements were identified by the audit team in respect of purchases cut-off, prompting adjustments to be made in last year's financial statements.

(a)   Briefly explain why cut-off is an important issue in the audit of inventory.   **(4 marks)**

(b)   Where a company uses a perpetual inventory counting system, describe the audit work that auditors would carry out to satisfy themselves that inventory was fairly stated.   **(6 marks)**

(Total = 10 marks)

82 Rocks Forever (AIR 12/05) (amended)   18 mins

You are the audit manager in the firm of DeCe & Co and are planning the audit of Rocks Forever. Rocks Forever purchases diamond jewellery from three manufacturers, then sells the jewellery. The jewellery is then sold from its four shops.

Inventory is the largest account on the statement of financial position with each of the four shops holding material amounts. Your firm has also employed specialist diamond valuers, who will also attend the inventory count. Due to the high value of the inventory, all shops will be visited and test counts performed.

With the permission of the directors of Rocks Forever, you have employed UJ, a firm of specialist diamond valuers who will also be in attendance. UJ will verify that the jewellery is, in fact, made from diamonds and that the jewellery is saleable with respect to current trends in fashion. UJ will also suggest, on a sample basis, the value of specific items of jewellery.

Counting will be carried out by shop staff in teams of two using pre-numbered count sheets.

Required

(a) Explain the factors you should consider when placing reliance on the work of UJ. **(5 marks)**

(b) Describe the audit procedures you should perform to ensure that jewellery inventory is valued correctly.

(5 marks)

(Total = 10 marks)

83 Whizee (12/07) (amended)   18 mins

Whizee Co assembles electrical domestic appliances from parts procured from a large number of suppliers. As part of the interim audit work two weeks prior to the company year-end, you are testing the procurement and purchases systems.

Procurement and purchases system

Parts inventory is monitored by the stores manager. When the quantity of a particular part falls below re-order level, an e-mail is sent to the procurement department detailing the part required and the quantity to order. A copy of the e-mail is filed on the store manager's computer.

Staff in the procurement department check the e-mail, allocate the order to an authorised supplier and send the order to that supplier using Electronic Data Interchange (EDI). A copy of the EDI order is filed in the order database by the computer system. The order is identified by a unique order number.

When goods are received at Whizee, the stores clerk confirms that the inventory agrees to the delivery note and checks the order database to ensure that the inventory were in fact ordered by Whizee. (Delivery is refused where goods do not have a delivery note.)

The order in the order database is updated to confirm receipt of goods, and the perpetual inventory system updated to show the receipt of inventory. The physical goods are added to the parts store and the paper delivery note is stamped with the order number and is filed in the goods inwards department.

The supplier sends a purchase invoice to Whizee using EDI; invoices are automatically routed to the accounts department. On receipt of the invoice, the accounts clerk checks the order database, matches the invoice details with the database and updates the database to confirm receipt of invoice. The invoice is added to the purchases database, where the purchase day book (PDB) and suppliers individual account in the payables ledger are automatically updated.

Required

List **five** audit procedures that an auditor would normally carry out on the purchases system at Whizee Co, explaining the reason for each procedure. **(10 marks)**

84 CAATs (12/12) (amended)   18 mins

You are the audit senior of Daffodil & Co and are responsible for the audit of inventory for Magnolia Co, a glass manufacturer. You will be attending the year-end inventory count on 31 December 20X2.

In addition, your manager wishes to utilise computer-assisted audit techniques for the first time for controls and substantive testing in auditing Magnolia's inventory.

Required

For the audit of the inventory cycle and year-end inventory balance of Magnolia:

(a)   Describe **four** audit procedures that could be carried out using computer-assisted audit techniques (CAATS).

(4 marks)

(b)   Explain the potential advantages of using CAATs.   **(3 marks)**

(c)   Explain the potential disadvantages of using CAATs.   **(3 marks)**

(Total = 10 marks)

85 Redburn (12/09) (amended)   18 mins

Redburn Co, a publisher specialised in poetry collections, has been a client of your firm of Chartered Certified Accountants for a number of years.

A material figure in the statement of financial position of Redburn Co is the amount attributed to inventory of books. Bookshops have the right to return books which are not selling well, but about 10% of these are slightly damaged when returned. The company keeps similar records of returns as it does for sales.

The management of Redburn Co have told you that inventory is correctly valued at the lower of cost and net realisable value. You have already satisfied yourself that cost is correctly determined.

Required

(a)   Define net realisable value.   **(2 marks)**

(b)   State and explain the purpose of **four** procedures that you should use to ensure that net realisable value of the inventory is at or above cost.   **(8 marks)**

(Total = 10 marks)

86 Tirrol (6/09) (amended)   18 mins

You are an audit manager for Cal & Co and are in charge of planning the audit of Tirrol Co for the year ended 30 June 20X9. Your firm has recently gained this audit following a competitive tender.

Tirrol Co provides repair services to motor vehicles from 25 different locations. All inventory, sales and purchasing systems are computerised, with each location maintaining its own computer system. The software in each location is the same because the programs were written specifically for Tirrol Co by a reputable software house. Data from each location is amalgamated on a monthly basis at Tirrol Co's head office to produce management and financial accounts.

Tirrol Co's internal audit department are going to assist with the statutory audit. The chief internal auditor will provide you with documentation on the computerised inventory systems at Tirrol Co. The documentation provides details of the software and shows diagrammatically how transactions are processed through the inventory system. This documentation can be used to significantly decrease the time needed to understand the computer systems and enable audit software to be written for this year's audit.

Required

(a)   Explain **four** benefits of using audit software in the audit of Tirrol Co.   **(4 marks)**

(b)   Explain how you will evaluate the computer systems documentation produced by the internal audit department in order to place reliance on it during your audit.   **(6 marks)**

(Total = 10 marks)

87 Obtaining evidence

18 mins

The auditor has a responsibility to design audit procedures to obtain sufficient and appropriate evidence. There are various audit procedures for obtaining evidence, such as external confirmation.

Required

Apart from external confirmation:

(i)   State and explain **five** procedures for obtaining evidence.

(ii)   For each procedure, describe an example relevant to the audit of purchases and other expenses.

(10 marks)

88 Letham (12/09) (amended)

18 mins

(a)   Describe **four** methods of selecting a sample of items to test from a population in accordance with ISA 530 *Audit Sampling*. **(4 marks)**

(b)   Letham Co is a large engineering company. The manufacturing process is capital intensive and the company holds a wide variety of plant and equipment.

The finance director prepares a detailed non-current assets budget annually. This annual budget, which is approved by the full board, is held on computer file and is the authority for the issue of a purchase order.

When the item of plant and equipment is delivered to the company, a pre-numbered goods received note (GRN) is prepared, a copy of which is sent to the accounting department, and used to update the non-current assets budget to reflect the movement. At the same time as the purchase invoice enters the purchasing system, a computerised non-current assets register is updated.

The internal audit department tests on a sample basis the operation of the system from budget preparation to entry in the non-current assets register.

As part of your work as external auditor, you are reviewing the non-current assets audit programme of the internal auditors and notice that the basis of their testing is a representative sample of purchase invoices. They use this to test entries in the non-current assets register and the updating movements on the annual budget.

Required

(i)   Explain why this is not a good test for completeness.

(ii)   State a more appropriate test to prove completeness of the non-current assets records, including the non-current assets register. **(6 marks)**

(Total = 10 marks)

89 Springfield Nurseries (AIR Pilot Paper) (amended)

18 mins

(a)   Auditors must obtain sufficient appropriate audit evidence to issue an audit opinion on the financial statements. In order to gain that evidence, auditors may use a combination of tests of controls and substantive procedures.

Required

Explain what is meant by:

(i)   A test of control
(ii)   A substantive procedure

And give one example of each that may be used when auditing the completeness of revenue. **(4 marks)**

(b)   Your firm is the auditor of Springfield Nurseries, a company operating garden centres which sell plants, shrubs and trees, garden furniture and gardening equipment (such as lawnmowers and sprinklers).

You are involved in the audit of the company's non-current assets for the year ended 31 December 20X8. The main categories of non-current assets are as follows:

(i)   Land and buildings (all of which are owned outright by the company, none of which are leased)
(ii)   Computers (on which an integrated inventory control and sales system is operated)
(iii)   A number of large and small motor vehicles, mostly used for the delivery of inventory to customers
(iv)   Equipment for packaging and pricing products.

The depreciation rates used are as follows:

(i)   Buildings   5% each year on cost
(ii)   Computers and motor vehicles 20% each year on the reducing balance basis
(iii)   Equipment   15% each year on cost

Required

Describe audit procedures you would perform to check the appropriateness of the depreciation rates on each of the three categories of non-current asset. **(6 marks)**

(Total = 10 marks)

90 Duck (12/11) (amended)   18 mins

You are an audit senior at Wither & Co, and are currently working on the external audit of Duck Co, a manufacturer of down bedding. The audit manager informs you of the following matters.

Duck Co has decided to outsource its sales ledger department and as a result is making 14 employees redundant. A redundancy provision, which is material, will be included in the draft financial statements.

Duck Co is considering establishing an internal audit (IA) department next year. The finance director has asked whether the work performed by the IA department can be relied upon by Wither & Co.

Required

(a)   Describe **five** substantive procedures you should perform to confirm the redundancy provision at the year end. **(5 marks)**

(b)   Explain the factors that should be considered by an external auditor before reliance can be placed on the work performed by a company's internal audit department. **(5 marks)**

(Total = 10 marks)

91 Audit procedures   18 mins

Audit evidence can be obtained using various audit procedures.

In respect of testing the accuracy of the time recording system for factory workers in a manufacturing business, explain **five** procedures used in collecting audit evidence and discuss whether the auditor will benefit from using each procedure. **(10 marks)**

92 MistiRead (AIR 6/07) (amended)   18 mins

You are an audit manager in Ron & Co. One of your audit clients, MistiRead Co, is a specialist supplier of crime fiction with over 120,000 customers. The company owns one large warehouse, which contains at any one time about 1 million books of up to 80,000 different titles. Customers place orders for books either over the internet or by mail order. Books are dispatched on the day of receipt of the order. Returns are allowed up to 30 days from the dispatch date provided the books look new and unread.

Due to the high inventory turnover, MistiRead maintains a perpetual inventory system using standard 'off the shelf' software. Ron & Co has audited the system for the last five years and has found no errors within the software. Continuous inventory checking is carried out by MistiRead's internal audit department.

You are currently reviewing the continuous inventory checking system with an audit junior. The junior needs experience in continuous inventory checking systems.

Required

(a)   Explain the advantages of using a perpetual inventory system.   **(4 marks)**

(b)   Describe the audit procedures you should perform to confirm the accuracy of the continuous inventory checking at MistiRead Co. For each procedure, explain the reason for carrying out that procedure.   **(6 marks)**

(Total = 10 marks)

93 First Light   18 mins

(a)   Describe the auditor's responsibilities in relation to the physical inventory count that will take place at the year end.   **(4 marks)**

You are the audit senior in a firm of chartered certified accountants, and are responsible for auditing the inventory of First Light Co, a manufacturer of awnings. You will be attending the year-end inventory count on 31 December 20X3.

Required

(b)   Describe **six** procedures to be undertaken by the auditor **during** the inventory count of First Light Co in order to gain sufficient appropriate audit evidence.   **(6 marks)**

(Total = 10 marks)

94 Mickey   18 mins

You are the audit manager of Donald & Co, responsible for the year end audit of Mickey Co. Mickey Co owns three offices. During the year, one of the company's properties was revalued from $203,000 to $238,000 by an independent expert valuer.

Required

(a)   Describe the factors Donald & Co should consider when placing reliance on the work of the independent valuer.   **(4 marks)**

(b)   (i)   Comment on the acceptability of the revaluation.   **(2 marks)**

        (ii)   Besides evaluating the independent valuer's report, describe **four** procedures the auditor should carry out to gain evidence over the adequacy of the value of the workshop and the related disclosures included in the financial statements.   **(4 marks)**

(Total = 10 marks)

95 Panda (6/13) (amended)   18 mins

Panda Co manufactures chemicals and has a factory and four offsite storage locations for finished goods.

Panda Co's year end was 30 April 20X3. The final audit is almost complete and the financial statements and audit report are due to be signed next week. Revenue for the year is $55 million and profit before taxation is $5.6 million.

The following two events have occurred subsequent to the year end. No amendments or disclosures have been made in the financial statements.

Event 1 – Defective chemicals

Panda Co undertakes extensive quality control checks prior to dispatch of any chemicals. Testing on 3 May 20X3 found that a batch of chemicals produced in April was defective. The cost of this batch was $0.85 million. In its current condition it can be sold at a scrap value of $0.1 million. The costs of correcting the defect are too significant for Panda Co's management to consider this an alternative option.

Event 2 – Explosion

An explosion occurred at the smallest of the four offsite storage locations on 20 May 20X3. This resulted in some damage to inventory and property, plant and equipment. Panda Co's management have investigated the cause of the explosion and believe that they are unlikely to be able to claim on their insurance. Management of Panda Co has estimated that the value of damaged inventory and property, plant and equipment was $0.9 million and it now has no scrap value.

Required

For each of the two events above:

(i)   Explain whether the financial statements require amendment.

(ii)   Describe audit procedures that should be performed in order to form a conclusion on any required amendment.

      Note: The total marks will be split equally between each event.   **(10 marks)**

96 Delphic (12/07)   36 mins

Delphic Co is a wholesaler of furniture (such as chairs, tables and cupboards). Delphic buys the furniture from six major manufacturers and sells them to over 600 different customers ranging from large retail chain stores to smaller owner-controlled businesses. The receivables balance therefore includes customers owing up to $125,000 to smaller balances of about $5,000, all with many different due dates for payments and credit limits. All information is stored on Delphic's computer systems although previous audits have tended to adopt an 'audit around the computer' approach.

You are the audit senior in charge of the audit of the receivables balance. For the first time at this client, you have decided to use audit software to assist with the audit of the receivables balance. Computer staff at Delphic are happy to help the auditor, although they cannot confirm completeness of systems documentation, and warn that the systems have very old operating systems in place, limiting file compatibility with more modern programs.

The change in audit approach has been taken mainly to fully understand Delphic's computer systems prior to new internet modules being added next year. To limit the possibility of damage to Delphic's computer files, copy files will be provided by Delphic's computer staff for the auditor to use with their own audit software.

Required

(a)   Explain the audit procedures that should be carried out using audit software on the receivables balance at Delphic Co. For each procedure, explain the reason for that procedure.   **(9 marks)**

(b)   Explain the potential problems of using audit software at Delphic Co. For each problem, explain how it can be resolved.   **(8 marks)**

(c)   Explain the concept of 'auditing around the computer' and discuss why this increases audit risk for the auditor.   **(3 marks)**

      (Total = 20 marks)

97 Tam (AIR 12/06) (amended)   36 mins

(a)   (i)   In the context of ISA 530 *Audit Sampling*, explain and provide examples of the terms 'sampling risk' and 'non-sampling' risk.   **(4 marks)**

      (ii)   Briefly explain how sampling and non-sampling risk can be controlled by the audit firm.   **(2 marks)**

Tam Co, is owned and managed by two brothers with equal shareholdings. The company specialises in the sale of expensive motor vehicles. Annual revenue is in the region of $70,000,000 and the company requires an audit under local legislation. About 500 cars are sold each year, with an average value of $140,000, although the range of values is from $130,000 to $160,000. Invoices are completed manually with one director signing all invoices to confirm the sales value is correct. All accounting and financial statement preparation is carried out by the directors. A recent expansion of the company's showroom was financed by a bank loan, repayable over the next five years.

The audit manager is starting to plan the audit of Tam Co. The audit senior and audit junior assigned to the audit are helping the manager as a training exercise.

Comments are being made about how to select a sample of sales invoices for testing. Audit procedures are needed to ensure that the managing director has signed them and then to trace details into the sales day book and sales ledger.

'We should check all invoices,' suggests the audit manager.

'How about selecting a sample using statistical sampling techniques,' adds the audit senior.

'Why waste time obtaining a sample?' asks the audit junior. He adds, 'taking a random sample of invoices by reviewing the invoice file and manually choosing a few important invoices will be much quicker.'

Required

(b)   Briefly explain each of the sample selection methods suggested by the audit manager, audit senior and audit junior, and discuss whether or not they are appropriate for obtaining a representative sample of sales invoices.   **(9 marks)**

(c)   Define 'materiality' and explain why the auditors of Tam Co must form an opinion on whether the financial statements are free from material misstatement.   **(5 marks)**

(Total = 20 marks)

98 BearsWorld (AIR 6/05)   36 mins

You are the auditor of BearsWorld, a limited liability company which manufactures and sells small cuddly toys by mail order. The company is managed by Mr Kyto and two assistants. Mr Kyto authorises important transactions such as wages and large orders, one assistant maintains the payables ledger and orders inventory and pays suppliers, and the other assistant receives customer orders and dispatches cuddly toys. Due to other business commitments Mr Kyto only visits the office once per week.

At any time, about 100 different types of cuddly toys are available for sale. All sales are made cash with order – there are no receivables. Customers pay using credit cards and occasionally by sending cash.

You are planning the audit of BearsWorld and are considering using some of the procedures for gathering audit evidence recommended by ISA 500 as follows:

(i)   Analytical Procedures
(ii)   Inquiry
(iii)   Inspection
(iv)   Observation
(v)   Recalculation

Required

(a)   For **each** of the above procedures:

    (i)   Explain its use in gathering audit evidence.   **(5 marks)**
    (ii)   Describe one example for the audit of BearsWorld.   **(5 marks)**

(b)   Discuss the suitability of each procedure for BearsWorld, explaining the limitations of each.   **(10 marks)**

(Total = 20 marks)

99 Wear Wraith (AIR 6/06)

36 mins

Wear Wraith (WW) Co's main activity is the extraction and supply of building materials including sand, gravel, cement and similar aggregates. The company's year end is 31 May and your firm has audited WW for a number of years. The main asset on the statement of financial position relates to non-current assets. A junior member of staff has attempted to prepare the non-current asset note for the financial statements. The note has not been reviewed by the senior accountant and so may contain errors.

	Land and buildings $	Plant and machinery $	Motor vehicles $	Railway trucks $	Total $
COST					
1 June 20X5	100,000	875,000	1,500,000	–	2,475,000
Additions	10,000	125,000	525,000	995,000	1,655,000
Disposals	–	(100,000)	(325,000)	–	(425,000)
31 May 20X6	110,000	900,000	1,700,000	995,000	3,705,000
Depreciation					
1 June 20X5	60,000	550,000	750,000	–	1,360,000
Charge	2,200	180,000	425,000	199,000	806,200
Disposals	–	(120,000)	(325,000)	–	(445,000)
31 May 20X6	62,200	610,000	850,000	199,000	1,721,200
Carrying amount					
31 May 20X6	47,800	290,000	850,000	796,000	1,983,800
Carrying amount					
31 May 20X5	40,000	325,000	750,000	–	1,115,000

- Land and buildings relate to company offices and land for those offices.

- Plant and machinery includes extraction equipment such as diggers and dumper trucks used to extract sand and gravel etc.

- Motor vehicles include large trucks to transport the sand, gravel etc.

- Railway trucks relate to containers used to transport sand and gravel over long distances on the railway network.

Depreciation rates stated in the financial statements are all based on cost and calculated using the straight line basis.

The rates are:

Land and buildings	2%
Plant and machinery	20%
Motor vehicles	33%
Railway trucks	20%

Disposals in the motor vehicles category relates to vehicles which were five years old.

Required

(a) Describe the audit work you should perform on railway trucks. **(10 marks)**

(b) You have just completed your analytical procedures of the non-current assets note.

Required

(i) Excluding railway trucks, identify and explain any issues with the non-current asset note.
(ii) Explain how each issue could be resolved. **(10 marks)**

Note. You do not need to re-cast the schedule.

(Total = 20 marks)

100 Tracey Transporters (AIR 6/05)   36 mins

You are the external auditor of Tracey Transporters, a public limited company (TT). The company's year end is 31 March. You have been the auditor since the company was formed 24 years ago to take advantage of the increase in goods being transported by road. Many companies needed to transport their products but did not always have sufficient vehicles to move them. TT therefore purchased ten vehicles and hired these to haulage companies for amounts of time ranging from three days to six months.

The business has grown in size and profitability and now has over 550 vehicles on hire to many different companies. At any one time, between five and 20 vehicles are located at the company premises where they are being repaired; the rest could be anywhere on the extensive road network of the country it operates in. Full details of all vehicles are maintained in a non-current asset register.

Bookings for hire of vehicles are received either over the telephone or via e-mail in TT's offices. A booking clerk checks the customer's credit status on the receivables ledger and then the availability of vehicles using the Vehicle Management System (VMS) software on TT's computer network. E-mails are filed electronically by customer name in the e-mail programme used by TT. If the customer's credit rating is acceptable and a vehicle is available, the booking is entered into the VMS and confirmed to the customer using the telephone or e-mail. Booking information is then transferred within the network from the VMS to the receivables ledger programme, where a sales invoice is raised. Standard rental amounts are allocated to each booking depending on the amount of time the vehicle is being hired for. Hard copy invoices are sent in the post for telephone orders or via e-mail for e-mail orders.

The main class of asset on TT's statement of financial position is the vehicles. The carrying amount of the vehicles is $6 million out of total shareholders' funds of $15 million as at 31 March 20X5.

Required

(a)   List and explain the reason for the audit tests you should perform to verify the completeness and accuracy of the sales figure in TT's financial statements.   **(10 marks)**

(b)   List and describe the audit work you should perform on the figure in the statement of financial position for vehicles in TT's financial statements for the year ended 31 March 20X5.   **(10 marks)**

(Total = 20 marks)

101 Duckworth Computers   36 mins

The firm of Chartered Certified Accountants you are employed by is the external auditor of Duckworth Computers, a privately owned incorporated business.

Accounting records are maintained on a computer using proprietary software.

You have worked on the audit for three years and this year you are in charge of the audit. Your assistant is a newly recruited business graduate who has done an accounting course but has no practical experience.

Because of the small size of the company there is limited opportunity for segregation of duties. You decide, as in previous years, that the appropriate audit strategy is to obtain evidence primarily through the performance of substantive procedures. You also plan to perform the audit around the computer as the proprietary software is known to be reliable and details of all transactions and balances can be readily printed out.

On arriving at the company's premises in December 20X9 to perform the final audit on the 31 October 20X9 financial statements, you obtain a copy of the year end bank reconciliation prepared by the bookkeeper and checked by the managing director. This is reproduced below.

Duckworth Computers
Bank Reconciliation 31 October 20X9

	$	$
Balance per bank statement 31 October 20X9		18,375.91
Deposits outstanding		
30 October	1,887.00	
31 October	1,973.00	3,860.00
		22,235.91
Outstanding cheques		
2696	25.00	
2724	289.40	
2725	569.00	
2728	724.25	
2729	1,900.00	
2730	398.00	
2731	53.50	
2732	1,776.00	
2733	255.65	5,990.80
		16,245.11
Cheque returned 'not sufficient funds' 29 October		348.00
Bank charges October		90.00
Balance per books 31 October 20X9		16,683.11

You have already obtained the bank confirmation and lists of cash (and cheque) receipts and payments printed out from the computer. These lists have been added and the totals agreed with ledger postings. You decide the first task to set for your assistant is the verification of the bank reconciliation.

Required

(a) (i) List the audit procedures to be followed by your assistant in verifying the bank reconciliation in sufficient detail for an inexperienced staff member to follow. **(6 marks)**

(ii) Explain the purpose of each procedure in terms of audit objectives. **(5 marks)**

(b) Discuss the reliability of bank statements as audit evidence. What steps can be taken if it is considered desirable to increase their reliability? **(3 marks)**

(c) (i) Distinguish between 'auditing around the computer' and 'auditing through the computer'. **(3 marks)**

(ii) Explain the circumstances when it would be inappropriate for the auditor to rely on auditing around the computer. **(3 marks)**

(Total = 20 marks)

102 Metcalf (AIR 6/07) (amended) 36 mins

ISA 500 *Audit evidence* states that the auditors objective 'is to design and perform audit procedures in such a way as to enable the auditor to obtain sufficient appropriate audit evidence to be able to draw reasonable conclusions on which to base the auditor's opinion'.

Required

(a) Describe the factors which will influence the auditor's judgement concerning the sufficiency of audit evidence obtained. **(4 marks)**

(b) You are the audit senior in charge of the audit of Metcalf Co, a company that has been trading for over 50 years. Metcalf Co manufactures and sells tables and chairs directly to the public. The company's year end is 31 March.

Current liabilities are shown on Metcalf Co's statement of financial position as follows.

	20X7	20X6
	$	$
Trade payables	884,824	816,817
Accruals	56,903	51,551
Provision for legal action	60,000	–
	1,001,727	868,368

The provision for legal action relates to a claim from a customer who suffered an injury while assembling a chair supplied by Metcalf Co. The directors of Metcalf Co dispute the claim, although they are recommending an out of court settlement to avoid damaging publicity against Metcalf Co.

Required

Describe the substantive audit procedures that you should undertake in the audit of current liabilities of Metcalf Co for the year ended 31 March 20X7. For each procedure, explain the purpose of that procedure.

Marks are allocated as follows.

(i)	Trade payables	**(8 marks)**
(ii)	Accruals	**(4 marks)**
(iii)	The provision for legal action	**(4 marks)**

(Total = 20 marks)

103 Have A Bite (12/09) (amended)   36 mins

(a)   Identify and explain **four** assertions relevant to accounts payable at the year-end date.   **(6 marks)**

You are the audit senior responsible for the audit of Have A Bite Co, a company that runs a chain of fast food restaurants. You are aware that a major risk of their sector is that poor food quality might result in damage claims by customers.

You had satisfied yourself at the interim audit that the company's control risk as regards purchases of food and its preparation in the kitchen was low. However, during the year-end audit, it comes to your attention that one month before the year-end, a customer has sued the company for personal injury caused by food poisoning, claiming an amount of $200,000 in compensation. This amount is material to the stated profit of the company, but management believes that it has good defences against the claim.

The overstatement of revenue has also been identified as an area of high audit risk.

Required

(b)   (i)   State **two** controls that the company should have in place to reduce the risk associated with purchases of food and its preparation in the kitchen.

        (ii)   State **two** audit procedures you should carry out during controls testing to satisfy yourself that control risk in this area is low.   **(4 marks)**

(c)   In respect of the potential claim state **three** items of evidence you should obtain and explain how they might enable you to form a conclusion on the likelihood of the claim being successful.   **(6 marks)**

(d)   Describe **four** substantive analytical procedures that you would carry out in respect of revenue.   **(4 marks)**

(Total = 20 marks)

104 FireFly Tennis Club (AIR 12/06) (amended)   36 mins

The FireFly Tennis Club owns 12 tennis courts. The club uses 'all weather' tarmac tennis courts, which have floodlights for night-time use. The club's year end is 30 September. Members pay an annual fee to use the courts and participate in club championships. The club had 430 members as at 1 October 20X5.

Income is derived from two main sources:

1   Membership fees. Each member pays a fee of $200 per annum. Fees for the new financial year are payable within one month of the club year end. Approximately 10% of members do not renew their membership. New members joining during the year pay 50% of the total fees that would have been payable had they been members for a full year. During 20X6, 50 new members joined the club. No members pay their fees before they are due.

2   Court hire fees: Non-members pay $5 per hour to hire a court. Non-members have to sign a list in the club house showing courts hired. Money is placed in a cash box in the club house for collection by the club secretary. All fees (membership and court hire) are paid in cash. They are collected by the club secretary and banked on a regular basis. The paying-in slip shows the analysis between fees and court hire income. The secretary provides the treasurer with a list of bankings showing member's names (for membership fees) and the amount banked. Details of all bankings are entered into the cash book by the treasurer.

Main items of expenditure are:

1   Court maintenance including repainting lines on a regular basis.
2   Power costs for floodlights.
3   Tennis balls for club championships. Each match in the championship uses 12 tennis balls.

The treasurer pays for all expenditure using the club's debit card. Receipts are obtained for all expenses and these are maintained in date order in an expenses file. The treasurer also enters the expenditure into the cash book and prepares the annual financial statements.

Under the rules of the club, the annual accounts must be audited by an independent auditor. The date is now 13 December 20X6 and the treasurer has just prepared the financial statements for audit.

Required

(a) Describe the audit work that should be performed to determine the completeness of income for the FireFly Tennis Club.   **(10 marks)**

(b) Describe the audit procedures that should be performed to check the completeness and accuracy of expenditure for the FireFly Tennis Club.   **(5 marks)**

(c) Discuss why internal control testing has limited value when auditing not-for-profit entities such as the FireFly Tennis Club.   **(5 marks)**

(Total = 20 marks)

105 Walsh (AIR 12/06) (amended)   36 mins

Walsh Co sells motor vehicle fuel, accessories and spares to retail customers. The company owns 25 shops.

The company has recently implemented a new computerised wages system. Employees work a standard eight hour day. Hours are recorded using a magnetic card system; when each employee arrives for work, they hold their card close to the card reader; the reader recognises the magnetic information on the card identifying the employee as being 'at work'. When the employee leaves work at the end of the day the process is reversed showing that the employee has left work.

Hours worked are calculated each week by the computer system using the magnetic card information. Overtime is calculated as any excess over the standard hours worked. Any overtime over 10% of standard hours is sent on a computer generated report by e-mail to the financial accountant. If necessary, the accountant overrides overtime payments if the hours worked are incorrect.

Statutory deductions and net pay are also computer calculated with payments being made directly into the employee's bank account. The only other manual check is the financial accountant authorising the net pay from Walsh's bank account, having reviewed the list of wages to be paid.

Required

(a) (i)   Describe the two main types of Computer-Assisted Audit Techniques.

     (ii) Using examples from Walsh Co, explain the benefits of using Computer-Assisted Audit Techniques to help the auditor to obtain sufficient appropriate audit evidence to be able to draw reasonable conclusions on which to base the audit opinion.   **(8 marks)**

(b) List six examples of audit tests on Walsh Co's wages system using audit software.   **(6 marks)**

(c) Explain how using test data should help in the audit of Walsh Co's wages system, noting any problems with this audit technique.   **(6 marks)**

(Total = 20 marks)

106 Pineapple (6/12)   36 mins

(a) (i)   Identify and explain **four** financial statement assertions relevant to account balances at the year end.

     (ii) For each identified assertion, describe a substantive procedure relevant to the audit of year-end inventory.   **(8 marks)**

(b) Pineapple Beach Hotel Co (Pineapple) operates a hotel providing accommodation, leisure facilities and restaurants. Its year end was 30 April 2012. You are the audit senior of Berry & Co and are currently preparing the audit programmes for the year end audit of Pineapple. You are reviewing the notes of last week's meeting between the audit manager and finance director where two material issues were discussed.

Depreciation

Pineapple incurred significant capital expenditure during the year on updating the leisure facilities for the hotel. The finance director has proposed that the new leisure equipment should be depreciated over 10 years using the straight-line method.

Food poisoning

Pineapple's directors received correspondence in March from a group of customers who attended a wedding at the hotel. They have alleged that they suffered severe food poisoning from food eaten at the hotel and are claiming substantial damages. Pineapple's lawyers have received the claim and believe that the lawsuit against the company is unlikely to be successful.

Required

Describe substantive procedures to obtain sufficient and appropriate audit evidence in relation to the above two issues.

Note: The total marks will be split equally between each issue.   **(8 marks)**

(c) List and explain the purpose of **four** items that should be included on every working paper prepared by the audit team.   **(4 marks)**

(Total = 20 marks)

107 Rose (12/12)

(a) Identify and explain each of the **five** fundamental principles contained within ACCA's *Code of Ethics and Conduct.* **(5 marks)**

(b) Rose Leisure Club Co (Rose) operates a chain of health and fitness clubs. Its year end was 31 October 20X2. You are the audit manager and the year-end audit is due to commence shortly. The following three matters have been brought to your attention.

(i) **Trade payables and accruals**

Rose's finance director has notified you that an error occurred in the closing of the purchase ledger at the year end. Rather than it closing on 1 November, it accidentally closed one week earlier on 25 October. All purchase invoices received between 25 October and the year end have been posted to the 20X3 year-end purchase ledger. **(6 marks)**

(ii) **Receivables**

Rose's trade receivables have historically been low as most members pay monthly in advance. However, during the year a number of companies have taken up group memberships at Rose and hence the receivables balance is now material. The audit senior has undertaken a receivables circularisation for the balances at the year end; however, there are a number who have not responded and a number of responses with differences. **(5 marks)**

(iii) **Reorganisation**

The company recently announced its plans to reorganise its health and fitness clubs. This will involve closing some clubs for refurbishment, retraining some existing staff and disposing of some surplus assets. These plans were agreed at a board meeting in October and announced to their shareholders on 29 October. Rose is proposing to make a reorganisation provision in the financial statements. **(4 marks)**

Required

Describe substantive procedures you would perform to obtain sufficient and appropriate audit evidence in relation to the above three matters.

Note*:* The mark allocation is shown against each of the three matters above. **(Total = 20 marks)**

108 Textile Wholesalers

Your firm is the auditor of Textile Wholesalers, a limited liability company, which buys textile products (eg clothing) from manufacturers and sells them to retailers. You attended the inventory count at the company's year-end of Thursday 31 October 20X6. The company does not maintain book inventory records, and previous years' audits have revealed problems with purchases cut-off.

Your audit procedures on purchases cut-off, which started from the goods received note (GRN), have revealed the following results:

	Date of GRN	GRN Number	Supplier's Invoice No	Invoice value $	On purchase ledger before year end	In purchase accruals at year end
1	28.10.X6	1324	6254	4,642	Yes	No
2	29.10.X6	1327	1372	5,164	Yes	Yes
3	30.10.X6	1331	9515	7,893	No	Yes
4	31.10.X6	1335	4763	9,624	No	No
5	1.11.X6	1340	5624	8,243	Yes	No
6	4.11.X6	1345	9695	6,389	No	Yes
7	5.11.X6	1350	2865	7,124	No	No

Assume that goods received before the year-end are in inventories at the year-end, and goods received after the year-end are not in inventories at the year-end.

A purchase accrual is included in payables at the year-end for goods received before the year-end when the purchase invoice has not been posted to the trade payables ledger before the year-end.

Required

(a)   At the inventory count:

    (i)   Describe the procedures the company's staff should carry out to ensure that inventories are counted accurately and cut-off details are recorded.

    (ii)   Describe the procedures you could carry out and the matters you would record in your working papers.   **(12 marks)**

(b)   From the results of your purchases cut-off test, described in the question:

    (i)   Identify the cut-off errors and produce a schedule of the adjustments which should be made to the reported profit, purchases and payables in the financial statements to correct the errors.   **(4 marks)**

    (ii)   Comment on the results of your test, and state what further action you would take.   **(4 marks)**

                       (Total = 20 marks)

REVIEW AND REPORTING

Questions 109 – 126 cover Review and Reporting, the subject of Part E of the BPP Study Text for F8.

109 Multiple choice questions

83 mins

1   As part of the review stage of an audit, the auditor will consider subsequent events.

Up to which date does the auditor have an active responsibility to perform procedures designed to identify subsequent events?

A   The reporting date
B   The date of the auditor's report
C   The date of issue of the financial statements
D   The date of approval of the financial statements   **(2 marks)**

2   Which of the following procedures will be performed by the auditor as part of a subsequent events review?

(1)   Request for written representations from management
(2)   Review of minutes of board meetings held after the date of the financial statements

A   (1) only
B   (2) only
C   (1) and (2)
D   Neither (1) nor (2)   **(2 marks)**

3   Is the following statement regarding the purpose of subsequent events true or false?

The purpose of the subsequent events review performed by the auditor is to ensure that the effects of all subsequent events identified are reflected in the financial statements.

A   True
B   False   **(1 mark)**

4   Is the following statement regarding the going concern assumption true or false?

Under the going concern assumption it is assumed that the business will never have cause to cease trading.

A   True
B   False   **(1 mark)**

5   Is the following statement regarding the auditor's responsibilities regarding going concern true or false?

It is the auditor's responsibility to assess an entity's ability to continue as a going concern.

A   True
B   False   **(1 mark)**

6   M Co has a year end of 31 December 20X4. The auditor has identified that management's assessment of M Co's ability to continue as a going concern covers the period to 30 June 20X5.

What action should the auditor take?

A   Request that management extends the assessment period to 30 September 20X5

B   Request that management extends the assessment period to 31 December 20X5

C   Request that management extends the assessment period to 31 December 20X6

D   No action is required provided the auditor is satisfied with management's assessment to 30 June 20X5

                                                                          (2 marks)

7   ISA 570 *Going concern* identifies events and conditions that may cast doubt about the going concern assumption.

Which of the following are identified by ISA 570 as financial factors?

(1)   Loss of key customers
(2)   Net liability position
(3)   Substantial operating losses
(4)   Shortages of key raw materials

A   (1) and (2)
B   (1) and (4)
C   (2) and (3)
D   (3) and (4)   **(2 marks)**

8   Z Co has a year end of 30 June 20X4. Management has assessed the ability of the company to continue as a going concern based on the period to 30 June 20X5.

Which of the following procedures **must** the auditor perform to identify factors that may affect Z Co's ability to continue as a going concern beyond 30 June 20X5?

A   Analysis of cash flow forecasts
B   Review of board minutes
C   Review of loan terms
D   Inquiry of management   **(2 marks)**

9   The auditor of S Co has concluded that the use of the going concern assumption is appropriate and that the material uncertainty has been adequately disclosed.

What is the impact of this conclusion on the audit report?

A   Adverse opinion
B   Modified opinion
C   Unmodified opinion without an emphasis of matter paragraph
D   Unmodified opinion with an emphasis of matter paragraph   **(2 marks)**

10 The auditor of Y Co has concluded that Y Co is not a going concern. The financial statements have been prepared on a going concern basis and management has refused to change them.

What form of audit opinion will be issued by the auditor?

A   An unmodified opinion
B   A modified opinion due to material misstatement
C   A modified opinion due to insufficient appropriate audit evidence
D   An adverse opinion   **(2 marks)**

11 T Co has a year end of 31 July 20X4. The auditor completed the audit work on 10 September 20X4 and the auditor's report was signed on 30 September 20X4. The financial statements were issued on 1 November 20X4.

Which of the following would be the most appropriate date for the directors to sign the written representations letter?

A   31 July 20X4
B   10 September 20X4
C   30 September 20X4
D   1 November 20X4   **(2 marks)**

12   Is the following statement regarding written representations true or false?

Written representations by management regarding specific assertions in the financial statements provide sufficient appropriate audit evidence in their own right.

A   True
B   False   (1 mark)

13   For which of the following matters **must** written representations be sought?

(1)   That management has fulfilled its responsibility for the preparation of the financial statements
(2)   That management has provided the auditor with all the information relevant to the audit
(3)   That accounts receivable are recoverable
(4)   That inventory is correctly valued at the lower of cost and net realisable value

A   (1) and (2)
B   (1) and (3)
C   (2) and (4)
D   (3) and (4)   (2 marks)

14   Which of the following statements regarding analytical procedures is correct?

A   Analytical procedures must be used as part of the overall review of the financial statements.
B   Analytical procedures may be used as part of the overall review of the financial statements.
C   Analytical procedures are only used as risk assessment procedures.

                                                                                                    (1 mark)

15   Misstatements can arise from error or fraud.

Which of the following statements is correct regarding the auditor's accumulation of identified misstatements?

A   The auditor must accumulate all misstatements identified during the audit.

B   The auditor must only accumulate individually material misstatements identified during the audit.

C   The auditor must accumulate misstatements identified during the audit, other than those that are clearly trivial.   (1 mark)

16   ISA 700 *Forming an opinion and reporting on financial statements* sets out the basic elements of an auditor's report.

Which of the following is **not** included in an unmodified auditor's report?

A   Management's responsibility for the financial statements
B   Auditors' responsibilities
C   Audit opinion
D   Deficiencies of internal controls   (2 marks)

17   The auditor of Q Co has completed the audit and has concluded that sufficient appropriate evidence has been obtained, which confirms that the financial statements are not materially misstated.

Which form of audit opinion will the auditor issue?

A   Adverse opinion
B   Qualified opinion
C   Unmodified opinion
D   A disclaimer of opinion   (2 marks)

18   ISA 705 *Modification to the opinion in the independent auditor's report* identifies three possible types of modification.

In which of the following circumstances would a disclaimer of opinion be issued?

A   The auditor concludes that the financial statements include misstatements which are material but not pervasive to the financial statements.

B   The auditor concludes that the financial statements include misstatements which are both material and pervasive to the financial statements.

C   The auditor has not been able to obtain sufficient appropriate audit evidence on which to base an opinion but has concluded that the possible effects of any undetected misstatements could be material but not pervasive.

D   The auditor has not been able to obtain sufficient appropriate audit evidence on which to base an opinion and has concluded that the possible effects of any undetected misstatements could be both material and not pervasive.   **(2 marks)**

19   The auditor of B Co has concluded that inventory is overstated as a number of lines have not been valued at the lower of cost and net realisable value. The overstatement is material but not pervasive to the financial statements. Management has refused to make an adjustment to the financial statements.

What form of modified opinion should the auditor issue?

A   Adverse opinion
B   Disclaimer of opinion
C   Qualified opinion due to a material misstatement
D   Qualified opinion due to insufficient appropriate evidence on which to base an opinion   **(2 marks)**

20   The financial statements of Z Co include a receivables balance of $20,000 which the auditors do not believe will be recovered. Materiality has been set at $100,000. There are no other unadjusted misstatements.

What form of audit opinion would be issued by the auditor?

A   Adverse opinion
B   Unmodified opinion
C   Disclaimer of opinion
D   Qualified opinion due to overstatement of receivables   **(2 marks)**

21   P Co is being sued by a customer for the supply of faulty products. At the year end the outcome of the legal case is still uncertain. The directors have fully disclosed the matter as a contingent liability and the auditors are satisfied with the treatment and the level of disclosure. The auditors have concluded that the uncertainty is fundamental to the understanding of the financial statements.

What form of audit opinion would the auditor give?

A   Disclaimer
B   Unmodified opinion with an emphasis of matter paragraph
C   Unmodified opinion without an emphasis of matter paragraph
D   Qualified opinion   **(2 marks)**

22   The auditor may wish to draw the users' attention to a matter which is not presented or disclosed in the financial statements but which is relevant to the users' understanding of the auditor's report.

How would this affect the auditor's report?

A   An emphasis of matter paragraph would be included.

B   The audit opinion would be qualified.

C   An other matters paragraph would be included.

D   The auditor's report would not be affected as the auditor's report only refers to matters presented or disclosed in the financial statements.   **(2 marks)**

23   The majority of the books and records of Q Co have been destroyed by a flood and the auditor has no other realistic means of obtaining sufficient, appropriate audit evidence.

Which form of opinion will the auditor issue?

A   An adverse opinion
B   A disclaimer of opinion
C   Qualified opinion on the basis that sufficient appropriate evidence is not available
D   Unmodified opinion with an emphasis of matter paragraph explaining the circumstances of the flood

(2 marks)

---

24   The statement of financial position of R Co includes a material amount of $200,000 in respect of costs capitalised in the year as development expenditure. The auditor has concluded that these costs are research expenditure.

If the auditor is to issue an unmodified opinion which financial statements will require adjustment?

A   Statement of financial position only
B   Statement of profit or loss only
C   Statement of financial position and statement of profit or loss
D   Neither the statement of financial position nor the statement of profit or loss   **(2 marks)**

---

110 Evaluating misstatements and responsibilities   18 mins

(a)   ISA 450 *Evaluation of misstatements identified during the audit* deals with the auditor's responsibilities to evaluate the effect of identified misstatements.

Required

Define 'uncorrected misstatement' and explain the auditor's responsibilities relating to uncorrected misstatements.   **(4 marks)**

(b)   ISA 580 *Written Representations* provides guidance on the use of written representations as audit evidence.

Required

List six items that could be included in a representation letter.   **(3 marks)**

(c)   Describe the three types of modified audit opinions.   **(3 marks)**

(Total = 10 marks)

---

111 Written representation and going concern (12/07) (amended)   18 mins

(a)   Towards the end of an audit, it is common for the auditor to seek written representations from the management of the client company. This is usually in the form of a letter from management to the auditors containing all of the required written representations. The auditors often draft the letter for the client to sign.

Required

Explain why auditors seek written representations and list the matters commonly included in the letter containing managements' written representations.   **(5 marks)**

(b)   ISA 570 *Going Concern* provides guidance to auditors in respect of ensuring that an entity can continue as a going concern.

Required

Explain the actions that an auditor should carry out to ascertain whether an entity is a going concern.

(5 marks)

(Total = 10 marks)

112 Corsco (AIR 12/03) (amended)
18 mins

Corsco is a large telecommunications company that is listed on a stock exchange. It is highly geared because, like many such companies, it borrowed a large sum to pay for a licence to operate a mobile phone network with technology that has not proved popular. The company's share price has dropped by 50% during the last three years and there have been several changes of senior management during that period. There has been considerable speculation in the press over the last six months about whether the company can survive without being taken over by a rival. There have been three approaches made to the company by other companies regarding a possible takeover but all have failed, mainly because the bidders pulled out of the deal as a result of the drop in share prices generally.

The company has net assets, but has found it necessary to severely curtail its capital investment program. Some commentators consider this to be fundamental to the future growth of the business, others consider that the existing business is fundamentally sound. It has also been necessary for the company to restructure its finances. Detailed disclosures of all of these matters have always been made in the financial statements. No reference has been made to the going concern status of the company in previous auditor's reports on financial statements and the deterioration in circumstances in the current year is no worse than it has been in previous years.

Required

(a)   On the basis of the information provided above, describe the auditor's report that you consider is likely to be issued in the case of Corsco, giving reasons. **(4 marks)**

(b)   Explain the difficulties that would be faced by Corsco and its auditors if Corsco's audit report made reference to going concern issues. **(6 marks)**

(Total = 10 marks)

113 Going concern and auditor's reports (AIR 12/03) (amended)
18 mins

(a)   Describe external auditor's responsibilities and the work that the auditor must perform in relation to the going concern status of companies. **(5 marks)**

(b)   Describe the possible auditor's reports that can be issued where the going concern status of a company is called into question; your answer should describe the circumstances in which they can be issued.

(5 marks)

(Total = 10 marks)

114 Greenfields (12/10) (amended)
18 mins

Greenfields Co specialises in manufacturing equipment which can help to reduce toxic emissions in the production of chemicals. The company has grown rapidly over the past eight years and this is due partly to the warranties that the company gives to its customers. It guarantees its products for five years and if problems arise in this period it undertakes to fix them, or provide a replacement product.

You are the manager responsible for the audit of Greenfields and you are performing the final review stage of the audit and have come across the following two issues.

Receivable balance owing from Yellowmix Co

Greenfields has a material receivable balance owing from its customer, Yellowmix Co. During the year-end audit, your team reviewed the ageing of this balance and found that no payments had been received from Yellowmix for over six months, and Greenfields would not allow this balance to be circularised. Instead management has assured your team that they will provide a written representation confirming that the balance is recoverable.

Warranty provision

The warranty provision included within the statement of financial position is material. The audit team has performed testing over the calculations and assumptions which are consistent with prior years. The team has requested a written representation from management confirming the basis and amount of the provision are reasonable. Management has yet to confirm acceptance of this representation.

Required

For each of the two issues above:

(i)   Discuss the appropriateness of written representations as a form of audit evidence.   **(4 marks)**

(ii)   Describe additional procedures the auditor should now perform in order to reach a conclusion on the balance to be included in the financial statements.   **(6 marks)**

(Total = 10 marks)

115 Tye (6/09)   **18 mins**

One of your audit clients is Tye Co a company providing petrol, aviation fuel and similar oil based products to the government of the country it is based in. Although the company is not listed on any stock exchange, it does follow best practice regarding corporate governance regulations. The audit work for this year is complete, apart from the matter referred to below.

As part of Tye Co's service contract with the government, it is required to hold an emergency inventory reserve of 6,000 barrels of aviation fuel. The inventory is to be used if the supply of aviation fuel is interrupted due to unforeseen events such as natural disaster or terrorist activity.

This fuel has in the past been valued at its cost price of $15 a barrel. The current value of aviation fuel is $120 a barrel. Although the audit work is complete, as noted above, the directors of Tye Co have now decided to show the 'real' value of this closing inventory in the financial statements by valuing closing inventory of fuel at market value, which does not comply with relevant accounting standards. The draft financial statements of Tye Co currently show a profit of approximately $500,000 with net assets of $170 million.

Required

(a)   List the audit procedures and actions that you should now take in respect of the above matter.   **(6 marks)**

(b)   There are many different types of accounting estimates in the financial statements. Describe the audit procedures required in respect of accounting estimates.   **(4 marks)**

(Total = 10 marks)

116 EastVale (amended)   **18 mins**

EastVale Co manufactures a range of dairy products (for example, milk, yoghurt and cheese) in one factory. Products are stored in a nearby warehouse (which is rented by EastVale) before being sold to 350 supermarkets located within 200 kilometres of EastVale's factory. The products are perishable with an average shelf life of eight days. EastVale's financial statements year-end is 31 July.

It is four months since the year-end at your audit client of EastVale and the annual audit of EastVale is almost complete, but the auditor's report has not been signed.

The following events have just come to your attention. Both events occurred in late November.

(a)   A fire in the warehouse rented by the company has destroyed 60% of the inventory held for resale.

(b)   A batch of cheese produced by EastVale was found to contain some chemical impurities. Over 300 consumers have complained about food poisoning after eating the cheese. 115 supermarkets have stopped purchasing EastVale's products and another 85 are considering whether to stop purchasing from EastVale. Lawyers acting on behalf of the consumers are now presenting a substantial claim for damages against EastVale.

Required

In respect of each of the events at EastVale Co mentioned above:

(i)   State, with reasons, whether or not the financial statements for the year-end require amendment.

(5 marks)

(ii)   Discuss the impact on the auditor's report, including whether or not the audit opinion should be modified.

(5 marks)

(Total = 10 marks)

117 ZeeDiem (12/08) (amended)   18 mins

The date is 3 December 20X8. The audit of ZeeDiem Co is nearly complete and the financial statements and the audit report are due to be signed next week. However, the following additional information on two material events has just been presented to the auditor. The company's year end was 30 September 2008.

Event 1 – Occurred on 10 October 20X8

The springs in a new type of mattress have been found to be defective making the mattress unsafe for use. There have been no sales of this mattress; it was due to be marketed in the next few weeks. The company's insurers estimate that inventory to the value of $750,000 has been affected. The insurers also estimate that the mattresses are now only worth $225,000. No claim can be made against the supplier of springs as this company is in liquidation with no prospect of any amounts being paid to third parties. The insurers will not pay ZeeDiem for the fall in value of the inventory as the company was underinsured. All of this inventory was in the finished goods store at the end of the year and no movements of inventory have been recorded post year-end.

Event 2 – Occurred 5 November 20X8

Production at the ShamEve factory was halted for one day when a truck carrying dye used in colouring the fabric on mattresses reversed into a metal pylon, puncturing the vehicle allowing dye to spread across the factory premises and into a local river. The Environmental Agency is currently considering whether the release of dye was in breach of environmental legislation. The company's insurers have not yet commented on the event.

Required

(a)   Explain the auditor's responsibility in respect of events after the reporting period according to ISA 560 *Subsequent events*.

(3 marks)

(b)   Explain the audit procedures that should be carried out with regards to:

(i)   Event 1   (4 marks)

(ii)   Event 2   (3 marks)

(Total = 10 marks)

118 Green (AIR 6/07) (amended)   18 mins

Green Co grows crops on a large farm according to strict organic principles that prohibit the use of artificial pesticides and fertilizers. The farm has an 'organic certification', which guarantees its products are to be organic. The certification has increased its sales of flour, potatoes and other products, as customers seek to eat more healthily.

Green Co is run by two managers who are the only shareholders. Annual revenue is $50 million with a net profit of 5%. Both managers have run other businesses in the last 10 years. One business was closed due to suspected tax fraud (although no case was ever brought to court).

Green Co's current auditors provide audit services. Additional assurance on business controls and the preparation of financial statements are provided by a different accountancy firm.

Last year, a neighbouring farm, Black Co started growing genetically modified (GM) crops, the pollen from which blows over Green Co's fields on a regular basis. This is a threat to Green Co's organic status because organic crops must not be contaminated with GM material. Green Co is considering court action against Black Co for loss of income and to stop Black Co growing GM crops.

You are an audit partner in Lime & Co, a 15 partner firm of auditors and business advisors. You have been friends with the managers of Green Co for the last 15 years, advising them on an informal basis. The managers of Green Co have indicated that the audit will be put out to tender next month and have asked your audit firm to tender for the audit and the provision of other professional services. The management of Green have made it clear that they expect the auditors they appoint to issue a 'clean' auditor's report otherwise they will put the audit out to tender again.

Required

(a)   In respect of the going concern concept:

(i)   Define 'going concern'.   **(1 mark)**

(ii)   Explain the directors' responsibilities and the auditors' responsibilities regarding financial statements prepared on the going concern principle.   **(4 marks)**

(b)   Describe **five** audit procedures that should be carried out to determine whether or not the going concern basis is appropriate for Green Co.   **(5 marks)**

(Total = 10 marks)

119 Minnie (6/11) (amended)   18 mins

You are the audit manager of Daffy & Co and you are briefing your team on the approach to adopt in undertaking the review and finalisation stage of the audit. In particular, your audit senior is unsure about the steps to take in relation to uncorrected misstatements.

During the audit of Minnie Co, a number of uncorrected misstatement has been noted.

Required

(a)   Explain the term 'misstatement' and describe the auditor's responsibility in relation to misstatements.

(4 marks)

(b)   The following issues have arisen during the course of the audit of Minnie Co. Profit before tax is $10m.

(i)   Minnie Co's computerised wages program is backed up daily, however for a period of two months the wages records and the back-ups have become corrupted, and therefore cannot be accessed. Wages and salaries for these two months are $1.1m.   **(3 marks)**

(ii)   Minnie Co's main competitor has filed a lawsuit for $5m against them alleging a breach of copyright; this case is ongoing and will not be resolved prior to the auditor's report being signed. The matter is correctly disclosed as a contingent liability.   **(3 marks)**

Required

Describe the impact on the auditor's report if the above issues remain unresolved.

Note: The mark allocation is shown against each of the three issues above. Auditor's report extracts are **not** required.   **(Total = 10 marks)**

120 Medimade (6/10)   18 mins

Medimade Co is an established pharmaceutical company that has for many years generated 90% of its revenue through the sale of two specific cold and flu remedies. Medimade has lately seen a real growth in the level of competition that it faces in its market and demand for its products has significantly declined. To make matters worse, in the past the company has not invested sufficiently in new product development and so has been trying to remedy this by recruiting suitably trained scientific staff, but this has proved more difficult than anticipated.

In addition to recruiting staff the company also needed to invest $2m in plant and machinery. The company wanted to borrow this sum but was unable to agree suitable terms with the bank; therefore it used its overdraft facility, which carried a higher interest rate. Consequently, some of Medimade's suppliers have been paid much later than usual and hence some of them have withdrawn credit terms meaning the company must pay cash on delivery. As a result of the above the company's overdraft balance has grown substantially.

The directors have produced a cash flow forecast and this shows a significantly worsening position over the coming 12 months.

The directors have informed you that the bank overdraft facility is due for renewal next month, but they are confident that it will be renewed. They also strongly believe that the new products which are being developed will be ready to market soon and hence trading levels will improve and therefore that the company is a going concern. Therefore they do not intend to make any disclosures in the accounts regarding going concern.

Required

(a) Explain the audit procedures that the auditor of Medimade should perform in assessing whether or not the company is a going concern. **(6 marks)**

(b) The auditors have been informed that Medimade's bankers will not make a decision on the overdraft facility until after the audit report is completed. The directors have now agreed to include going concern disclosures.

Describe the impact on the audit report of Medimade if the auditor believes the company is a going concern but a material uncertainty exists. **(4 marks)**

(Total = 10 marks)

121 Reporting (12/11) (amended)   18 mins

(a) ISA 705 *Modifications to the opinion in the independent auditor's report* sets out the different types of modified opinions.

Required

State **three** ways in which an auditor's opinion may be modified and briefly explain each modification.

(3 marks)

(b) ISA 700 *Forming an Opinion and Reporting on Financial Statements* provides guidance on the form and content of the auditor's report and should contain a number of elements.

Required

Describe **five** elements of an unmodified auditor's report. **(5 marks)**

(c) Describe the purpose of the emphasis of matter paragraph. **(2 marks)**

(Total = 10 marks)

122 Hood Enterprises (AIR 6/05) (amended)   18 mins

You are the audit manager of Hood Enterprises, a limited liability company.

Extracts from the draft auditor's report produced by an audit junior are given below:

'We have audited the accompanying financial statements of Hood Enterprises Limited which comprise........ We have also evaluated the overall adequacy of the presentation of information in the company's annual report.'

Auditor's Responsibility

....We conducted our audit in accordance with Auditing Standards. Those standards require that we comply with ethical requirements and plan and perform the audit so that we can confirm the financial statements are free from material misstatement. The directors however are wholly responsible for the accuracy of the financial statements and no liability for errors can be accepted by the auditor.

An audit involves performing procedures to obtain as much audit evidence as possible in the time available about the amounts and disclosures in the financial statements.

An audit also includes evaluating the appropriateness of accounting policies used and the reasonableness of all accounting estimates made by management as well as evaluating the presentation of the financial statements…...'

Required

Identify and explain the errors in the above extract.

Note. You are not required to redraft the report. **(10 marks)**

123 Galartha (12/07)

18 mins

(a) You are the audit manager in JonArc & Co. The audit work on one of your new clients, Galartha Co, has just been completed. During the course of the audit, the audit team identified that no depreciation has been provided on buildings in the financial statements, although International Financial Reporting Standards suggest that depreciation should be provided.

The financial statements are now due to be signed, but you have been unable to resolve the matter regarding depreciation of buildings. The directors insist on not providing depreciation. You have therefore drafted the following extracts for your proposed auditor's report.

(1) As discussed in Note 15 to the financial statements, no depreciation has been provided in the financial statements, a practice which, in our opinion, is not in accordance with International Financial Reporting Standards.

(2) The provision for the year ended 31 September 20X7, should be $420,000 based on the straight-line method of depreciation using an annual rate of 5% for the buildings.

(3) Accordingly, the non-current assets should be reduced by accumulated depreciation of $1,200,000 and the profit for the year and accumulated reserve should be decreased by $420,000 and $1,200,000, respectively.

(4) In our opinion, except for the effect on the financial statements of the matter referred to in the preceding paragraph, the financial statements present fairly, in all material respects ... (remaining words are the same as for an unmodified opinion paragraph).

The extracts have been numbered to help you refer to them in your answer.

Required

Explain the meaning and purpose of each of the above extracts in your draft auditor's report. **(8 marks)**

(b) State the effect on your auditor's report of the following alternative situation:

Depreciation had not been provided on any non-current asset for a number of years, the effect of which if corrected would be to turn an accumulated profit into a significant accumulated loss.

(**Note**. You are not required to draft any auditor's reports.) **(2 marks)**

(Total = 10 marks)

124 Humphries (12/11) (amended)

18 mins

Humphries Co operates a chain of food wholesalers across the country and its year end was 30 September 20X1. The final audit is nearly complete and it is proposed that the financial statements and auditor's report will be signed on 13 December. Revenue for the year is $78 million and profit before taxation is $7.5 million. The following events have occurred subsequent to the year end.

Lawsuit

A key supplier of Humphries Co is suing them for breach of contract. The lawsuit was filed prior to the year end, and the sum claimed by them is $1 million. This has been disclosed as a contingent liability in the notes to the financial statements; however correspondence has just arrived from the supplier indicating that they are willing to settle the case for a payment by Humphries Co of $0.6 million. It is likely that the company will agree to this.

Warehouse

Humphries Co has three warehouses; following extensive rain on 20 November significant rain and river water flooded the warehouse located in Bass. All of the inventory was damaged and has been disposed of. The insurance company has already been contacted. No amendments or disclosures have been made in the financial statements.

Required

For each of the two events above:

(i)   Discuss whether the financial statements require amendment.
(ii) Describe audit procedures that should be performed in order to form a conclusion on the amendment.
(iii) Explain the impact on the auditor's report should the issue remain unresolved.

Note: The total marks will be split equally between each event.

(Total = 10 marks)

125 Boggart (12/11) (amended)   18 mins

(a)   Describe the auditor's responsibility for subsequent events occurring between:

(i)   The year-end date and the date the auditor's report is signed.
(ii)   The date the auditor's report is signed and the date the financial statements are issued.   **(5 marks)**

(b)   Boggart Co operates a chain of food wholesalers and its year end was 31 December 20X1. The final audit is nearly complete and it is proposed that the financial statements and audit report will be signed on 13 March. Revenue for the year is $54.6 million and profit before taxation is $5.3 million.

Subsequent to the year end, a customer of Boggart Co has been experiencing cash flow problems and its year-end balance is $0.2 million. The company has just become aware that its customer is experiencing significant going concern difficulties. Boggart believe that as the company has been trading for many years, they will receive some, if not full, payment from the customer; hence they have not adjusted the receivable balance.

Required

In respect of the issue above:

(i)   Discuss whether the financial statements require amendment.

(ii)   Describe audit procedures that should be performed in order to form a conclusion on the amendment.

(iii) Explain the impact on the auditor's report should the issue remain unresolved.   **(5 marks)**

(Total = 10 marks)

126 Strawberry (6/12) (amended)   18 mins

You are the audit manager of Kiwi & Co and you have been provided with financial statements extracts and the following information about your client, Strawberry Kitchen Designs Co (Strawberry), who is a kitchen manufacturer. The company's year end is 30 April 20X2.

Strawberry has recently been experiencing trading difficulties, as its major customer who owes $0.6m to Strawberry has ceased trading, and it is unlikely any of this will be received. However the balance is included within the financial statements extracts below. The sales director has recently left Strawberry and has yet to be replaced.

The monthly cash flow has shown a net cash outflow for the last two months of the financial year and is forecast as negative for the forthcoming financial year. As a result of this, the company has been slow in paying its suppliers and some are threatening legal action to recover the sums owing.

Due to its financial difficulties, Strawberry missed a loan repayment and, as a result of this breach in the loan covenants, the bank has asked that the loan of $4.8m be repaid in full within six months. The directors have decided that in order to conserve cash, no final dividend will be paid in 20X2.

Financial statements extracts for year ended 30 April:

	DRAFT 20X2 $m	ACTUAL 20X1 $m
Current Assets		
Inventory	3.4	1.6
Receivables	1.4	2.2
Cash	–	1.2
Current Liabilities		
Trade payables	1.9	0.9
Overdraft	0.8	–
Loans	4.8	0.2

Required

(a) Describe the audit procedures that you should perform in assessing whether or not the company is a going concern. **(5 marks)**

(b) Having performed the going concern audit procedures, you have serious concerns in relation to the going concern status of Strawberry. The finance director has informed you that as the cash flow issues are short term he does not propose to make any amendments to the financial statements.

Required

(i) State Kiwi & Co's responsibility for reporting on going concern to the directors of Strawberry Kitchen Designs Co. **(2 marks)**

(ii) If the directors refuse to amend the financial statements, describe the impact on the audit report. **(3 marks)**

(Total = 10 marks)

Answers

1 Multiple choice answers

1 A Directors are stewards of the shareholders' investment.

2 A There are five elements in total: Criteria, Report, Evidence, Subject matter and Three-party relationship (remember CREST).

3 C This is the process by which the IAASB develops new standards.

4 B The shareholders of the company usually appoint the auditors at a shareholders' annual general meeting. In rare circumstances, the directors may appoint the auditors.

5 A The external audit is carried out by external auditors who are independent of the company so that they can provide an independent opinion on whether the company's financial statements are materially misstated. The principal aim of the audit is not in relation to the control system in place, although deficiencies and recommendations may be suggested by the external auditors as a by-product of the external audit in a report to management at the conclusion of the audit.

6 B The statement if false. The external audit provides only reasonable assurance on the truth and fairness of the financial statements. There are various reasons for this – the use of sampling to test transactions and balances, inherent limitations in the company's internal control, evidence being persuasive rather than conclusive, and the use of judgement.

7 A The correct answer is option A. The auditor does not have the right to attend and speak at directors' meetings and should not make or take part in any executive decisions on behalf of the company. Auditors do have the rights stated at (2) and (3).

8 A Risk management is a key feature of effective corporate governance.

9 B Integrity is one of the fundamental principles of professional ethics – the other options are threats to the fundamental principles. There are five threats in total, the remaining ones being self-review and intimidation.

10 B Where disclosure is permitted rather than required by law the auditor must obtain permission from the client. Where money-laundering is suspected the auditor is obliged to disclose this to the relevant authority.

11 B Rotation of audit partners is a safeguard against the familiarity threat.

12 D Bookkeeping services can be provided in an emergency. Assistance can be given in tax disputes provided the firm is not acting as an advocate of the client and the effect of the matter is material to the financial statements. Internal audit services can be provided except where this would result in the audit firm's personnel assuming management responsibility.

13 B The directors have ultimate responsibility. The board must set up procedures of internal control and monitor them regularly to ensure that they are operating effectively.

14 B The *UK Corporate Governance Code* recommends that companies should have an audit committee. This Code applies to all companies with a premium listing in the UK, therefore it does not generally apply to smaller companies. The Code also adopts a comply or explain approach which means that provisions may not be followed provided non-compliance is explained.

15 B An audit committee must comprise at least three independent non-executive directors (two for smaller companies). The role and responsibilities of the audit committee are set out in the terms of reference established by the company.

16 C The board of directors and audit committee should work together so the audit committee should not undermine the board. The fact that internal audit reports directly to the audit committee is a strength as this adds independence to the internal audit function.

17 D The ACCA *Code* does not allow the following to have a direct or indirect material financial interest in a client: the audit firm, a member of the audit team and an immediate family member of a member of the audit team.

18 B Economy, efficiency and effectiveness are sometimes referred to as the '3E's' of VFM audits.

19	A	2 & 4 are characteristics of an *external* audit.
20	B	The internal auditor plays a key role in organisational risk management, an important aspect of corporate governance. The internal auditor ensures that there are strategies in place to manage business risk and that they are effective. Audit risk is relevant to the external audit.
21	D	The internal auditor must ensure that policies are adequate and that they are operating effectively.
22	B	The format and content of the internal audit report will depend on the nature of the assignment. The form and content of the external audit report is governed by a combination of statute and ISAs.
23	C	As employees of the company the internal auditors will lack independence.
24	B	Whilst the day-to-day operations will be managed by the service provider, the company using the service will need to monitor activities to ensure that the service provided complies with the service agreement and is of a suitable quality.
25	C	The internal audit function is a review and monitoring function. It should not take operational responsibility for any part of the system.
26	B	The directors are responsible for identifying risks and implementing appropriate strategies. The internal auditor is responsible for assessing whether the risk management system is working, and that strategies to minimise risks are effective.
27	C	While the existence of an audit committee is likely to reduce audit risk, this is not necessarily the case. The level of audit procedures required must be determined by the external auditors, based on their own understanding of the entity's business as a whole and assessment of risk.
28	C	The advocacy threat arises because the bank may be given the impression that the auditor supports the client's proposed acquisition.
29	C	There is no blanket prohibition on disclosure, nor is there any general right of the police or taxation authorities to demand information. Auditors have an implied contractual duty of confidentiality. There is no statutory duty of confidentiality.

2 Audit regulation

Text reference. Chapter 2

Top tips. This question is a good test of your knowledge of audit regulation. There are two parts for five marks each so your answers need to be fairly detailed. The key is to make sure you stick to the correct time allocation – so don't spend longer than nine minutes on each part. Use short paragraphs in your answer.

Easy marks. This question should be straightforward to answer.

(a) **Development of ISAs**

ISAs are set by IAASB, the International Auditing and Assurance Standards Board, which is a technical standing committee of IFAC, the International Federation of Accountants.

ISAs are developed in consultation with interested parties within the profession and outside of it. They are also developed with due regard for national standards on auditing.

Subjects for detailed study are selected by a subcommittee established for that purpose. The IAASB delegates to the subcommittee the initial responsibility for the preparation and drafting of auditing standards and statements.

As a result of the study, an exposure draft is prepared for consideration. If approved, the exposure draft is distributed for comment by member bodies of IFAC and to other interested parties.

Comments received in response to the exposure draft are then considered and it may be revised as a result. If this revised exposure draft is approved, it is issued as a definitive International Standard on Auditing.

(b)   **Role of professional bodies in the regulation of auditors**

One of the key professional bodies is the ACCA.

The role of the ACCA varies from country to country depending on the legal requirements for the regulation of auditors in those countries.

In some countries governments regulate auditors directly, in others, the profession is self-regulating or a mixture of the two. In Europe, there is a tradition of government being directly involved in the regulation of auditors.

However, in the UK, regulation of the profession is devolved to Recognised Supervisory Bodies (RSB) and ACCA is one such RSB.

Training and entry requirements

The ACCA imposes certain requirements which must be fulfilled before a person can become a member of ACCA, and student members have to qualify by passing exams and fulfilling training requirements. There is also a commitment to Continuing Professional Development (CPD).

Ethics

The ACCA issues an ethical code which all students and members must comply with.

Investigation and discipline

The ACCA monitors its members' work and conduct and may impose punitive measures such as fines or exclusion from membership.

3 Regulation and ethics

(a)   **Importance of regulation**

A variety of stakeholders might read a company's financial statements. Some of these readers will not just be reading a single company's financial statements, but will also be looking at those of a large number of companies, and making comparisons between them.

It is important that the audit profession is regulated and that auditors follow the same standards because many of these readers want assurance that when making comparisons, the reliability of the financial statements does not vary from company to company.

This assurance will be obtained not just from knowing that each set of financial statements has been audited, but from knowing that this has been done in accordance with common standards.

(b)   (i)   **Advocacy threat**

Advocacy threats arise in those situations where the assurance firm promotes a client's position or opinion to the extent that its subsequent objectivity is compromised.

One example is where the firm acts as an advocate of an assurance client in litigation or disputes with third parties.

> **Top tip:** Advocacy threats might also arise if the firm promoted shares in a listed audit client.

(i)   **Close business relationships**

A close business relationship may result in a self-interest threat.

Examples of when an audit firm and an audit client have an inappropriately close business relationship include:

- Having a material financial interest in a joint venture with the assurance client
- Arrangements to combine one or more services or products of the firm with one or more services or products of the assurance client, and to market the package with reference to both parties

> **Top tip:** Another example you may have come up with is:
>
> • Distribution or marketing arrangements under which the firm acts as distributor or marketer of the assurance client's products or services or vice versa

(c)   **Review engagement**

A review engagement is an assurance engagement where the practitioner carries out limited procedures on certain financial information (for example, interim financial statements). The procedures are less extensive than those performed for an audit and less evidence is gained as a result.

As the procedures are limited, the practitioner will gain only enough evidence to provide **negative assurance**. This means the practitioner gives assurance that nothing has come to his or her attention which indicates that the financial information is not prepared, in all material respects, in accordance with the applicable financial reporting framework.

4 Assurance and regulation

(a)   **Accountability** is the quality or state of being accountable, that is, being required or expected to justify actions and decisions. It suggests an obligation or willingness to accept responsibility for one's actions.

Stewardship refers to the duties and obligations of a person who manages another person's property.

Agency refers to the relationship between principals and the agents employed to act on the principals' behalf. Agents are people employed or used to provide a particular service.

In a company, Directors act as **stewards** of the shareholders' investments. They are **agents** of the shareholders and are employed to manage the business to maximise the shareholders' returns on their investment. They are therefore **accountable** for the shareholders' investment.

(b)   (i)   **Objectives**

The objective of a **review engagement** is to enable a practitioner to state whether, on the basis of procedures which do not provide all the evidence that would be required in an audit, anything has come to the practitioner's attention that causes the practitioner to believe that the financial statements are **not** prepared, in all material respects, in accordance with an applicable financial reporting framework.

The objective of an **audit** of financial statements is to enable the auditor to express an opinion on whether the financial statements are prepared, in all material respects, in accordance with an applicable financial reporting framework.

(ii)   **Level of assurance**

From the objectives above it can be seen that an audit engagement requires the practitioner to gain a relatively high level of evidence as a basis for a **positive expression** of the practitioner's conclusion. Reasonable assurance is given in an audit engagement.

In contrast, in a review engagement results in a **negative conclusion** since the practitioner only reports if something comes to his/her attention to suggest that the financial statements are **not** prepared fairly in all material respects, or do not show a true and fair view. Therefore less evidence is sought than in an audit and only limited (negative) assurance is given.

(c)   **ISAs and national auditing standards**

ISAs are set by the IAASB and provide internationally recognised guidance for auditors. Individual countries may then adopt these standards or modify them for use locally so that they can be used with other applicable local legislation.

ISAs do **not** override the local regulations governing the audit of financial or other information in a particular country.

(i)   To the extent that ISAs **conform** with local regulations on a particular subject, the audit of financial or other information in that country in accordance with local regulations will automatically comply with the ISA regarding that subject.

(ii)   In the event that the local regulations **differ from**, or conflict with, ISAs on a particular subject, member bodies should comply with the obligations of members set out in the IFAC Constitution as regards these ISAs (ie **encourage changes** in local regulations to comply with ISAs).

5 Corporate governance

(a)   **Voluntary codes of corporate governance**

Advantages of voluntary codes	Disadvantages of voluntary codes
Allow organisation to maintain flexibility	Risk of non-compliance with the code
Irrelevant areas can be left unapplied	Results in lack of comparability between companies
Potential saving of unnecessary implementation costs	Difficult for shareholders to make investment decisions

(b)   **Requirements of the board**

- The board and its committees should have the appropriate balance of skills, experience, independence and knowledge of the company to enable them to discharge their respective duties and responsibilities effectively.

- There should be a formal, rigorous and transparent procedure for the appointment of new directors to the board.

- All directors should be able to allocate sufficient time to the company to discharge their responsibilities effectively.

- All directors should receive induction on joining the board and should regularly update and refresh their skills and knowledge.

- The board should be supplied in a timely manner with information in a form and of a quality appropriate to enable it to discharge its duties.

- The board should undertake a formal and rigorous annual evaluation of its own performance and that of its committees and individual directors.

- All directors should be submitted for re-election at regular intervals, subject to continued satisfactory performance.

(**Note**. Only four were required.)

(c)   **Audit committee**

An audit committee is a sub-committee of the board of directors of a company and should comprise at least three non-executive directors.

The objectives of such a committee include monitoring the integrity of the financial statements, reviewing the company's internal financial controls and risk management systems, monitoring the effectiveness of internal audit, monitoring the external auditor's independence and objectivity and making recommendations in respect of the appointment of the external auditor.

The UK Corporate Governance Code recommends that the board establishes an audit committee consisting of at least three (or, in the case of smaller companies, two) members who should all be independent non-executive directors.

6 Ethical issues

(a) **Threats to independence and objectivity**

Self-review

A self-review threat may occur when a previous judgement needs to be re-evaluated by members responsible for that judgement. Examples include providing internal audit and tax services to an external audit client.

Self-interest

A self-interest threat may occur as a result of the financial or other interests of members or of immediate or **close family** members. Examples include gifts and hospitality and overdue fees.

Advocacy

An advocacy threat arises when an audit firm promotes a position or opinion to the point that subsequent objectivity is compromised. An example would be acting as an advocate on behalf of an assurance client in litigation or disputes with third parties.

Familiarity

A familiarity threat arises when, because of a close relationship, members become too sympathetic to the interests of others. This can result in a substantial risk of loss of professional scepticism. An example would be long association with an audit client.

Intimidation

An intimidation threat arises when members of the assurance team may be deterred from acting objectively by threats, actual or perceived. Examples include family and personal relationships, litigation, and close business relationships.

(b) **Confidentiality**

The fundamental principle of confidentiality requires members of the ACCA to refrain from disclosing information acquired during the course of professional work. Information may only be disclosed where the client has given consent, there is a public duty to disclose, or there is a legal or professional right or duty to disclose. Information acquired in the course of professional work must not be used for personal advantage or for the advantage of a third party.

Obligatory disclosure

An accountant will report to the relevant authority if he or she believes a client is involved in:

- Money laundering
- Treason
- Drug-trafficking
- Terrorism

Voluntary disclosure

Voluntary disclosure is permitted when:

- Disclosure is necessary to protect the member's interests
- Disclosure is authorised by statute
- Disclosure is in the public interest
- Disclosure is to non-governmental bodies which have statutory powers to compel disclosure

7 True and fair, ISAs and assurance engagements

Text reference. Chapter 1

Top tips. This question is purely knowledge-based. Read the question carefully. Remember, this is an audit **and assurance** paper, so you should not neglect your study of assurance in general and other assurance engagements. Part (a) covers the concept of true and fair presentation and part (b) is concerned with the authority of International Standards on Auditing. If the auditor does not have a full understanding of these fundamental areas which form basis of the audit of financial statements, there is a real risk of giving an inappropriate opinion. In (a) there are really two concepts within one, and splitting your explanation into two parts – first explaining 'true' and then explaining 'fair' – helps in giving a complete answer. In part (c) you should know there are five elements of an assurance engagement which suggests one mark for each element, so only include a brief explanation for each element. Here you may have used the mnemonic CREST to remember the five elements.

Easy marks. This question is wholly knowledge-based so should be straightforward but make sure you stick to the time allocation. Use the mnemonic CREST in part (c) to generate five points.

Examiner's comments. Part (a) for 3 marks required candidates to explain the true and fair concept. Performance was mixed on this question. Candidates clearly are aware of the concept but struggled to explain it with sufficient clarity. A common answer was to describe true as being "truthful" and to explain fair in relation to "fairness." This does not answer the question. In addition a minority also confused their explanations between true and fair, for example, stating "true means unbiased". Also a significant minority, having gained credit for stating that true and fair means that there are no material misstatements in the financial statements, then went onto a detailed description of materiality which was not required.

Part (b) for 2 marks required an explanation of the status of ISAs. Candidates performed inadequately on this question. Many candidates did not seem to understand what was required and were confused by the word "status". However this requirement is taken from the study guide and relates to the authority of ISAs, what types of assignments they apply to, their content and also how they interact with other legislation.

For part (c) it was fairly apparent that many candidates had simply not studied the area of assurance.

Marking scheme

		Marks
(a)	Up to 1 mark per valid point	
	True – factual, conforms with reality	
	True – conforms with standards and legislation	
	True – correctly transferred from accounting records	
	Fair – clear, plain and unbiased	
	Fair – reflects commercial substance	
	Maximum marks	3
(b)	Up to 1 mark per valid point	
	Issued by IAASB	
	Apply to audits of financial historical information	
	Contain basic principles/essential procedures/explanatory material	
	If depart from ISA – justify	
	Maximum marks	2
(c)	Up to 1 mark per description of each element:	
	– **C** suitable criteria	
	– **R** assurance report	
	– **E** appropriate evidence	
	– **S** subject matter	
	– **T** three party relationship (responsible party, practitioner, intended user)	5
Total		**10**

(a) **True and fair presentation**

External auditors give an opinion on whether the financial statements prepared by management give a true and fair view. This is not an opinion of absolute correctness. 'True' and 'fair' are not defined in law or audit guidance, but the following definitions are generally accepted.

True: Information is factual and conforms with reality. In addition the information conforms with required standards and law. The financial statements have been correctly extracted from the books and records.

Fair: Information is free from discrimination and bias and in compliance with expected standards and rules. The accounts should reflect the commercial substance of the company's underlying transactions.

(b) **Status of International Standards on Auditing (ISAs)**

ISAs set out how an audit should be carried out and are produced by the International Auditing and Assurance Standards Board (IAASB). ISAs apply to the audit of historical financial information.

ISAs contain objectives, requirements which set out the minimum procedures an auditor must carry out to express the audit opinion, explanatory material referenced to the requirements and appendices.

ISAs provide a framework for auditors and the auditor must fully understand and comply with all of the ISAs relevant to the audit. Furthermore, the auditor must go beyond the requirements in the ISA if he or she considers it is necessary to achieve an ISA's objective. If in exceptional cases the auditor deems it necessary to depart from an ISA to achieve the overall aim of the audit, then this departure must be justified.

Top tips. You may have talked about other points here which may have been equally valid and gained you the marks you needed. For example you may have written about how many countries either follow ISAs or have incorporated them into their own national standards (including all countries in the European Union).

You could also have highlighted the fact an auditor following ISAs will be able to point to the fact that his or her work has been carried out in accordance with recognised standards and therefore should not be found guilty of negligence.

(c) The elements of an assurance engagement:

(1) **Suitable criteria**. The subject matter is evaluated or measured against criteria in order to reach an opinion.

(2) **An assurance report**. A report containing the practitioner's opinion is issued to the intended user.

(3) **Evidence**. Sufficient appropriate evidence needs to be gathered to support the required level of assurance.

(4) **A subject matter**. This is the data to be evaluated that has been prepared by the responsible party.

(5) **A three party relationship**. The three parties are the intended user requiring the assurance report, the responsible party (responsible for preparing the subject matter) and the practitioner, who will review the subject matter against the criteria and provide assurance.

8 NorthCee

Text references. Chapter 3.

Top tips. This is a 10 mark question on corporate governance considerations for a company which intends to obtain a listing. You need to apply your knowledge of a recognised code of corporate governance, such as the UK Corporate Governance Code, to the scenario in the question. You must explain your answers fully, not merely produce a list of points. In part (a), each action is worth one mark so make sure that you provide a sufficiently detailed answer to this part of the question. Similarly, in part (b), you need to submit four well explained points to score maximum marks.

Easy marks. The more straightforward marks are available in part (a) of this question but make sure you explain the actions, rather than just list them, in order to achieve maximum marks.

Marks

(a) Meeting corporate governance requirements, 6 marks. 1 mark for each point.

Chief executive officer (CEO)/chairman split	1
Appoint NED	1
NED with financial experience	1
NEDs to sub-committees of board	1
Internal audit	1
Internal control system	1
Contact institutional shareholders	1
Financial report information	1
Other relevant points (each)	1
Maximum marks	**6**

(b) Communication with audit committee, 4 marks. 1 mark for each point.

Independence from board	1
Time to review audit work	1
Check auditor recommendations implemented	1
Review work of internal auditor (efficiency, etc)	1
Other relevant points (each)	1
Maximum marks	**4**
	10

(a) **Actions required to meet corporate governance requirements**

The company should appoint a **Chairman and Chief Executive** for its board of directors and these must be different people with clear divisions of responsibility so that no one individual has unfettered powers of decision.

The company should appoint a **mixture of executive and non-executive directors** for the board. The ratio of non-executive directors to executive directors should be the same so that no individual or small group of individuals can dominate the board's decision taking. All directors should be subject to annual re-election.

The company should set up an **internal audit department** which can review its internal controls and risk management procedures and report findings to the audit committee.

The company should establish **remuneration and nomination committees**. The nomination committee should consist of a majority of non-executive directors and the remuneration committee should have at least three non-executive directors.

There should be a **terms of reference document** established to set out the scope of the audit committee.

The company should set up **procedures and policies** to establish sound risk management and internal control systems.

NorthCee should establish procedures to maintain contact with institutional (or any major) shareholders. The evening reception for shareholders should become a regular event.

(b) **Communication with audit committee**

Dark must communicate with NorthCee's audit committee for this and future audits so that the external auditors are reporting their findings and recommendations to a set of people which consists of an independent element (in the form of the non-executive directors).

The audit committee also provides a means for the external auditors to communicate with the company and raise issues of concern.

The audit committee will have more time to examine the external auditors' reports and recommendations and this provides comfort that recommendations and other matters are being considered and reviewed.

The audit committee provides a forum for Dark in the event of any disputes with the management of NorthCee.

9 International Standards on Auditing

Text reference. Chapter 2.

Top tips. Make sure you answer each requirement in turn and give your answer some structure.

Easy marks. Easy marks are available if your knowledge in this area of the syllabus is sound.

Examiner's comments. This question was based on a short scenario, but otherwise was essentially factual, requiring knowledge of the ISA setting process. Parts (a) and (b) were almost always well answered, with many candidates obtaining full marks. In part (c), most candidates correctly stated that auditors should follow ISAs.

Marking scheme

		Marks
One mark for each valid point		
(a)	Role of the IAASB Up to 1 mark per point to a maximum of	2
(b)	The process to issue an ISA Up to 1 mark per point to a maximum of	4
(c)	Extent to which auditor follows ISAs Up to 1 mark per point to a maximum of	4
		10

(a) **The role of the IAASB**

The International Auditing and Assurance Standards Board (IAASB), is a sub-committee of the International Federation of Accountants (IFAC).

The main role of the IAASB is to issue high quality auditing standards (ISAs) and assurance engagement standards (ISAEs) in order to give guidance to professional accountants when performing their work. This in turn aims to strengthen public confidence in the profession.

They also work to facilitate the convergence of international and national standards to enhance the quality and uniformity of practice throughout the world.

(b) **The process involved in issuing an ISA**

Initially, research and consultation will take place and normally a project task force is established to develop a draft ISA. The proposed standard is presented for discussion at an IAASB meeting.

Following agreement of the content of the **proposed** standard, an **exposure draft** is then widely distributed for public comment. It is circulated to the member bodies of the IFAC (such as ACCA) and any other interested parties. It is also published on the IAASB's website.

The IAASB receives **comments** on the exposure draft and the draft standard is revised as appropriate. If the changes made after exposure are significant, another exposure draft may be issued for further comment.

Once satisfied with the content of the standard, the final ISA is **approved** and made available on the IAASB website.

(c) The auditor must comply with all ISAs relevant to the audit. An ISA is relevant to the audit when the ISA is in effect and the circumstances addressed by the ISA exist.

In relation to the individual requirements within each ISA, the auditor ordinarily has to comply with each requirement unless the requirement is not relevant because it is conditional and the condition does not exist.

There may be **exceptional circumstances** under which the auditor may judge it necessary to depart from an ISA in order to achieve the objective of an audit more effectively.

In this case, the auditor must be prepared to **justify** and document the reason for the departure and this situation is likely to be the exception rather than the rule.

10 Jumper

Text reference. Chapter 3.

Top tips. Make sure you answer this question using a columnar format in order to make sure that you address both the corporate governance weaknesses and the recommendations to improve them. The best way to approach this question is to take each issue in turn from the scenario and deal with it separately. A detailed knowledge of the UK Corporate Governance Code is not required so don't panic. Use the clues in the scenario, for example, the company does not have an internal audit department, Mr Sheppard is both the Chief Executive and the Chairman of the company.

Easy marks. There aren't many easy marks as such in this question but use the question scenario to structure your answer and apply your knowledge of corporate governance.

Examiner's comments. The overall standard for this answer was quite good, with many candidates obtaining very high marks. However, common errors included providing a history of corporate governance regulations, not explaining the points made and providing detailed lists on the work of an audit committee.

Marking scheme

	Marks
1 mark for identifying the corporate governance weakness and 1 for each recommendation to address the weakness	
CEO and chairman	2
Composition of board	2
Director appointment	2
Review of board/director performance	2
Directors' remuneration	2
Internal control	2
Internal audit	2
Audit committee	2
Maximum marks	**10**

Corporate governance weaknesses and related recommendations

Weakness	Recommendation
Mr Sheppard is both the Chief Executive Officer and the Chairman of the Board of Directors. Corporate governance codes indicate that there should be a clear division of responsibilities between running the board of directors and running the company's business so that no individual has unfettered powers of decision.	SGCC should appoint a separate chairman who meets the independence criteria set out in the codes. This should ideally be an independent non-executive director.

Weakness	Recommendation
SGCC has only two non-executive directors compared with five executive directors. This means that non-executive directors comprise less than half the Board. This is clearly not an appropriate balance to ensure that board decisions are questioned and ultimately taken in the interests of the shareholders, and to prevent executives pursuing their own interests.	SGCC should appoint three more non-executive directors so that there is an equal number of executive and non-executive directors.
At present there are no formal targets or reviews of board policies/performance carried out. This means that SGCC does not have any means by which to appraise directors' performance and to identify training needs or poorly performing directors.	The board should set performance targets for each director and undertake a formal and rigorous review of its own performance and that of individual directors on an annual basis. The performance evaluation of the chairman should be undertaken by the non-executive directors. The fact that the review takes place should also be stated in the annual report.
Mr Sheppard decides the remuneration for all directors including himself. Furthermore remuneration is not based on performance. Directors should not set their own remuneration due to them having a clear self-interest which may prompt them to award themselves excessive pay packages.	A remuneration committee comprising at least three non-executive directors should be set up to determine the level of directors' remuneration. The remuneration of non-executive directors should be determined by the board itself (or the shareholders if required by the articles of association of the company). The remuneration policy should be fair and transparent.
SGCC does not have an internal audit department. This may mean that there are weaknesses in the way in which SGCC is directed and control as the internal audit department forms an important part of the entity's internal control system.	SGCC, should review the need for an internal audit department at least annually. Given the lack of formal controls at SGCC, an internal audit department should be established as soon as possible. It is not clear whether SGCC has an audit committee. If there is no audit committee then one should be established immediately and comprise at least three non-executive directors. The head of internal audit should report to the audit committee.

11 Conoy

Text references. Chapter 3.

Top tips. It is important you take account of Conoy's specific circumstances. You are given specific problems which an audit committee may help to alleviate, so these should form the basis of the benefits. For example, there is a lack of financial reporting expertise, so this is where an audit committee can add significant value, especially as both the auditors and the bank have expressed concerns in this area.

Easy marks. Knowing the role of the audit committee.

Examiner's comments. Some satisfactory answers showed how an audit committee could assist the company in the scenario were produced. Many answers, however, tended to list the benefits of an audit committee with little or no reference to the detail in the scenario. The main weakness in many answers was explaining the constitution of the audit committee or the work of other committees rather than the role of the audit committee and its benefit to Conoy.

Marks

Role of the audit committee and the benefits to Conoy

Up to 2 marks for each point. 1 for the role and 1 for applying that to suggest the benefit to Conoy.

- Assistance with financial reporting
- Enhance status of internal audit department
- Independence of on external auditors
- Platform/sounding board for the external auditors
- Enhance internal controls/best practice – corporate governance

<u>10</u>

Role of the audit committee and benefits to Conoy

Role of the audit committee	Benefits to Conoy
The audit committee should contain at least one member who has financial reporting expertise so that they can **monitor the integrity of the financial statements**.	Conoy's finance director has left and it appears that there is no-one else who has appropriate financial reporting knowledge to deal with the reporting needs of a company the size of Conoy. Therefore the establishment of an audit committee where at least one member has financial expertise would improve the quality of financial reporting and allowing the existing board members to concentrate on running the business.
The audit committee should monitor and **review the effectiveness of the entity's internal audit department**, provide input in to their work plan and meet regularly with the head of internal audit.	Currently Conoy's internal audit department is poorly supported and reports directly to the board who do not understand their reports. Establishing an audit committee will strengthen the position of the internal audit function and provide them with a greater degree of independence from management. It will also promote the need for a strong control environment to the board, which should then lead to implementation of an appropriate internal control system.
The audit committee should **recommend the appointment, reappointment and removal of the external auditor**, approve their remuneration and review and monitor their independence.	The external auditors are currently appointed by the board of Conoy Co. This could result in a familiarity threat to the independence of the external auditors if they develop too close a relationship with the board over time. An audit committee can recommend the appointment of the external auditors based on appropriate criteria only (quality of service, independence and competence for example). This will help prevent such an independence issue arising.
The audit committee should also be **available to the external auditor** should there be any unresolved audit issues.	Given that the findings of the internal audit department are not understood, it is likely the same is true of deficiencies reported by external auditors Anders & Co. The audit committee, if established, will strengthen the external auditor's position by providing a channel of communication and forum for issues of concern.
The audit committee is responsible for **reviewing the entity's internal controls and risk management systems** and these would include internal controls relating to the financial reporting process.	Conoy Co needs to raise external finance if the company is to expand. However the bank has concerns over Conoy's financial reporting practices. Establishing an audit committee should increase confidence in the credibility and objectivity of Conoy's financial statements. It will also demonstrate to the bank that although Conoy is not required to comply with specific corporate governance regulation, the company is prepared to take steps to move towards corporate governance best practice.

12 Goofy

Text references. Chapters 4 and 5.

Top tips. This question is scenario-based on ethics and outsourcing an internal audit department.

In part (a) you needed to realise that you had to explain safeguards limited to the conflict of interest issue rather than just regurgitate general safeguards you had learnt. Where possible you should have linked your answer to the scenario provided.

In part (b) you may be used to providing advantages and disadvantages of outsourcing internal audit from the client's point of view. However in this case you should have taken note that this question required them for both the client (Goofy) and the auditors (NAB & Co). The best approach here is to take each party in turn and discuss the advantages and disadvantages to each. The requirement contained the verb 'explain' so your answer needed to be of sufficient depth.

Easy marks. This question was, on the whole, straightforward. In particular you should have found part (b) on outsourcing the internal audit department relatively easy.

Examiner's comments. In part (a) most candidates were able to identify safeguards such as separate audit teams and informing both parties. However, many candidates then provided procedures which were a repeat of separate teams, such as separate engagement partners. In addition some candidates listed general ethical safeguards rather than focusing on the specific requirement of conflicts of interest.

Candidates performed well in part (b) on this question and most structured their answers to consider advantages and disadvantages for each of the two entities separately and this helped to generate a sufficient number of points. It was pleasing to see that many candidates used the small scenario provided to make their answers relevant, as this was not a general requirement, but one applied to Goofy and NAB. Where candidates did not score as well, this was mainly due to a failure to provide sufficient depth to their answers.

Marking scheme

		Marks
(a)	Up to 1 mark per well-explained safeguard	
	Notify Goofy Co and Mickey Co	
	Advise seek independent advice	
	Separate engagement teams	
	Procedures prevent access to information	
	Clear guidelines on security and confidentiality	
	Confidentiality agreements	
	Monitoring of safeguards	
	Maximum marks	4
(b)	Up to 1 mark per well-explained advantage/disadvantage	
	Staffing gaps addressed immediately	
	Skills and experience increased	
	Costs of training eliminated	
	Possibly reduced fees	
	Flexibility of service	
	Additional fees for NAB & Co	
	Knowledge of systems reduced	
	Existing internal audit department staff, cost of potential redundancies	
	Fees by NAB & Co may increase over time	
	Loss of in-house skills	
	Timing of work may not suit NAB & Co	
	Confidentiality issues	
	Independence issues NAB & Co	
	Control of department reduced	
	Maximum marks	6
		20

(a) **Safeguards to be implemented to manage the conflict of interest**

Goofy and Mickey's management should both be informed of the situation and asked to give consent for the NAB & Co to act for both.

NAB & Co should use separate engagement teams, with different engagement partners and team members for each audit. Employees that have worked on Goofy should be prevented from being on the audit of Mickey for an appropriate period of time and vice-versa.

NAB & Co should ensure the audit teams are provided with clear guidelines for members of each engagement team on issues of security and confidentiality.

Procedures should be put in place to prevent access to information, such as strict physical separation of both teams, confidential and secure data filing.

Top tips. Although only four safeguards needed explaining to gain full marks, other valid ones you may have come up with include:

- NAB & Co could advise one or both clients to seek additional independent advice.

- Confidentiality agreements could be drawn up and signed by employees and partners of the firm.

- A senior partner at NAB & Co who is not involved in either audit should regularly monitor the safeguards to ensure they are properly applied.

(b) **Outsourcing of Goofy's internal audit work to NAB & Co**

Advantages and disadvantages for Goofy

Advantages for Goofy	Disadvantages for Goofy
NAB & Co has expert knowledge and can provide skilled staff. Goofy may not be able to recruit staff with these skills and this may be especially relevant for ad hoc and specialist work Goofy appears to require.	Goofy will find it more difficult to monitor and control and outsourced internal audit department. Work and timings will need to be agreed further in advance.
The flexibility offered if internal audit work is outsourced means the staff from NAB & Co can be requested as and when work arises at Goofy. Again this has a cost implementation as employees need to be paid regardless of the workload.	Redundancy costs are likely to occur if the existing five employees are not given alternative roles.
NAB & Co's fees will increase as a result of the extra work.	A self review threat may be created as a result of NAB & Co acting as internal and external auditors. This is because they may seek to rely on their own work in gaining audit evidence. Appropriate safeguards (such as using different teams) would need to be put in place.

Top tips. The answer above contains sufficient advantages and disadvantages to gain full marks. However other valid ones you may have come up with include:

Advantages for Goofy:

- Cost-savings are made in terms of employee salaries, training costs and recruitment expenses.

- An immediate increase in the size of the internal audit department is provided if the department is outsourced to NAB & Co. Goofy would need time to recruit if the current department was expanded.

Disadvantages for Goofy:

- If the current internal audit team are not given alternative roles in Goofy, valuable in-house skills and experience may be lost. This will be difficult to get back if management has a change of mind later on and want to re-establish an internal department.

- The cost to Goofy on an hourly basis is likely to be significantly higher than for an internal employee.

- Frequent staff changes at NAB & Co could occur resulting in poor quality service being providing due to lack of understanding of Goofy's systems and operations.

- Goofy Co will be exposing more confidential data to NAB & Co leading to further risks of breach of confidentiality.

Disadvantages for NAB & Co:

- NAB & Co may find it difficult to provide the number and quality of staff needed by Goofy during busy periods.

13 L V Fones

Text reference. Chapter 4.

Top tips. This question is ethics based. A lot of the marks can be gained through purely drawing on the knowledge of ethical threats and safeguards, which you should have gained during your studies. The most likely cause of missing out on marks in a question like this is not addressing all of the requirements, or answering a different question to that asked. Remember to read the question very carefully and take a minute to make sure you have understood, and are ready to answer all the requirements.

In parts (a) and (b) you should notice that there are essentially two requirements – stating the five threats **and** listing one example of each. Don't lose out on half the marks here because of only stating the threats and not providing an example for each.

Easy marks. Explaining the ethical threats should have been quite straightforward as it is a largely knowledge based. Part (b) was more difficult as it required application of ethical knowledge to the scenario. Overall this question is a relatively straightforward question on ethical threats and safeguards.

Examiner's comments. Part (a) was well answered by most candidates. Some candidates did not explain the threats in sufficient detail, sometimes just identifying the issue and not explaining how this was an ethical threat.

Part (b) required methods for avoiding the threats, candidates performance here was generally satisfactory. Some answers tended to be quite brief and to include unrealistic steps, such as resigning as auditors to reduce the risk of fee dependence, not allowing the finance director and partner to be friends.

Marks

(a) and (b)

Up to 1 mark per ethical threat and up to 1 mark for each explanation of
safeguard
- Staff discount
- Secondment
- Total fee income
- Finance director and partner good friends
- Outstanding fees

Threats	5
Safeguards	5
	10

(a) and (b)

(a) Ethical threat rising	(b) How threat may be avoided
The audit team have previously been offered a 10% discount on luxury phones from LV Fones (LV) which will potentially have a high value. As only goods with a trivial and inconsequential value can be received, if the same discount is again offered, it will constitute a familiarity threat.	The offer for the discount should be declined if the value is significant.
An audit senior was seconded to LV to over the financial controller role for three months during the year. The audit senior probably prepared a significant proportion of the records to be audited; this creates a self-review threat as he will review his own work during the audit.	Only if it turns out the senior was only involved on areas unrelated to the financial statements being audited should be allowed to remain on the audit team, otherwise he should be removed from the assignment to avoid the threat to independence.
The fee income from LV is 16% of Jones & Co's total fees. If, after accounting for non-recurring fees such as the secondment, it remains at this percentage of total fees on a recurring basis there is likely to be a self interest threat because of undue dependence on this client. Where recurring fees exceed 15% for listed companies, objectivity is impaired to such an extent that mandatory safeguards are needed according to the ACCA *Code of Ethics and Conduct* (ACCA Code).	The firm should consider whether the further work should be accepted and also consider appointing an external quality control reviewer. Going forward, the firm needs to assess the recurring fee position for LV and consider refusing further offers of work where this will take them over the 15% threshold. If the threshold is breached for two consecutive years the threat can be mitigated by applying the mandatory safeguards of disclosing the position to the board and arranging an independent pre-issuance or post-issuance engagement review.
The partner and finance director of LV have been on holiday together and appear to have a longstanding close relationship. This results in a familiarity and self interest threat. Both are senior in their respective organisation and any onlooker would perceive independence to be threatened.	Ideally the partner should be rotated off the audit and replaced with another partner.

(a) Ethical threat rising	(b) How threat may be avoided
The overdue fees (20% of the total fee) may be perceived as a loan which is prohibited, but may also create a self-interest threat. This is because Jones & Co may be less robust than they should be when it disagrees with management out of fear they may not recover the fees.	The reasons for non payment should be determined, and if possible an agreement reached whereby LV repays the fees prior to the commencement of any further audit work.

14 Ethics

Text reference. Chapter 4.

Top tips. This question is ethics based. In part (a) you should notice that there are essentially two requirements – stating the five threats **and** listing one example of each. Don't lose out on half the marks here because of only stating the threats and not providing an example for each. Part (b) was knowledge based and you just needed to recall your knowledge of confidentiality in relation to disclosure of information. Your points should have been limited to confidentiality and the responsibility for the two types of disclosure and should not have included other irrelevant ethical rules or responsibilities.

Easy marks. Overall this question is a relatively straightforward question on ethical threats and obligatory and voluntary disclosure.

Marking scheme

Marks

(a) $\frac{1}{2}$ mark for each threat and $\frac{1}{2}$ per example of a threat
- Self-interest
- Self-review
- Advocacy
- Familiarity
- Intimidation

5

(b)   Up to 1 mark per valid point
ACCA's *Code of Ethics and Conduct* – auditors should not disclose information without client consent
Confidentiality implied term of engagement contract
Obligatory disclosure in certain circumstances
Statutory right or duty to disclose
Compelled by process of law
Voluntary disclosure in certain circumstances
Public interest
Protect member's interest
Authorised by statute/laws
Non-governmental bodies
Maximum marks   5
Total marks   10

(a)   **Ethical threats and examples**

Compliance with the fundamental principles of professional ethics may potentially be threatened by a wide range of different circumstances. These threats generally fall into five categories:

- Self-interest
- Self-review
- Advocacy
- Familiarity
- Intimidation

An example of a circumstance that may create each threat is given in the table below.

Threat category	Example
Self-interest	A financial interest in a client's affairs where an audit firm owns shares in the client.
Self-Review	A firm prepares accounting records and financial statements and then audits them.
Advocacy	Acting as an advocate on behalf of an assurance client in litigation.
Familiarity	Senior members of staff at an audit firm with a long association with a client.
Intimidation	Client threatens to sue the audit firm for previous work.

Tutorial note. There are a number of examples you could have stated for each threat category, however only one of each was needed.

(b)   **Confidentiality**

Due to confidentiality requirements set out in the *ACCA Code of Ethics and Conduct,* members have an obligation to refrain from disclosing information acquired in the course of professional work unless their client gives permission for them to do so. Confidentiality is an implied term of auditors' contracts with their clients and this obligation continues even after the professional relationship between the auditor and client has ended.

There are some exceptions to this rule. In certain circumstances, the auditor may be permitted to make a voluntary disclosure or may be obliged to make a disclosure without seeking client permission.

(i)   **Obligatory disclosure**

If the auditor knows or suspects his client to have committed money-laundering, treason, drug-trafficking or terrorist offences, the auditor is obliged to disclose all the information at his disposal to a competent authority.

In addition auditors must make a disclosure if compelled by a process of law (eg under a court order).

(ii)   **Voluntary disclosure**

Voluntary disclosure occurs when the auditor chooses to disclose but is not obliged to. This is permissible in the following situations.

- Disclosure is reasonably necessary to protect the member's interests, for example to enable him to sue for fees or defend an action for, say, negligence.

- Disclosure is authorised by statute

- Where it is in the public interest to disclose, say where an offence has been committed which is contrary to the public interest.

- Disclosure is to non-governmental bodies which have statutory powers to compel disclosure.

15 Code of Ethics and Conduct

		Marks
(a)	1 mark for each principle, ½ for stating the principle and ½ for brief explanation	
	– Integrity	
	– Objectivity	
	– Professional competence and due care	
	– Confidentiality	
	– Professional behaviour	5
(b)	½ mark for each threat and ½ mark per example of a threat:	
	– Self-interest	
	– Self-review	
	– Advocacy	
	– Familiarity	
	– Intimidation	5
Total marks		**10**

(a) **Fundamental principles**

Integrity	To be straightforward and honest in all business and professional relationships.
Objectivity	To not allow bias, conflicts of interest or undue influence of others to override professional or business judgements.
Professional competence and due care	To maintain professional knowledge and skill at the level required to ensure that a client or employer receives competent professional services based on current developments in practice, legislation and techniques and act diligently and in accordance with applicable technical and professional standards.
Confidentiality	To respect the confidentiality of information acquired as a result of professional and business relationships and, therefore, not disclose any such information to third parties without proper and specific authority, unless there is a legal or professional right or duty to disclose, nor use the information for the personal advantage of the professional accountant or third parties.
Professional behaviour	To comply with relevant laws and regulations and avoid any action that discredits the profession.

(b)   **Ethical threats to independence and objectivity**

Threat	Example
Self-interest	• Close business, family or personal relationships • Undue fee dependency on one client • % or contingent fees • Lowballing to win lucrative other work • Overdue fees • Gifts and hospitality • Employment with an assurance client • Partner on client board • Loans and guarantees • Financial interests in a client • Holding client assets
Self-review	• Provision of other non-audit services such as tax, internal audit, valuation services, corporate finance, IT systems services • Preparing financial statements and accounting records • Recent service with an audit client
Advocacy	• Promoting shares in a listed audit client • Acting as an advocate in a legal dispute • Commenting publicly on future events in particular circumstances
Familiarity	• Long association with an audit client • Close business, family or personal relationships • Gifts and hospitality
Intimidation	• Being threatened with removal as auditor • Dominant person in senior position within the client • Threat of litigation • Threat of other lucrative non-audit work not being awarded

Tutorial note. There are a number of examples you could have stated for each threat category, however only one of each was needed.

16 Stark

Text references. Chapter 4.

Top tips. This question is scenario-based on ethics. Use the information you've been given to help with your answer and remember the five types of threat identified in the ACCA's *Code of Ethics and Conduct*. You could present your answer to this part in a tabular format so you can link the threats and related safeguards together easily.

Easy marks. This question is relatively straightforward and there are many easy marks available here as you should be comfortable with the topic of professional ethics.

Examiner's comments. The standard of answers to this question was satisfactory. Not providing sufficient points was the main reason for a candidate not achieving a pass standard.

Marks

1 for each ethical threat and 1 for explanation of how to mitigate that threat

    = 2 marks per linked points

    Part (a) therefore is 5 marks total and part (b) is 5 marks total

    Engagement partner – time providing service

    Engagement partner's daughter takes part in audit

    Payment for investment advice

    Gift of balloon flight from client

    Contingent fee – taxation work

    Representing client in court

    Maximum marks   <u>10</u>

(a)   **Threats and safeguards**

(a) Ethical threats	(b) Possible safeguards
Familiarity	
Mr Son has been the engagement partner for Stark for the past nine years. This gives rise to a familiarity threat because of his long association with this one client which could impair his objectivity and independence.	Mr Son should be rotated off the audit. The ACCA's *Code of Ethics and Conduct* states that for listed companies, engagement partners should be rotated after no more than seven years and not return to that client until a further period of two years has elapsed. Although Stark is not stated as listed, partner rotation should be implemented.
Mr Son's daughter Zoe will be part of the audit team of Stark. This also gives rise to a familiarity threat because her father is the engagement partner and this may impair objectivity.	Whilst Mr Son is still the engagement partner for this audit, his daughter should not be part of the audit team of Stark.
Intimidation	
There may be an intimidation threat from the Finance Director of Stark who has made a statement regarding the calculation of the fees for taxation services. The audit firm may feel that it has to accept this in order to keep Stark as a tax client.	The engagement partner should explain to the Finance Director that although his firm can provide taxation services to Stark, the fees charged must be based on the time spent on the work.
Advocacy	
An advocacy threat may arise as the Finance Director is expecting Ali & Co to represent his company in a dispute with the taxation authorities.	There are no safeguards which could be put in place to mitigate this threat and so the firm must decline to represent Stark in this dispute.
Self-review	
The firm also provides taxation services to Stark and this may give rise to a self-review threat as staff may end up reviewing their own work. The extent of the threat will depend on the nature of the services and in particular how any matters advised on will be reflected in the financial statements.	Depending on the level of the threat, Stark could use separate engagement teams for the audit and tax work to mitigate any threat arising.

(a) Ethical threats	(b) Possible safeguards
Self-interest	
Mr Far, the audit senior, received investment advice from the company and intends to do so in the future. A self-interest threat may arise as a result which could impair his objectivity.	If Mr Far paid for the services received from Stark as any other customer would, there is potentially no problem. However, this should be discussed with the engagement and ethics partners and he may be advised not to use the services of Stark in the future.
The client is expecting the tax fee to be based on a % of tax saved – this is a form of contingent fees. This gives rise to a self-interest threat because the firm will want to save as much tax as possible in order to charge as high a tax fee as possible.	There are no safeguards that can be put in place to mitigate this threat and so the firm should not agree to the proposed fee arrangement for taxation services.
The client has arranged a balloon flight for the audit team. This could give rise to a self-interest threat in the form of gifts and hospitality.	The *Code of Ethics and Conduct* states that gifts and hospitality should only be accepted where the value is trivial and inconsequential. In this case, it would be appropriate to decline the balloon flight so as not to impair the firm's independence.

Tutorial note. You only needed to provide five threats and related safeguards to score maximum marks on this question. Also it was not necessary to group the threats under the headings of familiarity and so forth.

17 Governance

Text references. Chapters 3 and 5.

Top tips. Your explanations of corporate governance and why it is important in part (a) needed to be relatively short and to the point given that only three marks are available. You should not have talked at length about the different provisions of corporate governance codes as the requirement was to explain corporate governance and its importance in general, not to go into specifics. In part (b), don't just state the general benefits of having an internal audit department – make sure you can relate them to SPD Co, the company in the question.

Easy marks. This question is relatively straightforward and there are many easy marks available here. You should be comfortable with the definition of corporate governance and the many different functions which can be performed by the internal audit department especially if you use the scenario well.

Marking scheme

		Marks
(a)	Up to 1 mark per valid point	
	System by which companies are directed and controlled	
	Considers directors' responsibilities, board structure, importance of good internal controls and relationship with external auditors	
	Management run the business but shareholders own the company	
	Shareholders only have annual general meeting to raise concerns	
	Shareholders need process in place to ensure their needs met and kept informed	
	Maximum marks	3

(b)   1 mark per well-explained point
      Regulation
      Rapid growth
      Complex product portfolio
      Need for additional funding
      Imminent listing on a stock exchange
      Financial audits
      Liaison with external auditors
      Monitor effectiveness of internal control
      Risk assessment
      Maximum marks   7
      Total marks   10

(a)   **Corporate governance**

Corporate governance is the system by which companies are directed and controlled. The *UK Corporate Governance Code* states that 'the purpose of corporate governance is to facilitate effective, entrepreneurial and prudent management that can deliver the long-term success of the company'.

Corporate governance is concerned with the effective leadership of the business, a sound structure of the board, effective risk management and internal control implementation and monitoring, as well as promoting a good professional relationship with the external auditors.

Good corporate governance is necessary because although management and those charged with governance run the company, it is the shareholders who own the business. Therefore is important that the corporate governance in place protects the shareholders from management perusing their own interests at the expense of the owners. It is also important shareholders are kept informed and are able to raise concerns at times other than just at the annual general meeting.

(b)   **Benefits of an internal audit department**

SPD Co is a regulated business and so there is always a risk that the regulatory requirements may not be adhered to properly. An internal audit department could advise the Board on regulatory requirements and undertake testing to ensure that SPD Co is complying with all required legislation and regulation.

SPD Co has experienced rapid growth over the last 12 months and it is possible that its internal control system is no longer appropriate for the size of business. An internal audit department could examine the existing internal control system in operation at SPD Co and make recommendations to improve its effectiveness where there are deficiencies in controls.

The company is now offering a more complex range of products to clients and this increases the risk of mis-selling. An internal audit department could establish internal controls over the selling of new products and monitor compliance with these controls.

SPD Co is considering obtaining new funding from its bank, so having an effective internal audit department will increase the credibility off SPD Co's business and its financial management and financial reporting.

SPD Co is also considering obtaining a listing on a stock exchange. It is likely that SPD Co will be required to have an internal audit department if a listing is obtained, so establishing an internal audit department now will mean that they can make recommendations in respect of good corporate governance in advance of the listing taking place.

The internal auditors could undertake financial audits to substantiate information in management and financial reporting this may also be helpful for when SPD Co seeks to secure additional funding.

The external auditors might be able to rely on work undertaken by the company's internal auditors and this in turn could result in a reduced audit fee.

18 Serena

Marking scheme

	Marks
Up to 1 mark per well explained weakness and up to 1 mark per recommendation. Overall maximum of 5 for weaknesses and 5 for recommendations.	
Chairman is chief executive	
Two of six directors are non-executive, should be at least half	
Finance director alone reviews financial information and budgets	
Audit committee comprised of non-executives, chairman and finance director	
Finance director and chairman appoint and remunerate external auditors	
No internal audit function to save costs	
Finance director and chairman decide on the remuneration for the executive directors	
Remuneration all in form of salary and yearly bonus	
No director subject to re-election for the last five years	
Maximum marks	**10**

Corporate governance weaknesses and related recommendations

Weakness	Recommendation
There are only two non-executive directors which is less than half. This is clearly not an appropriate balance to ensure board decisions are questioned, ultimately taken in the interests of the shareholders and prevent executives pursuing their own interests.	Two more non-executives should be appointed so that there is an equal amount of executive and non-executive directors.
Only the finance director reviews the financial statements and budgets. These should be presented and explained to the whole board since the financial results of previous decisions should be known and these results will impact on the future decisions made by the board.	Financial statements and budgets should be presented to the board to allow directors to understand the financial position and performance. This will facilitate informed decision making.

Weakness	Recommendation
Daniel Brown is both Chairman and CEO. There should be a clear division of responsibilities at the head of Serena VDW and Daniel Brown should not be allowed to occupy both positions, remaining unchallenged and able to abuse his power.	Someone else should be appointed as chairman and in accordance with corporate governance best practice, this should be an independent non-executive.
The CEO/Chairman set up the audit committee and he and the finance director sit on it. This committee should consist of non-executive directors to maintain independence from the executive board members who have a self interest.	The audit committee should be reformed to only consist of non-executive directors. Daniel Brown and the finance director should resign from the committee.
Daniel Brown and the finance director decide the remuneration and appointment of auditors. This should be decided by an audit committee consisting of independent non-executives.	An audit committee consisting of non-executives should be responsible for the appointment of auditors and for setting their remuneration.
There is no internal audit department on the basis it would be too expensive. This decision should only be taken by an independent audit committee once the need to have an internal audit function has been assessed, taking into account both financial and non-financial benefits and drawbacks.	The newly formed independent audit committee should assess the need for internal audit taking both financial and non-financial factors into account. If it is decided that an internal audit function is not needed, the need for one should be assessed annually.
Daniel Brown and the finance director decide the remuneration for all directors. Directors should not set their own remuneration due to them having a clear self interest which may prompt them to award themselves excessive pay packages.	The remuneration policy should be fair and transparent. The non-executives should set the executives' pay and the finance director could set the non-executives' pay.
The annual revenue related bonus could encourage a short term view and ineffective decisions for the purposes of maximising long term shareholder wealth.	The remuneration of executives should be restructured to include an appropriate proportion linked to the long term performance of the company. For example awarding shares or share options instead of bonuses may encourage a longer term view.
Re-election of directors has not occurred for five years. The shareholders should review the performance of directors and have the opportunity not to re-elect them at regular intervals.	All directors should be submitted for re-election at the next AGM. After that directors should be submitted for re-election at regular intervals (not exceeding three years), subject to continued satisfactory performance.

(**Note**: Only five weaknesses and five related recommendations were needed to gain 10 marks.)

19 Orange

Text reference. Chapter 4.

Top tips. This question tests your knowledge of ethics and asks for an explanation of five ethical threats based on a scenario and for each threat, how it might be reduced to an acceptable level. A two column approach would work well here. Read through the information carefully identifying the problem. Make sure that you link the problem to a particular threat eg self-interest threat, self-review threat. When thinking about how the threat can be reduced consider appropriate safeguards. Remember in some cases safeguards will not be adequate to reduce the threat to an acceptable level.

Easy marks. There are few easy marks as such although part (a) is probably the most straightforward part of the question.

Marks

Up to 1 mark per ethical threat and up to 1 mark per managing method, max of 5
for threats and max 5 for methods

      Engagement partner attending listing meeting

      Preparation of financial statements

      Assistant finance director as review partner on audit

      Total fee income

      Pressure to complete audit quickly and with minimal issues

      Weekend away at luxury hotel

      Provision of loan at preferential rates

Maximum marks   **<u>10</u>**

Ethical threats and how they might be reduced

(a) Ethical threat	(b) How it might be reduced
The engagement partner has been asked to attend meetings with potential investors. This represents an advocacy threat as this may be interpreted as the audit firm promoting investment in Orange Financial Co.	This represents a significant threat to independence and it is unlikely that safeguards would be adequate to reduce it to an acceptable level. The request should be politely declined.
Current & Co have been asked to produce the financial statements of Orange Financials Co. This represents a possible self-review threat as Currant & Co would be both preparing and auditing the same information. As Orange Financials Co is not a listed company the preparation and audit of financial statements is not prohibited by ethical standards. However the company is in the process of seeking a listing which increases audit risk as it is likely that potential investors will rely on these financial statements to make investment decisions.	As the company is in the process of obtaining a listing the threat to independence may be assessed as too high if Currant & Co both prepares and audits the financial statements. If Currant & Co does choose to prepare the financial statements it should ensure that there are two separate teams, one which prepares the financial statements and one which performs the audit.
The assistant finance director of Orange Financials Co has joined Currant & Co as a partner and it has been suggested that he should be the independent review partner. This represents a self-review threat as the same individual would be responsible for reviewing the audit of financial statements which he has been involved in preparing.	This individual must not be involved in the audit of Orange Financials Co and another partner should be appointed as the review partner.
Current & Co would like to conduct other assignments for Orange Financials Co. This gives rise to a potential self-interest threat as the total fees generated from this client may form a substantial proportion of the fees of the firm which may have an impact on the firm's objectivity.	The other work will only be available when Orange Financials Co obtains its listing. The company will then be a public interest entity so Currant & Co will need to consider whether the these additional fees together with existing fees represent 15% of the firm's total fees for two consecutive years. Where this is the case disclosure must be made to those charged with governance and a review (pre or post issuance) must be conducted.

(a) Ethical threat	(b) How it might be reduced
Orange Financials Co has indicated that the other work will only be awarded to Currant & Co if it completes the audit with minimal issues. This gives rise to an intimidation threat as the audit team may feel under pressure not to perform a thorough audit in order to comply with this request.	The audit partner should explain to the finance director that the firm is required to perform the audit in accordance with auditing and quality control standards. As a result all relevant issues and questions will have to be investigated thoroughly in order to obtain sufficient appropriate evidence to form the audit opinion. The length of time this will take cannot be guaranteed. If the finance director is unwilling to accept this and continues to put undue pressure on Currant & Co the firm should consider resigning from the engagement.
The audit team has been offered a luxury weekend away once the stock exchange listing has been completed. This represents a self-interest threat as the independence of the audit team may be affected by their wish to go on the holiday.	As the value of the hospitality is unlikely to be inconsequential no safeguards would be adequate to reduce the threat to an acceptable level. The offer of the weekend away should be declined politely.
A senior member of the audit team has been offered a short-term loan at significantly reduced rates. This constitutes a self-interest threat as the decisions made by this member of the audit team could be influenced by a wish to take advantage of the offer.	If the loan had been made at normal commercial rates then the senior would be able to accept without any consequences for independence. In this case as the terms are preferential the loan must be declined.

Tutorial note: only five threats and safeguards were required to score 10 marks.

20 Internal audit function

(a) **Internal audit activities**

- Review of systems (internal control, management, operational, accounting)
- Monitoring of systems against targets and making recommendations
- Value for money, best value, information technology, financial audits
- Operational audits (for example, procurement)
- Monitoring or risk management
- Special investigations (for example, fraud detection)

(b) **Internal auditors versus external auditors**

Objectives

The objective of internal auditors is to add value and improve an organisation's operations, whereas the objective of external auditors is to express an opinion as to whether the financial statements of an organisation are true and fair (or presented fairly in all material respects).

Scope of work

Internal auditor's undertake work on the operations of an organisation, whereas external auditor's focus on the financial statements.

Reporting responsibilities

Internal auditors report to the board of directors or audit committee and produce reports that are private and for the use of directors and management only. External auditors report to the shareholders or members of the company as to the truth and fairness of the financial statements. The audit report produced by external auditors is publicly available.

(c) **Outsourcing**

'Outsourcing' is subcontracting a process to a third party company, that is, purchasing the service externally. Services that are typically outsourced include internal audit, accountancy and payroll functions.

Advantages of outsourcing internal audit	Disadvantages of outsourcing internal audit
Service provider has expert knowledge and can provide skilled staff.	Independence and objectivity issues if internal audit department is provided by same firm as external auditors.
Cost savings in terms of employee salaries, training costs, recruitment expenses.	Cost may be high enough to force entity to choose not to have an internal audit department at all.
Immediate internal audit department provided.	Frequent staff changes resulting in poor quality service being providing due to lack of understanding of client's systems and operations.

21 Internal audit responsibilities

Text references. Chapters 5 and 11.

Top tips. This question covers an important issue, fraud, and the role of both internal and external auditors in relation to it. It also covers reliance by the external auditor on internal audit work. It is important in this question that you do not get the timing wrong. This is critical on this question of the paper, especially, as it is very tempting to write down everything you know on the topics being examined.

Easy marks. This question is wholly knowledge-based so should be straightforward, proving your knowledge is sound. As stated above, make sure you stick to the time allocation so that lack of time does not affect your performance in subsequent questions.

Marking scheme

		Marks
(a)	Prevention, detection and reporting of fraud and error 1.5 marks per well explained point to maximum of	6
(b)	Reliance on internal audit work 1 mark per point to maximum of	4 10

(a) **Prevention, detection and reporting of fraud and error**

External auditors

Prevention and detection

The external auditors are bound by the requirements of ISA 240. This requires that auditors recognise that **fraud and error may materially affect the financial statements** and design procedures to ensure that the risk is minimised. The auditors have no specific requirement to prevent or detect fraud. However, they must maintain **professional scepticism** throughout the audit, recognising that circumstances may exist that cause the financial statements to be materially misstated.

By conducting the audit in accordance with ISAs the auditor obtains reasonable assurance that the financial statements are free from material misstatement caused by fraud or error. However, due to the nature of fraud the risk of not detecting fraud is higher than the risk of not detecting error.

Reporting

ISA 240 also sets out the requirements in relation to reporting fraud. If auditors suspect or detect a fraud, they must report it on a **timely basis** to the **appropriate level of management**.

If management are implicated the matter must be communicated to **those charged with governance**, unless the fraud necessitates immediate reporting to a **third party**.

The matter should only be referred to in the audit report if the opinion is modified on those grounds. It may also be that the matter is one which needs reporting to a relevant authority in the public interest. If the auditors feel that this is so, they should seek **legal advice** before taking any action, and request that the entity reports itself. If the directors refuse to make any disclosure in these circumstances, the auditors should make the disclosure themselves.

Internal auditors

Prevention and detection

It is likely that the internal auditors will have a role both in the prevention and detection of fraud. Indirectly, they play a role in their involvement with the **internal controls** of a business, which are set up to limit risks to the company, one of which is fraud. Directly, they may be engaged by the directors to carry out tests when a fraud is suspected, or routinely to discourage such activity. However, if a serious fraud was suspected, a company might bring in **external experts**, such as forensic accountants or the police.

Reporting

If internal auditors discovered issues which made them suspect fraud, they would **report it immediately** to their superiors, who would report to those charged with governance. In the event that an internal auditor suspected top level fraud, he might make disclosure to the relevant authority in the public interest.

(b) **Criteria to be considered when assessing whether to place reliance on internal audit work**

Extent to which its objectivity is supported

The auditor must consider the extent to which the internal audit function's objectivity is supported by its organisational status, relevant policies and procedures. The auditor should consider whom the internal auditors report to and whether they are subject to any conflicting responsibilities, constraints or restrictions. This will affect the capability of the internal auditors to communicate significant matters openly.

Scope of function

The external auditors should consider the extent and nature of assignments performed by the internal auditors and the action taken by management as a result of internal audit reports.

Level of technical competence

The external auditors should consider whether the internal auditors have adequate technical training and proficiency.

Whether a systematic and disciplined approach is taken (due professional care)

The external auditors should consider whether internal audit adopt a systematic and disciplined approach to planning, supervising, reviewing and documenting assignments. The auditor should consider whether the function has appropriate quality control procedures, audit manuals, work programs and internal audit documentation.

22 MonteHodge

Text reference. Chapter 5.

Top tips. This question relates to internal audit so you need to remember what the internal audit function does within an organisation before you attempt to tackle it.

For 10 marks, you must make sure your answer is relevant to the client, MonteHodge – don't launch into an answer that only discusses the advantages and disadvantages of internal audit departments in general. The question specifically asks you to consider the advantages and disadvantages for the company in the question scenario, therefore make sure that you do use the information provided – planning your answer first is therefore vital.

Marking scheme

Marks

Up to 1 mark for each well-explained point

For internal audit

– VFM audits
– Accounting system
– Computer systems
– Internal control systems
– Effect on audit fee
– Image to clients
– Corporate governance
– Lack of control
– Law change
– Assistance to financial accountant
– Nature of industry (financial services)
– Other relevant points

Against internal audit

– No statutory requirement
– Family business
– Potential cost
– Review threat
– Other relevant points

Maximum marks   **10**

Arguments for an internal audit department

There is currently a lack of internal control systems in place. An internal audit department could look at existing procedures and systems and make lots of useful recommendations to tighten up controls.

The internal audit department could make useful recommendations in respect of good corporate governance, even though the company is not required to comply with corporate governance guidelines. If the directors did decide to float the company in the future, it would have to comply with such guidelines.

The external auditors might be able to rely on internal audit work undertaken by the company's internal auditors and this in turn could result in a reduced audit fee.

The company will have to comply with additional financial services regulations in the future, so an internal audit department could undertake work to ensure that it is complying with all required legislation and regulations.

The presence of an internal audit department within the company would present a positive image to clients of the company.

The internal audit department could review the systems in place, such as the stock market monitoring system, and assess whether upgrades are required.

The internal audit department could provide benefit to the financial accountant, who is not qualified, in the areas of accounting regulations and the internal control system, for example.

Arguments against an internal audit department

Setting up an internal audit department from scratch could prove expensive in terms of both time and money. The company will incur recruitment costs and the cost of additional staff salaries.

The company does not have to have an internal audit department in place as it is not listed and therefore under no obligation to comply with recommended codes of corporate governance such as the *UK Corporate Governance Code*.

The company's shareholders consist of six members of the same family. There is therefore not the same requirement to provide assurance on systems and internal controls as there would be to shareholders in a public company.

Many accounting systems are not necessarily complex so the directors may not see the need for another department to review their operations.

The directors and senior management may feel threatened by the presence of internal auditors looking at systems and controls.

Top tips. Only ten arguments for and against (in total) were needed. There was no split in marks between the reasons for and against. For example, four reasons for having an internal audit department and four reasons against would have scored the same as five reasons for and three reasons against for this particular question.

---

23 Avocado

Text references. Chapters 1 and 5.

Top tips. Part (a) tests knowledge of the different levels of assurance obtained in an audit and other review assignments. This is a knowledge based question and should be relatively straightforward.

Part (b) examines your understanding of the differences between internal and external audit. A two column approach would be useful here as you can examine key issues eg scope of work, side by side. Make sure however that when you are using a columnar format your answer still contains a sufficient level of detail.

Part (c) asks for an explanation of the potential impact on the work performed by the auditor during the interim and final audits if the company established an internal audit department. This is a tricky requirement. The best approach is to think about the type of work that the internal audit function performs. Then consider the different emphasis for the external auditor at the interim and final audit stage. Can you see any connection or overlap between the internal audit work and the external audit procedures?

Easy marks. Easier marks are available in part (a) and part (b) of the question.

Examiner's comments. Parts (a) and (b) were answered well but the performance of candidates on (c) was unsatisfactory.

Where part (c) was attempted, many candidates failed to score more than 1 mark. What was required was an explanation of tasks that internal audit might perform that the external auditor might then look to rely on in either the interim or final audit. For example, they could utilise systems documentation produced by internal audit during the interim audit. Or they could rely on year-end inventory counts undertaken by internal audit as part of their inventory testing at the final audit.

Marking scheme

		Marks
(a)	Up to 1½ marks per well explained point	
	External audit – Reasonable assurance	
	Other review engagements – Negative assurance	2
(b)	Up to 1 mark per well explained point	
	Objective	
	Whom they report to	
	Reports – publicly available or not	
	Scope of work	
	Appointed by	
	Independence of company	4

(c) Up to 1 mark per well explained point
Interim audit
Systems documentation
Testing of systems such as payroll, sales, purchases
Risk assessment
Fraud and error, non-compliance with law and regulations
Final audit
Inventory count procedures

$$\frac{4}{\underline{10}}$$

(a) **Levels of assurance**

An audit engagement provides reasonable assurance. This is a high but not absolute level of assurance that the financial statements are free from material misstatement.

In other review engagements where an opinion is provided a moderate level of assurance is given. This is normally expressed in negative terms ie the practitioner states that nothing has come to his or her attention to suggest that the subject matter being reviewed contains material misstatements.

(b) **Differences between internal and external audit**

	Internal audit	External audit
Objective	The objective of internal audit is to add value and improve the organisation's operations.	The main objective of external audit is to enable the auditors to express an opinion on the financial statements
Reporting	Internal auditors report to the board of directors or other people charged with governance such as the audit committee. Reports are private and are for the directors and management of the company.	External auditors report to the shareholders or members of the company regarding the truth and fairness of the financial statements. The external audit report is publicly available to the shareholders and other interested parties.
Scope	The work performed relates to the operations of the organisation.	The work performed relates to the financial statements.
Relationship with the company	Internal auditors are often employees of the organisation although the internal audit function may be outsourced.	External auditors are independent of the company and its management. They are usually appointed by the shareholders.
Planning and collection of evidence	Planning and collection of evidence will depend on the nature of the assignment the internal auditor has been asked to carry out. Evidence will involve primarily inspection of internal documents and interviewing of staff.	Planning and evidence collection must be conducted in accordance with ISAs. Evidence sources will include external sources.

(c) **Impact on work performed by Lime & Co**

Assuming that Lime & Co have concluded that the work of the internal audit department can be relied upon, the impact on the audit would be as follows:

Interim audit

The focus of the interim audit is normally on controls work. Lime & Co will need to obtain an understanding of the system initially. If the internal auditors have produced systems notes the external auditor may be able to use these. The external auditor would need to perform walk-through tests to ensure that the system is operating as described.

Where the internal audit department has tested controls the external auditors may be able to reduce the extent of their procedures in this area. The external auditor would be required to re-perform a sample of the internal auditor's tests. Based on an evaluation of these results it may be possible to reduce the assessment of control risk.

Internal audit is often responsible for managing the risk of fraud and error and ensuring that the company complies with relevant laws and regulations. Lime & Co may be able to review the work performed by the internal auditors in this area as part of their own risk assessment process.

Final audit

At the final audit stage the focus of the external auditor will tend to be on substantive procedures. As internal audit is effectively part of the internal control of the business it is less likely that the internal auditor's work will be as relevant. However, internal audit procedures may be a source of substantive evidence in particular areas, such as year end inventory counting performed by internal audit. The external auditor would have to re-perform a sample of the procedures performed by the internal auditor and would still be required to obtain sufficient independent evidence.

24 Wood Industries

Text reference. Chapter 19.

Top tips. This question should be reasonably straightforward as you should be familiar with directors' and auditors' responsibilities and with the difference between reasonable and limited assurance.

Easy marks. Part (a) tests very basic knowledge so should have been reasonably easy.

Examiner's comments. Part (a) focused on a relatively small area of knowledge. Candidates need to focus points on the published financial statements. This section was well answered.

The overall standard in part (b) was high with most candidates correctly explaining reasonable and limited assurance and providing at least one benefit of limited assurance.

Marking scheme

		Marks
(a)	**Duties re financial statements**	
	Allow 1 mark for director responsibilities, and 1 for auditor responsibilities	
	Preparation of financial statements	2
	Fraud and error	2
	Disclosure	2
	Going concern	2
	Similar relevant points – each point	2
	Maximum marks	**6**
(b)	**Audit reports**	
	One mark per point	
	Meaning of reasonable assurance	1
	Meaning of limited assurance	1
	Advantages of limited assurance	
	Some comfort provided	1
	Credibility	1
	Cost effective	1
	Allow other relevant points	1
	Maximum marks	**4**
		10

(a) **Preparation of financial statements**

The directors have a legal responsibility to prepare financial statements giving a true and fair view. This implies that they have been prepared in accordance with the relevant IASs and IFRSs.

The auditor's duty is to carry out an audit (according to the International Standards on Auditing) and to give an opinion on whether a true and fair view is given (or whether the financial statements present fairly, in all material respects, the financial position of the entity). In doing this they will have to consider whether the relevant accounting standards have been properly followed.

Estimates and judgements and accounting policies

The directors have the responsibility for making the estimates and judgements underlying the financial statements and for selecting the appropriate accounting policies.

The auditor's responsibility is to assess the appropriateness of the directors' judgements and to modify the audit opinion in the case of any disagreement causing the auditors to conclude the financial statements are not free from material misstatement.

Fraud and error

The directors have a duty to prevent and detect fraud and error. This is a duty they owe to the shareholders and there is no 'materiality' threshold attached to their duty.

The auditor is responsible (under ISA 240) for obtaining reasonable assurance that the financial statements are free from material misstatement including material misstatement caused by fraud.

The auditor is responsible for maintaining **professional scepticism** throughout the audit, considering the possibility of management override of controls. The audit team must discuss how and where the entity's financial statements may be susceptible to material misstatement due to fraud, including how fraud might occur.

Disclosure

The directors are responsible for disclosing all information required by law and accounting standards.

The auditor's responsibility is to review whether all the disclosure rules have been followed and whether the overall disclosure is adequate. There are certain pieces of information, which, if not disclosed by the directors, must be disclosed by the auditor in his report. Examples of this are related party transactions and transactions with directors.

Going concern

The directors are responsible for assessing whether it is appropriate to treat the business as a going concern. In doing this they should look at forecasts and predictions for at least twelve months from the reporting date. They should also disclose any significant uncertainties over the going concern status of the company.

The auditors' responsibility is to consider whether there are any indicators of going concern problems in the company, and assess the forecasts made by directors and decide whether the correct accounting basis has been used and whether there is adequate disclosure of significant uncertainties.

The auditor must consider modifying the audit opinion in the auditor's report if:

(i)   The directors have considered a period of less than twelve months from the reporting date (this could result in a qualified opinion due to an inability to obtain sufficient appropriate evidence)

(ii)   The directors have used the going concern basis when the auditor believes that its use is not appropriate (this will be a result in an adverse opinion)

(iii)   The auditor agrees with the basis chosen by the directors but feels that the disclosures are inadequate (this will probably result in a qualified 'except for' opinion)

(iv)   The auditor agrees with the chosen basis, and that the disclosures are adequate but there are uncertainties over the going concern status of the company. In this case the opinion will be unmodified but an emphasis of matter paragraph will be added.

(b) Reasonable assurance is provided in a report where the auditor has obtained sufficient evidence to feel confident to give reasonable assurance that the information is free from material error. A normal audit opinion (giving reasonable assurance) takes a positive form of words, ie 'In our opinion the financial statements present fairly, in all material respects, (or give a true and fair view of) the financial position of..'

Limited assurance is provided where the auditor has obtained a lower level of evidence and can therefore give only a lower level of assurance. An opinion giving limited assurance would use a negative form of words. A review of a forecast would be an appropriate example of when this would be used. The auditor cannot be as confident about forward-looking information, based on the directors' assumptions.

A limited assurance opinion would be worded perhaps as 'nothing has come to our attention to suggest that the information is not based on reasonable assumptions...'

The advantages of the limited assurance would be:

- The bank will be able to place more reliance on the forecast as it has been subject to review by an independent professional. The level of comfort given will be less than that of an audit but forecast information cannot be verified to the same degree as historical information so the limited assurance is the best that could be expected in the circumstances.

- Limited assurance requires a lower level of work than a full scope audit so will be cheaper for the company.

25 Regulation and limitations

Text references. Chapters 1 and 2.

Top tips. Overall this is a relatively straightforward knowledge based question. In part (a) you only need three rights and you must be careful not to confuse auditors' rights with auditors' duties. In part (b) you need to consider the interaction between national standards and ISAs.

The limitations of audit in part (c) all stem from the fact not everything in the financial statements is checked and confirmed (eg only a sample of inventory costs is traced to invoice cost) and the auditor has to use judgement to provide only reasonable (and not absolute) assurance. In addition some items in the financial statements are based on estimates and can not be conclusively proven to be correct or incorrect.

Easy marks. As a knowledge based question there is an opportunity to score well on all parts of this question, however part (a) on auditors' rights is probably the most straightforward.

Marking scheme

		Marks
(a)	Up to 1 mark per well stated right, max of 3 rights	
	Right of access to books and records	
	Right to require information or explanations	
	Right to receive all written resolutions	
	Right to receive all notices of any general meeting	
	Right to attend any general meeting of the company	
	Right to be heard at the annual general meeting	3
(b)	Up to 1 mark per valid explanation	
	Maximum marks	4
(c)	Up to 1 mark per well explained limitation	
	Sampling	
	Subjectivity	
	Inherent limitations of internal control systems	
	Evidence is persuasive not conclusive	
	Audit report format	
	Historic information	3
		10

(a) **Rights of auditors**

The rights of auditors include:

- A right of access at all times to the books, accounts and vouchers of the company (in whatever form they are held)

- A right to require from the company's officers such information and explanations as they think necessary for the performance of their duties as auditors

- A right to attend any general meetings of the company and to receive all notices of and other communications relating to such meetings which any member of the company is entitled to receive

- A right to be heard at general meetings which they attend on any part of the business that concerns them as auditors

- A right to receive a copy of any written resolution proposed

(**Note:** Only three rights were required).

(b) ISAs must be applied in an audit of **financial statements** by an auditor. They need to be adapted as necessary in the circumstances when applied to audits of other historical financial information.

ISAs contain **auditor's objectives, basic principles** and **requirements** (including essential procedures), together with related guidance in the form of explanatory and other material.

The whole text of ISAs must be considered in order to understand and apply the basic principles and essential procedures.

It is important to note that ISAs do not override the national audit regulations in individual countries.

To the extent that ISAs conform with local regulations in regard to a particular subject, the audit in that country in accordance with local regulations will automatically comply with the ISA on that subject.

Where local regulations differ from or conflict with ISAs, member bodies should comply with the obligations of members in the IFAC constitution, ie encourage changes in local regulations to comply with ISAs.

(**Note:** Only four points were required).

(c) **Limitations of external audits**

Evidence on which the audit opinion is based is persuasive not conclusive as it involves estimates and judgements and cannot give a definite conclusion. For that reason only reasonable assurance can be given.

Some financial statement areas include estimates based on assumptions and judgements (such as provisions) and the auditors must therefore use their judgement when auditing such areas.

The auditor does not test every transaction, but instead only tests a sample of items making up certain financial statement balances. Therefore untested items may contain misstatements.

The internal control systems the auditor may seek to rely on are designed and operated by people, and are therefore susceptible to human error and management override. Employees can also collude to bypass controls.

The audit report is in a form and uses terminology that is not easily understood by non-accountants. There is therefore a risk the opinion given is also not understood.

The audit report may be issued a relatively long time after the year end, and so the client's current financial position may be significantly different from the position reported on. This makes the audit report less relevant and of less use.

(**Note:** Only three limitations were required).

26 Brampton

Text references. Chapters 1, 7 and 11.

Top tips. In part (a) you can use the requirements in ISA 610 *Using the work of internal auditors* (relating to assessing the adequacy of internal audit work) to structure your answer. It states that auditors must evaluate the extent to which internal audit's objectivity is supported, technical competence, whether the work is carried out in a systematic and disciplined manner with due professional care. Another consideration is whether there is likely to be effective communication between internal and external audit. You must remember to fully explain each point to gain full marks.

In part (b) think of how cash forecasts are constructed; they start with an opening balance and future cash flows are projected based on assumptions and plans. This should give you ideas for procedures. For example you will need to assess the validity of the assumptions somehow, and you need to verify the correct opening balance has been used.

Easy marks. In part (c) you should not have much difficulty in deciding the kind of assurance to be given.

Examiner's comments.

Part (a) was answered reasonably well by candidates. Some were able to take their knowledge of reliance on internal audit and provide an answer which covered areas such as independence, competence, professional care as well as scenario specific points such as the possibility of management pressure on internal audit in order to obtain the crucial loan finance. Some candidates tended to only focus on independence and so failed to generate a sufficient number of points.

Part (b) was unsatisfactorily answered by most candidates. Common errors included:

- Confusing a cash flow forecast and a cash flow statement

- Not appreciating that the forecast covered a future period as opposed to historic information, therefore it would not be possible to perform such procedures as 'agreeing revenue to sales invoices'

- Providing procedures which were unrealistic, such as 'compare the forecast to competitors cash flow forecast' it would not be possible to obtain the forecast of a competitor

- Providing procedures which are relevant for an audit as opposed to future information such as 'perform a receivables circularisation to confirm receivable balances'

- Not understanding that a cash flow forecast does not contain non-cash items such as depreciation

Few candidates understood that a forecast would be made up of assumptions and hence these needed to be reviewed in detail for reasonableness.

For part (c), it was pleasing to see that a significant proportion of candidates were able to correctly identify that limited assurance would be provided to the bank, and to state what this meant. However not many were able to explain why limited assurance was to be provided. Only some candidates were able to explain that it was due to the nature of forecasts being future information and hence reasonable assurance not being a practical option.

Marks

(a) **Work of internal audit**

Up to 1½ marks for each well-explained factor, but maximum 5
Independence – to whom report; links to audit committee
Competence – qualifications and experience
Effective communication – between internal and external auditors
Professional care – properly planned and performed
Maximum marks   5

(b) **Examination of forecast**

Up to 1 mark for each adequately described procedure, but maximum 3
Opening balance
Accuracy of past forecasts
Assumptions
Sales budgets
Non-current assets required
Increased working capital required
Maximum marks   3

(c) **Kind of assurance**

1 mark for each relevant point, but maximum 2
Not possible to give a report on accuracy and why
Limited assurance
What this kind of assurance means
Testing assumptions and reporting on validity
Forecast properly prepared on basis of assumptions
Maximum marks   2
                                                                                                      ──
                                                                                                      10
                                                                                                      ══

(a) **Relying on the work of internal auditors**

The external auditor has sole responsibility for the audit opinion expressed on the financial statements. However the work of internal audit may be used for the purposes of the external audit as long as the internal auditors are:

- **Independent** of the accounts department and have no conflicting responsibilities, constraints or restrictions. It seems that internal audit are reporting straight to the board, but this may include the finance director supervising the accounts department. Ideally internal audit would report to an audit committee.

- **Technically competent** and have had adequate training. Past experience of any internal audit work reviewed previously and knowledge of staff holding relevant professional qualifications should aid in the assessment of the competence of internal audit.

- Able to **communicate effectively** with external audit. Internal audit should be able to communicate openly with the external audit.

- Taking a **systematic and disciplined approach** and exercising due professional care. In order to rely on the work, the auditor must establish whether it was properly planned, supervised, documented and reviewed.

(b) **Examination of the cash flow forecast**

When examining the cash flow forecast, procedures undertaken would include the following:

- Agree the opening balance of the cash forecast to the closing cash book balance to ensure the correct opening balance has been used in the forecast.

- Consider how accurate previous company forecasts have been by comparing actual cash flows with previous forecasts. If previous forecasts are shown to have been accurate, it is more likely the current forecasts will be reliable.

- Review the assumptions made in preparing the forecasts and consider whether they are consistent with what is known about the business and its environment. For example costs have been increasing recently, so a decrease in costs in the forecasts would need to be investigated.

Top tips. There are other valid procedures, but only three were required to gain full marks. Other valid procedures include:

- Obtain evidence that the cash outflows for non-current assets needed to expand white bread facilities are included and the included investment is sufficient to generate any additional sales inflows projected. Ask production personnel what level of machinery investment is needed to expand production by a given proportion and then corroborate to current prices of this machinery (using supplier quotes if available).

- Consider the adequacy of the proposed working capital increase. Increased working capital would result in cash outflows so determining its adequacy is important.

(c) **Level of assurance**

It is not possible for the external auditors to confirm the accuracy of the forecast as requested by the bank. The forecast will be based on assumptions made by management and it would be impossible to gain enough evidence to confirm these are completely accurate.

Due to the uncertainties of the future cash flows included in the forecast, the bank should be informed that only a limited level of assurance can be provided in any report, expressed in the form of **limited assurance**.

The report will set out the types of procedures undertaken and the assumptions made by management. If no irregularities were found during the work performed, the report will state that nothing had come to the attention of the auditors that would cause them to believe that management's assumptions do not provide a reasonable basis for the cash forecast.

The auditor could also conclude in the report on whether the forecast has been properly prepared on the basis of the assumptions.

27 Multiple choice answers

1   D   The matters mentioned in option D relate specifically to business operations. The matters mentioned in the other options relate specifically to financial reporting A, investments B and financing C.

2   C   Statements 1 and 2 only are correct. Materiality may be based on other criteria, not just revenue, such as net assets and profit before tax. Materiality should be revisited throughout the audit and revised if necessary.

3   B   ISA 315 requires auditors to use analytical procedures and inquiry when obtaining an understanding of the entity and its environment. In addition, they should also use observation and inspection.

4   C   The risk of material misstatement at the assertion level is made up of inherent risk and control risk. Detection risk is the risk that the auditor's procedures will not detect a misstatement that exists in an assertion that could be material. Audit risk is the risk that the auditor gives an inappropriate audit opinion when the financial statements are materially misstated. Audit risk is made up of inherent risk, control risk and detection risk (AR = IR × CR × DR)

5   C   The main aim of planning is not to ensure the audit is completed within cost and time restraints but that it is carried out in an effective manner. All the other statements comprise the aims of planning.

6   C   Risk and exceptions identified influence the form and content of audit working papers. Other factors which do so are the nature of the procedures to be performed, extent of judgement required, significance of audit evidence obtained, and the need to document a conclusion not readily determinable from the documentation of work done or audit evidence obtained. Cost and the system used to document work are not valid factors.

7   B   The statement is false. Performance materiality levels are set lower than materiality for the financial statements as a whole.

8   D   Control risk (together with inherent risk) are components of the risk of material misstatement, which is governed by the circumstances of the audit client and therefore is outside the control of the auditor. Sampling risk is a component of detection risk, which is controlled by the auditor. The correct answer is therefore option D.

9   D   The audit strategy should be established before the audit plan is developed. The plan is more detailed than the overall audit strategy in that it includes the nature, timing and extent of audit procedures to be performed by engagement team members.

10   B   The statement is false. The risk of material misstatement is a function of inherent risk and control risk, calculated by multiplying these two factors. Audit risk is computed by multiplying the risk of material misstatement by detection risk.

11   C   Details in A and B would be included in the audit strategy document.

12   B   In accordance with ISA 330 *The auditor's responses to assessed risks* the auditor is more likely to perform procedures at the period end where there is a high risk of material misstatement.

13   D   Performance materiality must be lower than materiality for the financial statements as a whole.

14   C   Analytical procedures can be used throughout the audit but must be used as risk assessment procedures and at the review stage of the audit.

15   C   The external auditor is responsible for obtaining reasonable assurance that the financial statements are free from material misstatement whether caused by fraud or error. The internal audit function may assist management and those charged with governance in its monitoring and reviewing role but is not ultimately responsible.

16   C   A, B and D are overall responses.

17   C   The auditor cannot affect control risk or inherent risk. The auditor can reduce audit risk by manipulating detection risk. Increasing sample sizes and assigning more experienced staff to the audit will both reduce detection risk and therefore audit risk.

18 C The directors are ultimately responsible for the prevention and detection of fraud and error. The auditor needs to obtain reasonable assurance that the financial statements are not materially misstated.

19 B ACCA recommends a minimum retention period of seven years.

20 D Although the directors are responsible for the prevention and detection of fraud this is not one of the matters included in the agreement obtained by the auditors to establish that the preconditions of an audit exist in accordance with ISA 210 *Agreeing the terms of audit engagements*.

21 C In accordance with ISA 210 *Agreeing the terms of audit engagements* the expected form and content of any reports must be included. A, B and D however may be included but there is no requirement to do so.

22 A The responsibility for ensuring compliance with laws and regulations lies with management.

23 B Although the food hygiene regulations do not have a direct effect on the determination of material amounts in the financial statements, the external auditor must undertake audit procedures to help identify non-compliance, to the extent that such non-compliance may have a material effect on the financial statements.

    The auditor is required to obtain sufficient appropriate audit evidence about compliance, where the laws and regulations have a direct effect on the determination of material amounts and disclosures in the financial statements.

24 D ISA 250 distinguishes between laws and regulations which have a direct effect and those which have an indirect effect on the financial statements. The auditor must undertake specified audit procedures to help identify non-compliance with laws and regulations that may have a material effect on the financial statements.

28 Audit risk and planning

(a) Statutory audit objective

The objective of the statutory audit is to obtain reasonable assurance about whether the financial statements are free from material misstatement, thereby enabling the auditor to express an opinion on whether the financial statements are prepared, in all material respects, in accordance with an applicable financial reporting framework (such as IFRSs).

There is an International Standard on Auditing that deals with the overall audit objectives (ISA 200), but in addition each individual ISA has its own objective designed to aid in the achievement of the overall objective stated above.

Therefore, in most cases fully understanding and complying with the ISAs relevant to the audit will result in the auditor achieving each applicable ISA's objective and the overall objective.

To ensure objectives are met, ISA 200 states that the auditor must go beyond the requirements in a particular ISA if it is considered necessary to meet the objective.

The way in the audit is approached is very important, so ISA 200 stresses that in order to achieve the overall objective, auditors also need to plan and perform the audit with professional scepticism and apply professional judgement.

(b) Matters to be documented during audit planning

- Discussion amongst the audit team about the susceptibility of the financial statements to material misstatements
- Key elements of the understanding gained of the entity
- Identified and assessed risks of material misstatement
- Significant risks identified and related controls evaluated
- Overall responses to address the risks of material misstatement

- Nature, extent and timing of further audit procedures linked to the assessed risks at the assertion level

- Where reliance is to be placed on the effectiveness of controls from previous audits, conclusions on how this is appropriate

(**Note.** Only six were required.)

(c) **Factors affecting the form and content of audit working papers**

- The size and complexity of the entity

- The nature of the audit procedures to be performed

- The identified risks of material misstatement

- The significance of the audit evidence obtained

- The nature and extent of exceptions identified

- The need to document a conclusion or basis for a conclusion not readily determinable from documentation of work performed or audit evidence obtained

- The audit methodology and tools used

(**Note.** Only six were required.)

29 Interim audit

Text reference. Chapter 7.

Top tips. Pay attention to the requirements in the question. Where you are asked to explain something make sure you provide full sentences if you want to gain full marks. As always, stick to time on this knowledge based question or you will not leave enough for the other questions on the paper.

Easy marks. Part (a) is easier than the other parts since you are asked to explain the types of audit procedures carried out during the interim audit.

(a) During the interim audit the auditor may conduct the following audit procedures.

Detailed testing on the elements of the entity's internal control system which are relevant to the audit.

Analytical procedures such as variance analysis and ratio analysis on the entity's performance to date and any key ratios/trends.

Review of any reports produced by the internal audit department which are relevant to the audit.

Detailed substantive procedures on transactions which have occurred during the first part of the year.

(b) **Impact of interim audit work on internal controls on the final audit**

If the auditors are to place reliance on internal controls they must obtain evidence that controls have operated effectively throughout the period.

If the auditor obtains audit evidence about the operating effectiveness of controls at the interim audit, when it comes to the final audit, instead of having to gain evidence over controls covering the whole year the auditor can focus on obtaining audit evidence about significant changes to those controls subsequent to the interim period.

The auditor will need to determine the extent of the additional audit evidence to be obtained for the remaining period.

(c) **Factors to consider when determining the extent of further work on internal controls at the final audit**

At the final audit the auditor will need to gain additional audit evidence about controls that were operating during the period between the interim audit and the year end. When determining the extent of the additional work needed the auditor will take into account:

- The significance of the assessed risks of material misstatement at the assertion level.

- The specific controls that were tested during the interim period, and significant changes to them since they were tested, including changes in the information system, processes, and personnel.

- The degree to which audit evidence about the operating effectiveness of those controls was obtained.

- The length of the remaining period.

- The extent to which the auditor intends to reduce further substantive procedures based on the reliance of controls.

- The strength of the control environment.

30 Audit planning

(a) The purpose of the **audit strategy** is to set the overall scope, timing and direction of the audit.

Matters that would be considered in establishing an overall audit strategy include:

- Characteristics of the engagement:
    - The entity's applicable financial reporting framework
    - Any industry-specific reporting requirements
    - The nature of the business
    - Availability of the client's data and staff (including internal audit)
    - The potential for using Computer Assisted Audit Techniques

- Reporting objectives, timing of the audit and nature of communications.

- Knowledge gained from previous audits and during the preliminary risk assessment.

- Nature, timing and extent of resources in terms of using appropriate personnel.

(b) The auditor will take the overall audit strategy and convert it into a more detailed audit plan. The plan includes the nature, timing and extent of audit procedures to be performed by engagement team members in order to obtain sufficient appropriate audit evidence to reduce audit risk to an acceptably low level.

Examples of items included in the audit plan could be:

- A timetable of planned audit work
- Details of the allocation of work to audit team members
- Audit procedures for each major account area (eg inventory, receivables, cash etc)
- Materiality for the financial statements as a whole and performance materiality

Tutorial note: only **two** examples were needed.

(c)   Performance materiality is the amount or amounts set by the auditor at less than materiality for the financial statements as a whole to reduce to an appropriately low level the probability that the aggregate of uncorrected and undetected misstatements exceeds materiality for the financial statements as a whole.

Performance materiality also refers to the amount or amounts set by the auditor at less than the materiality level or levels for particular classes of transactions, account balances or disclosures.

Having set the materiality for the financial statements as whole, usually using appropriate benchmarks and percentages (for example 5% of profit before tax), a lower level of performance materiality is determined by the auditor using his or her professional judgement.

The performance materiality level is affected by the auditor's understanding of the entity and the nature and extent of misstatements identified in prior audits.

31 Mason Air Services

Text reference. Chapter 6.

Top tips. This question includes a requirement type commonly used in F8. You need to make sure you identify and describe audit risks that have a clear impact on the financial statements rather than general business risks. Make sure your auditor's responses to each risk are explained in sufficient detail.

Easy marks. These are available for the description of each audit risk.

Audit risks and responses

Audit risk	Response(s) to risk
The company charges an annual fee which is payable in advance based on the contract date. There is a risk that the revenue for the annual fees is not properly recognised in the period to which it relates leading to revenue and deferred income being misstated in the financial statements.	Obtain copies of all contracts and use the terms to calculate the annual charge for each. Then compare this with the revenue recorded for annual charges in the financial statements. Investigate any discrepancies.
The flying hour charge per hour used on the invoice is not based on the relevant contract but instead on the last invoice. As a contract has been renewed in the year for the ambulance service, the historic charge may have been incorrectly included on invoices and therefore revenue recorded may not reflect the value of services provided. There is also a risk of errors in one invoice being repeated in subsequent invoices.	Inspect both the old and new air ambulance contracts to establish when the new hourly rate should have been charged. For a sample of invoices after that date ensure the new rate was applied and recorded. Review a sample of invoices during the year for other contracts to ensure the rate charged is as per the contract in case contract revisions in previous years have been missed.
Mason Air Services has only four customers and each makes up a significant proportion of revenue (as contracts are of a similar value). Given profits are $500k and one quarter of revenue is $11m, the loss of one customer will make Mason loss making and may threaten the company's ability to continue as a going concern.	Each contract should be reviewed for break clauses and end date to assess the risk that contracts may not continue for the foreseeable future. Board minutes and correspondence should be reviewed for evidence of customer dissatisfaction or evidence the contracts will not be renewed.

Audit risk	Response(s) to risk
The contract with the police force runs out in March 20X1 and the police are trying to substantially reduce the contract charges. The reduction of the contract charges or the loss of the contract to a competitor could threaten the going concern of the company. There is therefore a risk that the basis of, or disclosure in, the financial statements is incorrect.	Enquire of management as to the progress of contract negotiations and inspect board minutes/correspondence for evidence of discussions on this matter. If figures are available for the proposed decrease in charges, estimate the impact on revenue and profits to assess the effect on going concern. Review any disclosures in relation to this matter for compliance with IFRSs.
There is a risk that the cost of re-fitting, replacement and adding of specialist equipment to the aircraft has been incorrectly treated as revenue expenditure when it should have been capital expenditure, or vice versa. This would result in the non-current assets or repairs costs being misstated in the financial statements.	An analysis of these costs should be reviewed and traced to invoices. The invoice descriptions and supporting documents should be reviewed to assess the nature of the expenditure. Once established as either capital or revenue, it should be traced to the general ledger and the financial statements to ensure it has been classified correctly as an asset or repairs.
Approximately $500k (= $2m/4) of equipment included in inventory has been replaced, suggesting such equipment is no longer fit for purpose, even though it may be functional. In addition, the value of the replaced equipment has been estimated by the directors and there is a risk that inventory is not recorded at the lower of cost and NRV. Inventory could therefore be materially overstated.	Enquire of management whether there is any alternative use or market for the equipment and the likely selling price in any alternative market. Establish the cost of the equipment by referring to previous year's files or to original purchase invoices. Compare the cost with the NRV and see if the lower of the two shows the director's estimate to be reasonable. If there is no alternative market and the equipment is unlikely to be used going forward, discuss the need for a write down with management. If the asset can continue to be used in the business (eg for training) consider whether it should be classified as a non-current asset rather than as aircraft spares within inventory.

Tutorial note: only **five** risks and responses were required to score 10 marks.

32 Bingsby

Text references. Chapters 7 and 11.

Top tips. Part (a) requires a list of the main sections of an audit strategy document, an explanation of the purpose of each section and an example relevant to the company in the scenario. A tabular approach using the three mini requirements as headers will help you structure your answer and make sure you answer the question fully. Don't worry if the examples you came up with are not the same as those listed, as long as they are relevant you will be awarded marks.

In part (b), you need to apply your knowledge of auditing service organisations to the information contained in the scenario.

Marks

(a) **Audit strategy document**

½ for each section of audit strategy document, ½ for explaining the purpose of that section, 1 for the relevant example from the scenario.

Procedure
- Understand the entity's environment
- Understand the accounting and control systems
- Risk and materiality
- Timing and extent of audit procedures
- Co-ordination, supervision and review of work
- Other relevant points

Maximum marks 6

(b) **Service organisation**

Nature of services
Nature and materiality of transactions
Degree of interaction between service organisation and user entity
Nature of relationship with service organisation
Controls at Bingsby that relate to service provided
1 mark each for each valid point

Maximum marks $\frac{4}{10}$

(a) **Audit strategy document**

Section	Purpose	Example relevant to Bingsby
Characteristics of the engagement	Provides details of the industry and regulatory environment the client operates in. Describes the entity's activities.	Bingsby runs a chain of gastro pubs. As a result, it will need to comply with significant food hygiene and health and safety regulations.
Reporting objectives, timing of the audit engagement and nature of communications	Provides details of the client's reporting dates, the proposed timetable and dates for proposed meetings with management.	The audit is being planned less than a month before the end of the period to be audited. It may be necessary to schedule an initial meeting with management before year end, to ensure any necessary year end testing can be carried out (eg non-current asset verification, food and beverages inventory count.)
Significant factors, preliminary engagement activities, and knowledge gained on other engagements	Identifies areas where there is a greater risk of material misstatement and a greater susceptibility to fraud. Details management's commitment to design, implementation and maintenance of a sound internal control environment. Details the basis for setting materiality.	Bingsby makes cash sales. This increases the susceptibility to fraud. An approach which can appropriately test the completeness of income is needed.

(b) **Audit team's responsibilities to obtain an understanding of the services provided**

Ricks & Co is a service organisation because it is an external organisation that provides a service to Bingsby that could be done internally (it is managing the payroll function for Bingsby). Under ISA 402 *Audit considerations relating to an entity using a service organisation*, Bingsby is the user entity and Sams Co is the user auditor.

As the user auditor, Sams Co must obtain an understanding of the services provided by the service organisation (Ricks & Co) including:

(i) The nature of the services provided and the significance of these to the Bingsby, including the effect on Bingsby's internal control

(ii) The nature and materiality of transactions processed or financial reporting processes affected

(iii) The degree of interaction between Ricks & Co and Bingsby

(iv) The nature of the relationship including the contractual terms in place between Ricks & Co and Bingsby

When obtaining an understanding of the internal control relevant to the audit, Sams Co must evaluate the design and implementation of relevant controls at Bingsby that relate to the services provided by Ricks & Co.

33 Risks and professional scepticism

Text reference. Chapter 6.

Top tips. Part (a) requires you to recall your knowledge of professional scepticism and judgement. In part (b), notice that your examples of areas to apply professional judgement should be limited to the planning stage. Part (c) for 4 marks required a discussion of the importance of assessing risk at the planning stage of an audit. Remember that assessing risk would lead to an effective audit with the focus of testing being on high risk areas only.

Easy marks. In part (b), easy marks are available for explaining professional scepticism and defining professional judgement. Part (c) is a relatively straightforward requirement that does not require application to the scenario. A good knowledge of the importance of risk assessment will enable you to gain the majority of the marks on this part.

(a)   **Professional scepticism**

Professional scepticism is an attitude that includes having a questioning mind, being alert to conditions which may indicate possible misstatement due to error or fraud, and subjecting audit evidence to a critical assessment rather than just taking it at face value.

It is important that professional scepticism is maintained throughout the audit to reduce the risks of overlooking unusual transactions, of over-generalising when drawing conclusions, and of using inappropriate assumptions in determining the nature, timing and extent of audit procedures and evaluating the results of them.

Professional scepticism is necessary to the critical assessment of audit evidence. This includes questioning contradictory audit evidence and the reliability of documents and responses from management and those charged with governance.

(b)   **Professional judgement**

Professional judgement is the application of relevant training, knowledge and experience in making informed decisions about the appropriate courses of action in the circumstances of the audit engagement. The auditor must exercise professional judgement when planning an audit of financial statements.

Professional judgement will be required in many areas when planning. For example the determination of materiality for the financial statements as a whole and performance materiality levels will require professional judgement.

Professional judgement will also be required when deciding on the nature, timing and extent of audit procedures.

(c)   **Importance of assessing risks at the planning stage**

ISA 315 states that the auditor shall identify and assess the risks of material misstatement at the financial statement level and at the assertion level for classes of transactions, account balances and disclosures.

It is very important that auditors carry out this risk assessment at the planning stage because:

- It helps the auditor gain an understanding of the entity for audit purposes
- It helps the auditor focus on the most important areas of the financial statements (where material misstatements are more likely), therefore increasing efficiency
- The risk assessment will form the basis of the audit strategy and the more detailed audit plan
- Once the risks have been assessed, audit team members of sufficient skill and experience can be allocated to maximise the chance of those risks being addressed.

> **Top tips.** Other valid points could have been made here, such as risk assessment as aiding in assessing going concern and the assessment of fraud risks. However stating the ISA 315 requirement along with four valid points relating to the importance of risk assessment would have gained full marks on this question.

34 Sleeptight

> **Text reference.** Chapter 6.
>
> **Top tips.** This is a common requirement where you are asked to explain audit risks and then suggest appropriate responses. Audit risks will be related to potential material misstatements of the financial statements and this should be in the forefront of your mind throughout when you are answering this part of the question. When you are explaining your risk you should therefore state how the financial statements are affected.
>
> Responses are the auditor's responses, not management responses. These will therefore be procedures or actions the auditor will carry out to mitigate the risks.

Marks

Risks and responses

1 mark per well explained risk (maximum of 5) and 1 mark for   5

each valid response (maximum of 5) up to a total maximum of   5

Maximum marks   <u>10</u>

Audit risk	Auditor's response
The directors only work part time at Sleeptight and there is no finance director. This may promote a weak control environment, resulting in undetected errors or frauds.	The controls will need to be documented and evaluated. If these are weak the level of substantive testing will need to be increased accordingly.
The requirement for customers to pay 40% on ordering and the remainder following delivery could result in revenue recorded before it should be, if the deposit is recorded as a sale and not deferred until delivery. This would result in revenue being overstated. Alternatively, revenue could be understated if the final payment were only recognised when it is received, rather than on delivery of the bed.	Enquire of management the point at which revenue is actually recognised, and review the system of accounting for deposits to ensure they are not included in revenue until goods delivered and signed for. For a sample of transactions within 8 weeks of the year end, ensure the revenue recorded is only in respect of beds delivered to customers in the same period and ensure they have been signed for.
The two year guarantee on the beds gives rise to a provision, the measurement of which involves a high degree judgement, and therefore carries a risk of misstatement. This risk is increased by the fact the loan covenants are profit-related and there is an incentive to manipulate areas of the financial statements based on judgements.	Establish the basis of the amount provided for and assumptions made by the financial controller. Re-perform any calculations and establish the level of warranty costs in the year, and compare with the previous provision. Review the level of repair costs incurred post year-end and use these to assess the reasonableness of the provision.
The current year raw materials costs for materials also in inventory last year are based on prices at least a year old. They should be based on the actual cost or reasonable average cost. Given that prices fluctuate the value of year end raw materials may be over or undervalued due to price rises/decreases occurring during the year.	For a sample of materials to include the cost of wood, compare material costs to actual prices on invoices. Investigate and resolve any significant differences and evaluate the potential impact on the inventory value in the financial statements.
The finished goods value is to be estimated by Anna Jones, who appears to be basing her estimate on order value rather that applying the IAS 2 rule that goods should be valued at the lower of cost and NRV. This could result in inventory being overstated in the financial statements.	For beds awaiting dispatch, establish the lower of cost and NRV and compare with the figures provided by Anna Jones. Investigate any differences evaluate the potential impact on the inventory value in the financial statements.
The new workshop is undergoing refurbishment that could result in inappropriate treatment of capital or non capital items, potentially misstating non-current assets, or repair costs in the statement of profit or loss. Again, this risk is increased by the fact the loan covenants are profit related and there is an incentive to manipulate areas of the financial statements based on judgements.	Obtain a breakdown of the related costs and establish which are included as non-current assets and which are treated as repair costs. Review the nature of items included in non-current assets to ensure only capital items included and review repairs to ensure no capital items are included.

(**Note:** Only **five** risks and **five** related responses were needed to gain 10 marks.)

35 Materiality and documentation

Marking scheme

		Marks
(a)	Up to 1 mark per valid point:	
	Definition	
	Amount	
	Nature, or both	
	Small errors aggregated	
	Judgement, needs of users	
	Performance materiality	
	5% profit before tax or 1% revenue	
	Maximum marks	5
(b)	Up to 1 mark per valid point:	
	Evidence of conclusions	
	Evidence of compliance with ISAs	
	Helps team to plan and perform audit	
	Helps supervision	
	Team is accountable	
	Record of matters of continuing significance	
	Maximum marks	5
		10

(a) **Materiality**

Materiality for the financial statements as a whole (referred to from now on as 'overall materiality') and performance materiality must be determined for all audits.

In the context of the financial statements, a matter is material if its omission or misstatement would reasonably influence the economic decisions of users taken on the basis of the financial statements.

Performance materiality is a materiality level set by the auditor for particular transactions, account balances and disclosures.

Ultimately, both overall and performance materiality are determined using the auditors judgement as to how the users will be affected by misstatements for a particular area. However it is useful to use benchmarks as a starting point, such as 5% of profit before tax, or 1% of total assets.

When setting performance materiality, the possibility of a number of misstatements with a low value aggregating to high overall value must be considered. This results in it being lower than overall materiality.

(b) **Benefits of documenting audit work**

- It provides evidence of the auditor's basis for a conclusion about the achievement of the overall audit objective.

- It provides evidence that the audit was planned and performed in accordance with ISAs and other legal and regulatory requirements.

- It assists the engagement team to plan and perform the audit.

- It assists team members responsible for supervision to direct, supervise and review audit work.

- It allows a record of matter of continuing significance to be retained.

> **Top tips.** Only five benefits were needed, but other valid benefits of documenting audit work include:
>
> - It enables the team to be accountable for its work.
> - It enables the conduct of quality control reviews and inspections (both internal and external).

36 Interim v final audit

> **Text reference.** Chapter 7.
>
> **Top tips.** This question is clearly sub-divided. The requirement asks about the interim and final audit and the body of the question lists out the main procedures at each of these stages. You should be able to use this as a plan for your answer.
>
> Notice that it is not **enough** to list procedures; the requirement asks you to '**explain**'. Re-read the points you have made to check that each is **explained**.
>
> **Easy marks.** Easy marks can be found by looking at each stage of the audit flagged in the question and explaining one or two basic procedures for each.
>
> **Examiner's comments.** This question was answered well where candidates provided an overview of the procedures and processes. The main area where comment was not expected in answers was on the initial process of client acceptance, as the implication was that the client had been accepted and the interim audit was commencing. A common error was spending too much time on one area, especially the determination of audit risk and explanation of the risk model.

Marking scheme

	Marks
Main audit procedures and processes: interim and final audit	
Up to 1 mark per point to a maximum of	10

Main audit procedures and practices during the interim audit

(1) The auditor will obtain a thorough knowledge of the business by discussion with client management and reading relevant trade publications.

(2) Preliminary analytical procedures will be performed on interim accounts in order to identify any major changes in the business or unexpected trends.

(3) The client's accounting systems will be documented, or documentation prepared in prior year audits will be updated.

(4) An assessment will be made of **inherent risk** and **control risk**.

(5)   Appropriate **materiality** levels will be estimated.

(6)   The information obtained during the planning stage will be **documented** along with an outline of the audit strategy to be followed.

(7)   If control risk has been assessed as low in particular areas, then **controls testing** will need to be performed on the controls to confirm the initial assessment of the risk. These tests of controls will be started at the interim audit although they will generally need to be performed on a sample of items extending right over the accounting period so may need to be completed at the final audit.

(8)   The **detailed audit approach** should be prepared. Programmes of audit procedures, both tests of controls and substantive procedures, will be designed to show the work that needs to be done and to enable subsequent review of audit completion.

(9)   If substantive procedures are to be performed that involve auditing a sample of transactions selected to cover the whole accounting period, it is likely that some of these procedures will also be started at the interim audit, but these will again be completed at the final audit.

Main audit procedures and practices during the final audit

(1)   The tests that were started at the interim visit, both tests of controls and substantive procedures should be completed.

(2)   Year-end balances may be verified through confirmations obtained from third parties such as:
- Receivables
- Payables
- Banks

(3)   If the client has carried out a year-end inventory count, detailed procedures will be carried out to verify the accuracy of the compilation of the year-end inventory listing and also to follow up any evidence gathered by the auditor when attending the inventory count.

(4)   Detailed calculations will need to be obtained of any estimates the client has made at the year-end such as allowances for receivables, depreciation and provisions. Procedures will need to be performed to:
- Assess the reasonableness of the methods used to make the estimates;
- Re-perform the calculations; or
- Develop point estimates to evaluate management's point estimates.

(5)   Analytical procedures will be performed on the draft accounts to consider whether the view given by the financial statements is in line with the auditor's understanding of the business.

(6)   The auditor must review the directors' assessment of whether the business is a going concern. The auditor must consider whether the assumptions made by the directors are reasonable and whether it is appropriate to prepare the accounts on the going concern basis.

(7)   A review of events after the reporting period must be performed in order to assess whether any appropriate adjustments or disclosures as required by IAS 10 have been dealt with correctly.

37 Donald

Text reference. Chapter 6.

Top tips. This is a common scenario related requirement where you needed to identify and describe **audit** risks and then explain the auditor's response to each risk. A tabular format would help ensure both mini requirements are addressed.

Note that we have emphasised that the risks are **audit** risks. For a risk to be an audit risk rather than just a general business risk it needs to have an impact on the financial statements being audited. Therefore you should include the assertion or area of the financial statements affected. If you do this it should become apparent if you have not come up with a audit risk as you will be unable to make the link. Make sure your responses to risks in a question like this are responses of the auditor, not of management.

Easy marks. There were easy marks in this question if you used the information in the scenario effectively.

Examiner's comments. Many candidates performed inadequately on this question. As stated in previous examiner's reports, audit risk is a key element of the Audit & Assurance syllabus and candidates must understand audit risk.

A number of candidates wasted valuable time by describing the audit risk model along with definitions of audit risk, inherent risk, control and detection risk. This generated no marks as it was not part of the requirement.

The main area where candidates continue to lose marks is that they did not actually understand what audit risk relates to. Hence they provided answers which considered the risks the business would face or 'business risks,' which are outside the scope of the syllabus. Audit risks must be related to the risk arising in the audit of the financial statements and should include the financial statement assertion impacted.

The issue of the call centre closing and hence the workforce being made redundant was misunderstood by many. These candidates felt that this must mean that the company was having going concern issues, but there was no indication of this in the scenario. The risk related to the completeness of the redundancy provision.

Even if the audit risks were explained many candidates failed to provide a relevant response to the audit risk, most chose to give a response that management would adopt rather than the auditor.

Future candidates must take note audit risk is and will continue to be an important element of the syllabus and must be understood, and they would do well to practice audit risk questions.

Marking scheme

	Marks
Up to 1 mark per well explained risk and up to 1 mark per response, overall maximum of 10.	
Planes ordered may not exist at year end	
Refurbishment of planes – capital or repairs	
Loan of $25m not received yet	
Recoverability of receivables	
Completeness of income	
Customer refunds	
Redundancy provision	
Maximum marks	<u>**10**</u>

Audit risks and responses

Audit risk	Response to risk
Six planes have been ordered pre year end and it appears as though they may be delivered close to the year end. On average they are $3.33m each and there is a risk the assets and/or related liabilities are recorded in the wrong period, understating or overstating non-current assets.	Due to the monetary value of each aircraft all aircraft should be inspected and matched to those included in the Donald's accounting records. This will immediately highlight any planes recorded not received (ie those that don't exist at the year end date). It could also help to identify an asset received but not recorded.
The company has spent $15m on refurbishing aircraft. In order to classify this expenditure correctly (as either capital or revenue) accounting knowledge and judgement is required. Management at Donald may have classified the expenditure incorrectly either overstating or understating profit in the statement of profit or loss as a result.	An analysis of the refurbishment costs should be reviewed and traced to invoices. The invoice descriptions and supporting documents should be reviewed to assess the nature of the expenditure. Once established as either capital or revenue it should be traced to the general ledger and the financial statements to ensure it has been classified correctly as an asset or repairs.
Donald Co has capital commitments to fulfil having already ordered the planes, but has not yet secured funding because the bank loan of $25m has not been approved. This could cause going concern problems if the funding is refused.	Inquiries should be made as to the status of the loan application and progress in securing the funding should be monitored. A detailed going concern review is required.
Some of Donald's customers (the travel agents) are struggling to pay the amounts they owe to the company. This could result in irrecoverable debts not being written off and doubtful debts not being provided for. As a result the receivables balance and profit in the financial statements may be overstated.	The detailed aged receivables analysis should be discussed with management and a value for a provision estimated for any potentially irrecoverable or doubtful debts. The review of amounts received by customers in respect of year end debts should be extended as far as possible.
Donald Co is making staff redundant as a result of the closure of their call centre which occurred pre-year end. There is a risk a redundancy provision has not been set up for staff not paid before the year end as required by IAS 37 *Provisions, contingent liabilities and contingent assets*. Profits may be overstated and provisions understated.	The auditor needs to establish the full redundancy cost through discussion with management and should corroborate to supporting evidence where necessary. The calculated redundancy cost should be compared to the actual provision included in the financial statements to ensure it is reasonable.

Top tips. Only five risks and five responses were needed to gain full marks, but other valid risks and responses are set out below.

Audit risk	Response to risk
Donald Co's website has consistently encountered difficulties with recording sales. This could result in sales of income recorded in the financial statements being incomplete.	Controls testing over the sales cycle should be increased to assess the extent of any potential understatement of revenue. Detailed testing should be performed over the completeness of income.
Tickets have been sold twice and some customers will require refunds. There is a risk that the tickets to be refunded have not been removed from sales.	The cut-off treatment of customer refunds should be reviewed around the year end to ensure that sales to be refunded are not included in the revenue figure in the financial statements.

38 Bridgford Products

(a)   Auditors should plan their work so that:

   (i)   Attention is **devoted** towards the **key audit areas**. These will be areas which are **large** in **materiality** terms, where there is significant risk of material misstatement, or which have had **significant problems** in previous years.

   (ii)   **Staff** are **briefed**. The audit strategy should provide enough detail about the client to enable staff to carry out the detailed work effectively. Budgets should ensure that appropriate time is spent on each audit area.

   (iii)   The **efficiency** of the **audit process** should be **enhanced**. Good planning should ensure that the **right staff** are **selected**, that **information technology** is used **appropriately,** and that maximum use is made of schedules prepared by the client and of the work of internal audit if applicable.

   (iv)   The **timing** of the audit is **appropriate**. Staff will need to be available to carry out an inventory count and circularisation of receivables at the year-end. If use is to be made of work done by the client or internal audit, then this work will need to have been completed in time for the final audit. The timing should also allow sufficient time for the audit to be completed so that the financial statements can be signed on the date desired by the client.

   (v)   **Review** is **facilitated**. Setting out an audit plan and budgets at the planning stage means that the reviewer has measures against which the work can be examined at the end of the assignment.

   Tutorial note: only four reasons were required to score full marks.

(b)

Matters to consider	Further action
Whether data was accurately transferred in to the new system on 1 June 20X8 and whether the computerised inventory system is reliable for determining the quantity of inventory at the year end.	The auditor will need to determine the process by which information was input in to the new system and the level of testing which was done by the client to ascertain the accuracy of the transfer.
	The auditor will also need to document the new system.
	If they are to rely on to gather audit evidence they will also need to test the system using computer assisted audit techniques.
Whether the entity's inventory count procedures are sufficiently reliable to verify the accuracy of the inventory system.	The auditor should determine how often inventory counts are performed and the level of corrections required and the procedures to ensure that corrections are accurately made and authorised.
	The auditor should also attend one or more of the inventory counts during the year.

Matters to consider	Further action
Whether there are provisions required in the financial statements which have not been provided for. These could relate to provisions for legal claims, provisions for legal fees, allowances against receivables and provisions to reduce the carrying amount of inventory to the lower of cost and net realisable value.	The auditor should obtain an understanding of the nature of the legal claims and review correspondence with the entity's solicitor to determine the likely outcome of the cases. They should also consider the outcome of any legal action in the post year end period in order to determine whether any write downs need to be made to the carrying amounts of both receivables and inventory.
Whether the extended credit offered to new customers may lead Bridgford to experience cash flow difficulties and ultimately raise concern over the entity's ability to continue as a going concern.	The auditor should examine Bridgford's cash flow position at the year end and its cash flow forecasts for the future (at least 12 months) in order to assess whether it is likely to struggle to meet its obligations as they fall due. They should also consider whether there is a risk that the extended credit terms may mean that there is an increase risk that receivables may not be recoverable.

Tutorial note: only three matters were required to score full marks.

39 Cinnamon

Text reference. Chapter 4.

Top tips. Although a very brief scenario is given, this is essentially a knowledge-based question. Part (a) is divided into two sub-requirements. Make sure that you do not make the same points for both.

Easy marks. There are plenty of easy marks in this question, particularly in part (b).

			Marks
(a)	(i)	Up to 1 mark per well described point.	
		– Compliance with ACCA's *Code of Ethics and Conduct*	
		– Competent	
		– Reputation and integrity of directors	
		– Level of risk of Cinnamon audit	
		– Fee adequate to compensate for risk	
		– Write to outgoing auditor after obtaining permission to contact	
		– Previous auditor permission to respond	
		– Review response for any issues	5
	(ii)	Up to 1 mark per valid point.	
		– Determination of acceptable framework	
		– Agreement of management responsibilities	
		– Preparation of financial statements with applicable framework	
		– Internal controls	
		– Provide auditor with relevant information and access	
		– If preconditions are not present discuss with management	
		– Decline if framework unacceptable	
		– Decline if agreement of responsibilities not obtained	3

(b)   ½ mark per valid point.
–   Objective/scope
–   Responsibilities of auditor
–   Responsibilities of management
–   Identification of framework for financial statements
–   Form/content reports
–   Elaboration of scope
–   Form of communications
–   Some misstatements may be missed
–   Arrangement for audit
–   Written representations required
–   Fees/billing
–   Management acknowledge letter
–   Internal auditor arrangements
–   Obligations to provide working papers to others
–   Restriction on auditor's liability
–   Arrangements to make draft financial statements available

$$\frac{2}{10}$$

(a)   **Client acceptance procedures**

(i)   **Prior to accepting the audit**

Prior to accepting Cinnamon as an audit client, Curcuma should carry out the following procedures.

(1)   Ensure the firm is professionally qualified to act: Curcuma will need to consider whether it could be disqualified to audit Cinnamon on legal or ethical grounds. This includes evaluating any threats to auditor independence and ensuring that the engagement is compliant both with the ACCA's *Code of Ethics and Conduct* and with local legislation.

(2)   Ensure existing resources are adequate: Curcuma will need to ensure that it has the staff and technical expertise required to perform the audit competently within the timescale agreed.

(3)   Obtain references: Curcuma will need to verify the identity, reputation and integrity of Cinnamon's directors. If necessary, references should be obtained for the directors.

(4)   Consider the associated risk: Based on the knowledge obtained about Cinnamon's business and its directors, Curcuma will need to determine the level of risk associated with the audit engagement. It will need to assess whether the level of risk is acceptable to the firm, and whether the proposed audit fee is appropriate in the light of the associated risk.

(5)   Communicate with the predecessor auditors: Curcuma should enquire about Cinnamon's reason for not reappointing its previous auditor. It should obtain permission from Cinnamon's directors to contact the outgoing auditor, and then communicate with the outgoing auditor to confirm whether there have been any actions by the client which would on ethical grounds preclude Curcuma from accepting the engagement. The outgoing auditor will also require the directors' permission to respond to Curcuma's request.

If the directors refuse to allow Curcuma to communicate with the outgoing auditor, or withholds permission for the outgoing auditor to respond, Curcuma should not accept the audit engagement.

(ii)   **Preconditions for the audit**

Auditors must only accept a new audit engagement if the preconditions for the audit are present.

To determine whether the preconditions for the audit are present, Curcuma should do the following.

•   Determine whether Cinnamon's financial reporting framework is acceptable. Factors to consider include the nature of the entity, the purpose of the financial statements, the nature of the financial statements, and whether law or regulation prescribes the applicable financial reporting framework.

- Obtain agreement from Cinnamon's management that it acknowledges and understands its responsibilities for the following:
  - Preparing the financial statements in accordance with the applicable financial reporting framework
  - Instituting a system of internal control sufficient to enable the preparation of financial statements which are free from material misstatement
  - Providing Curcuma with access to all information of which management is aware that is relevant to the preparation of the financial statements, with additional information that the auditor may request, and with unrestricted access to entity staff from whom the auditor determines it necessary to obtain audit evidence

If these preconditions are not present, the auditor shall discuss the matter with Cinnamon's management. Curcuma should not accept the audit engagement if:

- It has determined that the financial reporting framework to be applied is not acceptable.
- Management's agreement referred to above has not been obtained.

(b) **Matters to be included within an audit engagement letter**

ISA 210 *Agreeing the Terms of Audit Engagements* requires the audit engagement letter to include the following:

- The **objective and scope** of the audit
- The **auditor's responsibilities**
- **Management's responsibilities**
- Identification of the **applicable financial reporting framework** for the preparation of the financial statements
- Reference to the **expected form and content of any reports** to be issued by the auditor and a statement that there may be circumstances in which a report may differ from its expected form and content.

In addition to the above, an audit engagement letter may also make reference to the following matters:

- **Elaboration of scope of audit**, including reference to legislation, regulations, ISAs, ethical and other pronouncements
- Form of **any other communication** of results of the engagement
- The fact that due to the inherent limitations of an audit and those of internal control, there is an **unavoidable risk that some material misstatements may not be detected**, even though the audit is properly planned and performed in accordance with ISAs
- **Arrangements regarding planning and performance**, including audit team composition
- Expectation that management will provide **written representations**
- **Agreement** of management to provide **draft financial statements** and other information in time to allow auditor to complete the audit in accordance with proposed timetable
- **Agreement** of management to inform auditor of **facts** that may affect the financial statements, of which management may become aware from the date of the auditor's report to the date of issue of the financial statements
- **Fees and billing arrangements**
- Request for management to **acknowledge receipt** of the letter and agree to the terms outlined in it
- Involvement of **other auditors and experts**
- Involvement of **internal auditors and other staff**
- Arrangements to be made with **predecessor auditor**

- Any **restriction of auditor's liability**

- Reference to **any further agreements** between auditor and entity

- Any **obligations to provide audit working papers** to other parties.

(**Note:** Only **four** matters are required to be identified in the exam, but we have listed additional possible answers for your reference.)

40 Cardamom

Text reference. Chapter 4.

Top tips. Although a very brief scenario is given, this is essentially a knowledge-based question. Part (a) is divided into two sub-requirements. Make sure that you do not make the same points for both.

Easy marks. There are plenty of easy marks in this question, particularly in part (b).

Marking scheme

		Marks
(a)	Responsibilities of those charged with governance	
	– ½ mark for identification of responsibility and a further ½ if adequately described, but maximum 2.	
	– Strategic direction	
	– Accountability obligations	
	– Financial reporting process	
	Maximum marks	2
(b)	2 marks for each independence factor. 1 for explaining the issue and 1 for mitigating that factor.	
	– Reporting system	
	– Scope of work	
	– Actual audit work	
	– Length of service of internal audit staff	
	– Appointment of chief internal auditor	
	– External auditor assistance with internal audit? (additional to answer)	
	– Other relevant points	
	Maximum marks	8
		10

(a) **Responsibilities of those charged with governance**

Those charged with governance are responsible for overseeing the strategic direction of the entity and obligations related to the accountability of the entity. The obligations relating to accountability will include overseeing the financial reporting process.

(b) **Limitations and recommendations**

(i) *Limitation*

The internal audit department implements controls within the accounting systems. This impairs independence as the internal audit department is effectively responsible for auditing control systems which it has implemented. It is unlikely that the internal audit department will be able to be fully objective in assessing these.

Recommendation

The internal audit department should not establish controls within the accounting systems. Where this has already occurred a different member of the internal audit staff should audit the controls.

(ii) *Limitation*

All internal audit staff have been employed by Cardamom for between 5-15 years. This long length of service may lead to over-familiarity with the systems and controls being reviewed, making it more difficult for the internal auditors to identify errors or areas where improvements could be made.

Recommendation

There should be a system of staff rotation into the accounting departments, with other staff being brought into the internal audit department.

(iii) *Limitation*

The CEO appoints the chief internal auditor. This limits the independence of the internal audit department as it is possible that the CEO will choose someone who he believes will be less critical of his work and the way in which the company operates.

Recommendation

The chief internal auditor should be appointed by the audit committee. If there is no audit committee the appointment should be approved by the board of directors.

(iv) *Limitation*

The chief internal auditor reports to the finance director. This limits independence because the chief internal auditor is reporting to the individual responsible for many of the systems and processes which the internal audit department audits. The chief internal auditor may be intimidated by the fact that he is effectively reporting on his direct superior and may not feel that he is able to highlight all of his concerns.

Recommendation

The chief internal auditor should report to an audit committee or the board collectively.

(v) *Limitation*

The finance director is involved in deciding the scope of the work of the internal audit department. This limits independence as the finance director can influence the areas which the internal auditors will work on. The finance director could use this influence to ensure that attention is not directed towards issues which are contentious and which he does not want to be audited.

Recommendation

The chief internal auditor should decide the scope of the internal audit work. If there is an audit committee it could advise the internal audit department's work.

(**Note:** Only four limitations and recommendations are required for eight marks.)

41 South

Text references. Chapters 6, 8 and 10.

Top tips. When you read the requirements you should spot that this is a very practical question. You need to identify the tasks you are being given in the requirements then read the scenario information carefully to find practical points to make.

Easy marks. These are available in part (a).

Marks

(a) **Understanding entity and environment**
1 mark for identification of reason and a further 1 mark for explanation,
but maximum 4
Risks of material misstatement
Design and performance of audit procedures
Identification of assertions
Maximum marks 4

(b) Risks and responses
1 mark per risk and 1 mark per response to a maximum of $\underline{6}$
$\underline{\underline{10}}$

(a) **Importance of understanding the entity and its environment**

Understanding the entity and its environment (including the entity's internal control), is important to the auditor because it allows the auditor to:

- Identify and assess the risks of material misstatement, whether due to fraud or error, at both the assertion and the financial statement level.

- Assess the reliance that can be placed on internal control

- Design and perform further audit procedures in response to the assessed risks such that detection and audit risk can be reduced to an acceptable level.

- Establish a frame of reference for exercising audit judgement, for example, when setting audit materiality.

(b) **Audit risks and responses to risks**

Audit risk	Response(s) to risk
The firm has recently been appointed as auditor. There is a lack of cumulative knowledge and understanding of the business, which may result in a failure to identify events and transactions which impact on the financial statements. Furthermore, opening balances may be misstated.	Adopt procedures to ensure opening balances are properly brought forward and corresponding amounts are correctly classified and disclosed. Review the previous auditor's working papers and consider performing additional substantive procedures on opening balances.
The company installed a new till system in all supermarkets four months before the year end. This is likely to be very material expenditure and will include integration costs. There is a risk that costs have been incorrectly recorded or classified.	Obtain a schedule of all costs related to the till installation (including integration and testing costs) and agree values back to invoices. Ensure the amounts of scheduled items have been properly recorded as an asset and are only included in non-current assets if they meet the criteria set out in IAS 16. Also for items expensed to the statement of profit or loss, verify that they should not have been included as an asset.

Audit risk	Response(s) to risk
North are likely to rely on the new till system to record revenue which could cause revenue to be misstated if insufficient testing was carried out. Also, staff may not have got to grips with using the till properly, meaning the data entered into the till initially could be incorrect.	Enquire of management what controls they have put in place to ensure the automatic postings are working as intended, and to ensure staff are using the tills correctly. Observe and test relevant controls over the till system and its transfer of data into the accounting system. Perform analytical procedures by comparing daily/weekly sales by store with previous years and expectations to see if any unusual pattern occurs following installation of the new system.
Incorrect accounting treatment or disclosures may be included in the financial statements as a result of the legal claims against South. Given the uncertainty this would appear to be a contingent liability and should be disclosed.	Enquire of management their views on the likely outcome of the legal action, and corroborate responses to legal correspondence. Review disclosures or accounting entries made and assess whether they are reasonable based on the information available and the requirements of IAS 37.

Note: Only three risks and three responses were needed for full marks.

42 Planning, analytical procedures and interim audit

(a) **Benefits of planning**

In accordance with ISA 300 *Planning an audit of financial statements* the benefits of audit planning are as follows:

- It helps the auditor devote appropriate attention to important areas of the audit
- It helps the auditor identify and resolve potential problems on a timely basis
- It helps the auditor organise and manage the audit so that it is performed in an effective manner
- It assists in the selection of appropriate team members and assignment of work to them
- It facilitates the direction, supervision and review of work
- It assists in the coordination of work done by auditors of components and experts

(b) **Factors to consider when using analytical procedures at the planning stage of the audit**

- The objectives of the analytical procedures and the extent to which their results are reliable
- The degree to which information can be analysed
- The availability of information
- The reliability of the information available
- The relevance of the information available
- The source of the information available
- The comparability of the information available
- Knowledge gained from previous audits

(**Note:** Only four were required.)

(c) **Difference between the interim audit and the final audit**

Auditors usually carry out their audit work for a financial year in one or more sittings. These are referred to as the **interim audit(s)** and the **final audit**. The final audit opinion will be a result of conclusions based on evidence obtained during both the interim and final audit.

The interim audit

Interim audit visits are carried out during the period of review and work typically carried out includes:

- Re-assessing the risk assessment made at the planning stage
- Tests of controls and systems, although substantive audit procedures may also be carried out

The final audit

The final audit visit is at the year-end or shortly after and work focuses on the audit of the financial statements. Some audit procedures can only be performed at the final audit visit, such as:

- Agreeing the financial statements to the accounting records and examining adjustments made during the process of preparing the financial statements

- A subsequent events review

The auditor will also carry out testing to ensure any conclusions from interim audit are still valid at the year end.

43 Specs4You

Text reference. Chapter 7.

Top tips. This is a question on audit working papers. Part (a) was a straightforward test of knowledge of the purposes of audit working papers. You may have thought of purposes other than those in the answer below and any three valid purposes would gain full marks. In part (b), you could present your answer in a tabular format – eight marks are available here so make sure you describe the information you expect from each document. In part (c), there are nine marks available so try to generate at least six well-explained points and you will be well on your way to passing this part of the question.

Easy marks. Easy marks are available in part (a) of this question – you should be able to achieve the maximum three marks available without any problems. Part (b) should also be straightforward as long as you think about the client you are auditing and the types of documentation that a company would hold that would be useful to an auditor at the planning stage of an audit.

Examiner's comments. The overall standard of answers to part (a) was satisfactory, but some candidates misinterpreted the question and wrote about types of test, such as analytical procedures or listed the types of working papers.

In part (b) the requirement left candidates with a wide range of points to make, from the previous year's audit file to company brochures. Many provided good lists of documents but common errors included:

- Not explaining the information to be obtained from each document
- Listing non-documentary sources of evidence
- Not providing sufficient points. The full eight marks could not be obtained with only three or four points
- Focusing on the current audit file in too much detail

In part (c) candidates who took the approach of mentioning anything that appeared to be 'strange' such as the lack of initial of a preparer correctly identified the problems with the working paper. Again errors included the failure to explain the points made. For example, stating that the working paper did not have a page number, but then not explaining that this meant that it could not be filed or retrieved easily from the audit file.

Marking scheme

		Marks
(a)	1 mark per point	
	Assist planning	1
	Assist supervision	1
	Record of audit evidence	1
	Other relevant points	1
	Maximum marks	**3**

		Marks
(b)	½ for document, ½ for information obtained	
	Memo and articles	1
	Financial statements	1
	Management accounts	1
	Organisation chart	1
	Industry data	1
	Financial statements similar companies	1
	Prior year audit file	1
	Internet news sites	1
	Permanent audit file	1
	Board minutes	1
	Other relevant points	1
	Maximum marks	**8**

		Marks
(c)	1 mark per relevant point (½ for area, ½ for explaining why working paper poor quality)	
	Page reference	1
	Year end	1
	No preparer signature	1
	Poor job from reviewer	1
	Vague test objective	1
	Not an audit assertion	1
	Sufficient audit evidence obtained?	1
	Lack of appropriate referencing	1
	Test results unclear	1
	Conclusion not consistent with results found	1
	Other relevant points (each)	1
	Maximum marks	**9**
		20

(a) **Purposes of working papers**

- To assist the audit team to plan and perform the audit

- To assist relevant team members to direct, supervise and review audit work

- To provide a tangible record of the audit evidence obtained to support the auditor's opinion as to the truth and fairness of the financial statements

(b) **Specs4You documentation**

Prior year audit file

This will provide useful information on the audit approach used, results of testing, areas of concern etc which were encountered in the previous year.

Prior year financial statements

These will provide valuable information on the statement of profit or loss and statement of financial position and allow the auditor to undertake an analytical review at the planning stage to identify potential areas of risk. They will also provide information on the accounting policies used by the company.

Current year budgetary information and latest management accounts

These will allow the auditor to see how the company is progressing in the current year and also provide budgetary information that can be used to carry out analytical review.

Organisation chart

This will allow the auditor to see how the company is structured and will highlight key personnel that will be useful for the audit.

Details of store locations

The auditor can see where the stores of Specs4You are located which will be useful for the year-end inventory count and other visits.

Staff listing

The staff listing will be useful as it will provide contact details for key staff that the audit team may need to speak to during the course of the audit.

Internet site of Specs4You

If the company has an internet site, this can provide valuable background information and also highlight current news.

Memorandum and articles of association

These will provide information on the objectives of the company and how it is structured.

(c) **Working paper**

The working paper does not identify who prepared it so it makes it difficult for the reviewer to follow up any queries arising during the review.

The working paper has not been dated by the person who prepared it.

The working paper does not completely state the year-end that the audit relates to. This means that the working paper could be filed in an incorrect audit file.

The audit assertion has not correctly been identified so does not tell the reviewer what the work is trying to achieve.

The audit assertion has been confused with the objective of the audit work.

The working paper does not tell the reviewer where the details of the items tested can be found – there should be adequate cross-referencing so that the reviewer does not have to go through all the working papers to find these.

The method of sample selection and number to test have not been clearly explained in the working paper. It simply states that 15 purchase orders were selected, but not the basis for the selection of this number nor how the sample was selected.

The conclusion reached contradicts the results of the audit work, since errors were found in the testing but the conclusion states that purchase orders are completely recorded in the purchase day book.

The working paper does not appear to have been referenced in accordance with the firm's agreed referencing system which means it may be incorrectly filed.

44 Tempest

Text references. Chapters 6 and 7.

Top tips. When a question includes both narrative and numerical information, you must take time to read all of the information several times to identify all the points that you can develop in your answer. While you should not get too bogged down in number crunching, a little bit of basic ratio analysis here, eg profit margins and day's sales in receivables will give you some more practical points to raise in your audit strategy.

If you need to do detailed calculations, such as the ones for materiality in this answer, it is a good idea to put them into an appendix.

Easy marks. The only genuinely easy marks here were in part (a) where sound knowledge of ISA 300 could give you full marks.

Examiner's comments. Part (a) was answered well although there was a tendency for some students to provide answers that were far too detailed for the marks available. In part (b), where a risk was identified, not all students succeeded in explaining why the risk was important. Some answers to part (b) did not take into account the scenario, ie the type of company and its business.

		Marks
(a)	**ISA 300 – Planning**	1
	Audit work performed in an effective manner	1
	General approach and strategy for audit	1
	Attention to critical areas	1
	Amount of work	1
	Discussion with audit committee	1
	Basis to produce audit programme	1
	Other relevant points	1
	Maximum marks	5
(b)	**List of tests at 1 mark per relevant point**	
	Audit strategy	
	Type of audit	1
	ISAs to be used	1
	Overview of Tempest	1
	Key dates for audit	1
	Overview of approach	
	Industry details	1
	Fall in GP%	1
	Materiality	
	How determine	1
	Risk areas (state with reason for risk)	
	COS	1
	Inventory	1
	Trade receivables	1
	Non-current assets	1
	Long term liabilities	1
	Audit approach	
	Compliance testing	1
	New inventory system – transfer of balances	1
	New inventory system – test end of year balances	1
	New inventory system – test during year	1
	Other risk areas	
	Information on going concern	1
	Related party transactions	1
	Inventory count assistance	1
	Any other general points ½ mark	
	Maximum marks	15
		20

(a) Audit planning is important for the following reasons:

- It ensures that **appropriate attention** is devoted to important areas of the audit. For example, overall materiality and performance materiality will be assessed at the planning stage and this will mean that when the detailed audit plan is drawn up, more procedures will be directed towards the most significant figures in the financial statements.

- Planning should mean that **potential problems are identified and resolved** on a timely basis. This could be in the sense of identifying financial statement risks at an early stage, so allowing plenty of time to gather sufficient relevant evidence. It could also relate to identifying practical problems relating to the gathering of evidence and resolving those through actions such as involving other experts being built into the detailed audit plan.

- Planning helps ensure that the audit is **organised and managed in an effective and efficient manner**. This could relate to, for example, ascertaining from the client when particular pieces of information will be available so that the timings of the audit are organised so as to minimise waste of staff time and costs.

- Planning assists in the **proper assignment of work** to engagement team members. Once the main risk areas have been identified at the planning stage, the engagement partner can then make sure that staff with suitable experience and knowledge are allocated to the engagement team.

- Planning **facilitates direction, supervision and review** of the work done by team members. Once procedures have been designed and allocated to members of the team, it is easier for the manager and partner to decide when work should be completed and ready for review. It will also make it easier for them to assess during the audit whether work is going according to the original plan and budget.

(b)   **Audit strategy**

Client: Tempest
Year-end: 31 December 20X7
Prepared by: A. Manager

Scope of audit

Tempest is subject to a normal statutory audit. It cannot take advantage of any reporting or audit exemptions.

The financial statements are prepared under IFRS.

The audit will be carried out under International Standards on Auditing.

Tempest trades in fittings for ships and stores its inventory at ten different locations. As in previous years, we have carried out year-end procedures at the three locations with the most significant inventory balances plus three others on a rotational basis, using staff from our most conveniently located offices. This year, due to the change in accounting systems we will carry out year-end procedures at all of the locations.

Timings

- Interim audit
- Final audit
- Audit staff planning/briefing meetings
- Meeting with directors (or audit committee, if one exists)
- Approval of financial statements by the board
- Issue of audit report

Materiality for the financial statements as a whole

Preliminary calculations of materiality for the financial statements as a whole are based on the forecast financial statements and are set out in Appendix 1. These materiality levels will need to be reassessed when the actual financial statements for the year ended 31 December 20X7 are available and performance materiality levels will also need to be determined.

Materiality for statement of profit or loss items should be set in the region of $40,000 (being at the upper end of the range based on profit before tax).
Materiality for statement of financial position items should be set in the region of $200,000, based on total assets.

Materiality levels for the financial statements as a whole are generally lower than those for the prior year, suggesting performance materiality levels will also be lower. This is likely to increase sample sizes for procedures; this is appropriate in light of the indications that there may an increased risk of error this year.

Higher risk areas

(i)   **Inventory**

The forecast year end inventory figure is significantly lower than in the prior year. Coupled with the mid-year change in the accounting system for inventory there is a risk of material error in inventory quantities or valuation.

(ii)   **Sales**

Sales are forecast to have increased by 12% over the prior year. Compared to the average year on year growth of only 7% for the industry in general there is a risk that sales may be overstated.

(iii)   **Profit**

Gross profit margin has fallen to 17.3% (20X6 21.9%) and net profit margin has fallen to 0.9% (20X6 4.1%). This could indicate errors in cut off or allocation or that the company has been cutting prices in order to win market share and has let profitability suffer. Although there is no specific indication of immediate going concern difficulties, this strategy may not be sustainable in the longer term.

(iv)   **Receivables**

Days' sales in receivables are forecast to have increased to 47 days (36 days in 20X6). This may indicate problems with the recoverability of the receivables and a risk that impairments in value of the receivables' balances are not recognised.

(v)   **Non-current assets**

There is a decrease in this balance of $900,000. This is far in excess of what could be explained by depreciation of assets that comprise mainly properties. It may be that there have been disposals in the year. This raises the possibility of incorrect accounting or inadequate disclosures.

Also in relation to the non-current assets, if the inventory balance has genuinely decreased to approximately 15% of its previous level, some of the storage locations may be redundant. It could be that the reduction relates to impairment write-downs and it could be the case that further write-downs are needed.

(vi)   **Related party transactions**

Given the information that one of the directors purchased a yacht during the year it may be that he has purchased fittings from Tempest Co. There is a risk that any related party transactions have not been fully disclosed.

Audit approach

Where possible evidence should be obtained from tests of control so that detailed substantive procedures can be reduced.

Special emphasis will be needed in respect of inventory accounting.

Procedures will include:

- Obtaining an understanding of how the transfer of balances to the new system was carried out. Direct testing of balances from the old to new systems may be needed as well as reviewing evidence of control procedures carried out by the client at the point of changeover.

- A sample of sales and purchase transactions should be traced through the new system to establish whether additions to and deletions from inventory are being made correctly.

- Test counts of inventory at the various locations should be performed at the year-end and agreed to the inventory records as at that date.

Testing of items in the statement of profit or loss will need to include:

- Consideration of the revenue recognition policies being used
- Cut-off testing on sales and costs of sales
- Comparison of expense classifications from year to year

The review of events after the reporting period should focus on:

- Any substantial adjustments to the inventory figure
- Evidence of recoverability of receivable balances
- Any information suggesting further reductions in profitability of the business
- Management accounts and cash flow projections for the post year end period

Appendix 1

Materiality ($'000)

½ -1% of revenue (½% × 45,928 – 1% × 45,928)	230	to	459
5-10% of profit before tax (5% × 436 – 10% × 436)	22	to	44
1-2% of total assets (1% × 10,300 – 2% × 10,300)	103	to	206

45 EuKaRe

Text references. Chapters 6, 9 and 17.

Top tips. This question is about audit risk in the context of a charitable organisation so when you come to part (b) on the areas of inherent risk, you must bear in mind the type of organisation you are dealing with. Part (b) is on inherent risk areas and is worth 12 marks so you should be able to come up with six risk areas. Make sure you explain the effect of each risk on the audit approach, if you want to score well.

Part (c) should be straightforward on the control environment as long as you keep in your mind the fact that the client is a charity and bear in mind the particular issues relevant to not-for-profit organisations.

Easy marks. Part (a) is straightforward knowledge and you should be very familiar with the audit risk model. There is no reason why you shouldn't be able to score the four marks available here. You should also be able to score well in part (c) on the control environment at the charity.

Examiner's comments. In part (a) common errors included explaining audit risk in terms of errors in the financial statements rather than inappropriate audit reports and omitting to explain that inherent risk is linked to the nature of the entity. In (b) the standard of the answer varied considerably. It appeared that the use of a charity was marginally concerning, although this was within the bounds of study. In part (c) the standard of answers was inadequate. Common errors included restating points from part (b) as also relevant to part (c) and omitting the question completely from the candidate's answer.

Marks

(a) 1 mark for explanation of each term
Audit risk
Inherent risk
Control risk
Detection risk
Maximum marks   4

(b) 1 mark for each area of inherent risk and 1 mark for explaining the effect on the
audit = 2 marks per linked points
Income voluntary only
Completeness of income

	Marks
Funds spent in accordance with charity objectives	
Taxation rules	
Reporting of expenditure	
Donation for specific activities	
Maximum marks	12

(c) 1 mark for each point on weak control environment

Lack of segregation of duties
Volunteer staff
Lack of qualified staff
No internal audit
Attitude of trustees

	Marks
Maximum marks	4
Total marks	20

(a) **Audit risk**

Audit risk is the risk that the auditor expresses an inappropriate audit opinion when the financial statements are materially misstated. Audit risk is a function of the risk of material misstatement and the risk that the auditor will not detect such misstatement (detection risk). The risk of material misstatement has two components: inherent risk and control risk. Audit risk can be summarised by the following equation:

Audit risk = Inherent risk × Control risk × Detection risk

Inherent risk is the susceptibility of an assertion to a misstatement that could be material, individually or when aggregated with other misstatements assuming that there were no related internal controls.

Control risk is the risk that a misstatement that could occur in an assertion and that could be material, individually or when aggregated with other misstatements, will not be prevented or detected and corrected on a timely basis by the entity's internal control.

Detection risk is the risk that the auditor's procedures will not detect a misstatement that exists in an assertion that could be material, individually or when aggregated with other misstatements.

(b) **Inherent risk areas**

Detailed constitution

The charity has a detailed constitution which sets out how money may be spent. This increases the inherent risk of the audit.

The auditors will need to spend time examining and becoming familiar with the constitution and design their audit procedures with this in mind.

Limit on administration expenditure

The constitution states that administration expenditure cannot exceed 10% of income in any year. This increases inherent risk as management may be tempted to misstate income or administration expenditure so this limit is not breached.

Special attention will need to be devoted to income and expenditure to ensure that the 10% limit is not breached legitimately.

Uncertainty of future income

The charity relies wholly on voluntary donations for its income which means that it cannot be assured of receiving a minimum level of income from one year to the next. This increases the risk of it not being able to continue.

The auditors must bear in mind whether the charity can continue as a going concern when carrying out their final review procedures. This will involve discussion with management and examination of budgetary information.

Cash donations

Some of the donations received will be in the form of cash collected from the public. There is a risk of misappropriation of cash as a result.

Controls over cash should be examined as this is an area open to misappropriation and theft.

Donations from individuals

Some donations have clauses about how the money can be spent. This again increases inherent risk because money may be misspent without regard for the conditions in place.

Where donations have been received with clauses attached, the auditors will need to do detailed work to ensure the conditions have not been breached.

Taxation legislation

There are complex rules in place regarding the taxation of charities.

The audit team will need to familiarise itself with the taxation rules for charities to ensure that this area is correctly dealt with.

(c) **Control environment**

The control environment at EuKaRe may be weak for a number of reasons.

The staff working at the charity may be volunteers who may not have accounts experience and who may also not work there full-time. There may also be a high staff turnover because of the nature of the work.

There may be a lack of segregation of duties in place due to the number of staff working at the charity. This means that trustees may play a role in the day to day running of the charity and there is therefore a risk of override of any controls that are in place.

The charity may not have an internal audit department in place due to its size or the equivalent of an audit committee to monitor its effectiveness.

There may also be a lack of budgetary information being produced on a timely basis which increases the control risk from the auditor's point of view.

46 Serenity

Text references. Chapters 1, 4 and 6.

Top tips. Part (a) of this question should be straightforward as you are asked to explain the purpose of risk assessment procedures and outline sources of audit evidence that can be used for this part of the audit. In part (b), you have to identify issues to be considered during the planning stage of an audit. There are lots of clues in the question scenario so the best way to approach this part of the question is to go through the scenario line-by-line, jotting down issues as you go. This will give more structure to your answer, as will the use of sub-headings for each issue you identify.

Easy marks. These are available for basic technical knowledge in part (a) for six marks on risk assessment procedures and sources of evidence and part (c) for four marks on explaining what negative assurance means.

		Marks
(a)	One mark per point	
	(i) Purpose of risk assessment – understand client	1
	Material misstatements	1
	Knowledge of classes of transactions	1
	Association risk	1

		Marks
(ii)	Evidence from inquiry (with example)	1
	Analytical review (with example)	1
	Observation (with example)	1
	Maximum marks	6
(b)	One mark per point	
	Skills necessary?	1
	Self-review threat	1
	Acceptance non-audit work	1
	Fee income	1
	Internal audit – fee pressure	1
	Client growth	1
	Association threat	1
	Advocacy threat	1
	Report on cash flow	1
	Possible going concern	1
	Other relevant points (each)	1
	Maximum marks	10
(c)	Key points one for each point = knowledge outside scenario	
	Accuracy of cash flow not confirmed	1
	'Reasonable' – not T&F	1
	Nothing to indicate cash flow is incorrect	1
	Forecast relates to future – uncertainty	1
	Conditions may not turn out as expected	1
	Other relevant points (each)	1
	Maximum marks	4
		20

(a) (i) Risk assessment procedures are performed at the planning stage of an audit to obtain an understanding of the entity being audited and to identify any areas of concern which could result in material misstatements in the financial statements. They allow the auditor to assess the nature, timing and extent of audit procedures to be performed.

(ii) Sources of audit evidence that can be used as part of risk assessment procedures.

- Inquiries of management
- Prior year financial statements
- Current year management accounts and budgets
- Analytical procedures
- Observation and inspection

(b) *Poor internal controls and rapid growth*

The accounting systems of Serenity Co are changing rapidly and the control systems are difficult to maintain as the company continues to grow. This indicates that the **internal controls are likely to be poor** so control risk and the risk of material misstatements in the accounts will be high. Therefore a **fully substantive audit** is likely and Mal & Co must ensure it has enough time and resources to obtain sufficient audit evidence to support the figures in the financial statements.

Reliance on internal audit department

Serenity Co has only **recently established** its internal audit department so Mal & Co needs to be very careful in deciding whether it can place reliance on the work performed by internal audit and ultimately in a reduced external audit fee, as desired by the financial controller. Additional time and work would be required to assess internal audit so an immediate reduction in the fee is very unlikely.

Additional services required

Serenity Co requires additional services of review and implementation of control systems but Mal & Co must consider whether it has sufficiently skilled **resources** to carry out this additional work as it is a small firm with a number of clients in different sectors.

Fee income

The additional work required by Serenity Co will result in increased fee income to Mal & Co. The audit firm must ensure that its **fee income** from this one client does not breach the guidelines set by the ACCA's Code of Ethics. These state that the fee income from an unlisted client should not exceed 15% of the firm's total fees.

Self-review threat

The additional work required on the review and implementation of control systems at Serenity Co could result in the risk of **self-review**. Mal & Co must ensure it implements appropriate safeguards to mitigate this risk, such as separate teams to carry out the review work and the external audit.

This may be difficult in a small audit firm. It would also be essential to ensure that the client makes all the management decisions in relation to the systems.

Legal status of new mobile

The legal status of the new mobile product is not known – it may be illegal. Any **adverse publicity** generated as a result will impact on Mal & Co as the auditors of the company. The audit firm needs to consider carefully whether it wants to be associated with Serenity Co. The fact that the company is planning to make a product of dubious legality raises questions about the **integrity of the directors**, and the audit team should be cautious in relying on any written representations provided by the directors.

Reliance on cash flow statement for licence

The granting of the licence to market the mobile is dependent on the financial stability of the company. Mal & Co may be asked to provide a report on the company's cash flow statement for the following financial year. This needs to be considered carefully – Mal & Co must ensure it has sufficient experienced **resources** for this work and determine what kind of **assurance** is required.

Going concern assumption

The company is **growing rapidly** and is relying on the granting of a licence for the new mobile, whose legal status is not known. These factors may indicate a possible **going concern risk** which should be monitored carefully.

(c)　'Negative assurance' refers to when an auditor gives an assurance that nothing has come to his or her attention which indicates that the financial statements have not been prepared according to the identified financial reporting framework, ie the auditor gives his or her assurance in the absence of any evidence to the contrary.

Negative assurance is given on review assignments such as the review of a company's cash flow forecast.

A cash flow forecast relates to the future so is based upon assumptions that cannot be confirmed as accurate. The auditor cannot confirm positively that the statement is materially true and fair (or presented fairly in all material respects).

This is because the conditions assumed when preparing the cash flow statement may not turn out as expected and it is not possible to gain the level of evidence expected to express absolute or reasonable assurance.

47 Redsmith

Text references. Chapters 4 and 6.

Top tips. Part (a) is a knowledge based requirement on the process to assess whether the preconditions of an audit are present. Notice the focus of the question – it is the **process** that you should have concentrated on in your answer, it is **not** simply asking what the preconditions of an audit are. Simply describing the preconditions would not have been sufficient.

Again in part (b) take note of the question being asked. You should have confined your answer to matters to be considered when obtaining an understanding of the entity. You were asked to **list** the factors, so you didn't need to go into too much detail. Four were required, so you should only have included four.

In part (c)(i) you needed to draw on your knowledge of common accounting ratios. You should have been thinking about the risks arising for part (c)(ii) as you worked out your five ratios that you thought would be useful for planning purposes. You should have also been thinking about how each confirmed the risks arising from the information in the scenario, for example the extension of the credit period for customers is consistent with increased receivables days.

For part (c)(ii) it is vital you read the question properly. You should not have confined your answer to risks arising from the ratios, as the question clearly points out that all information should be taken into account. A tabular approach to the answer could be taken here to help present a clear and full answer.

Easy marks. Listing matters to consider when obtaining an understanding in part (b) should have been straightforward. You should also have had little problem calculating five relevant ratios in (c)(i).

Examiner's comments. Part (a) tested a new topic from the revised ISA 210 *Agreeing the Terms of Audit Engagements* and a large number of candidates did not attempt this question. Where it was attempted it was inadequately answered. It was fairly apparent from the answers provided that many candidates had simply not studied the new syllabus area of preconditions and hence were unable to score any marks at all. In addition many candidates wrote at considerable length for a 3 mark requirement. This put them under significant time pressure for later questions. Candidates must note the total number of available marks and provide an answer in line with this.

Part (b) was unrelated to the scenario and was a knowledge based question. In general candidates performed satisfactorily.

Part (c) for 15 marks required a calculation of 5 ratios each for 2 years and an explanation of the related audit risks and responses. The ratios requirement was answered well by the majority of candidates. A significant minority confused the calculation of inventory days using inventory divided by revenue rather than cost of sales. Candidates are reminded that as part of an analytical review, going concern or audit risk question they must be able to calculate and then evaluate relevant ratios.

The question then required audit risks and responses for 10 of the 15 marks. Many candidates performed inadequately on this part of the question. Audit risk is a key element of the Audit & Assurance syllabus and candidates must understand audit risk.

The main area where candidates lost marks is that they did not actually understand what audit risk relates to. Hence they provided answers which considered the risks the business would face or 'business risks', which are outside the scope of the syllabus. Audit risks must be related to the risk arising in the audit of the financial statements. If candidates did not do this then they would have struggled to pass this part of the question as there were no marks available for business risks. In addition many candidates chose to provide an interpretation of accounts and the ratios calculated rather than an assessment of audit risk. Comments such as "revenue has increased by 28% this could be as a result of the bonus scheme introduced" would not have scored any marks as there was no identification of the audit risk, which is overstatement of revenue.

Even if the audit risks were explained many candidates then failed to provide a relevant response to the audit risk, most chose to give a response that management would adopt rather than the auditor. For example, in relation to the risk of valuation of receivables, as Redsmith Co had extended their credit terms to customers, many candidates suggested that customers should not be accepted without better credit checks, or offering an early settlement discount to encourage customers to pay quicker. These are not responses that the auditor would adopt, as they would be focused on testing valuation through after date cash receipts or reviewing the aged receivables ledger. Also some responses were too vague such as "increase substantive testing" without making it clear how, or in what area, this would be addressed. Audit risk is an important element of the syllabus and must be understood.

Marks

(a) Up to 1 mark per valid point
ISA 210 provides guidance
Determination of acceptable framework
Agreement by management that internal controls in place
Preparation of financial statements with applicable framework
Internal controls
Provide auditor with relevant information and access
If preconditions are not present discuss with management
Decline if framework unacceptable
Decline if agreement of responsibilities not obtained   3

(b) ½ marks per example of matter to consider in obtaining an
understanding of the nature of the entity   2

(c) (i) ½ marks per ratio calculation per year
Gross margin
Operating margin
Operating expenses as % of revenue
Inventory turnover
Inventory days
Receivable days
Payable days
Current ratio
Quick ratio   5

(ii) Up to 1 mark per well explained audit risk, 1 mark per audit response
Management manipulation of results
Sales cut-off
Revenue growth
Misclassification of costs
Inventory valuation
Receivables valuation
Going concern risk   <u>10</u>
                                                                        <u>20</u>

(a) **Assessing whether the preconditions for an audit are present**

The preconditions for an audit are the use by management of an acceptable financial reporting framework in the preparation of the financial statements and the agreement of management and, where appropriate, those charged with governance to the premise on which an audit is conducted.

ISA 210 *Agreeing the terms of audit engagements* provides guidance as to how the auditor determines whether the preconditions for an audit are present. The auditor must:

- Determine whether the financial reporting framework is acceptable. Factors to consider include the nature of the entity, the purpose of the financial statements, the nature of the financial statements, and whether law or regulation prescribes the applicable financial reporting framework.

- Obtain management's agreement that it acknowledges and understands its responsibilities for the following.

  - Preparing the financial statements in accordance with the applicable financial reporting framework

  - Internal control that is necessary to enable the preparation of financial statements which are free from material misstatement

– Providing the auditor with access to all information of which management is aware that is relevant to the preparation of the financial statements, with additional information that the auditor may request, and with unrestricted access to entity staff from whom the auditor determines it necessary to obtain audit evidence

> **Top tips.** The above answer would have been enough to gain the three marks available, however other valid points you may have made are as follows:
>
> If the preconditions are not present, the auditor shall discuss the matter with management. The auditor shall not accept the audit engagement if:
>
> - The auditor has determined that the financial reporting framework to be applied is not acceptable.
> - Management's agreement referred to above has not been obtained.

(b) **Understanding the entity – matters to consider**

- Industry, regulatory and other external factors, including the applicable financial reporting framework
- Ownership and governance
- Entity's selection and application of accounting policies
- Key suppliers and customers

> **Top tips.** There are a number of other matters you could have come up with (such as markets, competition and financing), but only four were required.

(c) (i) **Five ratios for 2010 and 2009 to assist in planning**

Ratio	2010	2009
Gross margin (gross profit/revenue × 100%)	52.2%	44.4%
Operating margin (PBIT/revenue × 100%)	19.6%	22.2%
Inventory days ([inventory/COS] × 365)	70 days	58 days
Receivable days ([receivables/revenue] × 365)	71 days	61 days
Current ratio (Current assets/current liabilities)	2.6	5.8

> **Top tips.** Other ratios you may have used include payable days (53 in 2010, 44 in 2009), the quick ratio (1.8 in 2010, 4.4 in 2009), inventory turnover (5.2 in 2010, 6.3 in 2009) and operating expenses as a percentage of revenue (33% in 2010, 22% in 2009).

(ii) **Audit risks and responses**

Audit risk	Response(s)
Redsmith's management may be biased in financial statement areas involving judgement because 2009 results were disappointing. They may use accounting estimates to artificially improve presented results.	The audit team must be alert to the increased risk of bias and focus on financial statement estimates that require management to exercise judgement. Careful review must be undertaken of any such area.
The introduction of a sales related bonus scheme may incentivise employees to push post year end sales back into the current year, overstating revenue for 2010.	Increase the sample sizes for any substantive sales cut off testing and extend the time period from which the sample is selected.
Receivables balances may not be recoverable given that receivable days have increased by 10 days and credit periods for customers have increased.	A review of aged receivable balances should be carried out and there will be an increased focus on recoverability through extended post year end cash receipts testing.

Audit risk	Response(s)
The current ratio decrease by 55%, lack of cash (an overdraft in 2010) and sales increase indicates potential liquidity problems due to overtrading, which could impact on the company's ability to continue as a going concern.	Increased emphasis on a detailed going concern review. Discussions with management as to the ability of Redsmith to continue as a going concern and careful attention paid to the post year end period.
Inventory could be overvalued as a result of the new policy to include more overheads in inventory. This is consistent with the 10 day increase in inventory days.	Review the inventory calculations to identify the overheads included and ensure they are valid production overheads. Discuss the reasons for including them with the finance director.

Top tips. Five well explained risks and responses would have been sufficient here, but you may have also come up with the following:

Audit risk	Response(s)
Costs of sales may have been omitted or incorrectly included as operating expenses. This may be the reason for gross margin increasing by 7.8% but operating margin decreasing by 2.6%.	Cost of sales and operating expenses to be compared to prior year and expectations on a line by line basis to identify any instances of change in classification of expenses.

48 Abrahams

Text references. Chapters 6 and 13.

Top tips. The first requirement in part (a) was straightforward and you should have been able to explain each component (inherent risk, control risk and detection risk) in turn. Note that the definition of audit risk itself was not required. The example of a factor which would **increase** audit risk in relation to each component required more thought as often auditors think of how to **reduce** these risks. However if you know what decreases the risk, it is not difficult to work out what increases it. For example, increasing sample sizes can decrease detection risk, so not selecting an appropriate sample size will increase it. There are a number of factors to choose from in each case, but only one example was required for each – so only give one and then move on.

Part (b) tested the important area of identifying and responding to audit risks. It should be clear from your answer how each risk impacts on a financial statement assertion or area, since this is the nature of an audit risk. If there is no clear link the chances are you have identified a business risk that may not be a relevant audit risk. Your response should be clear and include a specific action rather a general response of, for example, 'do more work on this area'.

Part (c) asks for substantive procedures in relation to gaining evidence over two specific aspects of inventory (inventory held by a third party and standard costs used in the inventory valuation). In (ii) there is always a danger that standard costs are not updated enough to take account of movements in actual costs so your tests should focus on this, for example comparing standard costs with actual costs per invoices or wages records.

Easy marks. Easy marks were available in (a) for explaining the components of audit risk.

Examiner's comments. Part (a) was knowledge based and candidates performed well.

Part (b) for 10 marks required a description of five audit risks and responses for Abrahams. Many candidates performed inadequately on this part of the question. As stated in previous examiner's reports, audit risk is a key element of the Audit & Assurance syllabus and candidates must understand audit risk. The main area where candidates continue to go wrong is that they did not actually understand what audit risk relates to. Hence they provided answers which considered the risks the business would face or 'business risks', which are outside the scope of the syllabus.

Part (c) was answered unsatisfactorily by most candidates, especially (ii) on standard costs. Candidates seemed to see 'inventory valuation' in the requirement and so produced generic tests for verifying that inventory should be at the lower of cost and NRV. This was not what the question required. Candidates did not seem to understand that standard costing was an acceptable option for calculating the cost of inventory and hence they needed to test how close an approximation to actual cost standard cost was.

Marking scheme

		Marks

(a) Up to 1 mark for each component of audit risk (if just a component is given without an explanation then just give ½) and up to 1 mark for each example of factor which increases risk.
  Inherent risk
  Control risk
  Detection risk   6

(b) Up to 1 mark per well explained risk and up to 1 mark for each well explained response. Overall max of 5 for risks and 5 for responses.
  Development expenditure treatment
  Standard costing for valuation of inventory
  Expert possibly required in verifying work in progress
  Third party inventory locations
  New accounting system introduced in the year
  Lack of support by IT staff on new system may result in errors in accounting system
  New finance obtained; loans and equity finance treatment
  Loan covenants and risk of going concern problems
  Revaluation of land and buildings
  Reduced reporting timetable   10

(c) 1 mark per well explained procedure, maximum of 2 marks for each of (i) and (ii)
  (i) Third party locations
    Letter requesting direct confirmation
    Attend inventory count
    Review other auditor reports and documentation   2
  (ii) Standard costing
    Discuss with management basis of standard costs
    Review variances
    Breakdown of standard costs and agree to actual costs   2
                                                                                    20

(a) Audit risk is made up of the following components:

Inherent risk is the susceptibility of an assertion to a misstatement that could be material individually or when aggregated with other misstatements, assuming there were no related internal controls.

Factors which may increase inherent risk include:

- Changes in the nature of the industry the company operates in
- A high degree of regulation over certain areas of the business
- Going concern issues and loss of significant customers
- Expanding into new territories
- Events or transactions that involve significant accounting estimates

- Developing new products or services, or moving into new lines of business
- The application of new accounting standards
- Accounting measurements that involve complex processes
- Pending litigation and contingent liabilities

Control risk is the risk that a material misstatement, that could occur in an assertion and that could be material, individually or when aggregated with other misstatements, will not be prevented or detected and corrected on a timely basis by the entity's internal control.

The following factors may increase control risk:

- Changes in key personnel such as the departure of key management
- A lack of personnel with appropriate accounting skills
- Deficiencies in internal control
- Changes in the IT environment
- Installation of significant new IT systems related to financial reporting

Detection risk is the risk that the procedures performed by the auditor to reduce audit risk to an acceptably low level will not detect a misstatement that exists and that could be material, individually or when aggregated with other misstatements.

Detection risk is affected by sampling and non-sampling risk. Factors which may result in an increase include:

- Poor planning
- Inappropriate assignment of personnel to the engagement team
- Failing to apply professional scepticism
- Inadequate supervision and review of the audit work performed
- Incorrect sample sizes
- Incorrect sampling techniques performed

(**Note:** Only one example of a factor increasing the relevant risk was needed for each component.)

(b) **Audit risks and responses**

Audit risk	Response
Abraham's finance director intends to capitalise the $2.2 million of development expenditure incurred. This material amount should only be capitalised if the related product can generate future profits as set out in IAS 38 *Intangible Assets*. There is a risk at least some of the expenditure does not meet the criteria. This will mean assets and profits are overstated.	An analysis showing developments costs in relation to each product should be obtained and reviewed. Testing should be carried out to ensure the technical and commercial feasibility of each product and where it can't be proven that future economic benefits will result from the product developed, the related costs should be expensed.
At the year end it is anticipated that there will be significant levels of work in progress, likely to constitute a material balance. The pharmaceuticals production process is likely to be complex and the audit team may not be sufficiently qualified to assess the quantity and value of work in progress. Therefore they be unable to gain sufficient evidence over a material area of the financial statements.	Nate & Co should assess their ability to gain the required level of evidence and if it is not sufficient, they should approach an independent expert to value the work in progress. This should be arranged after obtaining consent from Abrahams' management and in time for the year-end inventory count.

Audit risk	Response
Abrahams use standard costing to value inventory and under IAS 2 *Inventories* the standard cost method may be used for convenience, but only if the results approximate actual cost. However, standard costs have not been updated since the product was first manufactured, leading to a risk that standard costs are out of date. If they are, this could mean inventory is over or under valued in the statement of financial position.	Standard costs used for inventory valuation should be compared to actual cost for an appropriate sample of inventory items. Any significant variations should be discussed with management to gain evidence that the valuation is reasonable and inventory is fairly stated.
Approximately one-third of the warehouses storing finished goods for Abrahams belong to third parties. Sufficient and appropriate audit evidence will need to be obtained to confirm the quantities of inventory held in these locations in order to verify existence and completeness.	Additional procedures, including attending inventory counts at third party warehouses, will be required to ensure that inventory quantities have been confirmed across all locations.
In September a new accounting package was introduced. The fact the two systems were not run in parallel increases the risk that errors occurring during the changeover were not highlighted, and all areas of the financial statements could potentially be affected.	The new system will need to be fully documented by the audit team including relevant controls. Testing should be performed to ensure the closing data on the old system was correctly transferred as the opening data on the new system, and that transactions have not been duplicated on both systems and therefore include twice.
The IT manager who developed the bespoke system left the company two months after the changeover and his replacement is not due to start until just before the year end. Without an IT manager's support in the interim, errors may occur and may not be picked up due to a lack of knowledge or experience of the system. This could potentially result in misstatements in many areas of the financial statements.	This audit team will need to ascertain from the finance director how this risk of misstatement is being mitigated. During the audit the audit team should remain alert throughout the audit for evidence of errors, particularly when testing transactions occurring between September and January.
$1 million of equity finance and $2.5 million of long-term loans has been raised during the year. The accounting treatment and disclosure of these can be complex with the equity finance to be allocated correctly between share capital and share premium, and the loan to be properly presented as a non-current liability. Disclosures need to be sufficient to comply with IFRSs.	The audit team must ensure the split of the equity finance is correct and that total financing proceeds of $3.5 million were received. Disclosures relating to the equity and loan finance should be reviewed to ensure compliance with relevant IFRSs.
The loan has covenants attached to it. If these are breached then the loan would be repayable straight away and would need to be classified as a current liability, potentially resulting in a net current liability position on the statement of financial position. If the company did not have sufficient cash available to repay the loan balance the going concern status of the company could be threatened.	Obtain and review (or re-perform) covenant calculations to identify any breaches. If there are any the likelihood of the bank demanding repayment will need to be assessed and the potential impact on the company. The need to avoid breaching the covenants reinforces the audit team's need to maintain professional scepticism in areas that could be manipulated.

Audit risk	Response
The finance director has announced that all land and buildings will be revalued as at the year end. The revaluation surplus or deficit is likely to be material and if the revaluation is not carried out and recorded in accordance with IAS 16 *Property, Plant and Equipment*, non-current assets may be under or over-valued.	Review the reasonableness of the valuation and assess the competence, experience and independence of the individual performing the valuation. The surplus/deficit should be recalculated to ensure that land and buildings are included at a reasonable amount in the statement of financial position.
The already short reporting timetable for Abrahams is likely to be reduced. This could increase detection risk because there is pressure on the team to obtain sufficient and appropriate evidence in a shorter time scale, which could adversely influence judgement on the size of samples and the extent of work needed.	If it is confirmed with the finance director that the time available at the final audit is to be reduced then the ability of the team to gather sufficient appropriate evidence should be assessed. If it is not realistically possible to perform all the required work at a final audit then an interim audit should take place in late December or early January to reduce the level of work to be done at the final audit.

(**Note:** Only five risks and five related responses were needed to gain 10 marks.)

(c) (i) **Substantive procedures for inventory held at third party warehouses**

- Attend any inventory count at the third party warehouses to review the controls in operation, to ensure the completeness and existence of inventory and to perform any necessary test counts.

- Request direct written confirmation of quantities of inventory balances held at year end from the third party warehouse providers and request confirmation of any damaged or slow moving goods.

- Review any available reports by the auditors of the third parties owning the warehouses in relation to the adequacy of controls over inventory.

- Inspect any documentation relating to third party inventory.

(ii) **Substantive procedures to confirm standard costs used for inventory valuation**

- Obtain an analysis of the standard costs used in inventory valuation and compare them with the costs shown on actual invoices or in wages records to see if they are reasonable

- Analyse the variances between standard and actual costs and discuss the reason for these with management and the action taken in respect of any variances.

- Discuss with management how standard costs are formulated and applied to the inventory valuation, and the procedures in place to ensure these are updated to account for movements in actual cost when necessary.

49 Sunflower

Marking scheme

Marks

(a)   ½ mark for source of documentation and ½ mark for information expect to obtain, max of 2½ marks for sources and 2½ marks for information expect.
    Prior year audit file
    Prior year financial statements
    Accounting systems notes
    Discussions with management
    Permanent audit file
    Current year budgets and management accounts
    Sunflower's website
    Prior year report to management
    Financial statements of competitors 5

(b)   Up to 1 mark per well explained risk and up to 1 mark for each well explained response. Overall max of 5 marks for risks and 5 marks for responses.
    Treatment of $1.6m refurbishment expenditure
    Disposal of warehouse
    Bank loan of $1.5m
    Attendance at year-end inventory counts
    Inventory valuation
    Transfer of opening balances from supermarkets to head office
    Increased inherent risk of errors in finance department and new financial controller 10

(c)   Up to 1 mark per well described point
    Costs versus benefits of establishing an internal audit (IA) department
    Size and complexity of Sunflower should be considered
    The role of any IA department should be considered
    Whether existing managers/employees can undertake the roles required
    Whether the control environment has a history of control deficiencies
    Whether the possibility of fraud is high 5
20

(a)   **Information sources**

Information source	Expect to obtain:
Permanent audit file	Information on matters of continuing importance for the company and the audit team, such as governing documents, share certificates and ongoing contractual agreements.
Prior year audit file	An awareness of issues arising in the prior year audit and the implications for the current year audit, especially the risk assessment where issues in the prior year suggest a particular area is more susceptible to misstatements.
Prior year financial statements	Information on the historic performance of the entity and its accounting policies. Last year's financial statements can help the auditor form expectations for the purposes of performing analytical procedures.
Systems notes/Internal control questionnaires	Information on how each of the key accounting systems is designed, how it operates and how robust the internal controls are.
Company website	Information on recent developments or press activity which could impact on the risk assessment.
Financial statements or financial information relating to competitors	Information from which the auditor can develop expectations when undertaking preliminary analytical procedures and undertaking the risk assessment.
Company budgets	A reference point for expected performance which can be compared with actual performance.
Prior year report to management	Information on deficiencies identified last year and auditor recommendations. If the deficiencies are unresolved this will impact on the risk assessment.
Discussions with management	Information in relation to any important issues arising or changes to the company during the period under review.

(**Note:** Only five sources were required)

(b)   **Audit risks and responses**

Audit risk	Response
The $1.6m spent on refurbishing may have been incorrectly analysed between non-current assets and repairs. There is therefore a risk that non-current assets and expenses are misstated.	Obtain and review an analysis of the costs, tracing to invoices and other supporting documents to establish the nature of the expenditure. Then accounting entries should be reviewed to ensure revenue expenditure has been charged to the statement of profit or loss and capital expenditure is included in non-current assets.
The 5 year loan of $1.5m from the bank may have been incorrectly analysed between current and non-current liabilities.	The allocation of the loan between current and non-current liabilities and the related disclosures for the loan should be reviewed to assess whether it is presented in accordance with IFRSs.

Audit risk	Response
If Sunflower has given the bank a charge over its assets as security for the loan, the related financial statement disclosures may be incomplete or inadequate.	The loan agreement should be obtained and reviewed for evidence that security has been given. A bank confirmation should be obtained including details of any security Financial statement disclosures relating to security should be reviewed to ensure they are complete and in accordance with IFRSs.
The warehouse disposed of during the year may have been incorrectly accounted for resulting in a potential overstatement of non-current assets and the related profit on disposal.	The non-current asset register should be reviewed to ensure that the asset has been removed. Disposal proceeds should be agreed to bank statements and the profit on disposal should be recalculated.
Due to Sunflower conducting numerous inventory counts simultaneously on 31 December it may not be possible to attend all counts. As a result there is a risk sufficient appropriate audit evidence may not be gained over inventory in the financial statements.	A sample of sites should be visited with those holding material inventory, including the warehouse, prioritised. Supermarkets with a history of inventory count issues should also be visited.
Sunflower's inventory valuation policy is selling price less average profit margin. Although IAS 2 *Inventories* allows this as an inventory valuation method it is only permitted if it proves a close approximation to cost. If this is not the case, inventory could be under or overvalued.	Valuation testing should include a comparison of the cost of inventory with the selling price less margin to assess it the method used does result in a close approximation to cost. The actual NRV (rather than anticipated selling price) for some items should be tested to ensure it does not fall below recorded values.
Transfer of opening balances to head office may not have been performed completely and accurately. If the opening balances are misstated, for some statement of financial position accounts (such as non-current assets) the closing balances may also be misstated.	Enquire of management how the data was transferred, what controls were in place and which procedures were performed to confirm the transfer was complete and accurate. Review the journal(s) made to transfer the opening balances and compare with the prior year financial statements to ensure they were as expected.
The increased workload for the finance department has forced the financial controller to leave and his replacement will not start until late December. The increased workload increases the risk of staff making errors. In addition the new financial controller's lack of experience of Sunflower's systems and accounting records may mean he or she is more likely to produce financial statements with misstatements or incorrect disclosures. In addition audit queries may be less likely to be resolved.	Sample sizes and the level of substantive procedures may need to be increased in light of the increased inherent risk of overworked staff and an inexperienced financial controller. A request that the finance director be available to answer audit questions should be made in anticipation that the new financial controller may not be able to resolve audit issues relating to events during the year. The audit team should remain alert to the possibility of errors.

(**Note:** Only five risks and five related responses were needed to gain 10 marks.)

(c) **Factors to be considered before establishing an internal audit department**

Before establishing an internal audit department the finance director would consider:

(i)   *The costs of establishing an internal audit department*

These are likely to be significant and should be weighted against the benefits and future cost savings.

(ii)   *The size and complexity of Sunflower*

As Sunflower has numerous supermarkets, a central warehouse and a head office, its size and complexity could benefit from an IA department.

(iii) *The effectiveness of the current control environment and past experience of control deficiencies*

The less effective the controls in the organisation, the greater the need for an internal audit department.

(iv)   *The role of the proposed internal audit department*

The finance director needs to establish the nature of the assignments to be carried out by internal audit. These could be compliance based reviews, control reviews, or observing controls and test counting at the inventory counts.

(v)   *The ability of current employees in current roles carry out proposed internal audit assignments*

It may be that the relevant expertise and time exists within the organisation already to fulfil the objectives that would be set for an internal audit department.

(vi)   *The susceptibility of the business to fraud*

The more susceptible the business is to fraud the greater the need for an internal audit department (eg to review relevant controls and assist in fraud investigations). Supermarkets collect large sums of cash so Sunflower is likely to be relatively susceptible and will need robust controls to prevent fraud. These controls will need to be monitored.

50 Multiple choice answers

1   B   Even the most effective internal control system can only provide reasonable assurance that control objectives are met due to its inherent limitations. These include in particular human error and the possibility of fraud.

2   A   An internal control evaluation questionnaire asks questions to determine whether there are controls which prevent or detect specified errors or omissions. A flowchart is a diagram showing the physical flow of information through the system.

3   D   Records of program changes and virus checks are general IT controls.

4   A   One for one checking and hash totals are application controls.

5   B   This means that customers are not able to exceed their credit limits and are therefore more likely to be able to pay. A helps to ensure that goods are sold at the right price. C & D are effective controls regarding the recovery of debts but do not prevent sales being made to customers who are unlikely to pay as the sale has already been made by this stage.

6   B   Matching of suppliers' invoices to purchase orders and goods received notes ensures that liabilities are only recognised for goods which have been received by the company. The reconciliation of the payables control account and purchase ledger and checking of calculation of invoices are accuracy checks. Sequential numbering of documentation helps to ensure completeness.

7   B   Personnel records are documentary evidence of the existence of an employee. Segregation of duties between staff involved in HR and payroll helps to prevent the creation of bogus employees with subsequent payroll payments being made.

8   D   Counting inventory is one of the key controls for ensuring the existence of inventory. Controls to protect inventory from theft reduce the risk that inventory is recorded in the inventory records but is no longer held by the company. Sequential documentation provides confidence regarding completeness. Procedures to identify obsolete and damaged inventory provide confidence regarding valuation.

9   C   Although it is possible for two individuals to collude the risk of fraud and/or theft is reduced. The control is only effective at the point it occurs so it will not have any effect on the subsequent recording or banking of the cash.

10   A   Capital expenditure will often involve significant amounts. It is important therefore that it is for valid business purposes and that appropriate decisions are made by senior individuals.

11   B   Tests of controls are performed to obtain evidence about the effectiveness of the design of controls in preventing, detecting and correcting material misstatements and about their operation throughout the period.

12   D   This is a substantive procedure.

13   C   The direction of the test is important here. The sample is taken from goods received notes as these represent deliveries. The auditor can then check that each delivery is supported by a valid order. If the sample is chosen from purchase orders (Answer A) the test would confirm whether orders have been fulfilled. B and D are tests of controls regarding completeness of accounting information.

14   A   The control helps to ensure sales are valid as sales are only recognised for goods which have been dispatched.

15   A   A range check helps to confirm that the data has been input correctly. A sequence check is a completeness control. Password protection and authorisation are general controls and therefore they do not impact directly on the input of data.

16   C   The matching of dispatch notes to an invoice ensures that for all goods dispatched an invoice has been raised. If this is not the case sales and trade receivables may be understated. For answer B an appropriate control would be to match dispatch notes to invoices. Matching dispatch notes and invoices would not prevent orders being dispatched incorrectly (A) or prevent invoices being input incorrectly (D).

17   C   This is in accordance with guidance given in ISA 265.

18   D   Staff numbers are likely to be lower in a small company making segregation of duties more difficult. The external auditor will assess the attitudes, awareness and actions of management as part of the assessment of the control environment. Although controls may be less sophisticated in a small company the auditor may be able to rely on controls in some areas depending on the overall assessment and results of tests of controls (Option 1). Controls are likely to be operated less formally therefore documentary evidence is less likely to exist (Option 3).

19   B   Internal control evaluation questionnaires (ICEQs) are used to determine whether there are controls which prevent or detect specified errors or omissions. Internal control questionnaires (ICQs) are used to ask whether controls exist which meet specific control objectives.

20   A   ISA 265 *Communicating deficiencies in internal control to those charged with governance and management* states that consideration of internal control is to enable suitable audit procedures to be designed, not to enable the auditor to express an opinion on the effectiveness of controls.

21   B   Significant deficiencies must be reported in writing. Other deficiencies which are not significant but which warrant management attention may be reported in writing or orally.

51 Documenting internal controls

Text reference. Chapter 9.

Top tips. In these knowledge-based questions the biggest danger is not answering the question set and instead answering the question you hoped would come up on the area being examined. The best way to avoid this is to make sure you read the requirement and any related information very carefully.

In this case for part (a) you needed to describe advantages and disadvantages for two methods used to document internal control systems. It was important to establish which methods you needed to focus on and ignore other possible methods. If you read the supplementary information first and then the requirement you would have noticed that the methods are stated twice so should have been in no doubt as to where to focus your answer. As you were asked to 'describe' you should have realised short bullet points would not be sufficient.

In part (b), as long as you are familiar with control activities there are a number of different ones to select from, apart from control accounts which you are specifically asked not to include.

Easy marks. This is a knowledge-based question and you should have been able to score a good proportion of marks on each part.

Examiner's comments. In part (a) a significant minority of candidates did not understand the question requirement fully, and so instead of providing advantages and disadvantages for notes and then for ICQs, they provided answers which were of a general nature and just covered advantages and disadvantages of documenting the internal control system. It is possible that these candidates did not carefully read the scenario paragraph preceding the requirement. Candidates must take the time to read and understand any scenario paragraphs; these are intended to help candidates understand the question requirements.

Those candidates who understood the requirement often made the following mistakes:

- Lack of detail, the requirement was to "describe" and often candidates provided bullet point notes.

- Some candidates were confused as to who prepared the systems documentation, thinking that ICQs were produced by management, and so identified irrelevant advantages and disadvantages.

- Providing definitions and explanations of what notes and ICQs are, rather than answering the question requirement.

- Listing points in relation to internal control evaluation questionnaires (ICEQ)s rather than ICQs.

Part (b) was answered well by most candidates with many scoring full marks.

Marks

(a)   Up to 1 mark per valid point

Notes
- Simple to understand
- Facilitate understanding by all team
- Cumbersome especially if complex system
- Difficult to identify missing controls

Questionnaires
- Quick to prepare and hence cost effective
- All internal controls considered and missing controls identified
- Easy to complete and use
- Easy to overstate controls
- Easy to misunderstand controls and miss unusual controls

Maximum marks   6

(b)   Up to 1 mark per well explained control activity
Segregation of duties
Information processing
Authorisation
Physical controls
Performance reviews
Arithmetical controls
Account reconciliations

Maximum marks   4
                                                                                 10

(a)   **Narrative notes**

Advantages	Disadvantages
They are relatively simple to record and can facilitate understanding by all audit team members.	Describing something in narrative notes can be a lot more time consuming than, say, representing it as a simple flowchart, particularly where the system follows a logical flow.
They can be used for any system due to the method's flexibility	They are awkward to update if written manually.
Editing in future years can be relatively easy if they are computerised.	It can be difficult to identify missing internal controls because notes record the detail of systems but may not identify control exceptions clearly.

Internal control questionnaires

Advantages	Disadvantages
If drafted thoroughly, they can ensure all controls are considered.	The principal disadvantage is that they can be drafted vaguely, hence misunderstood and important controls not identified.
They are quick to prepare.	They may contain a large number of irrelevant controls.

Advantages	Disadvantages
They are easy to use and control.	They may not include unusual controls, which are nevertheless effective in particular circumstances.

(**Note:** Only six valid points were needed to obtain full marks)

(b)

Control activities include:	
Approval and control of documents	Transactions should be approved by an appropriate person (eg overtime should be approved by departmental managers).
Checking the arithmetical accuracy of records	For example, checking to see if individual invoices have been added up correctly.
Reconciliations	Reconciliations involve comparison of a specific balance in the accounting records with what another source says the balance should be, for example, a bank reconciliation. Differences between the two figures should only be reconciling items.
Segregation of duties	Allocating roles and responsibilities to two or more different people such that the risk of an individual being able to perpetrate fraud is reduced.
Comparing internal data with external sources of information	For example, comparing records of goods dispatched to customers with customers' acknowledgement of goods that have been received.
Limiting physical access to assets and records	Only authorised personnel should have access to certain assets (particularly valuable or portable ones) eg ensuring that the inventory stores locked are unless store personnel are there.
Controls over information processing	Computer controls are put in place including general IT controls. These cover a range of applications and support the overall IT environment and application controls, which can be manual or automated controls and which operate on a cycle/business process level.
Performance reviews	A comparison or review of the performance of the business is carried out by looking at areas such as budget v actual results.

52 Flowers Anytime

Text references. Chapters 9, 10 and 11.

Top tips. This question is demanding as it examines internal controls in the context of a scenario. The key here is to ensure you consider the elements of the cycle mentioned in the question (ie receipts, processing and recording of orders and collection of cash) and that you both **describe** and **explain the purpose** of the controls you would expect to see.

Examiner's comments. Candidates lost marks for failing to address all aspects of the requirement. For example, part (a) asked for controls regarding the receipt, processing **and** recording of orders.

Marking scheme

		Marks
Internal controls		
(a)	Receipt, processing and recording Up to 1 mark per point to a maximum of	6
(b)	Collection of cash Up to 1 mark per point to a maximum of	4
		10

Internal control activities

(a) *Receipts, processing and recording of orders*

All orders should be recorded on **pre-printed sequentially numbered documentation**. This could be a four part document, one copy being the order, one copy being the dispatch note, one copy being sent to the customer as evidence of the order and the last copy retained by the accounts receivable clerk.

To ensure completeness of orders a **sequence check** should be performed on the documents either manually or by computer. Any missing documents should be traced.

As the clerk inputs the order the system should automatically check whether the customer remains within its **credit limit**. Any orders which exceed the credit limit should be rejected.

In exceptional circumstances where credit limits are to be exceeded this should be authorised by the department manager. Orders should also be rejected if the customer has a significantly overdue balance.

As the order is being input the system should check whether the item required is **in inventory**. This is possible as the ordering and inventories systems are integrated. If items are unavailable the order should be rejected. This will enable the clerk to inform the customer which will enhance customer service.

Periodically an **independent review should be performed of the standing data on the system**. A sample of credit limits should be checked to ensure that they have been calculated in accordance with the standard formula. Any breaches should be investigated. Similarly the price of flowers should be matched against an up to date price list.

Sales invoices should be posted automatically to the sales daybook and accounts receivable ledger. An accounts receivable control account reconciliation should be performed on a monthly basis and any discrepancies should be investigated and dealt with.

Customer statements should be generated by the system automatically. Any queries raised by the customer on receipt of these should be investigated promptly. Any resulting credit notes should be authorised.

(b) *Collection of cash*

Details of all **bank transfers** received should be input into the cash book/bank control account and the accounts receivable ledger and accounts receivable control account.

Entries in the accounts receivable ledger should be **matched** against specific invoices. Any unallocated cash should be investigated via an exception report.

On a monthly basis a **bank reconciliation** should be performed. Together with the accounts receivable control account reconciliation and the following up of queries on customer statements this will help to ensure that the cash is correctly recorded and allocated.

On a monthly basis an **aged receivables** listing should be generated. The company should have procedures in place for the chasing of debts which the credit controller would follow ranging from a telephone reminder to the threat of legal action.

53 North

Text reference. Chapter 10.

Top tips. This is a very practical question. You need to identify the tasks you are being given in the requirements then read the scenario information carefully to find practical points to make.

You should have picked up on the controls in place relatively easily. Then it was really a case of thinking how you could confirm these controls were actually working as they should, as this is what tests of controls are all about. Your reason will always be linked to gaining evidence for the audit as you want to use the results to reduce other substantive testing.

Marks

Five tests of controls and reasons
1 mark per test of control and 1 per reason to a maximum of   10

Test of control	Reason
Inspect a sample of timesheets for evidence of signature by an appropriate supervisor.	To verify that only valid employee timesheets (and therefore hours worked) are processed.
For a sample of employee payroll entries, trace back to timesheet and ensure that the entries were made from a timesheet signed by a supervisor.	To gain evidence that the payroll clerk is only processing authorised timesheets, and ultimately only those hours worked are recorded and paid.
For a sample of employees, recalculate the gross pay, deductions and net pay and compare with the amounts shown on the payroll printout.	To ensure the payroll system calculations (including any standing data) are accurate, therefore giving evidence over the completeness and accuracy of the payroll charge.
Reperform or observe the check of hours carried out by the chief accountant for a sample of employees.	To gain evidence over the completeness and accuracy of hours (and therefore payroll cost) recorded in the payroll records.
Compare the journals with the payroll printout and make sure they are consistent with the totals on it.	To gain evidence that the amounts to be entered into the general ledger accurately reflect the checked printout, and therefore gain comfort over the accuracy of the wages related balances in the ledger.
Enter a false password into the online banking system to ensure it is not accepted.	To gain evidence that only authorised and valid payments are made and recorded.

Note: Only **five** tests and reasons were required.

54 Value for money audit

Text references. Chapters 5 and 10.

Top tips. This is a question on deficiencies in the purchases system of a company, but from an internal audit point of view. Don't be put off by this – stay focused and use the information in the scenario to generate your answer. A good way to set out your answer is by using a columnar format – this ensures that you link deficiencies to recommendations and gives more structure to your answer.

Easy marks. Easy marks are available if you use the scenario to generate the internal control deficiencies.

Marks

1 mark for identifying and explaining the deficiency and 1 mark for a
recommendation to overcome that deficiency.

Transfer info – purchase requisition to order form	2
Purchase requisition destroyed	2
Order form no copy in ordering department	2
No copy order form in goods inwards department	2
GRNs filed in part number order	2
Other relevant points (each)	2
Maximum marks	**10**

(i) Internal control deficiency	(ii) Recommendation
A clerk transfers information from the order requisition to an order form. This could result in errors in orders being made after the buyer has authorised the requisition.	The order form should be signed off as authorised to confirm that the details on the requisition match those on the order form.
The order requisition is thrown away once the chief buyer has authorised it. Any subsequent queries on orders cannot be traced back to the original requisition.	The order requisition form should be retained with the order form in case of query or dispute regarding items ordered.
No copy of the order form is retained by the ordering department. This means that goods could be ordered twice in error or deliberately. It also means that queries on deliveries cannot be chased up.	A three-part pre-numbered order form should be used and one copy should be retained by the ordering department with the requisition form.
The Goods Inward Department does not retain a copy of the Damaged Goods note. If the note is lost on the way to the ordering department, or there is a query, the Goods Inward Department has no record of goods returned.	Four copies of the Damaged Goods note should be retained. One copy could be retained by the Goods Inward Department, one sent to the ordering department, one to the department who requested the goods, so they are aware that there will be a delay and one to the supplier.
The Ordering Department does not keep a record of goods received, so is unable to confirm which orders are closed or to chase up suppliers.	The Ordering Department should match orders to GRNs and mark orders as closed once all goods have been received.
The Goods Inwards Department files GRNs in order of the supplier's goods reference. This could make it difficult to find a GRN at a later date if the department is not aware of the supplier's reference.	GRNs should be filed in date order, or by PO number.

Tutorial note: only five deficiencies and recommendations were required to score 10 marks.

55 ICQs and ICEQs

(a) The auditor should obtain an understanding of internal controls relevant to the audit.

They should:

- Obtain an understanding of the entity and the risks it is exposed to

- Ascertain the nature of the entity's internal control system and assess the impact of this on the level of audit risk

- Decide whether the internal control system is sufficient to gather audit evidence through tests of control with reduced substantive testing or whether full substantive testing is required

- Report any significant deficiencies in internal control to those charged with governance

(b) Narrative notes and flow charts.

(c) **Internal Control Questionnaires (ICQs)**

IQCs are used to ask whether controls exist which meet specific control objectives. They comprise a list of questions designed to determine whether desirable controls are present, and are formulated so that there is one to cover each of the major transaction cycles.

An ICQ is therefore designed to help evaluate the system as well as to record it. One of the most effective ways of designing the questionnaire is to phrase the questions so that all the answers can be given as 'YES' or 'NO' and a 'NO' answer indicates a deficiency in the system.

For example, one question in respect of the purchases cycle might be 'Are purchase invoices matched and compared to goods received notes before being passed for payment?'

Internal Control Evaluation Questionnaires (ICEQs)

ICEQs have a different focus from ICQs and are concerned with assessing whether specific errors (or frauds) are possible, rather than establishing whether certain desirable controls are present. This is achieved by reducing the control criteria for each transaction stream down to a handful of key questions (or control questions).

The characteristic of these questions is that they concentrate on the significant errors or omissions that could occur at each phase of the appropriate cycle if controls are weak (deficient).

For example, one of the questions in the purchases cycle might be 'Is there reasonable assurance that goods or services could not be received without a liability being recorded?'

56 Smoothbrush

Text references. Chapters 9 and 10.

Top tips. This question has two separate requirements: First to identify and secondly to explain suitable controls. Make sure you do both. Also limit your answer to controls over the assertions specified in the question. When answering questions like this, commit to memory the fact that you want controls over completeness and accuracy only, otherwise you may find yourself listing and explaining controls over all assertions, many of which will be gaining no marks.

Examiner's comments. This question for 10 marks required an identification and explanation of controls over the continuous/perpetual inventory counting system in order to ensure completeness and accuracy of the inventory records. This question proved to be challenging for a number of candidates and there were some unsatisfactory answers. Many identified controls, such as "the inventory team should be independent of the warehouse staff" but failed to then explain these controls, this would have restricted their marks to ½ mark per control as opposed to the 1½ marks available for an identification and explanation.

Marking scheme

Marks

½ mark for each identification of a control and up to 1 mark per well explained
description of the control
- – Team independent of warehouse
- – Timetable of counts
- – Inventory movements stopped
- – No pre-printed quantities on count sheets
- – Second independent team
- – Direction of counting floor to records
- – Damaged/obsolete goods to specific area
- – Records updated by authorised person

Marks   <u>10</u>

Controls over inventory system: completeness and accuracy

Suitable controls	Explanation
An inventory count team independent of the warehouse team is used.	There should be segregation of duties between those who have day-to-day responsibility for inventory and those who are checking it to help prevent fraud and error. The current team including a member of warehouse staff is inadequate and two internal auditors should be used if possible.
Pre-printed inventory sheets are used stating code/descriptions, but without quantities.	Using sheets with quantities already filled in means counters could potentially agree the current quantities to avoid counting and save time. The lack of quantities forces a count to be undertaken in each case.
Damaged/obsolete goods are moved to a designated area for inspection, but left on the sheets. They are provided for if necessary.	Rather than removing damaged/obsolete items from the sheet (and losing the audit trail), they should be written down or provided against to ensure that they are included at the lower of cost and NRV. A member of the finance team should make the assessment as to what needs writing down.
Movements of inventory are not allowed into or out of the area being counted during inventory counts.	Allowing movements in and out of inventory during counts could result in double counting, or inventory not being counted at all. Therefore such movements should be stopped during the count.
A sample of independent checks of the counts carried out by a separate team. Items to be checked are determined after the first count has been completed.	By counting a sample of inventory lines again this should help to ensure completeness and accuracy of the counts, and act as an incentive for the first team to carry out counts more accurately initially.
As a separate exercise after the counts of items on the sheets, teams check a sample of items that are physically present are correctly included on the sheets.	A count performed from the records to the warehouse will only test for existence or overstatement of inventory line quantities. Testing for completeness requires a different approach where inventory in the warehouse is compared to the records to identify goods physically present but not recorded.
Inventory count sheets are compared with the inventory records after the count. Where adjustments are needed, the reason for them is investigated and they are processed on a timely basis by appropriate personnel.	Only authorised individuals should be able to amend the records in which year end inventory will be based. On a periodic basis, senior finance team members should review the types and levels of adjustments for indications of fraud.

Tutorial note. You may have come up with other valid controls here. As long as they meet the control objective for the assertions specified in the question, and are adequately explained, you will have gained marks for these. Other valid controls include the monitoring of timetabling of the counts to ensure all areas are covered at least once a year.

57 Lily (12/12) (amended)

Text references. Chapters 10 and 13.

Top tips. This case-study style question is based on procedures at an inventory count. You need to fully explain each deficiency before you move on to providing relevant recommendations. As you read through the scenario ask yourself what could go wrong and to what extent the inventory count procedures do, or do not, address these issues. This will help you explain your deficiencies as your explanation will include the possible consequences of the missing or ineffective control.

Easy marks. You should have been able to identify and explain deficiencies.

Marking scheme

Marks

Up to 1 mark per well explained deficiency and up to 1 mark per recommendation.
If not well explained then just give ½ mark for each.
Warehouse manager supervising the count
No division of responsibilities within each counting team
Internal audit teams should be checking controls and performing sample counts
No flagging of aisles once counting complete
Additional inventory listed on sheets which are not sequentially numbered
Inventory sheets not signed by counters
Damaged goods not moved to central location
Movements of inventory during the count
Warehouse manager not qualified to assess the level of work-in-progress
Warehouse manager not experienced enough to assess the quantities of raw materials

<u>10</u>

(i) Deficiency	(ii) Recommendation
The warehouse manager will supervise the inventory count and is not independent as he has overall responsibility for the inventory. He therefore has an incentive to conceal or fail to report any issues that could reflect badly upon him.	An independent supervisor should be assigned, such as a manager from the internal audit department.
Aisles or areas counted will not be flagged. This could result in items being double counted or not counted at all.	Once areas have been counted they should be flagged. At the end of the count the supervisor should check all areas have been flagged and therefore counted.
There is no-one independent reviewing controls over the count or test counting to assess the accuracy of the counts.	Instead of the internal auditors being involved in the count itself, they should perform secondary test counts and review controls over the count.
Damaged goods are being left in their location rather than being stored separately. This makes it more difficult for finance to assess the level of damage to the goods and establish the level of write down needed. Also, if not moved, damaged goods could be sold by mistake.	Damaged goods should be clearly marked as such during the count and at the end of the count they should be moved to a central location. A manager from the finance team should then inspect these damaged goods to assess the level of allowance or write down needed.

(i) Deficiency	(ii) Recommendation
Due to the continuous production process, there will be movement of goods in and out of the warehouse during the count, increasing the risk of double counting or failing to count inventory. This could mean inventory in the financial statements is under or overstated.	Although it is not practicable to disrupt the continuous production process, raw materials (RM) required for 31 December should be estimated and separated from the remainder of inventory. These materials should be included as part of work-in-progress (WIP). Goods manufactured on 31 December should be stored separately, and at the end of the count should be counted once and included as finished goods. Goods received from suppliers should also be stored separately, counted once at the end and included in RM. Goods dispatched to customers should be kept to a minimum during the count.
The warehouse manager is going to estimate WIP levels. The warehouse manager is unlikely to have the necessary experience to estimate the WIP levels which is something the factory manager would be more familiar with. Alternatively a specialist may be needed to make the estimate. This could ultimately result in an inaccurate WIP balance in the financial statements.	A specialist should be used assess the work-in-progress.
The warehouse manager is going to approximate RM quantities. Although he is familiar with the RM, and on the basis that a specialist has been required in the past, the warehouse manager may not have the necessary skill and experience to carry out these measurements. This could result in an inaccurate RM balance in the financial statements.	As in previous years, a specialist should assess the quantities of raw materials, or at least check the warehouse manager's estimate to give comfort that the manager's estimates will be reasonable going forward.
There is no indication that inventory sheets are signed or initialled by the counting team, nor a record kept of which team counted which area. This means it will be difficult to follow up on any anomalies noted, as the identity of the counters may not be known.	Inventory sheets should be signed by both team members once an aisle is completed. The supervisor should check the sheets are signed when handed in.
Inventory not listed on the sheets is to be entered onto separate sheets. These sheets are not sequentially numbered and the supervisor will be unable to ensure the completeness of all inventory sheets.	Every team should be given a blank sheet on which they can enter any inventory counted which is not on their sheets. The blank sheets should be sequentially numbered with any unused sheets returned at the end of the count. The supervisor should then check the sequence of all sheets.
The responsibilities of each of the two staff members within a counting team is unclear. It does not appear that one has been told to count and the other to check. Therefore errors in counting may not be picked up.	For each area one team member should be asked to count and the second member asked to check that the inventory has been counted correctly. The roles of each can then be reversed for the next area.

(**Note:** Only five deficiencies and five related recommendations were needed to gain 10 marks.)

58 Shiny Happy Windows

Text references. Chapter 9, 10, 11, 14 and 15.

Top tips. Part (a) is unrelated to the scenario. Read the question carefully and answer the question being asked as concisely as possible, as both (i) and (ii) are worth just two marks each and you do not want to run over your time allocation. The definitions of tests of control and substantive procedures are essential knowledge and you should have no problems in recalling these.

Parts (b) (i) and (ii) are concerned with identifying deficiencies in a cash received cycle for a window cleaning company, and suggesting appropriate controls. These sorts of requirements are commonplace. You can ask yourself – what could go wrong? At each stage of the cycle to help you identify the deficiencies, then ask yourself - how could that be prevented?

This will help you come up with controls. For example, Cash is sent in by post which is opened by a junior clerk. What could go wrong? – the clerk could steal it and not record it in the cash received log (deficiency). How could this be prevented? – by having two people present when the post is opened, one opening the post and one recording the cash receipts in the log (suggested control).

For part (b)(iii) you need to assume the controls you suggested are in place, and test that they are operating properly. In other words you are happy with the design of the control, but need to ask – How can I test that the control is working as expected? Observe the mail opening and recording (test of control) is the obvious answer for the control just suggested.

Easy marks. Part (a) is core knowledge and you should be able to answer these in full and obtain the majority, if not all of the marks available on these parts. There are lots of clues in part (b) as to what deficiencies are present and part (i) at least is relatively straightforward.

Examiner's comments. For part (a) candidates were required to define a substantive procedure and a test of control and then provide an example of each procedure relevant to sales invoicing. A large number of candidates could not provide valid definitions. Most were able to define test of control, but struggled with substantive procedure.

The attempts by most candidates at providing examples of tests of control and substantive procedures were unsatisfactory. Many provided controls rather than how to test the controls and the substantive procedures were weak in relation to the level of detail provided. Obtaining evidence is a core part of the syllabus and for candidates to not be able to provide examples and definitions for substantive procedures and tests of control is unsatisfactory. Future candidates must ensure that they are mindful of the importance of this topic area.

Part (b) for 9 marks had three sub-requirements; an identification and explanation of deficiencies in the cash cycle, controls to address these deficiencies, and tests of controls to assess the effectiveness of the controls. The first two parts of these three sub-requirements were answered well by almost all candidates, many scored full marks.

The third sub-requirement for tests of controls was not well answered. Following on from comments made in relation to (a), candidates do not seem to understand what a test of control is and how it operates.

Marking scheme

		Marks
(a)	1 mark for stating that significant deficiencies must be reported	
	1 mark each for matters to consider:	
	– Whether misstatement has occurred	
	– Likelihood of misstatements occurring	
	– Potential magnitude of misstatement	4

(b) Up to 1 mark for each deficiency identified and explained, up to 1 mark for
     each suitable control and up to 1 mark per test of control.
     –   Junior clerk opens post
     –   Small locked box
     –   Cash not banked daily
     –   Cashier updates cash book and sales ledger   Max 2 for deficiencies
     –   Bank reconciliation not performed monthly   Max 2 for controls
                                                                Max 2 for test of controls
                                                                         6
     Total marks   10

(a) **Significant internal control deficiencies**

ISA 265 requires the auditor to determine whether one or more deficiencies in internal control have been
identified and if so, whether these constitute **significant deficiencies** in internal control. All significant
deficiencies should be reported to those charged with governance.

The significance of a deficiency depends on whether a misstatement has occurred and also on the likelihood
of a misstatement occurring and its potential magnitude. ISA 265 includes examples of matters to consider
when determining whether a deficiency in internal control is a significant deficiency:

- The **likelihood** of the deficiencies resulting in material misstatements in the financial statements in
  the future

- The **susceptibility to loss or fraud** of the related asset or liability

- The **subjectivity and complexity** of determining estimated amounts

- The **amounts** exposed to the deficiencies

- The **volume of activity** that has occurred or could occur

- The **importance of the controls** to the financial reporting process

- The **cause and frequency** of the exceptions identified as a result of the deficiencies

- The **interaction** of the deficiency with other deficiencies in internal control

(b)

(i) Deficiency	(ii) Control	(iii) Test of control
A junior clerk opens the post on his/her own. This could result in cash being stolen and not recorded in the log.	Another accounts staff member should be present when the mail is opened. One person should open the post and the others should record the cash received.	Observe the opening of the mail (without announcing it in advance) to assess if the control is operating as expected.
Cash and cheques are secured in a small locked box. This is a weak physical control inadequate to prevent theft of significant cash sums	Cash and cheques should be stored in a secure safe, and access to this safe should be restricted to supervised individuals.	Inspect the location where unbanked cash/cheques are stored to ensure it is secure. Confirm access is supervised or restricted.
Bank reconciliations are not performed every month and there is no evidence of an independent review by a senior member of the finance department. Errors may not be discovered on a timely basis.	Bank reconciliations should be performed monthly and reviewed by a senior member of the finance department.	Review the reconciliations for the year, making sure there is one prepared each month, evidenced by the date on the reconciliation. Inspect the reconciliation for evidence of review (eg signature and date of senior member of finance department.

59 SouthLea

Text references. Chapters 9, 10 and 11.

Top tips. There are eight marks available for identifying the control deficiencies and suggesting controls to overcome them. The best way to present your answer is in a columnar format because this allows you to link each deficiency with a recommendation.

Make sure you explain the deficiencies you have identified fully, as required by the question. Go through the scenario carefully, noting down potential deficiencies as you do so.

Marking scheme

	Marks
Control deficiencies and recommendations. 8 marks. 1 for explanation of deficiency and 1 for internal control recommendation. Maximum 2 per deficiency/recommendation.	
Maximum marks	**10**

(a) **Wages system – deficiencies and recommended controls**

(i) Deficiency	**(ii) Internal control recommendation**
The foreman is in a position to set up fictitious employees onto the wages system as he has authority to issue temporary employee numbers. This would allow him to collect cash wages for such bogus employees.	The issue of new employee numbers should be authorised by a manager and supported by employee contract letters etc.
The two wages clerks are responsible for the set up and maintenance of all employee records. They could therefore, in collusion, set up bogus employees and collect cash wages from them.	The list of personnel should be matched with the payroll by a manager and all new employee records should be authorised before being set up on the system.
The wages clerks are responsible for making amendments to holidays and illness etc. They could make unauthorised amendments which affect individual staff members' pay.	Any amendments to standing data on the wages system should be done by an authorised manager so that unauthorised amendments are not made. A log of amendments should be regularly reviewed.
The computer system calculates gross pay and any deductions but these are hand-written by the wages clerks for the staff pay packets, so errors could be made and incorrect wages issued.	A payslip should be generated by the computer system and included in the wage packet to reduce the chance of errors in deductions and gross pay being made.
The computer automatically calculates gross pay and deductions, however there is no check to ensure the calculations are accurate.	One of the wages clerks should check the gross pay and deductions for a sample of employees to gain assurance that the computer is calculating amounts correctly.
The foreman distributes cash wages to the employees. He could therefore misappropriate any wages not claimed.	The distribution of wages should be overseen by another manager. Unclaimed wages should be noted on a form and returned to the wages department.

60 Burton Housing

(i)   **Rental income**

Internal controls over the system for recording rents are weak because there are no real checks on the work of the bookkeeper who could therefore easily commit a fraud or make undiscovered errors.

The main controls that should be in place here are as follows.

(1)   There should be **segregation of duties** between recording invoices, recording cash, receiving cash and banking cash.

(2)   **Authorisation of bad debt write offs** should rest with the chief executive not the housing manager.

(3)   An **independent check** is required to compare amounts received to expected rent based on occupancy levels.

My audit procedures will be greater in the areas of where there are deficiencies in internal control and I will perform the following procedures:

(1)   **Compare rental income to previous levels and to budget**. Analytical review can be used to check occupancy, the level of empty flat/weeks and the level of bad debts. The theoretical rental income is 50 × weekly rent (ie on full occupancy).

$$\therefore \text{Occupancy (\%)} = \frac{\text{Actual rental income}}{\text{Theoretical rental income}}\ \%\text{, so:}$$

Empty flat rate (%) = 100 − Occupancy (%)

The level of occupancy can be checked to the housing manager's reports and compared to prior years. Investigate discrepancies between calculated occupancy and reported occupancy.

(2)   Select a sample of weeks from the year and **check** the **posting** of all **invoices** for rent for all flats to the sales ledger. Where there is no invoice I will check to the occupancy report that the flat was empty. This will check that the invoices have been posted to the correct sales ledger account.

(ii)   **Control over receipt and recording of rent**

Control activities which should be in operation here include the following.

(1)   **Reception** staff should **issue receipts** for rent, reconciling cash to copy receipts before handing over the money to the bookkeeper. **Differences** between cash and receipts should be **investigated** and a note kept of the cash handed over.

(2)   A **check** should be made by a senior (independent) official, eg the chief executive, between the **cash received** by the reception staff and the **cash** banked and **posted** to the sales ledger.

(3)   **Complaints** from residents about rent payments should be **investigated** by an independent member of the management committee, particularly where residents claim to have paid rent, but it has not been received. (The use of rent books for residents might avoid the loss of individual receipts.)

Main audit checks to be carried out

(1) Select a sample of days from during the year and **check** from the **reception staff's receipts** and record of cash to the **banked cash** and the postings to the sales ledger. Check that the money is banked promptly.

(2) **Check** that **disputes** about rent are **investigated** independently and a written report made to the management committee.

(3) **Investigate** any **problems** found. Any weaknesses in the system should be reported to the management committee.

(iii) **Postings of credit notes/bad debts/adjustments**

There should not be too many adjustments of this type. The controls in place should include:

(1) Write off of bad debts and other non-routine adjustments should need chief executive authorisation.

(2) A periodic **review** of these adjustments should be carried out by the chief executive for any that are unauthorised or indicate fraudulent activity.

I will select a sample of all these items (probably based on size) and carry out the following procedures.

(1) **Agree to supporting documentation** (explaining why rents returned, or steps to recover rent before writing it off).

(2) **Check authorisation** has been given by the chief executive (for all these items).

(3) **Adjustments** to correct errors will be **checked** to the original entry and the calculations redone.

(4) Where a **credit note** has been issued, I will **check** that the **resident was originally charged** for that period and that amount.

(5) For **bad debts**, I will check that the **debt was old** and that the **resident had left**; also check that the Association tried to chase the customer and collect the money.

At the year end, any credit balances which exist may indicate overpayment by residents. I will also **look** for any **old balances** which may need to be written off. These bad debts should be checked by the chief executive to ensure that they are not a result of misappropriation by staff.

61 Matalas

Text references. Chapters 5, 10 and 15.

Top tips. This question deals with internal audit and controls in the petty cash system. The emphasis in this question is on your ability to apply your knowledge so you must read the scenario very carefully. Make sure that your answer is tailored specifically to the circumstances which are described.

You are asked to identify deficiencies in the petty cash system and to make recommendations to overcome each deficiency. A two-column format here would be useful. There are a number of different methods you can use to help you to identify deficiencies. As you read through the information try to think of the controls you would ideally want to see in a petty cash system. Do these controls exist in Matalas' system? Alternatively you might want to think of the different categories of control (eg authorisation, physical controls). Does the current system include these? Having identified the deficiency you should then be able to recommend a control to overcome the problem.

Examiner's comments. Candidates had to explain the deficiencies in the petty cash system and recommend a control to mitigate that deficiency. Some candidates failed to provide an adequate explanation of the points made. Others suggested deficiencies that were not mentioned in the scenario. Where recommendations were required, some candidates made suggestions that were completely impractical. It is therefore important for candidates to consider the type of client when thinking about ways to overcome deficiencies in systems.

Marks

2 marks for each control deficiency. 1 for explaining the deficiency and 1 for
control over that deficiency.
- Size of petty cash balance
- Security of petty cash box
- High value petty cash expenditure – individual items
- Authorisation of petty cash expenditure
- Counting of petty cash
- No review of petty cash vouchers – signing of imprest cheque
- Vouchers not pre-numbered
- Other relevant points

Maximum marks   <u>10</u>

Deficiency	Control
The amount of cash held in the petty cash box is high ($5,000) in comparison to the average monthly expenditure of ($1,538). This increases the risk that the cash will be stolen or that errors will be made in counting.	The amount of the petty cash balance at each branch should be reviewed. Based on an average monthly expense of $1,538, a balance of $2,000 would seem reasonable.
The petty cash box is not physically secure as it is kept on a bookcase in the accounts office. This increases the risk of theft.	The petty cash box should be kept in the branch safe or in a locked drawer in the accountant's desk.
Reimbursement for petty cash expenditure takes place without evidence of the expenditure being incurred eg receipt. This may result in false claims being made.	All petty cash claims should be supported by a receipt.
The petty cash vouchers are not authorised – they are only signed by the individual claiming reimbursement.	All petty cash vouchers should be authorised by the accounts clerk.
In some instances significant items are purchased through petty cash (up to $500). These are not authorised prior to the purchase being made. This could result in unnecessary expense being incurred.	Expenditure over a certain limit (eg $50) should be authorised in advance.
There is no indication that the vouchers are pre-numbered, meaning that the branch cannot confirm completeness of the vouchers. Unauthorised claims could be made and then blamed on missing vouchers.	Petty cash vouchers should be pre-numbered. On entry into the petty cash book the sequential numbering should be checked to ensure that all expenditure has been completely recorded.
There is a lack of segregation of duties. The petty cash is counted by the accounts clerk who is also responsible for the cash balance. There is no additional independent check on the petty cash balance.	The accountant should check the petty cash count to confirm the accuracy of the balance and ensure that the asset is safeguarded.
Whilst the accountant confirms that the cheque to reimburse petty cash agrees to the journal entry to the general ledger, the petty cash vouchers are not reviewed to support the amounts involved.	The petty cash vouchers should be reviewed by the accountant to confirm that the monthly petty cash expenditure agrees to the reimbursement cheque and journal entries.

62 Bluesberry

Text reference. Chapter 5.

Top tips. The most important thing is to understand the requirement. Don't be fazed by the fact you are asked for strengths instead of weaknesses or deficiencies. The scenario actually gives examples of problems that have been solved by certain procedures, so you should have recognised that these were strengths (for example the overtime scheme has seen reliance on expensive temporary staff reduced). As you were pulling out the strengths in the operating environment you could also have been considering the areas for improvement to help in answering part (b). In fact a good approach would have been to lay out your answer so that you could answer (a) and (b) together.

Examiner's comments. This question required identification and explanation of four strengths within the hospital's operating environment and a description of an improvement to provide best value for money for the hospital. Candidates performed well in the explanations of the strengths within Bluesberry with many scoring full marks. Where candidates failed to score well this was due to a failure to explain their strengths. The requirement was to "identify and explain", where a strength was identified then ½ mark was available, another 1 mark was available for a clear explanation of each strength. In addition, a significant minority misread the question requirement and identified weaknesses rather than strengths.

The second part of this question required improvements to the strengths identified. Performance on this question was adequate. The majority of candidates attempted this part of the question, and were able to identify a few relevant points. However answers were often too vague or unrealistic.

Marking scheme

		Marks
(a)	½ mark for identification and up to 1 mark for explanation of each well explained strength.	
	Internal audit department	
	Centralised buying department buys from lowest cost supplier	
	Authorisation of all purchase orders by purchasing director	
	Reduction in use of temporary staff	
	Employee clocking in cards to monitor hours worked	
	New surgical equipment leading to better recovery rates	
	Capital expenditure committee	6
(b)	Up to 1 mark per improvement.	4
		10

(a) Strength	(b) Improvement
The buying department researches the lowest price from suppliers before raising a purchase order. This helps with economy of the process, attaining resources at the lowest cost.	In order to also ensure the goods are of the required quality, an approved list of suppliers could be built up, with purchases only being permitted from those suppliers on the list.
Overtime rates have been increased and this has incentivised staff to fill staffing gaps. As a result the hospital has saved money by decreasing the level of expensive temporary staff. Additionally, the permanent staff may be more effective as they are familiar with the hospitals systems and the level of patient care expected at Bluesberry.	The increased hours will affect overall efficiency given that the same staff are now carrying out extended shifts, as overtime rates are higher than basic rates, even though overtime cost appears to be lower than temporary staff.

There is also an increased risk of mistakes due to tiredness which could have adverse effects on the reputation of the hospital. Ideally the hospital should recruit enough permanent staff of the required level to fill shifts without then working overtime. |

(a) Strength	(b) Improvement
The hospital has implemented time card clocking in to ensure employees are only paid for those hours worked. It also provides a means for recording hours worked which is valuable management information. Before this there would have been no definitive record of actual hours worked.	The system appears to allow payable overtime to accumulate simply because an employee clocks out late, even if there is no staff gap to fill. The system should be set to automatically clock out after the normal number of shift hours. Staff will then need to clock back in for their overtime if they have an authorised shift. Overtime hours each month should be reviewed by the department head for consistency with agreed extra shifts.
A capital expenditure committee of senior managers has been set up to authorise significant capital expenditure items. This will help prevent cash out flows for unnecessary assets, or assets not budgeted for.	In a hospital there will be very expensive equipment purchases, such as the recently acquired new surgical equipment. It is better that these are authorised at board level rather than by senior managers. An authorisation policy should be drawn up setting out the different levels of authorisation needed (the highest being at board level) depending on the amount of expenditure for capital items.

Top tips. You were only asked for four strengths and related improvements. Others you may have come up with in place of those given in the answer above are:

(a) Strength	(b) Improvement
The hospital has an internal audit department monitoring the internal control environment and advising on value for money.	The remit of internal audit could be extended to advising on implementation.
Orders are authorised by a purchasing director to help ensure expenditure incurred is necessary expenditure.	The volume of forms (200 per day) will no doubt take valuable time away from the director which could be used on more pressing matters. Orders below a certain monetary level should be authorised by the next level (down) of management. Orders over the specified monetary value should still be reserved for purchase director authorisation.
New surgical equipment purchased has improved the rate of operations and patient recovery rates. This is an improvement in the effectiveness of the hospital.	The equipment is not used as efficiently as it could be due to lack of trained medical staff. The hospital should look at providing targeted training for existing medical staff and look to recruit staff that have the appropriate skills.

63 Chuck

Text references. Chapters 6, 10 and 16.

Top tips. You should notice you are given the deficiency and need to explain the implications and suggest recommendations. Therefore a two column tabular approach will be appropriate, one column for implications and one for recommendations. You will find that if you properly explain the implication the deficiency itself will be evident. There is no need to describe the deficiency – no marks are available for the deficiencies, although you could have listed them briefly as headings to help structure your answer. The marks are awarded for implications and recommendations, not identification of the deficiencies already given.

Examiner's comments. The scenario contained an abundance of deficiencies and so on the whole candidates were able to easily identify enough points. A small minority of candidates provided implications and recommendations for general deficiencies which were not specified within the scenario; these points would not have gained credit as the question requirement clearly stated that points needed to be raised for the deficiencies identified in the scenario. A significant proportion of candidates wasted time by writing out the deficiencies from the scenario; there were no marks available for deficiencies, only for the implications and recommendations.

Marks

Up to 1 mark per well explained implication and up to 1 mark for each well
explained recommendation

Multiple employees can be clocked in

Weaker control environment

Unauthorised overtime hours

Payroll system errors not identified

Night shift wages susceptible to risk of theft

Factory supervisor not independent

Absent night shift employees' pay not secure over weekend

Joiners/leavers notified on timely basis

<u>10</u>

Chuck Industries – payroll system implications and recommendations

Implication	Recommendation
Lack of monitoring of clocking in:	
The lack of monitoring of the clocking in/out process allows other employees to clock in colleagues resulting in a payroll cost in excess of that expected for the actual hours worked.	Clocking in and out should be monitored by a supervisor of an appropriate level.
The lack of supervision over clocking in and out also gives employees the opportunity to delay clocking out (or to clock in before starting work) to increase their overtime, leading to invalid payroll costs being incurred.	Payment of overtime hours should only be made on authorisation by a supervisor who has reviewed the overtime hours for reasonableness and compared them to production volumes and observed working patterns.
The absence of clocking in/out monitoring may result in a weak control environment as it promotes an attitude where it is acceptable to override controls.	Formal communications should be made on the importance and purpose of the company's policies and procedures in relation to clocking in and out, and the importance of adhering to company controls in general.
Payroll calculations not reviewed:	
Since payroll calculations are not checked and the system is entirely trusted, any errors made as a result of standing or underlying data being incorrect or occurring during payroll processing would not be discovered. Overpayments or underpayments (and incorrect payroll costs) may result and lead to losses or disgruntled employees.	A payroll supervisor should periodically recalculate the net pay based on the gross pay and expected deductions, then compare the result with the computer generated figures for a sample of employees. The review should be evidenced by a signature and wages should not be paid until this signed review is completed.
Factory supervisor distribution of wages:	
The factory supervisor is trusted with substantial cash sums in advance of distribution of wages to the night shift. This cash is susceptible to theft and loss while not with employees or securely stored.	Payroll officials should be available for certain hours during the night shift to distribute wages.
The factory supervisor keeps absent employee's wages over the weekend before handing back to payroll and this further increases the risk of loss or theft of cash wages.	Any amounts not paid out on Fridays should be kept by payroll in a safe or other secure means until Monday when the employee can collect from Payroll.

Implication	Recommendation
The supervisor entrusted with the wages is not independent and may take it upon him/herself to reallocate the wages as he/she deems necessary.	The supervisor should not be responsible for distribution of cash wages. Payroll should distribute these and should consider the proposal of operating for at least part of the night shift.
Poor communication of joiners/leavers:	
The lack of procedures in place to ensure timely notification of joiners/leavers means leavers may still be paid in error and joiners may not be paid on time. The payroll records will not reflect accurate wages costs at least temporarily.	HR staff duties and responsibilities should be reallocated when staff are ill or on holiday, including the responsibility of immediate communication of new joiners/leavers to payroll. In addition new joiner forms showing start date should be completed and authorised and passed to payroll so they are aware of the need to update the payroll records.

(**Note:** Only five well explained implications and five related recommendations were needed to gain full marks.)

64 Rhapsody

Text references. Chapters 3 and 10.

Top tips. Part (a) of this question is on deficiencies in the sales system and you should find it reasonably straightforward. You've been asked to set out four deficiencies so work on the basis that there are three marks available for each deficiency, implication and recommendation, plus a further two marks overall for your presentation. Setting out your answer to this part in a tabular format would be sensible since this enables you to link deficiencies, implications and recommendations easily. When making recommendations, bear in mind your knowledge of the client from the question scenario so that your recommendations are pertinent and sensible – think about what you would recommend if you were working in the internal audit department of this company for real.

Easy marks. Easy marks are available in part (b) of this question on the advantages of audit committees. However, you should also be able to score two easy marks in part (a) as you are told in the requirement that two marks are available for presentation – don't throw these away by preparing a poorly presented answer.

Examiner's comments. The overall standard of answers to part (a) was satisfactory. Common errors included:

*   Not obtaining the format marks
*   Including deficiencies not included in the scenario
*   Not linking the deficiency, its effect and a recommendation
*   Writing too much. A sentence or two for each deficiency, effect and recommendation was sufficient

In part (b) many candidates provided between four and six points with appropriate explanation. Common errors included:

*   Not explaining the point made. For example, stating 'better communication' without explaining why this was an advantage
*   Providing a lengthy introduction explaining the role of non-executive directors and audit committees

Marks

(a) Content of report – 1 mark each for
 Identifying deficiency
 Effect of deficiency
 Recommendation to remove deficiency
 Recording of orders   3
 Control over orders and packing lists   3
 Obtaining payment   3
 Completeness of orders   3
 No check on goods in inventory when ordered   3
 Two part packing slip insufficient   3
 Sales invoice not sent to customer   3
 Inventory only updated on dispatch   3
 Other relevant points   3
 Maximum marks   15
 Format of answer – appropriate headings   1
 Format of answer – report format   1
                                                                          2
 Maximum marks this section   17

Marks

(b) 1 mark per relevant point
 Independent reporting   1
 Help internal audit implement changes   1
 Shareholder/public confidence   1
 Directors' obligations   1
 Communication external auditors   1
 Independence external auditor   1
 Other relevant points (each)   1
 Maximum marks this section   3
                                                                         20

(a) **Report**

 To: Audit committee, Rhapsody
 From: Internal audit department
 Subject: Deficiencies in the sales system, Seeds Division
 Date: Today

 The deficiencies we found from our work on the sales system, the implications of those deficiencies and possible recommendations to mitigate them are set out below.

(i) Deficiency	(ii) Implication	(iii) Recommendation
Orders placed on the internet are manually transferred onto the inventory control and sales system.	Errors could be made when this transfer is made, resulting in incorrect inventory figures and the wrong orders being sent to customers, resulting ultimately in loss of customers and goodwill.	The systems should be integrated so that once the order is placed, it automatically updates the inventory and sales systems.

(i) Deficiency	(ii) Implication	(iii) Recommendation
A random code is generated for each order, which is based on the name of the employee inputting the details, the date and the products ordered.	There is no easy way to track orders because the coding system is random so any queries may take a long time to resolve and orders not yet dispatched will be difficult to monitor.	If the systems are automated, the computer should generate a numerical code automatically once the order is placed and this will mean orders can be monitored more easily.
Customers' credit cards are charged after dispatch of the order has taken place, rather than when they place the order.	If payments are rejected, then the company will lose out on sales income, resulting in increased levels of bad debts and falling profit margins.	The credit card should be charged as soon as the customer has placed the order over the internet. This will reduce the level of bad debt and ensure payment is received before the goods are sent out.
There is no control in place to monitor orders that have not been dispatched or those that remain uninvoiced.	Outstanding orders will result in queries from customers and ultimately result in loss of these customers and a loss in income.	Orders should be monitored on a regular, weekly basis to identify any that have not been dispatched so that queries can be dealt with on a timely basis.
The packing lists are only two-part rather than three. The only packing list retained internally is with accounts and no record is kept at the warehouse.	If accounts misplace this copy there is no physical record of documentation sent to the customer in case of dispute. This may lead to financial loss.	A three-part packing list should be used with a copy also retained at the warehouse.
There is no confirmation that goods are in inventory at time of ordering nor a check on condition of goods dispatched (eg torn seed packets).	Goods of sufficient quality may not be dispatched on a timely basis to customers. This could lead to customer refunds.	Inventory checks should be carried out to ensure the correct goods of a sufficient quality are dispatched.

(**Note:** Only five deficiencies, implications and recommendations were needed to gain full marks.)

(b)   **Advantages of an audit committee**

- They can improve the **quality** of financial reporting by reviewing the financial statements on behalf of the Board of Directors.

- They have the potential to create a **climate of discipline and control** which may reduce the opportunity for fraud occurring within the company.

- They allow non-executive directors to contribute an **independent judgement** and play a positive role in the organisation.

- They assist the Finance Director by providing a **forum** in which he can raise issues of concern.

- They strengthen the position of the external auditor by providing a **channel of communication** and a forum for issues of concern.

- They strengthen the position of internal audit by providing a greater degree of **independence** from management.

- They may **increase public confidence** in the credibility and objectivity of the financial statements.

65 Fitta

Marking scheme

		Marks
(a)	Objectives in the payroll system	
	Correct employees paid	2
	Paid the correct amount	2
	Ensure the deductions calculated correctly	2
	Correct accounting for the cost and deductions	2
	No fraud or error	2
	Maximum 2 points for each objective must be adequately explained	10
(b)	1 mark per sensible correction of a deficiency identified in section (i)	
	Restricted to a maximum	10
		20

(a) and (b)   Objectives and improvements

(a)	(b)
Objective: To ensure the right employees are paid.	
Achieved?	**Improvements**
Amounts are paid directly into bank accounts via direct transfer, and this eliminates any cash mishandling problems.	Mr Grimshaw should perform the transmission of data by using a password known only to him and the review should cover the areas mentioned.
The autopay list is reviewed before transmission although it is not clear what for.	
Unusual amounts, employees, duplicate sort codes may not be identified.	
Mr Grimshaw reviews the list before Michelle transmits the details to the bank. This gives Michelle the opportunity to change the details before transmission.	Mr Grimshaw should also receive the printout from the bank, review to ensure accuracy of transmission, initial the form as evidence of review and then pass to Michelle for filing.

(a)	(b)
Objective: To ensure only genuine employees are paid and are paid correctly for all work done.	
Achieved?	**Improvements**
Michelle reviews the timesheets for completeness which should ensure they are all received.	
Michelle ensures that the appropriate supervisor has authorised the hours worked.	
However, she then enters the details and is the only one to verify that the hours have been entered correctly. This could result in errors of numbers of hours processed.	An independent review using total hours and sample of employees should be performed after input to the system. Batch control totals may be sued to ensure completeness and accuracy of input.
Michelle does not appear to perform any review for reasonableness of the timesheets to ensure number of hours claimed are feasible.	A review of all timesheets independent of supervisors should be performed to ensure reasonableness of hours claimed.
	Total number of hours of overtime claimed should be reviewed for reasonableness.
	Reconciliation of basic hours claimed should be performed each week by an independent person (from Michelle and supervisor).
Objective: To ensure that net pay and deductions are calculated correctly.	
Achieved?	**Improvements**
Amendments to be made to personnel records are detailed on a standard form by supervisors.	Amendment forms should be pre-numbered and breaks in the sequence should be investigated promptly.
There does not seem to be any verification of completeness or accuracy of processing.	Printout obtained by Michelle should be reviewed by employee or supervisor or accountant as appropriate to check accuracy.
Michelle appears to have access to standing data and can therefore make unauthorised changes.	Master file changes should be made only by Mr Grimshaw who should periodically check sample of payslips for details back to source documentation.
Objective: To ensure that accounting for cost and deductions is accurate in the financial statement and in returns sent to the taxation authority.	
Achieved?	**Improvements**
Cumulative details are stored on disc in a safe ensuring that returns can be filed even if data is last from the system.	Storage of the CDs could be more secure off-site (eg bank deposit box).
Mrs Duckworth reviews the monthly figures for tax and should identify any obvious errors.	The review could be more thorough and encompass all deductions with calculations of estimated costs and monthly reviews performed to identify fluctuations.
Objective: To ensure duties are adequately segregated.	
Achieved?	**Improvements**
There is very little segregation of duties with Michelle performing most tasks.	More appropriate segregation has been noted above but generally more use of other personnel staff would achieve this objective.

66 Greystone

Marking scheme

	Marks

(a) Up to 1 mark per well explained deficiency, up to 1 mark per implication and up to 1 mark per recommendation. If not well explained ½ mark for each.
2 marks for presentation, 1 for address and intro, 1 for conclusion
Purchasing manager orders goods without consulting store
Purchase order reviewed in aggregate by purchasing director
Store managers re-order goods
No inter-branch transfer system
Deliveries accepted without proper checks
Sales assistants produce the goods received note
Goods received but not checked to purchase orders
Manual matching of goods received notes to invoice
Purchase invoice logged late   17

(b) Up to 1 mark per well explained point
Cash controls testing
Mystery shopper
Financial/operational controls
Fraud investigations
IT systems review
Value for money review
Regulatory compliance   3
                                                                                                        ––
                                                                                                        20
                                                                                                        ══

(a)

ABC & Co
Certified Accountants
29 High Street

The Board of Directors
Greystone Co
15 Low Street

8 December 20X0

Members of the board,

Financial statements for the year ended 30 September 20X0

We set out in this letter deficiencies in the purchases system which arose as a result of our review of the accounting systems and procedures operated by your company during our recent audit. The matters dealt with in this letter came to our notice during the conduct of our normal audit procedures which are designed primarily for the purpose of expressing our opinion on the financial statements.

Determination of inventory levels

(i)   *Deficiency*
      The purchasing manager determines store inventory levels without consulting those who are best place to judge the local market; the store or sales managers.

(ii) *Implication*
      Certain clothes and accessories may be initially over-ordered and may need to be sold at reduced prices. This may also result in overvalued inventory (if held at cost) in the management accounts and ultimately the financial statements. Also some inventory may not be ordered in enough volume to meet demand and the reputation of Greystone may suffer.

(iii) *Recommendation*
      The purchasing manager should consult (in a meeting or by conference call) the store managers and a joint decision should be made on the initial inventory levels to be ordered for clothes/accessories.

Re-ordering

(i)   *Deficiency*
      Store managers are responsible for re-ordering through the purchases manager and it can take four weeks for goods to be received.

(ii) *Implication*
      The reliance is on Store managers to be proactive and order four weeks before a potential stock out. Without prompting they may order too late and inventory may run out for a period of up to four weeks, resulting in lost revenue.

(iii) *Recommendation*
      Realistic re-order levels should be established in the inventory system. When inventory is down to the pre-determined level, the purchasing manager should be prompted to raise a purchase order (for example the system may generate an automatic re-order request which is e-mailed to the purchasing manager).

Internal ordering

(i)   *Deficiency*
      Stores can not transfer goods between each other to meet demand. Customers are directed to try other stores/the website when an item of clothing is sold out.

(ii) *Implication*
      Revenue is lost because the system is inconvenient for the customer, who may not follow up at other stores, but may have purchased if the goods were transferred to their local store. Additionally the perceived lack of customer service may damage the store's reputation.

(iii) *Recommendation*

An internal ordering system should be set up which allows for the transfer of goods between stores. In particular, stores with very low inventory levels should be able to obtain excess inventories from those with high levels to meet demand while goods are re-ordered.

Checking of goods received

(i) *Deficiency*

Goods received are not checked against purchase orders.

(ii) *Implication*

Goods which were not ordered in the first place could be received. Once received, it may be difficult to return these goods and they may need to be paid for. In any case there is a potential unnecessary administrative cost. Additionally, some goods ordered may not be received leading to insufficient inventory levels and potential lost revenue.

(iii) *Recommendation*

A copy of authorised orders should be kept at the relevant store and checked against GRNs. If all details are correct, the order should be marked completed and sent to head office. The purchasing clerk should review the purchase orders at regular intervals for incomplete items and investigate why these are not completed.

Review of purchase orders

(i) *Deficiency*

The purchase orders reviewed and authorised by the purchasing director are aggregated by region.

(ii) *Implication*

The lack of detail does not allow the purchasing director to make an informed assessment of the buying policies and they may be unsuitable for specific markets within regions.

(iii) *Recommendation*

A country by country review of orders should be carried out by the purchasing director. Where appropriate, discussions should take place between the purchasing director and local purchasing managers before authorisation of orders.

This letter has been produced for the sole use of your company. It must not be disclosed to a third party, or quoted or referred to, without our written consent. No responsibility is assumed by us to any other person.

We should like to take this opportunity of thanking your staff for their co-operation and assistance during the course of our audit.

Yours faithfully

ABC & Co

Top tips. The answer to (a) includes four well explained deficiencies, implications and recommendations as four were needed to gain 12 marks. Together with the 2 marks available for presentation, this would be enough for the full 14 marks.

Please note however, there were a number of alternative deficiencies/implications/recommendations you may have identified, including those shown in the table below.

(i) Deficiency	(ii) Implication	(iii) Recommendation
Quality of goods is not checked by sales assistants, only quantity.	Poor quality clothes are accepted and may not be saleable (also inventory may be temporarily overvalued).	Goods should be checked on arrival for quantity and quality prior to acceptance.
Purchase invoices and GRNs are manually matched, which is time	The manual process of such a high volume of documents is prone to human error. Invalid	A purchasing system should be adopted which allows for logging of GRNs against original invoices, and then electronic/automatic matching of

(i) Deficiency	(ii) Implication	(iii) Recommendation
consuming.	invoices may be processed as a result.	invoices against GRNs. A regular review by the purchasing clerk should then be focused on unmatched items.
A purchase invoice is not put on the system until it is ready for authorisation by the purchasing director	The purchase ledger will not have all invoices posted, understating liabilities. Also payables may be paid late.	Invoices not matched should be filed separately, as should those not posted. These should be reviewed at period ends and accrued for to ensure completeness of payables.

(b) **Additional assignments for internal audit**

Testing of controls over cash

Retail stores have a significant amount of cash at each shop and need robust controls over the cash receipts process. Internal audit could test the design and operation of these controls at each store on a periodic basis. They could also conduct cash counts at the same time they carry out inventory counts.

Fraud investigations

A retailer such as Greystone with large sums of cash and desirable, easily moveable, inventory is more susceptible to fraud than many other businesses. Internal audit assignments may therefore include reviewing the fraud risk areas and suggesting controls to mitigate these risks. Where fraud is uncovered, internal audit could also investigate these instances of fraud.

Value for money review

Internal audit could undertake value for money audits examine the economy, efficiency and effectiveness of activities and systems, such as the just in time ordering system recently introduced.

Overall review of financial/operational controls

Internal audit could undertake reviews of central controls at head office, making recommendations to management over, for example the sales, purchases and payroll systems.

Review of information technology (IT) systems

Greystone may have complex computer systems linking tills in the stores to head office. If internal audit has an IT specialist, they could be asked to perform a review over the computer controls for this system or other computer systems.

Compliance with laws and regulations

Like all businesses, Greystone will be subject to law and regulation, which will vary depending on the part of the world a store is operating in. The internal audit department could review compliance with these laws and regulations.

> **Top tips.** Six other assignments were needed for full marks. An alternative you may have come up with is the assignment of an internal auditor to test the customer experience in stores by posing as a customer. The level of perceived customer satisfaction is then fed back to each shop to improve customer service and form the basis for any further training that is required.

67 Blake

Marking scheme

		Marks
(a)	Management letter – 1 mark for each deficiency, 1 for each possible effect and 1 for each recommendation = 3 marks × 4 sets of points = 12 marks	
	Logging in process not monitored	
	Overtime not authorised	
	Poor password control (cat's name)	
	Transfer total wages not checked	
	Employees leaving details sent on e-mail	
	Other valid points	
	5 points × 3 marks each =	15
	Letter format	1
	Introduction and conclusion to letter	1
	Maximum marks	**17**
(b)	1 mark for each valid procedure	
	Total salary cost	
	Average salary	
	List of payments each month	
	Other valid points	
	Maximum marks	**3**
	Total marks	**20**

(a)   **Wages system management letter**

ABC & Co
Certified Accountants
29 High Street

The Board of Directors
Blake Co.
10 Low Street

December 20X8

Members of the board,

Deficiencies in internal control

We set out in this letter deficiencies in the wages system which arose as a result of our review of the accounting systems and procedures operated by your company during our recent audit. The matters dealt with in this letter came to our notice during the conduct of our normal audit procedures which are designed primarily for the purpose of expressing our opinion on the financial statements.

(i) Deficiency	(ii) Consequence of deficiency	(iii) Recommendation
Shift workers can log in and out just by using their electronic identification cards.	Workers can be paid even if they are not working because the time recording system logs them in and out when their cards are scanned and they are paid from and to this time.	The shift manager should agree the number of workers with the computer records at the start and end of the shift.
Overtime is not authorised appropriately or monitored.	Workers could be paid at overtime rates when they are not actually working and could collude with the shift foreman for extra overtime without actually working it.	All requests for overtime must be authorised by the shift manager. Overtime costs should also be monitored regularly.
The code word for the time recording system is generally known within the department.	Unauthorised individuals could log onto the system and enter extra hours so that they are paid more than they should be. Fictitious employees could also be set up on the system.	The code word should be changed immediately to one containing random letters and numbers. The system should be set up so that the code word has to be changed on a regular basis, such as every six weeks.
Payments into workers' bank accounts are made by one member of accounts staff, without any authorisation.	Unauthorised payments into workers' and fictitious bank accounts could be made.	The payroll should be authorised by the Finance Director or another senior manager prior to payments being made.
Review of wages payments is done every few weeks by the financial accountant, seemingly on an ad hoc basis.	There is no regular monitoring of wages by senior management.	The Finance Director should review payroll costs on a weekly basis so that he can assess whether they are reasonable and any unusual amounts can be investigated.

This letter has been produced for the sole use of your company. It must not be disclosed to a third party, or quoted or referred to, without our written consent. No responsibility is assumed by us to any other person.

We should like to take this opportunity of thanking your staff for their co-operation and assistance during the course of our audit.

Yours faithfully

ABC & Co

(b)   **Substantive analytical procedures**

(i)   Perform a proof in total of the salaries charge for the year using the prior year charge and increasing it for the pay increase and taking account of any starters or leavers in the period.

The figures should be comparable with the exception of the salary increase and any starters or leavers in the year.

(ii)   Perform a comparison of the annual charge to the prior year and to the budgeted figure. Where the variance is significant, investigate further to ascertain why.

The figures should be comparable with the exception of the salary increase of 3%.

(iii)   Review monthly salaries month by month.

The figures should be about the same each month, except for July and November when the pay rise and annual bonus were paid respectively. Any starters or leavers would also be reflected in the relevant month.

68 Tinkerbell

Text references. Chapters 9, 10 and14.

Top tips. Read the examiner's comments below carefully in relation to part (a). You must be able to differentiate between a test of control and a substantive procedure or you risk losing a high proportion of marks on some questions. A test of control must provide evidence that a control is operating effectively (or otherwise).
Parts (b) and (d) were relatively straightforward and you should have been able to come up with enough procedures to gain the majority of marks. You should use the scenario to help you to generate tests, for example identifying procedures in relation to the discounts offered to large customers.
Part (c) could be answered in a tabular format to help address both mini requirements – (1) identify and explain controls, (2) describe how the risk of fraud is mitigated. The description of the 'teeming and lading' fraud uncovered in the year pointed out the current lack of controls, so this could form the basis of your controls which should fill the gap. For example customer statements were not sent out and this is one of the reasons the fraud was not uncovered before, so making sure that they are sent out in the future is a valid control.

Easy marks. These are available in parts (b) and (d) where you are asked for substantive procedures in relation to receivables and revenue.

Examiner's comments. In part (a) most candidates performed inadequately. The main problems encountered were that candidates struggled to differentiate between tests of control and substantive tests and hence often provided long lists of substantive procedures, which scored no marks. In addition a significant minority of candidates did not read the question carefully, and instead of providing tests of controls, gave control procedures management should adopt. The approach candidates should have taken was to firstly identify from the scenario the controls present for Tinkerbell, they then should have considered how these controls could be confirmed by the auditor. In addition candidates' explanations of tests were vague such as; "check that credit limits are set for all new customers." This procedure does not explain how the auditor would actually confirm that the control for new customer credit limits operates effectively. Tests that start with "check" are unlikely to score many marks as they do not explain how the auditor would actually check the control. Future candidates should practice generating tests; both substantive and tests of controls, which do not start with the word "check".

The second part of this requirement was to explain the objective of the test of control provided. Again, this was not answered well. A common answer was to state that the objective was "to ensure that the control is operating effectively." This was far too vague. Instead, candidates should have considered the aim of the specific control being tested. Therefore the objective of a test over credit limits is "to ensure that orders are not accepted for poor credit risks".

As noted in previous examiner's reports candidates are often confused with the differences between tests of controls and substantive tests. Candidates must ensure that they understand when tests of controls are required and when substantive procedures are needed. They need to learn the difference between them and should practice questions requiring the generation of both types of procedures. A significant number of candidates presented their answers in a columnar format and this seemed to help them to produce concise and relevant answers.

Part (b) required substantive procedures the auditor should perform on year-end receivables. This was answered well by many candidates. Candidates were able to provide variety in their procedures including both tests of detail and analytical review tests.

The most common mistakes made by some candidates were providing tests of control rather than substantive procedures, providing substantive procedures for revenue rather than receivables and describing the process for a receivables circularisation at length (this was not part of the question requirement.)

Part (c) required identification and explanation of controls that Tinkerbell should adopt to reduce the risk of fraud occurring again, as well as an explanation of how this control would mitigate the fraud risk. This question was answered well by most candidates, with some scoring full marks.

The scenario provided details of a "teeming and lading fraud" which had occurred during the year and candidates needed to think practically about how Tinkerbell could reduce the risk of this occurring again. However, candidates' performance on the second requirement to describe how the control would mitigate the risk of fraud occurring again was mixed.

The main problem was that answers were not specific enough, frequently vague answers such as "this will reduce the risk of fraud and error occurring" were given.

Part (d) required substantive procedures the auditor should perform on Tinkerbell's revenue. This requirement was not answered well. Some candidates confused this requirement with that of 1b, which required receivables tests, and so provided the same tests from 1b again. In addition a significant number of candidates provided procedures to confirm bank and cash rather than revenue.

Those candidates who performed well were able to provide a good mixture of analytical procedures such as, "compare revenue to prior year or to budget" and "review monthly sales against prior year" and also detailed tests such as confirming cut-off of sales.

Marking scheme

Marks

(a) Up to 1 mark per well explained point and up to 1 mark for each objective
     Process order for fictitious order
     Sales order over credit limit
     Inspect credit applications
     Agree prices used to relevant price list
     Confirm discounts used on invoices agree to customer master file
     Attempt to process a discount for a small customer
     Inspect orders to confirm order acceptance generated
     Observe sales order clerk processing orders to see if acceptance generated
     Observe goods dispatch process
     Agree goods dispatch notes (GDN) to invoices
     Sequence checks over invoices
     Maximum marks   10

(b) Up to 1 mark per well explained procedure
     Trade receivables circularisation, follow up any non-replies
     Review the after date cash receipts
     Calculate average receivable days
     Reconciliation of sales ledger control account
     Cut-off testing of GDN

Aged receivables report to identify any slow moving balances
Review customer correspondence to assess whether there are any invoices in dispute
Review board minutes
Review post year-end credit notes
Review for any credit balances
Agree to GDN and sales order to ensure existence
Maximum marks 3

(c) Up to 1 mark per well explained control and up to 1 mark for how it mitigates risk
Relatives not permitted to work in the same department
Cash receipts processed by two members of staff
Monthly customer statements sent
Bank reconciliations reviewed by responsible official
Rotation of duties within finance department
Sales ledger control account reconciliation regularly performed
Consider establishing an internal audit department
Maximum marks 4

(d) Up to 1 mark per well explained procedure
Analytical review over revenue compared to budget and prior year
Analytical review of major categories of toy sales compared to prior year
Gross margin review
Recalculate discounts allowed for larger customers
Recalculate sales tax
Follow order to goods dispatched note to sales invoice to sales ledger
Sales cut-off
Review post year-end credit notes $\underline{3}$
Total marks $\underline{20}$

(a) **Tinkerbell – Tests of control and test objectives for the sales cycle**

Test of control	Test objective
Enter an order for a fictitious customer account number and ensure the system does not accept it.	To ensure that orders are only accepted and processed for valid customers.
Inspect a sample of processed credit applications from the credit agency and ensure the same credit limit appears in the sales system.	To ensure that goods are only supplied to customers with acceptable credit ratings.
For a sample of invoices, agree that current prices have been used by comparing them with prices shown on the current price list.	To ensure that goods are only sold at authorised prices.
For a sample of invoices showing discounts, agree the discount terms back to the customer master file information.	To ensure that sales discounts are only provided to those customers the sales director has authorised.
For a sample of orders ensure that an order acceptance email or letter was generated.	To ensure that all orders are recorded completely and accurately.

Top tips. Five tests of controls and five objectives such as those shown above were enough to gain the 10 marks available. However, other valid tests and objectives you may have come with are shown below.

Test of control	Test objective
Visit a warehouse and observe whether all goods are double checked against the GDN and dispatch list before sending out.	To ensure that goods are dispatched correctly to customers and are of an adequate quality.
With the client's permission, attempt to enter a sales order which will take a customer over the agreed credit limit and ensure the order is rejected as expected.	To ensure that goods are not supplied to poor credit risks.
Attempt to process an order with a sales discount for a customer not normally entitled to discounts to assess the application controls.	To ensure that sales discounts are only provided to valid customers.
Observe the sales order clerk processing orders and look for proof that the order acceptance is automatically generated (eg e-mail in sent folder)	To ensure that all orders are recorded completely and accurately.
Inspect a sample of GDNs and agree that a valid sales invoice has been correctly raised.	To ensure that all goods dispatched are correctly invoiced.
Review the latest report from the computer sequence check of sales invoices for omissions and establish the action taken in respect of any omissions found.	To ensure completeness of income for goods dispatched.

(b) **Substantive procedures to confirm Tinkerbell's year-end receivables balance**

- Circularise trade receivables for a representative sample of the year-end balances. If authorised by Tinkerbell's management, send an e-mail or reminder letter to follow up non-responses.

- Review cash receipts after the year-end in respect of pre year-end receivable balances to establish if anything is still outstanding. Where amounts are unpaid investigate whether an allowance is needed.

- Review the reconciliation of the receivables ledger control account (sales ledger control account) to the list of receivables (sales ledger) balances and investigate unusual reconciling items.

> **Top tips**. Three substantive procedures like the ones shown above were enough to gain the 3 marks available. However other valid procedures you may have come with are shown below.

- Review the aged receivables report to identify any old balances and discuss the probability of recovery with the credit controller to assess the need for an allowance.

- Calculate average receivable days and compare this to prior year and expectations, investigating any significant differences.

- Select a sample of goods dispatched notes just before and just after the year end ensure the related invoices are recorded in the correct accounting period.

- Review a sample of credit notes raised after the year end to identify any that relate to pre year-end transactions and confirm that they have not been included in receivables.

- Review the aged receivables ledger for any credit balances and inquire of management whether these should be reclassified as payables.

- For slow moving/aged balances, review customer correspondence files to assess whether there are any invoices in dispute which require an allowance.

- Review board minutes to assess whether there are any material disputed receivables.

- Select a sample of year-end receivable balances and agree back to a valid GDN and sales order to ensure existence.

(c) **Controls to reduce the risk of fraud re-occurring and explanation of how the risk is mitigated**

Control	Explanation of how risk is mitigated by control
Related members of staff should not be allowed to work in the same department where they can seek to override segregation of duty controls.	The risk of related staff colluding and being able to commit a fraud without easily being discovered will be reduced.
Customer statements should be sent out each month to all customers. The receivables ledger supervisor should check that all customers have been sent statements.	Customers receiving statements may notice anomalies in the allocation of payments (either timing or amount) and may alert the company of these anomalies. This may draw attention to the sort of fraud that occurred at Tinkerbell (known as 'teeming and lading').

Top tips. Two controls such as those shown above along with two explanations were enough to gain the 4 marks available. However other valid controls and explanations are given below.

Control	Explanation of how risk is mitigated by control
Bank reconciliations should be reviewed regularly by an appropriate level of management who is not involved in its preparation. Unreconciled amounts should be investigated and resolved at the time of review.	Any compensating material balances netted off to a small difference on the bank reconciliation will be discovered quickly, increasing the probability of uncovering fraud on a timely basis.
Two members of staff should process cash receipts.	This would mean another collusion would be necessary (on top of the one that has already occurred) to steal cash receipts. This therefore reduces the risk of re-occurrence.
Staff within the finance department should rotate duties on a regular basis.	Rotation will act as a deterrent to fraud. This is because staff will be less likely to commit fraudulent activities due to an increased risk of the next person to be rotated to their position uncovering any wrongdoing.
The receivables ledger should be reconciled to the receivables ledger control account on at least a monthly basis. The reconciliation should be reviewed by a responsible official and anomalies investigated.	This will increase the chance of discovering errors in the receivable balances and help to create a strong control environment likely to deter fraud.
Management should consider establishing an internal audit department to assess and monitor the effectiveness of controls, identify any deficiencies, and carry out specific fraud investigations.	The presence of an internal audit department would help to deter employees committing fraud and identification of fraud would be more likely due to ongoing monitoring of internal controls.

(d) **Substantive procedures to confirm Tinkerbell's revenue**

- Compare the total revenue with that reported in previous years and the revenue budgeted, and investigate any significant fluctuations.

- For a sample of customer orders, trace the details to the related dispatch notes and sales invoices and ensure there is a sale recorded in respect of each (to test the completeness of revenue).

- For a sample of sales invoices for larger customers, recalculate the discounts allowed to ensure that these are accurate.

- Select a sample of dispatch notes in the month immediately before and month immediately after the year end. Trace these through to the related sales invoices and resultant accounting entries to ensure each sale was recorded in the appropriate period.

- Obtain an analysis of sales by major categories of toys manufactured and compare this to the prior year breakdown and discuss any unusual movements with management.

- Calculate the gross profit margin for Tinkerbell for the year and compare this to the previous year and expectations. Investigate any significant fluctuations.

- Recalculate the sales tax for a sample of invoices and ensure that the sales tax has been correctly applied to the sales invoice.

- Select a sample of credit notes issued after the year end and trace these through to the related sales invoices to ensure sales returns were recorded in the proper period.

69 Pear

Text references. Chapters 1, 5, 9, 10 and 12.

Top tips. This case-study style question tests a range of issues including controls, substantive procedures, assurance and internal audit.

Part (a) asks you to identify and explain control deficiencies in a scenario, recommend a control to address each deficiency and finally to describe a test of control which would be performed by the auditor. The most logical approach to this requirement is to use a three column format. Work through the information systematically identifying each deficiency as you read through the information. In this question the deficiencies are fairly clearly indicated. Make sure your answer explains the deficiency ie the effect of the weakness identified, rather than simply repeating the information in the question. Control suggestions should be relevant to the deficiency and should be clearly explained. Try to describe what should actually take place (ie who does what and when) rather than what the control is trying to achieve. Tests of controls are a bit trickier. Think about how the control works and what the auditor would need to do to prove that the control is operating effectively.

Part (b) requires a description of substantive procedures that would be performed on plant and equipment additions and disposals. Try to avoid simply listing out all the substantive procedures you can think of that apply to plant and equipment. Ensure that your procedures take into account the specific nature of additions and disposals. Also note that you are asked to 'describe' the procedure so check that your answer is sufficiently detailed and precise.

Examiner's comments. Most candidates performed well on part (a) of the question. They were able to confidently identify five deficiencies from the scenario. However, many candidates did not address the question requirement fully as they did not 'identify and explain'. Candidates identified, but did not go on to explain why this was a deficiency. The requirement to provide controls was generally well answered, but the requirement to provide tests of control was not. Many candidates simply repeated their controls and added "to check that" or "to make sure". These are not tests of control.

Performance was mixed on part (b) of the question. There were two available marks for addition tests and two marks for disposal tests. Candidates who scored well often did so by providing a number of tests for each area, each test was average and so scored ½ mark each and so they managed to attain full marks in this way. However, some candidates provided detailed procedures and so achieved the 1 mark available per test. This is better utilisation of time. The requirement verb was to 'describe' therefore sufficient detail was required to score 1 mark per test. Candidates are reminded that substantive procedures are a core topic area and they must be able to produce relevant detailed procedures. Many tests given were just too brief.

Marks

(a)   Up to 1 mark per deficiency, up to 1 mark per well explained control and up to 1
       mark for each well explained test of control, max of 5 for deficiencies, max of 5
       for controls and max of 5 for tests of control.
       Website not integrated into inventory system
       Customer signatures
       Unfulfilled sales orders
       Customer credit limits
       Sales discounts
       Supplier statement reconciliations
       Purchase ledger master file
       Surplus plant and equipment
       Authorisation of capital expenditure   15

(b)   Up to 1 mark per substantive procedure, max of 2 for additions and max of 2
       for disposals.

       Additions
       Cast list of additions and agree to non-current asset register
       Vouch cost to recent supplier invoice
       Agree addition to a supplier invoice in the name of Pear to confirm rights and
       obligations
       Review additions and confirm capital expenditure items rather than repairs and
       maintenance
       Review board minutes to ensure authorised by the board
       Physically verify them on the factory floor to confirm existence

       Disposals
       Cast list of disposals and agree removed from non-current asset register
       Vouch sale proceeds to supporting documentation such as sundry sales
       invoices
       Recalculate the profit/loss on disposal   5
                                                                                      ──
                                                                                      20

(a)   **Internal controls**

(i) Deficiency	(ii) Control	(iii) Test of control
As the website is not integrated with the inventory system inventory levels are not checked before an order is accepted. This means that orders may be accepted when goods are not in inventory resulting in delay in delivery. This could lead to loss of customer goodwill and/or loss of sales.	The website and the inventory system should be integrated so that inventory levels are checked before the order is processed. For items which are not in inventory customers should be given an indication of how long the delay will be.	Test data should be input into the order system via the website for items which are both in inventory and out of inventory. Only orders for items in inventory should be processed. Those out of inventory should be indicated as such.

(i) Deficiency	(ii) Control	(iii) Test of control
Local couriers do not always obtain proof of receipt of goods from customers. Customers could claim that they have not received the goods when in fact they have and Pear may have to dispatch the goods again.	Pear should bring the matter to the attention of the courier companies and remind them of the importance of obtaining a customer signature on delivery of the goods. Pear could refuse to pay for any deliveries which are made without a signature.	A sample of dispatches made by the courier companies should be taken. These should be matched to goods dispatched notes returned by the couriers and reviewed for evidence of a signature.
Sales orders are not always fulfilled promptly. This may harm the reputation of the company and result in lost sales.	When goods are dispatched the sales order and dispatch note should be matched as evidence that the order has been fulfilled. Unmatched orders should be flagged by the system after a predetermined period eg one week. A report of unmatched items should be reviewed by a supervisor and outstanding items followed up.	For a sample of orders which are not on the unmatched item report agree to the dispatch note and verify that the date of delivery is within the time limit set by the company. Review the report of unmatched items to assess whether there is still a significant delay. Discuss the report with the supervisor and obtain an explanation as to why sales orders are still outstanding.
Credit limits are set by the sales ledger clerks. The sales ledger clerks are unlikely to be senior enough to make this type of decision. Also as more than one clerk is involved inconsistent decisions may be taken. If limits are too high this may lead to irrecoverable debts. If limits are too low sales may be lost as a result.	Credit limits should be set by the sales ledger department supervisor or manager, or another suitably senior member of staff.	The credit limits of a sample of new customers should be looked at to ensure that they are within the guidelines set and that they have been authorised by the relevant senior member of staff.
Sales discounts are determined by individual members of the sales team. This increases the risk that inappropriately high discounts may be given by the sales staff in order to achieve a sale. Profits would be reduced as a result.	A standard discount policy should be put in place by the sales director to be implemented by the sales staff. This should be reviewed on a regular basis. Any discounts in excess of these amounts should be authorised by the sales manager or sales director.	The discount policy document should be reviewed to confirm that it has been drawn up by the sales director and is regularly assessed. A sample of sales should be selected and any discounts given should be agreed to the discount policy. Where the discount exceeds the set limit evidence of authorisation by an appropriate member of staff should be inspected.

(i) Deficiency	(ii) Control	(iii) Test of control
Supplier statement reconciliations are not performed. This may mean that there are errors in the purchases and payables accounts which are not identified.	Supplier statement reconciliations should be performed on a monthly basis. Any major discrepancies should be reviewed by a senior member of staff.	Review the reconciliations to ensure that they are being performed on a monthly basis and that significant issues are being followed up by a senior member of staff.
The purchase ledger master file can be changed by the purchase ledger clerks. This increases the risk of error as master file information may be updated incorrectly. It also increases the risk of fraud as fictitious suppliers could be created and bogus payments made.	Only the supervisor should be able to change standing data on the master file. Hierarchical passwords should be used allowing clerks to access the master file but not to change the data. A report of changes to standing data on the master file should be produced on a monthly basis and reviewed by a senior staff member eg the purchasing manager. This review should be evidenced by signature.	Attempts should be made to change standing data on the master file using the hierarchical passwords. Only passwords with the appropriate authority should allow the data to be changed. The report of changes to the master file should be inspected for evidence of review by a suitable senior member of staff.
Pear has surplus plant and equipment. This indicates an inefficient use of company resources. For example these items could be sold and cash reinvested.	A capital expenditure plan needs to be developed by senior management which details not only the requirements for new plant and machinery but also details plans for the disposal of old or surplus items. The factory manager should perform a documented review of the plant and equipment held by Pear on a regular basis (eg quarterly) to identify old or surplus items.	Select a sample of capital expenditure forms and verify that the details comply with management policy. Inspect the plant and equipment review document and follow through the treatment of old or surplus items.
Purchase requisitions for new equipment are authorised by production supervisors. Production supervisors are not senior enough to authorise major items of capital expenditure. The company may be committed to the purchase of capital items not required.	Capital expenditure limits should be set so that major items of capital expenditure are authorised by the board. Production supervisors should only be able to authorise the purchase of low value items. Capital expenditure authorised by production supervisors should be reviewed on a regular basis by senior management.	Obtain a sample of capital expenditure forms and ensure that authorisation has been made by staff of an appropriate level based on the limits set.

(**Note:** Only five deficiencies were required to achieve full marks)

(b) **Substantive procedures**

(i) **Additions**

- Cast the list of additions and agree the details to the non-current assets register to ensure that additions have been completely recorded

- For significant additions review the board minutes to ensure that the purchase has been authorised

- For a sample of additions physically inspect the asset to confirm existence

- For a sample of additions agree the cost of the asset to the purchase invoice to confirm their value

- For a sample of additions verify that the purchase invoice is made out in the name of Pear International to confirm rights and obligations

- Review the nature of additions to confirm that revenue expenditure has not been capitalised in error.

(ii) **Disposals**

- Cast the list of disposals and agree the details to the non-current assets register

- For a sample of disposals agree the sale proceeds to supporting documentation and trace receipt of payment to the cash book and bank statements

- Recalculate profits or losses on disposal and confirm that they have been correctly recorded

- For major disposals inspect the board minutes for authorisation of the sale

70 DinZee

Text references. Chapters 10 and 13.

Top tips. This 20 mark question is split into three parts so it is very important that you spend the appropriate amount of time on each part – don't get bogged down on one part and then find out that you do not have enough time to answer the other parts of the question.

In part (a) you must read the requirement carefully. Notice you are asked to specify the procedures you would perform **prior to** attending the inventory count, **not during** the count.

Part (b) asks you to identify deficiencies in the control system for counting inventory, to explain the deficiency and to recommend improvements. Make sure that your answer addresses all three requirements. A tabular format is a particularly useful way of presenting your answer.

Part (c) tests you knowledge of the difference between a test of control and a substantive procedure and then requires you to apply this knowledge. You should find this relatively straightforward.

Easy marks. Overall you should feel that you can tackle this question with confidence. Easy marks can be found in part (a) and part (b) provided you have a good understanding of the inventory count. You should also feel that you can score good marks in part (c).

Examiner's comments. Part (a) was an audit procedures prior to attending an inventory count. The key issue here was the requirement for procedures to undertake **prior** to the count – no marks were awarded for listing procedures relevant to actually attending the inventory count. Other weaknesses included not stating the procedure in sufficient detail or writing too much when the requirement was to 'list'.

Part (b) was generally well answered, although the main issues were not linking weaknesses (deficiencies) to explanations/recommendations and providing impractical solutions.

Part (c) was answered very poorly by a significant number of candidates, demonstrating a worrying lack of knowledge about substantive procedures and tests of controls. This is an important area which needs to be addressed.

Marks

(a) **Audit procedures prior to inventory count attendance**
1 mark for each procedure
Procedures
- Review prior year working papers for problems
- Contact client
- Book audit staff to attend the inventory counts
- Obtain copy of inventory count instructions from client
- Ascertain whether any inventory is held by third parties
- Obtain last year's inventory count memo
- Prepare audit programme for the count
- Other relevant points

Maximum marks 2

(b) **Deficiencies in counting inventory**
1 for each deficiency, 1 for explaining the reason for the deficiency and 1 for
stating how to overcome deficiency. 3 max therefore per deficiency.
Deficiencies
- Inventory sheets stating the quantity of items expected to be found in the store
- Count staff all drawn from the stores
- Count teams allowed to decide which areas to count
- Count sheets not signed by the staff carrying out the count
- Inventory not marked to indicate it has been counted
- Recording information on the count sheets in pencil
- Count sheets for inventory not on the pre-numbered count sheets where only
  numbered when used
- Other relevant points

Maximum marks 15

(c) 1 mark for explaining the aims of a test of control and a substantive procedure
1 mark each for:
Explaining test of control relevant to inventory count
Explaining substantive procedure relevant to inventory count

Maximum marks 3
___
20

(a) Audit procedures performed prior to attending the inventory count

   (i)   Review prior year working papers and obtain an understanding of the nature and volume of inventory.

   (ii)   Obtain a copy of the inventory count instructions prepared by the client and discuss any significant issues arising from these with the client.

Top tips. The answer only required two procedures, however, the following additional points could have been made:

- Assess the implications of the locations at which the inventory is held eg inventory held by third parties.
- Book the necessary audit staff to attend the count.
- Review internal control relating to inventory in order to identify potential problem areas eg cut-off
- Perform analytical procedures and discuss with management any significant changes in inventory
- Obtain last year's inventory count memo
- Prepare the audit programme for the count
- Consider the need for expert assistance

(b)

(i) Deficiency	(ii) Effect	(ii) Recommendation
The count sheets show the amount of inventory currently recorded on the perpetual inventory records.	This may encourage the counters to try to match the figure provided rather than to carry out the count as an independent exercise.	The count sheets should not show the perpetual inventory records balance. The count staff should record the number of items they have physically counted.
All count staff are drawn from the inventory warehouse.	These staff are not independent of the count. It would be possible for the counters to disguise errors or to cover up theft of inventory.	Count teams should consist of staff from other departments.
The teams are allowed to choose which inventory they count within each area of stores.	This lack of detailed organisation may lead to certain inventory items being counted more than once whilst some items may not be counted at all.	Each team of counters should be given specific instructions regarding which area of the stores they are responsible for.
There is no system for marking items which have been counted.	Again this increases the risk that inventory will be double counted or omitted completely.	All inventory should be marked systematically to indicate that it has been counted eg by the use of stickers.
Information on the count sheets is recorded in pencil.	This increases the risk that the information could be amended after the count without authorisation, resulting in inventory being incorrectly stated.	Results of all counts on the count sheets should be recorded in ink.
Additional count sheets are not pre-numbered.	The pre-numbering of the count sheets allows control over the completeness of the information. If the staff using the separate sheets do not number them as they are used there is no means of identifying that all sheets issued have been returned. Lost count sheets may then go unnoticed.	All count sheets should be pre-numbered before they are issued.
Count sheets are not signed by the count teams.	It may be difficult to identify who is responsible for the count of specific items if subsequent questions arise. The signature also encourages the counters to take responsibility for the counting they have performed.	All count sheets should be signed by the members of the count team.

(c)   (i)   The aim of a test of control is to demonstrate that a control exists and operates effectively in preventing, or detecting and correcting material misstatements.

The aim of a substantive procedure is to detect material misstatements at the assertion level in the financial statements.

(ii)   Test of control: Observation of the count teams to ensure that they are conducting the count in accordance with the inventory count instructions.

Substantive procedure: Identify and record details of damaged items of inventory to ensure that this is taken into account in the final valuation of inventory.

71 Multiple choice answers

1   D   There are two types of substantive procedure: tests of details of transactions, account balances and disclosures and analytical procedures. Analytical procedures can be used throughout the audit including as an analytical procedure.

2   A   Liabilities and income would be tested for understatement.

3   A $(160/420) \times 365$

4   A   As set out in ISA 530 *Audit sampling*.

5   B   Where the sample has not provided the auditor with a reasonable basis for forming an audit conclusion the auditor must tailor the nature, timing and extent of further procedures to achieve the required assurance. In this case further tests of control and/or substantive procedures would be appropriate.

6   D   Computer-assisted audit techniques cannot replace the skill of judgement used by the auditor.

7   C   A, B and D relate to activities which would use test data. Test data is used for tests of controls.

8   A   Audit software assists with substantive procedures, while test data assists with tests of control.

9   C   An auditor's expert may be an internal or an external expert. In addition to assessing the competence of the expert the auditor must consider their capabilities and competence, obtain an understanding of their field of expertise and evaluate the adequacy of their work before concluding on the extent to which they can rely on any audit evidence provided.

10 A   In accordance with ISA *610 Using the work of internal auditors* the external auditor is prohibited from using the work of internal audit in this situation as the risks to the quality of the evidence provided are too great.

11 A   This is a requirement of ISA 610 *Using the work of internal auditors*.

12 B   The vehicle registration document records the details of the legal registered owner of the vehicle.

13 A   If the inventory listing does not include the items test counted by the auditor at the inventory count this indicates that the final inventory figure is not complete.

14 C   Management are responsible for organising the inventory count, not the auditor. If the results of the auditor's test counts are not satisfactory the auditor can request that inventory is recounted but cannot insist. However, if management refuse the auditor's request the auditor will need to consider the implications of this on the audit opinion.

15 B   As the goods have been received and included in inventory the liability for the goods must be recognised at the period end. As a purchase invoice has not been received and the invoice amount has not been accrued for liabilities are understated. Inventory is unaffected.

16 D   Responses must be sent directly to the auditor. Under the positive method the customer confirms the accuracy of the balance or details the extent to which there is a disagreement.

17 C   If supplier statements do not agree with the payables ledger balance any discrepancies will be investigated and any understatement identified. A and B provide evidence that liabilities recognised are valid. D provides evidence of the accuracy of recording of liabilities.

18 A   In accordance with ISA 501 *Audit evidence – specific considerations for selected items*.

19 B   The registrar provides an external source of evidence.

20 C   If the paying-in slips show that the remittances have been paid in to the bank after the year end a cut-off error has been made and cash at bank is overstated. This could be a sign of window-dressing.

21 A   Numerical controls over collection boxes allow the charity to identify whether any boxes are missing. Sealing of the boxes at the end of each shift prevents cash being removed before it is counted. Matching of paying-in slips to bank statements provides evidence of accuracy but not necessarily completeness.

22	A	This is referred to as a type 1 report.
23	A	For the test to provide evidence of existence the sample should be selected from the asset register ie the auditor would be looking to confirm that all assets recorded on the register exist. Rights and obligations (ownership) would be tested by reference to purchase/legal documentation. Accuracy and valuation relates to presentation and disclosure.
24	B	Confirmation would be sought from the bank regarding the existence of bank balances.
25	B	This is defined in ISA 315.
26	A	Sufficiency is the measure of quantity.
27	C	Inspecting supporting documentation tests whether a transaction has occurred.
28	B	The verification of trade receivables by direct confirmation provides evidence of existence and rights and obligations. It does not provide evidence of valuation. If a debtor confirms the amount due, this does not necessarily mean that they will pay the balance.

72 Expert

Text references. Chapters 11 and 12.

Top tips. Part (a) draws on your accounting knowledge relating to non-current assets. You need to apply IAS 16 to the information in the scenario to highlight the audit issues arising.

Part (b) is largely a knowledge based requirement.

Easy marks. Using your knowledge of IAS 16 would have helped you generate points in part (a). Also in part (b) you may have used the mnemonic SODIT to give you ideas.

Marking scheme

		Marks
(a)	Audit issues arising from revaluation and non-depreciation Up to 1 mark per point to a maximum of	7
(b)	1 mark for each factor Professional qualification Experience and reputation Objectivity Other valid points	
	Maximum marks	<u>3</u>
	Total marks	<u><u>10</u></u>

(a)   **Audit issues arising**

(i)   *Revaluation of shop*

IAS 16 *Property, Plant and Equipment* permits non-current assets to be revalued. However, if an item of property, plant and equipment is revalued, the **entire class of property**, plant and equipment to which that asset belongs must be revalued.

Truse Co are therefore entitled to revalue the shop, but they will also need to revalue all of the shops to comply with IAS 16.

The intended treatment to only revalue one shop is not compliant and the auditor will need to ask management to revise their proposed treatment, explaining the reason for the request. If management refuses, the auditor will need to assess the implications for their report when they undertake the audit.

If management agrees to revalue all properties, the reliability and basis of the valuation will need to be determined. IAS 16 states that valuations of property are normally undertaken by professionally qualified valuer. The auditor will need to assess whether or not this is the case.

The revaluation will result in the creation of a revaluation surplus and various related disclosures are required by IAS 16. The auditor will have to review the disclosures in order to assess whether they are complete and reasonable.

The change also constitutes a change in accounting policy, and the auditors will need to consider the adequacy of the disclosures made in respect of this.

(ii) *Non-depreciation of shop*

Under IAS 16 all non-current assets used by the entity should be depreciated, even if the fair value is in excess of the carrying amount. Depreciation is the systematic allocation of the depreciable amount of an asset over its useful life. As the building has a useful life it should be depreciated.

Repair and maintenance of an asset does not negate the need to depreciate it, so management's argument that the shop building does not need to be depreciated because it is maintained to a high standard is not a valid one.

This means the depreciation charged is likely to be misstated and the auditor will need to assess the materiality of that misstatement.

The auditor will also need to look at the adequacy of any disclosures required relating to the change in depreciation method.

(b) **Factors to consider when assessing competence and objectivity of an auditor's expert**

The auditor should consider whether the expert is certified or licensed by an appropriate professional body or has membership of such a professional body.

The auditor should also consider the expert's experience and reputation in the field in which he is seeking audit evidence.

Finally the auditor should consider whether the expert is employed by the audited entity or is related in some other way such as by being financially dependent on the entity or having investments in it. Such relationships would impair the expert's objectivity.

73 Audit techniques

(a) **Statistical sampling** is any approach to sampling that involves random selection of a sample, and the use of probability theory to evaluate sample results, including measurement of sampling risk.

Non-statistical sampling is where the auditor does not use statistical methods and draws a judgemental opinion about the population.

Sample selection methods include the following:

(i) **Random selection** ensures that all items in the population have an equal chance of selection. It often involves selection of a sample with the use of random number tables or random number generators.

(ii) **Systematic selection** involves selecting items using a constant interval between selections, the first interval having a random start.

(iii) **Haphazard selection** may be an alternative to random selection provided auditors are satisfied that the sample is representative of the entire population. It is selection of a sample without following any particular structured technique and requires care to guard against making a selection which is biased.

(iv) **Block selection** may be used to check whether certain items have particular characteristics. For example an auditor may use a sample of 50 consecutive cheques to test whether cheques are signed by authorised signatories rather than picking 50 single cheques throughout the year.

(b)   Where an error is identified in a sample, the auditor will:

- Record the error on their schedule of uncorrected misstatements

- Investigate the reason for the error and determine whether it is an anomalous (one-off) error or a recurrent one.

- Extrapolate the non-anomalous errors and determine the projected error for the population as a whole.

Where sampling is being used to perform tests of controls the auditor will compare the error rate to the level of tolerable error (tolerable error rate).

Where sampling is being used to perform substantive testing the monetary value of the error will be extrapolated and compared to the monetary value of tolerable error.

74 Evidence and assertions

Text reference. Chapter 8.

Top tips. In (a), remember that only factors affecting sufficiency and reliability are needed. Do not be tempted to write about relevance. In part (b) you are only required to explain four assertions so don't waste time listing more than that.

Easy marks. This is a knowledge based question and if you are familiar with the two relevant ISAs, you should obtain the majority or all of the marks here.

Examiner's comments. In part (b) most candidates provided four valid points; however, there was significant confusion regarding which assertions related to classes of transactions even though study material clearly makes that distinction.

Marking scheme

Marks

(a)   Up to 1 mark per properly explained factor up to a maximum of 6.
Sufficient:
Risk assessment
Nature of accounting and internal control systems
Materiality
Experience of previous audits
Results of audit procedures
Reliability:
Independent source
Effective controls
Evidence obtained directly by auditor
Written evidence
Original documents
Maximum marks   6

(b)   1 mark per properly explained assertion.
- Occurrence
- Completeness
- Accuracy
- Cut-off
- Classification
Maximum marks   4
                                                                                                                      ──
                                                                                                                      10

(a) The sufficiency of audit evidence relates to the quantity of evidence required by the auditor.

The sufficiency of audit evidence is influenced by:

- The **risk assessment** of the audit – a high risk audit will require more evidence to be gathered.

- The **materiality** of the item – a material item will require more audit evidence.

- The **results of audit procedures** – where results of audit procedures are consistent with each other and assess the auditor's initial expectations then less additional audit evidence is required.

The reliability of audit evidence is influenced by the source of the audit evidence.

- Audit evidence from **external sources** is more reliable than that obtained from the entity's records because it is from an independent source.

- Evidence obtained **directly by auditors** is more reliable than that obtained indirectly.

- Evidence in the form of **documents (paper or electronic)** or **written representations** are more reliable than oral representations, since oral representations can be retracted.

(b) **Assertions**

Assertions from ISA *315 Identifying and assessing the risks of material misstatement through understanding the entity and its environment* relating to classes of transactions and events include:

Occurrence: transactions and events that have been recorded have actually occurred and pertain to the entity.

Completeness: all transactions and events that should have been recorded have been recorded.

Accuracy: amounts and other data relating to recorded transactions and events have been recorded appropriately.

Cut-off: transactions and events have been recorded in the correct accounting period.

Tutorial note. Classification is another assertion that could have been listed and explained relating the recording of transactions.

75 External confirmations

(a) Positive circularisations require a response, whatever the response may be whereas negative circularisations only require a response from the customer if he disagrees with the balance stated as outstanding on the circularisation letter. The negative method is used less frequently and only when internal controls within the audited entity are considered to be strong.

There are two types of positive circularisation. The first is where the amount is stated on the letter and the customer is asked whether he agrees or disagrees with this amount. If he disagrees, he is asked to give reasons. This has the disadvantage that the customer might just agree to the balance without checking or agree because it is less than what is actually owed. The advantage is that disagreements might bring other matters to the auditor's attention such as faulty inventory or pricing issues.

The second method is where the customer is asked to confirm the amount owed. This method is likely to result in fewer responses because more effort is required to obtain the balance.

(b) External confirmations can be used for the following:

- Bank balances and other information from bankers
- Inventory held by third parties
- Property title deeds held by lawyers for safe custody or as security
- Investments purchased from stockbrokers but not delivered at the year-end date
- Loans from lenders
- Accounts payable balances

(c)   The bank confirmation letter could ask for the following information:

- Balances due to or from the client on current, deposit, loan and other accounts
- Any nil balances on accounts
- Accounts closed during the period
- Maturity and interest terms on loans and overdrafts
- Unused facilities
- Lines of credit/standby facilities
- Any offset or other rights or encumbrances
- Details of any collateral given or received
- Contingent liabilities
- Confirmation of securities and other items in safe custody

(**Note:** Only six were required.)

76 Accounting estimates

Text references. Chapters 11 and 14.

Top tips. To answer this question you need a good knowledge of ISA 540 *Audit of accounting estimates, including fair value accounting estimates, and related disclosures*. To score well in this type of question you need to identify the key issues. In this case you are dealing with balances which are estimates made by management. The focus of your audit work will therefore be to establish how management estimated the figure, and then to determine how reasonable this is.

Easy marks. The easier marks were available in (a) for explaining the auditor's approach in relation to accounting estimates.

(a)   **Approaches to gaining audit evidence re estimates**

The auditor will need to review and perform procedures on the process used by management to arrive at the accounting estimate.

The auditor can also develop an auditor's point estimate for comparison with management's point estimate, and investigate further if the two are significantly different.

The auditor should also review subsequent events which provide evidence on the accuracy of the estimate made.

(b)   **Specific allowance for potentially irrecoverable debts**

(i)   Obtain a list of the doubtful debts that are deemed potentially irrecoverable.

(ii)   Cast the list to ensure it has been correctly totalled and agree the total to the general ledger balance for the allowance.

(iii)   Discuss these debts with the credit controller to ascertain why these are considered to be potentially irrecoverable.

(iv)   Review the correspondence with the customer to ascertain whether the customer intends to pay or not.

(v)   If there is no correspondence, consider why. If the client has not chased the debt, it suggests that they expect to receive the money.

(vi)   Review cash receipts after the year end date to ensure that the amount is still outstanding by inspecting bank statements and remittance advices.

(vii)   Scrutinise lists of companies going into receivership up to the date of signing to ensure none of them are customers of the company.

(viii) Ask the company solicitors whether they have started legal proceedings against any receivables against which allowances have been made.

(ix)   If they have, review correspondence with solicitor or inquire of solicitor the likelihood of the debt being recovered.

(x) Ascertain whether the customer is 'on stop'. If not, enquire why the company is still trading with the customer. It may be because the debt is not really doubtful.

(xi) Scrutinise board minutes since the end of the reporting period to ascertain whether any subsequent events require the provision to be changed.

(xii) Review credit notes issued since the end of the reporting period and consider if any of them mean that the provision should be changed.

(xiii) Ensure that the allowance has been scrutinised and authorised by the directors by inspecting the relevant documentation.

(xiv) Taking all evidence into account, estimate a reasonable allowance (auditor's point estimate) and compare with management's allowance.

77 Porthos

Text reference. Chapter 11.

Top tips. The important thing here is to read the question and apply your knowledge to the requirements.

The other thing to remember here is that you can get a long way with common sense. You may not have much audit experience but the chances are that you have ordered goods (not necessarily tennis racquets!) over the internet. In part (b) you should think about what you'd expect to happen when you do that. Once you have thought about it in this way it should be much easier to think what sort of test data the auditor could use to test the system.

Easy marks. This was a fairly tough question but a basic knowledge of CAATs would help you get started on part (a).

Examiner's comments. The standard of answers to this question varied considerably. Part (a) was answered very well. In part (b), areas of weakness included confusing test data and audit software and relating answers to the scenario.

Marking scheme

		Marks
(a)	**Advantages of CAATS – 1 mark each**	
	Test program controls	1
	Test more items quickly	1
	Test actual records	1
	Cost effective after initial setup	1
	Supplement traditional testing	1
	Other relevant points	1
	Maximum marks	4
(b)	**Examples of test data ½ for test and ½ for explanation**	
	Negative quantities	1
	High quantities	1
	Lack of payment details	1
	Invalid inventory code	1
	Invalid credit card details	1
	Invalid address	1
	Other relevant points	1
	Maximum marks	6
		10

Advantages of Computer-Assisted Audit Techniques (CAATs)

Time savings

Potentially time-consuming procedures such as checking casts of ledgers can be carried out much more quickly using CAATs.

Reduction in risk

Larger samples can be tested, giving greater confidence that material errors have not been missed.

Testing programmed controls

Without CAATs many controls within computerised systems cannot be tested, as they may not produce any documentary evidence. This gives greater flexibility of approach.

Cost effective

Many CAATs have low set-up costs, such as where information is downloaded from the client's system onto the auditor's copy of the same system. Even where CAATs have had to be written specially for a particular audit, the on-going costs will be minimal as they can be reused until the client changes its systems.

(b)

Test data	Reason
Order for unusually high quantities, eg 20 racquets	This would identify whether any reject controls requiring special authorisation for large orders are effective. This control would also prompt the customer to recheck the quantity if they had accidentally keyed in the wrong quantity.
Orders with fields left blank	This would give evidence as to whether orders could be accepted that prove impossible to deliver because, for example, the name of the town has been omitted from the delivery address.
Orders with invalid credit card details	This will identify whether the controls over the ordering system will protect the company from losses arising from credit card frauds.
Orders with details of customers on retailers' 'blacklists' or of cards that have been reported as stolen	This will identify whether the company has effective procedures to ensure that their system is regularly updated for security. This should reduce the risk of bad debts.
Order with invalid inventory code	This will show whether the system will alert the customer to the code error and prompt them to check it. This should ensure that the correct goods are dispatched.
Order with complete and valid details	This order should be accepted by the system so will allow the auditor to inspect the order confirmation to determine whether the order details are transferred accurately into the dispatch system.

78 Newthorpe

Text references. Chapters 12, 13 and 16.

Top tips. This is a relatively difficult question for 10 marks. Note that you should have verified the completeness of the client's schedules, a test that would not be necessary here for inventory in (b) because of the satisfactory results of the inventory counting. You should have considered separately in inventory and non-current assets that had been sold, and inventory and non-current assets that had not been sold.

(a) *Plant and equipment*

(1) Perform a reconciliation of the **non-current assets register** with the **accounting records** to help confirm it is complete.

(2) Select a sample of **non-current assets** in the non-current asset register to agree to the **client's schedule** to ensure that the client's schedule is **complete.**

(3) For items that are shown as sold, **agree** the **value** of the **sales proceeds** to **supporting documentation,** confirming that title has been transferred, the sales price and date of completion. Confirm payment to the cash book.

(4) For items that have yet to be sold **obtain evidence** of likely **sales prices** and **review correspondence** with possible buyers to assess likelihood of items being sold. Sales/scrap values are likely to be low. Any expensive, specialised machinery may be hard to sell. **Use trade press** to **verify sales/scrap values** considering age, condition etc.

(5) Review costs of disposal and consider whether any **costs of disposal** will be **significant** (will the assets have to be moved piece-by-piece, or are transportation costs significant).

(b) *Inventories*

(1) **Agree** the **selling prices** of **inventories sold since the year-end** to **sales invoices** and the **cash book.** If a number of different items have been sold at the same time, review the basis of allocation of sales proceeds and consider if it appears to be reasonable.

(2) **Assess** the **reasonableness** of **management's point estimates** of realisable value of inventories that has not yet been sold by **reviewing sales before** the **year-end, comparing** the **values** with **inventories** that has been **sold since** the year-end and considering **offers** made which have not yet been finalised.

(3) For unsold inventories, **assess** reasonableness of **provisions for selling expenses** by comparison of selling expenses with inventories sold.

(4) **Review** the **records of inventory counting** for any items noted as **damaged, obsolete** or **slow-moving** and confirm that the realisable value of these items is appropriate (in most cases it is likely to be zero).

(5) **Discuss** with management any **significant disagreements** in estimates of net realisable value, and how inventory where there is little recent evidence of sales value was valued.

(c) *Redundancy costs*

(1) For **employees** appearing on the **payroll** when the factory was shut, make sure they either **appear** on the **schedule** of **redundancy payments** or on the **payroll** of **another factory**.

(2) Examine pre-closure payrolls to ensure that **employees** who appear on the **schedule of redundancy payments** were actually **employed** by the **factory** that has **shut**.

(3) Re-perform the **redundancy pay** calculations to make sure they are correct and ensure employees have received their **statutory** or **contractual** entitlement.

(4) **Verify** that the **figures used** in the **calculation** of **redundancy pay** are **correct**. For employees whose redundancy package is based on service and salary, **agree** details of **service** to **personnel records** and **final salary** to the **last payroll.** For employees whose redundancy payment is based on their service contract, confirm details to service contract.

(5) **Agree payments on the schedule of redundancy payments** to **cash book** to confirm that payments have been made as indicated on the schedule.

(6) For **redundancy payments** that are **in dispute**, **review correspondence** and **obtain legal advice** about the likely outcome.

79 Analytical procedures and bank confirmations

Marking scheme

		Marks
(a)	**Analytical procedures**	
	1 mark for each valid, well explained point	
	(i) – Obtain information, on client situation	
	– Evaluation financial information	
	(ii) – Comparison prior periods	
	– Comparison actual/anticipated results	
	– Comparison industry information	
	– Specific procedures for individual account balances (eg receivables)	
	– Ratio analysis eg GP% year on year	
	– Proof in total eg total wages = employee × average wage	
	(iii) – Risk assessment procedures	
	– Substantive procedures	
	– End of analytical procedures	
	Maximum marks	7
(b)	**Bank letter**	
	1 mark for each audit procedure	
	– Evaluate need for letter	
	– Prepare bank letter – standard form	
	– Client permission	
	– Refer to standing authority at bank	
	– Letter direct to bank	
	Maximum marks	3
		10

(a) **Analytical procedures**

(i) Analytical procedures consist of the analysis of significant ratios and trends including the resulting investigations of fluctuations and relationships that are inconsistent with other relevant information or which deviate from predictable amounts.

(ii) Types of analytical procedures

- The consideration of comparisons with similar information for prior periods, anticipated results of the client from budgets or forecasts, predictions prepared by the auditor, and industry information

- Analytical procedures between elements of financial information that are expected to conform to a predicted pattern based on the client's experience, such as the relationship of gross profit to sales

- Analytical procedures between financial information and relevant non-financial information, such as the relationship of payroll costs to the number of employees

(iii)   Use of analytical procedures

Analytical procedures can be used at all stages of the audit, and must be used at:

- The planning stage in accordance with ISA 315 *Identifying and assessing the risks of material misstatement through understanding the entity and its environment;* and

- The final review stage in accordance with ISA 520 *Analytical procedures.*

During the audit planning stage, analytical procedures are used as a risk assessment procedure to obtain an understanding of the entity and its environment and to help determine the nature, timing and extent of audit procedures.

Analytical procedures can be used as substantive audit procedures during audit fieldwork when their use can be more effective or efficient than tests of details in reducing the risk of material misstatement at the assertion level to an acceptably low level.

Analytical procedures must be used at the final review stage of the audit where they assist the auditor in forming an overall conclusion as to whether the accounts are consistent with his understanding of the entity.

(b)   **Bank confirmation letter**

- The client must give the bank explicit written authority to disclose the information requested to the auditor.

- The request letter should be written on the audit firm's headed paper.

- The auditor's request must refer to the client's letter of authority and the date of that authority.

- The request letter should reach the branch manager of the bank at least a month in advance of the client's year-end and should state that year-end and the previous year-end.

- The letter should state that the information should be sent directly to the auditor.

80 Zak

Text references. Chapters 11 and 15.

Top tips. It is not enough to simply calculate a few numbers without explaining them – there are ten marks available here so make sure that where you identify significant fluctuations, you can provide reasonable explanations for them.

Easy marks. You ought to be able to perform a few relevant calculations to gain some marks but remember to try and support them with some pertinent explanations.

Examiner's comments. This question was not answered well due to lack of well-explained points and some basic calculations, as well as answers lacking structure and providing too much detail on the cash and bank balances which was not required.

Marks

Risks – statement of profit or loss

½ mark, for identifying unusual changes in statement of profit or loss.

Award up to 1 more mark. Total 1½ marks per point.

- Net profit
- Revenue
- Cost of sales
- Gross profit
- Administration
- Selling and distribution
- Interest payable
- Interest receivable (must be linked to the change in bank balance)

Maximum marks   **10**

Zak Co

Revenue

Although the directors have indicated that the company has had a difficult year, revenue has increased from the previous year by 18%. The auditors need to establish the reason for this increase as it does not correlate with the directors' comments.

Cost of sales

Cost of sales has fallen by 17% in comparison to the previous year – this is strange given that revenue has increased, as one would expect cost of sales to similarly increase. The reason for this decrease needs to be ascertained. It could be as a result of closing inventory being undervalued.

Gross profit

Gross profit has increased dramatically by 88% in comparison to the previous year. The reason for this needs to be examined, given that revenue has increased but cost of sales has decreased.

Administration costs

Administration costs have fallen slightly by 6%. This appears unusual given that revenue has increased from the previous year, as one would expect the increased revenue to lead to increased administration costs. Expenditure in this area may be understated perhaps as a result of incorrect cut-off being applied.

Selling and distribution costs

Selling and distribution costs have increased significantly by 42%. An increase is expected given that revenue has also increased, however the increase is not comparable. There may have been a misallocation between administration and selling and distribution costs – again this will need to be investigated thoroughly.

Interest payable

It is surprising that Zak has a reasonable cash surplus this year but still continues to pay a similar level of interest. The interest payable may be overstated and the reasons for interest payments not decreasing despite the absence of the large overdrawn balance seen last year must be established. One explanation for this might be a cash injection immediately prior to the year end.

81 Perpetual inventory system

Text reference. Chapter 13.

Top tips. This question deals with the year-end inventory count and cut-off procedures, a frequently-examined topic. You should know the audit procedures required in respect of perpetual inventory counting systems.

(a) **Importance of cut-off in the audit of inventory**

Cut-off is a key issue in the audit of inventory. All purchases, transfers and sales of inventory must be recorded in the correct accounting period as inventory can be a material figure for many companies, particularly those engaged in manufacturing.

The points of purchase and receipt of goods and services are particularly important in order to ensure that cut-off has been correctly applied. The transfer of completed work-in-progress to finished goods is also important as is the sale and dispatch of such goods.

Incorrect cut-off can result in misstatements in the financial statements at the year-end and this can be of particular concern where inventory is material. Auditors therefore need to consider whether the management of the entity being audited have implemented adequate cut-off procedures to ensure that movements into and out of inventory are properly identified and reflected in the accounting records and ultimately in the financial statements.

(b) **Perpetual inventory counting systems**

Perpetual inventory counting systems are where an entity uses a system of inventory counting throughout the year and are commonly used by larger organisations.

Where such a system is in place, the auditors should carry out the following work:

- Talk to management to establish whether all inventory lines are counted at least once a year.

- Inspect inventory records to confirm that adequate inventory records are kept up-to-date.

- Review procedures and instructions for inventory counting and test counts to ensure they are as rigorous as those for a year-end inventory count.

- Observe inventory counts being carried out during the year to ensure they are carried out properly and that instructions are followed.

- Where differences are found between inventory records and physical inventory, review procedures for investigating them to ensure all discrepancies are followed-up and resolved and that corrections are authorised by a manager not taking part in the count.

- Review the year's inventory counts to confirm the extent of counting, the treatment of differences and the overall accuracy of records, and to decide whether a full year-end count will be necessary.

- Perform cut-off testing and analytical review to gain further comfort over the accuracy of the year-end figure for inventory in the financial statements.

82 Rocks Forever

Text references. Chapters 11 and 13.

Top tips. Part (a) asks for factors to consider when placing reliance on the work of the expert. For five marks you need about five points so you will need to generate a few ideas. If you are not familiar with ISA 620 don't panic. You should be able to produce a reasonable answer with a bit of common sense.

For part (b) the key is your accounting knowledge. Inventory should be valued at the lower of cost and net realisable value. Approach this part by thinking about the ways in which the cost of inventory can be confirmed. Then think about the way in which net realisable value can be established.

> **Easy marks.** Overall this is a reasonably straightforward question looking at aspects of the audit with which you should be familiar. All the marks are reasonably achievable, which is good news although you do need to apply your knowledge to the scenario. Part (a) is probably the most straightforward as you can use your knowledge of ISA 620 *Using the work of an auditor's expert* to structure your answer.

Marking scheme

		Marks
(a)	Factors to consider when placing reliance on UJ	
	Up to 1 mark per point to a maximum of	5
(b)	Audit procedures to ensure jewellery is valued correctly	
	Up to 1 mark per point to a maximum of	5
		10

(a) **Factors to consider**

- The need for an auditor's expert

  The auditor must consider the risk of material misstatement and whether there is the required expertise within the audit firm. In this case as inventory is material and this is the only client in the diamond industry which the firm has it would seem appropriate to use an expert. This need is increased by the specialised nature of the client's business.

- The competence of the expert

  The expert should be a member of a relevant professional body. The auditor should also consider the individual's experience and reputation in his field.

- The objectivity of the expert

  The opinion of UJ could be clouded if for example, if they were related in some manner to Rocks Forever. This could be a personal relationship or one of financial dependence.

- The scope of the expert's work

  If the auditor is to rely on this evidence it must be relevant to the audit of inventory. In this case UJ is considering issues which will impact on the valuation of inventory. This is of great importance to the auditor and is therefore relevant.

- Evaluation of the work performed

  The auditor will need to assess the quality of the work performed by the expert. The auditor will consider the following:

  – Source data used

  – Assumptions and methods used and their consistency with previous years

  – The consistency of the results of UJ's work with other audit evidence taking into account DeCe's overall knowledge of the business.

  In spite of the fact that the auditor's expertise is limited in this field DeCe may test the data used by UJ. For example comparative price information may be available from other shops or industry sources.

(b) **Inventory valuation: audit procedures**

The key principle is that inventory should be valued at the lower of cost and net realisable value.

Cost

For a sample of items agree the cost price to the original purchase invoice. Care should be taken to ensure that the invoice relates specifically to the item in question.

Net realisable value

Review the report produced by UJ for any indication that items are fake. (This is unlikely to be the case but should be confirmed.)

For a sample of items sold after the year end verify that the sales price exceeds cost. Where this is not the case the item should be written down to its net realisable value.

Confirm that items valued by the valuer have been included in the inventory total at this valuation. If there are discrepancies the inventory balance should be revised to include UJ's valuation.

Obtain a schedule of the ageing of inventory. For items identified as slow moving discuss with management the need to make an allowance.

83 Whizee

Text references. Chapters 10, 13 and 16.

Top tips. This question is very structured as you are told specifically the number of points which you are required to make. Ensure you do follow these instructions. It asks for procedures and explanation – 6 of the 12 marks available will be awarded for the explanation so make sure you do not miss out this step. Read the scenario carefully and tailor your answer specifically to the system described. The examiner wants to see that you have understood the information that you have been given and that you can design procedures accordingly.

Examiner's comments. This question was generally not well answered. Common errors included writing about testing general controls instead of controls over the purchases system, including procedures for the payments system rather than the purchases system, insufficiently detailed answers, and stating what the purchase system should do without stating any audit procedures. Students must be comfortable with the sales and purchases systems and the need to be able to provide clear audit procedures and explanations for those procedures – this will remain a key element of the audit and assurance paper.

Marking scheme

Marks

Audit procedures procurement and purchases system
1 mark for stating procedure and 1 for the reason for that procedure. Limit marks to ½ where the reason is not fully explained. Maximum 2 marks per point.
Procedure
– E-mails to order database
– Order database to delivery note
– Orders to inventory database
– Paper goods receipt notes to inventory database
– Orders database to payables ledger database
– Computerised purchase invoice details to record of purchase invoice
– Details of purchase invoice database to EDI purchase invoice received
– Purchase invoice record to payables database
– CAATs – cast PDB, trace to nominal ledger
– Other relevant procedures
Maximum marks <u>10</u>

Audit procedure	Reason
(1) For a sample of emails filed on the store manager's computer match the details to a corresponding order filed on the order database.	To ensure that orders are completely and accurately recorded.
(2) For a sample of orders taken from the order database match the details to a corresponding paper delivery note and then to the entry in the perpetual inventory system.	To confirm that all goods ordered are subsequently received and then completely and accurately recorded in the inventory database.

Audit procedure	Reason
(3) For a sample of purchase invoices agree the details to the corresponding order and confirmation of receipt on the order database.	To ensure that liabilities are only recognized in respect of goods ordered and received.
(4) For a sample of orders confirmed as received and invoiced on the order database trace and match the details to the corresponding entry in the payables ledger.	To confirm the completeness of the liability recorded in the payables ledger.
(5) Review the order database for orders received but not yet invoiced.	To ensure that the year end accrual for goods received not invoiced has been calculated correctly.
(6) For a sample of purchase invoices trace the entry of the liability to the individual account in the payables ledger and confirm that the correct account has been credited.	To confirm that liabilities are allocated to the correct supplier account.

Top tips. In this case the answer only asked for five audit procedures. Other valid points include:

For a sample of orders agree the allocated supplier to the authorized supplier list	To ensure that goods are only purchased from suppliers authorized by management
For a sample of delivery notes seek evidence that the physical inventory has been agreed to the details on the delivery note eg a signature	To ensure that the goods delivered correspond to the goods actually received
For a sample of purchase invoices trace to the entry on to the purchases database	To ensure the completeness of purchases recorded on the purchases database

84 CAATs

Marks

(a) Up to 1 mark per well described procedure, max of 4 procedures
Calculate inventory days
Produce an aged inventory analysis to identify any slow moving goods
Cast the inventory listing
Select a sample of items for testing to confirm net realisable value (NRV) and/or cost
Recalculate cost and NRV for sample of inventory
Computer-assisted audit techniques (CAATs) can be used to confirm cut-off
CAATs can be used to confirm whether inventory adjustments noted during the count have been updated to inventory records.

4

(b) Up to 1 mark per well explained advantage
Test a large volume of inventory data accurately and quickly
Cost effective after setup
CAATs can test program controls as well as general IT controls
Test the actual inventory system and records rather than printouts from the system
CAATs reduce the level of human error in testing
CAATs results can be compared with traditional audit testing
Free up audit team members to focus on judgemental and high risk areas

3

(c)   Up to 1 mark per well explained disadvantage

Costs of using CAATs in this first year will be high

Team may require training on the specific CAATs to be utilised

Changes in the inventory system may require costly revisions to the CAATs

The inventory system may not be compatible with the audit firm's CAATs

If testing the live system, there is a risk the data could be corrupted or lost

If using copy files rather than live data, there is the risk that these files are not genuine copies

Adequate systems documentation must be available

$\frac{3}{\underline{\underline{10}}}$

Computer assisted audit techniques

(a)   **Audit procedures**

Software can be used to cast the inventory listing to confirm the total is complete and accurate.

Audit software could be used to extract a statistical sample of inventory items in order to verify their cost or net realisable value (NRV).

Calculations of inventory days or inventory turnover could be carried out by audit software, before being used to compare against the same ratios for the prior year or of competitors. This will help to assess the risk of inventory being overstated.

Audit software could be used to help extract an aged inventory analysis. This could in turn be used to identify any obsolete or slow moving items, which may require a write down or an allowance.

Audit software can be used to perform calculations during testing of inventory, such as recorded cost (eg weight or quantity multiplied by cost per kg or unit).

CAATs can be used to confirm whether inventory adjustments recorded during attendance at the count have been correctly recorded in the final inventory records forming the basis of inventory in the financial statements.

CAATs can be used to verify cut-off by testing whether the dates of the last GRNs and GDNs recorded relate to pre year end, and that any with a date after the year end have been excluded from the inventory records.

(**Note:** Only four procedures were required.)

(b)   **CAATs – Advantages**

- CAATs allow the audit team to test a large volume of inventory data more accurately and more quickly than if tested manually.

- CAATs decrease the scope for human error during testing and can provide evidence of a higher quality.

- By using CAATs, auditors can test actual inventory transactions within the system rather than working on printouts from spool or previewed files which are dependent on other software (and therefore could contain errors or could have been tampered with following export).

- Assuming the inventory system remains unchanged, CAATs used in the audit of Magnolia year on year should bring time (and therefore cost) savings in the long term, which should more than compensate for any set up costs.

- Auditors can utilise CAATs to test programme controls as well as general internal controls associated with computers.

- Results from CAATs can be compared with results from traditional testing. If the results correlate, overall confidence is increased.

- The use of CAATs allows audit team members more time to focus on risk areas and issues requiring judgement, rather than performing routine calculations that can be carried out by audit software.

(**Note:** Only three advantages were needed to gain full marks.)

(c)   **CAATs – Disadvantages**

- Setting up the software needed for CAATs in the first year is likely to be time consuming and expensive.

- Audit staff working on Magnolia's audit will need to be trained so they have a sufficient level of IT knowledge to apply CAATs when auditing the inventory system.

- If testing is performed on data in the live inventory system, there is a risk that live client data may be corrupted and lost.

- If the inventory system at Magnolia changed then it may be expensive and time consuming to re-design the CAATs.

- If the inventory system at Lily is not compatible with Daffodil & Co's CAATs then they will need to be tailored to Magnolia's system, which may be costly.

- If testing is performed on data from copies of the live files rather than the live data itself, there is the risk that these files have been affected by the copying process or have been tampered with.

- If there is not adequate systems documentation available, it will be difficult to design appropriate CAATs due to a lack of understanding of the inventory system at Magnolia.

(**Note:** Only three disadvantages were needed to gain full marks.)

85 Redburn

Text reference. Chapter 13.

Top tips. Part (b) is quite tricky. Although stating the procedures is straightforward, you must add sufficient explanation to gain full marks. Because there are eight marks available you will need to include sufficient detail in respect of each of the general procedures.

Easy marks. There are easy marks available in part (a) for defining net realisable value.

Examiner's comments. It was pleasing to see that a significant proportion of candidates could clearly provide the definition of NRV from IAS 2 *Inventories*. However, there were a large number of candidates who did not understand what NRV was. The second part of this question was not answered well. Perhaps due to the misunderstandings over what NRV involved, many candidates could not provide any relevant procedures.

Marking scheme

		Marks
(a)	Define net realisable value	
	½ mark for each element of the definition	
	IAS 2	
	Selling price	
	Less estimated costs to completion	
	Less estimated costs to make the sale	
	Maximum marks	2
(b)	Four procedures	
	Up to 1 mark for stating procedure and up to 1 further	
	mark for explanation, but maximum 8.	
	On sales price	
	On costs to completion	
	On selling and distribution cost	
	Discussion with management	
	Maximum marks	8
		10

(a) **Definition of NRV**

IAS 2 *Inventories* defines NRV as 'the estimated selling price in the ordinary course of business, less the estimated costs of completion and the estimated costs necessary to make the sale'.

(b) **Procedures**

Procedures appropriate to assess that NRV is at or above cost are as follows:

(1) Develop an estimate of (or obtain actual) sales prices and proceeds in respect of inventory held at the year end. This is done to provide the sales price for the NRV calculation and should involve the following:

- Inspecting post year end sales invoices to obtain actual sales prices for year end inventory

- If there are no sales of the inventory line being tested, obtain management's estimated sales price. The auditor should assess the reasonableness of this, for example by inspecting current price lists or looking at the sales reports from sales staff.

- Having identified slow moving or damaged items from the sales reports and results of inventory counts, the auditor should ensure that these are assigned a nil value.

(2) Establish an estimate of costs to completion (to include in the NRV calculation). This will involve the following:

- The books may be complete, but if not (for example the books are unbound) the auditor must determine the cost to completion using actual post year end cost records or budgeted costs. Any further costs for returned books to make them saleable should also be taken into account.

(3) Determine directly attributable selling, distribution and marketing costs (to form part of the NRV calculation).

- Estimate these costs for the books being tested and whether any apportionment of costs to inventory lines is reasonable (for example apportionment by weight or size for distribution costs).

(4) Combine the three elements above (1 less 2 and 3) to arrive at NRV and compare with the cost. Discuss your findings and estimates with management and other informed staff to gain comfort that conclusions are reasonable.

86 Tirrol

Text references. Chapters 5 and 11.

Top tips. The Study Text contains a list of benefits of using Computer Assisted Audit Techniques (or CAATs), but in part (a) you should link these to the scenario by using those most relevant to the situation given. For example being able to test more inventory items quickly and accurately.

In part (b) you must maintain a focus on evaluating the systems documentation. Although internal audit has prepared the documentation and their ability must be evaluated, your answer must include the steps you would take to evaluate the accuracy of the documentation itself.

Easy marks. Use your knowledge of CAATs to generate points in part (a). Also using the mnemonic SODIT will help you generate ideas in part (b) but you must apply these to the computer systems documentation.

Examiner's comments. In part (a), most candidates demonstrated basic knowledge of the use of audit software explaining the 'standard' benefits of time, cost, use of actual data in the computer etc. A few candidates made some good links to the scenario, for example, explaining how data could be amalgamated to avoid having to visit the 25 branches in the company.

In part (b) the main area of weakness related to candidates spending too much time explaining the appointment and general work of internal audit rather than placing reliance on this function.

Marks

(a) **Benefits of audit software**

1 mark per properly explained benefit.
- Standard systems
- Use actual computer files
- Test more items
- Cost
- Other relevant points

Maximum marks 4

(b) **Reliance on internal audit documentation**

1 mark per point
- Appropriate qualifications
- Produced according to plan
- Problems with use noted
- Documentation logical
- Compare to live system
- Use documentation to amend audit software
- Other relevant points

Maximum marks 6
  10

(a) **Benefits of using audit software**

(1) **Ability to test all locations**

The software in each of the 25 different locations is the same; therefore the audit software will not need to be adapted for each location resulting in time (and therefore cost) savings.

(2) **Ability to gain more evidence**

It will be possible to test more transactions using the audit software than simply manually scanning print outs. For example the audit software can search all items for exceptions, such as negative or very high quantities. The additional information will give the auditor increased comfort that the inventory figure is reasonably stated.

(3) **Source files tested**

The actual computer files will be tested from the originating programme, rather than print outs from spool or previewed files which are dependent on other software (and therefore could contain errors or could have been tampered with following export).

(4) **Long term cost-effectiveness**

Using audit software is likely to be cost-effective in the long-term if the client does not change its systems.

(b) **Evaluation of internal audit documentation**

The external auditor should consider:

Scope of work:

- Whether the work performed by the internal audit department is relevant to the external audit.

- Here the documentation relates to the computerised systems which the auditor wants to test and so it would appear that their work is relevant.

Organisational status:

- Whether the internal audit department's findings are taken seriously and their action plans implemented.

- Establish how the documentation is used in internal audit work, obtaining evidence of its use and finding out if it has been updated where problems have been found.

Due skill and care:

- Whether the internal audit department's work has been properly performed.

- Establish how this and other projects to produce systems documents is planned and tested (for example are testers independent of those producing the documents).

- Compare the document with the actual system (by following a transaction through the system using the diagram) to ensure it is an accurate record.

- Ensure the diagram includes clear and consistent symbols and keys throughout.

- Ensure the documents contain evidence of proper review and authorisation by senior internal audit personnel.

Independence:

- Determine whether the internal auditors testing the systems are separate individuals from those who have implemented the systems.

Technical competence:

- Obtain details of relevant IT or accountancy qualifications held by the internal auditors to determine whether they are competent to undertake the work.

87 Obtaining evidence

Text references. Chapters 8 and 16.

Top tips. This is a knowledge based question and unrelated to a scenario. As long as you read the question correctly you should have scored well on this.

Easy marks. This is a straightforward question.

Marks

Up to 1 mark per well explained procedure (i) and up to 1 mark for a valid audit
test (ii), overall maximum of 2 marks per type of procedure and test.

Inspection
Observation
Analytical procedures
Inquiry
Recalculation
Performance
Maximum marks | **10**

Procedures to obtain audit evidence and examples relevant to auditing purchases and other expenses

Inspection

This is the examination of documents and records, both internal and external, in paper, electronic or other forms.

In the audit of purchases the auditor may inspect a sample of purchase invoices to ensure they agree to the amount posted to the general ledger.

Observation

This involves watching a procedure or process being performed.

An auditor may observe the checking of goods received against purchase orders in the goods received department.

Inquiry

This involves seeking financial or non-financial information from client staff or external sources.

An auditor may discuss with management whether there have been any changes in the key suppliers used and compare this to the purchase ledger to assess completeness and accuracy of purchases.

Recalculation

This consists of checking the mathematical accuracy of documents or records and can be performed through the use of IT.

The auditor may recalculate accruals and prepayments to gain evidence that other expenses are not over or understated.

Reperformance

This is the auditor's independent execution of procedures or controls that were originally performed as part of the entity's internal control.

The auditor may re-perform the payables ledger control account reconciliation to ensure it has been properly carried out.

Analytical procedures

This is evaluating and comparing financial and/or non-financial data for plausible relationships. Also include the investigation of identified fluctuations and relationships that are inconsistent with other relevant information or deviate significantly from predicted amounts.

The auditor could review expenses on a monthly basis to identify significant fluctuations and discuss them with management.

(**Note:** You may have come up with other valid examples relevant to purchases and expenses.)

88 Letham

Text references. Chapters 10 and 12.

Top tips. Remember to focus on completeness in part (b).

Easy marks. Part (a) offers some easy marks for basic knowledge.

Examiner's comments. This question provided many inadequate answers. Many candidates choose to criticise the test in part (b) because the auditor had used a representative sample, and so they suggested that all non-current assets should be tested. This demonstrates a lack of understanding of the principles of sampling and of the aim of audit procedures. In addition, a significant proportion criticised the test as they stated that it was not a good test for existence. The requirement of the question was for completeness and not existence, yet many candidates wrote at length about the need for existence tests.

Marks

(a) 1 mark for each method. ½ for stating the method and ½ for brief
explanation.
 – Random
 – Systematic
 – Haphazard
 – Sequence
 – MUS
 – Judgemental
Maximum marks 4

(b) **Test for completeness**
Up to 1 mark for what the current test does and 2 marks
for an adequate explanation.
1 mark for identification of a more appropriate test and
2 marks for an explanation why it is more appropriate
Maximum marks 6
10

(a) **Sampling methods**

Methods of selecting a sample acceptable according to ISA 530 *Audit Sampling*:

Random selection ensures that all items in the population have an equal chance of selection, eg by use of random number tables or random number generators.

Systematic selection involves selecting items using a constant interval between selections, the first interval having a random start.

Haphazard selection is selection of a sample without following any particular structured technique. It may be an alternative to random selection provided auditors are satisfied that the sample is representative of the entire population.

Block selection may be used to check whether certain items have particular characteristics. For example an auditor may use a sample of 50 consecutive cheques to test whether cheques are signed by authorised signatories rather than picking 50 single cheques throughout the year.

> **Top tip. Monetary unit sampling** is the other principal method given by ISA 530.

(b) **Completeness testing**

(i) **Purchase invoice based testing**

Comparing a representative sample of purchase invoices to non-current assets register and the annual budget proves only that those particular invoices are accurately recorded and gives little evidence over completeness.

Purchase invoices form the basis of the entries on the asset register (they are updated simultaneously) and testing one to the other will not detect missing purchase invoices.

Similarly testing from the invoices to the budget will only aid in highlighting an asset not recorded on the budget if that asset was delivered **and** the invoice was received. However it will not identify missing asset entries for items that have been delivered but no purchase invoice has received.

(ii)   **Appropriate completeness test**

In order to test completeness of non-current asset records effectively, any sample should be selected from the goods received notes (GRNs) because:

- This document is used to update the annual budget.
- GRNs will include equipment delivered even if no purchase invoice has been received.
- At the point of delivery you would expect acceptance of a corresponding liability.

To test completeness, GRNs should be traced to the purchase invoices to make sure initially that there are not related missing purchase invoices. Then the GRNs and invoices should be traced to the budget and non-current asset register to ensure none have been omitted.

Tutorial note. An equally valid test would involve tracing visible assets to entries in the non-current assets register and budget movements (ie confirming on the budget that they are noted as purchased).

89 Springfield Nurseries

Text references. Chapters 8, 12 and 14.

Top tips. Many students struggle with the difference between tests of control and substantive procedures so make sure that you can give specific examples of each. Part (b) is typical of the sort of question you should expect on any of the main classes of assets or liabilities on your exam paper. You need to be able to explain issues and identify audit tests to gain sufficient evidence about them. Remember to relate your answer to information provided in the scenario where possible.

Easy marks. Part (b) is the more straightforward part of the question.

(a)   **Procedures**

(i)   *Tests of controls*

Tests of controls are performed to obtain audit evidence about the operating effectiveness of controls preventing, or detecting and correcting, material misstatements at the assertion level.

A test of control that may be carried out when auditing completeness of revenue is observing or verifying the process of matching of goods dispatch notes (GDNs) to invoices. The auditor should also enquire how unmatched GDNs are investigated to ensure related sales are recorded where necessary.

(ii)   *Substantive procedures*

Substantive procedures are audit procedures performed to detect material misstatements at the assertion level. They are generally of two types:

- Substantive analytical procedures
- Tests of detail of classes of transactions, account balances and disclosures

An example of a substantive procedure is comparing monthly revenue with prior years, budgets and expectations (eg for expected seasonal peaks) and investigating any significant deviations.

(b) **Procedures re depreciation**

The purpose of depreciation is to write off the cost of the asset over the period of its useful economic life.

(i) *Buildings*

To assess the appropriateness of the depreciation rate of 5%, the auditor should:

- Consider the physical condition of the building and whether the remaining useful life assumption is reasonable.
- Review the minutes of board meetings to ensure there are no relocation plans.
- Consider the budgets and ensure that they account for the appropriate amount of depreciation. If they do not, they may give an indication of management's future plans.

(ii) *Computers and motor vehicles*

The reducing balance basis seems reasonable, given that computers and their software are updated frequently and therefore do wear faster early on in life, however the auditor should consider whether 20% is an appropriate rate given the speed at which technology develops.

The auditor should enquire and observe whether the assets are still in use.

The auditor should review the board minutes to ascertain whether there are any plans to upgrade the system.

The auditor should estimate the average age of the motor vehicles according to their registration plates and consider whether the life is reasonable in light of average age and recent purchases. Given that a number of vehicles are delivery vehicles and likely to heavily used, the auditor should look at recent profits and losses on disposals to see if large losses on disposal give an indication the 20% rate might be too low.

The auditor should ask management what the replacement policy of the assets is.

(iii) *Equipment*

The equipment is depreciated at 15% per year, or over 6-7 years.

The auditor should consider whether this is reasonable for all the categories of equipment, or whether there are some assets for which the technology advances more quickly than others. Such assets may require a higher rate of depreciation.

Note: Only six procedures were required for six marks.

90 Duck

Text references. Chapters 11 and 16.

Top tips. Part (a) was on the auditor's responsibility in relation to laws and regulations. Remember the auditor's opinion will be on the financial statements, so the auditor's responsibility will be focused on those laws and regulations that could have a material effect on the financial statements, whether direct or indirect.

Part (b) was relatively straightforward in relation to reliance on internal audit as long as you knew the four key factors of objectivity, technical competence, due professional care and communication.

Easy marks. Easy marks are available in both parts of this question, provided you are familiar with the topics.

Examiner's comments. Part (a) was answered unsatisfactorily by most candidates. Most candidates focused on management's responsibility for preparing financial statements and implementing controls and auditors' responsibility to provide a true and fair opinion. These points are not related to laws and regulations.

Marks

(a)   Up to 1 mark per substantive procedure
       Discuss with directors whether formal announcement made of
       redundancies
       Review supporting documentation to confirm present obligation
       Review board minutes to confirm payment probable
       Cast breakdown of redundancy provision
       Recalculate provision and agree components of calculation to supporting
       documentation
       Review post year-end period to compare actual payments to amounts
       provided
       Written representation to confirm completeness
       Review disclosures for compliance with IAS 37 *Provisions, contingent
       liabilities and contingent assets*   5

(b)   Up to 1 mark per well explained point
       Objectivity – independence, status and to whom report
       Technical competence – qualifications and experience
       Due professional care – properly planned and performed
       Communication – between internal and external auditors   5
                                                                               ___
                                                                                10

(a)   **Substantive procedures – Redundancy provision**

- Obtain an analysis of the redundancy calculations (cost by employee) and cast it to ensure completeness.

- Obtain written representation from management confirming the completeness of the provision.

- In order to establish that a present obligation exists at the year end, ask the directors whether they formally announced their intention to make the sales ledger department redundant during the year.

- If the redundancies have been announced pre-year end, review any documentation corroborating that the decision has in fact been formally announced.

- Review the board minutes to assess the probability the redundancy payments will be paid.

- Recalculate the redundancy provision to confirm completeness and agree components of the calculation to supporting documents.

- Confirm whether any redundancy payments have been made post year end and compare any amounts paid to amounts provided to assess the adequacy of the provision.

- Review the disclosure of the redundancy provision to ensure it complies with IAS 37 *Provisions, Contingent Liabilities and Contingent Assets*.

(**Note:** Only five procedures were needed to gain full marks.)

(b)   **Factors to consider – Reliance on work performed by internal audit**

The following important criteria will be considered by the external auditors when determining if the work of internal auditors is likely to be adequate.

Extent to which its objectivity is supported

The auditor must consider the extent to which the internal audit function's objectivity is supported by its organisational status, relevant policies and procedures. Considerations include to whom internal audit reports, any conflicting responsibilities, any constraints or restrictions, whether those charged with governance oversee employment decisions regarding internal auditors and whether management acts on recommendations made.

Level of technical competence

The auditor must consider whether internal auditors are members of relevant professional bodies, have adequate technical training and proficiency and whether there are established policies for hiring and training.

Whether a systematic and disciplined approach is taken (due professional care)

The auditor must also consider whether internal audit activities are systematically and properly planned, supervised, reviewed and documented; and whether suitable audit manuals, work programmes and internal audit documentation exist.

Effectiveness of communication

Communication will be most effective when internal auditors are free to communicate openly with external auditor, meetings are held regularly and where the external auditor has access to relevant internal audit reports.

Scope of internal audit work

The internal audit work will need to cover areas providing evidence over the financial statement areas relevant to the external auditor. If the internal audit work is largely limited to operational or IT issues, it may not provide the audit evidence needed to replace the planned external audit procedures.

91 Audit procedures

Text references. Chapters 8, 9 and 10.

Top tips. This is a knowledge-based question, but make sure your comments relate to the time-recording system.

Easy marks. This question should provide easy marks as long as you don't just provide a list of types of procedure – you need to explain each procedure and how they can benefit the auditor.

Marking scheme

	Marks
1 mark for explaining each procedure and 1 mark for discussing the use of that procedure = 2 marks for each	
Procedure	
Confirmation	
Observation	
Inquiry	
Recalculation	
Reperformance	
Analytical procedures	
Inspection	
Maximum marks	**10**

Audit procedures

Observation

Observation consists of looking at a process or procedure being performed by others. It could be used here to observe employees scanning their cards when they start and finish a particular shift. However, its use is limited because it only provides evidence that the process happened at the time of observation. It should be used in conjunction with other audit procedures.

Inquiry

Inquiry consists of seeking information of knowledgeable individuals, both financial and non-financial, throughout the entity or outside the entity. This can be used to find out how the time recording system works by interviewing relevant staff so would be a good procedure to use.

Recalculation

Recalculation consists of checking the mathematical accuracy of documents or records. It could be used to calculate the hours worked according to the information on the time recording system.

Reperformance

Reperformance is the auditor's independent execution of procedures or controls that were originally performed as part of the entity's internal control, either manually or using computer-assisted audit techniques. The auditor could test the controls in place within the time recording system using CAATs.

Analytical procedures

Analytical procedures consist of evaluations of financial information by studying plausible relationships among both financial and non-financial data. They can be used in this case to compare the time recorded per the system to the standard hours per employee plus any overtime worked.

Inspection

Inspection involves examining records or documents, in paper form, electronic form, or other media. It also refers to the physical examination of an asset. Inspection of records and documents provides audit evidence of varying degrees of reliability, depending on their nature and source. The auditor could inspect the reports produced by the system in respect of overtime worked, for evidence of authorisation from responsible management.

(**Note**: Only five were required.)

Tutorial note: Confirmation would not be a valid procedure in this question because confirmation is a type of inquiry where a representation of information or of an existing condition is obtained directly from a third party.

92 MistiRead

Text reference. Chapter 13.

Top tips. This is a question on inventory and ethics. Part (a) should be straightforward on the advantages of a perpetual inventory system. In part (b), make sure that as well as listing the audit procedures to perform, you also explain why you are doing them – use the clues in the scenario to help you generate specific audit procedures – for example, you are told that internal audit carries out continuous inventory checking so make sure you address this in your answer.

Easy marks. You should be able to score well on part (a) on the advantages of a perpetual inventory system.

Examiner's comments. Answers to part (a) were sometimes more in a list format than providing an explanation of the advantages of a perpetual inventory system, stating advantages rather than explaining them. For example, stating an advantage as 'increased control over inventory' without mentioning the advantage of decrease in theft. In part (b) the key point to note was that the procedures could place at any time in the year, not simply at the year end. The point became the main weakness in many answers as candidates wrote all they knew about inventory checking – at the year end.

		Marks
(a)	1 mark each advantage	
	No disruption	1
	Identify slow moving damaged inventory quicker	1
	Always have actual inventory details available	1
	Increased control storekeepers	1
	Limit audit tests	1
	Other relevant points	1
	Maximum marks	4
(b)	1 for procedure, 1 for explaining purpose	
	Meeting with internal audit	2
	Continuous inventory > book inventory	2
	Book inventory > continuous inventory	2
	Condition of books	2
	Opinion on accuracy continuous inventory system	2
	All lines counted once per year	2
	Computer record amendment to actual inventory levels	2
	Acceptable procedures on return of inventory	2
	Other relevant points	2
	Maximum marks	6
		10

(a) **Advantages of a perpetual inventory system**

- Allows a year-end count to be avoided as inventory is counted throughout the year, thereby minimising disruption at the year-end

- Enables the company to maintain greater control over inventory because inventory balances are known at any time

- Errors can be investigated quickly and corrected and slow-moving or obsolete inventory can be identified more quickly

- External auditors can rely on the system, thus reducing the level of substantive work required on inventory at the year-end

(b) **Audit procedures to confirm accuracy of continuous inventory checking at MistiRead**

Audit procedure	Reason
Review the results of continuous inventory checking carried out by internal audit, including a review of working papers.	To confirm that the work has been carried out appropriately and that external auditors can rely on the results of that work.
Examine the procedures in place for carrying out continuous inventory checking.	To ensure that policies and procedures regarding continuous inventory checking are adequate.
Observe the continuous inventory checking being carried out during the year.	To confirm that inventory checking is being carried out properly and in accordance with documented procedures.
Follow-up the inventory counts observed.	To ensure that all discrepancies are fully investigated and resolved.

Audit procedure	Reason
For a sample of inventory items on the system, agree it to book inventory and for a sample of items in inventory, agree them to the inventory records.	To ensure that the company maintains adequate inventory records.
Discuss the programme of inventory counting with internal audit staff and review the year's inventory counts.	To provide assurance that all inventory lines are counted at least once a year.

(**Note:** Three audit procedures and three reasons were sufficient to gain full marks.)

93 First Light

Text reference. Chapter 13.

Top tips. In (b) your procedures must be those that can realistically be carried out during the inventory count, not before or after. These will therefore include observing the teams to make sure they are following instructions, test counting and making notes of GRNs and GDNs. Your procedures should not include standard inventory tests that would be carried out later during the detailed audit fieldwork, such as reconciling quantities from the final listing back to the inventory count sheets.

Easy marks. You should find part (a) straightforward.

Marking scheme

		Marks
(a)	Up to 1 mark per point	4
(b)	Up to 1 mark per well described procedure	
	Observe the counters to confirm if inventory count instructions are being followed	
	Perform test counts inventory to sheets and sheets to inventory	
	Confirm procedures for damaged goods are operating correct	
	Inspect damaged goods to confirm whether the level of damage is correctly noted	
	Observe procedures for movements of inventory during the count	
	Obtain a photocopy of the completed inventory sheets	
	Identify and make a note of the last goods received notes and goods dispatched notes	
	Observe the procedures carried out by warehouse manager in assessing the level of work-in-progress	
	Discuss with the warehouse manager how he has estimated the raw materials quantities	
	Identify inventory held for third parties and ensure excluded from count	6
		10

(a) ISA 501 *Audit evidence – specific considerations for selected items* sets out the responsibilities of auditors in relation to the physical inventory count. It states that where inventory is material, auditors shall obtain sufficient appropriate audit evidence regarding its existence and condition by attending the physical inventory count.

At the count attendance, the auditors will need to evaluate management's instructions and procedures for recording and controlling the result of the physical inventory count.

They must also observe the performance of the count procedures to assess whether they are properly carried out.

In addition, the auditors should inspect the inventory to verify that it exists and look for evidence of damaged or obsolete inventory. They will also perform test counts to assess the accuracy of the counts carried out by the company.

The auditors are also required by ISA 501 to perform audit procedures over the entity's final inventory records to determine whether they accurately reflect the count results.

(b) **Procedures undertaken during the inventory count**

- For a sample of inventory items, carry out test counts from aisle to inventory sheet to test completeness and from inventory sheets to aisle to test existence.

- Obtain and record details of the last goods received notes (GRNs) and goods dispatched notes (GDNs) for 31 December to form the basis for cut-off procedures at the audit.

- Observe whether teams carrying out the count are adequately following the inventory count instructions.

- For a sample of items marked as damaged on the inventory sheets, inspect the items to verify that the level of damage has been correctly recorded.

- Observe the procedures for movements of inventory in and assess the risk that raw materials or finished goods have been missed or double counted.

- Photocopy the inventory sheets for follow up and use when performing procedures at the final audit.

- Ascertain how the level of work-in-progress is assessed by observing the assessment and by reviewing the assumptions made, and consider how consistent this estimate is with observed levels.

- Make enquiries of staff to ascertain how the raw materials quantities are estimated and review the calculations and any assumptions for reasonableness. Re-perform a sample of the measurements of height and width forming the basis of any calculation to see if they are accurate.

- Confirm any third party inventory observed has been excluded from the count.

- Confirm that the procedures for identifying and separately storing damaged goods are operating effectively.

(**Note:** Only six procedures were needed to gain full marks).

94 Mickey

Text reference. Chapter 12.

Top tips. This question contains a mixture of knowledge based requirements and requirements which need you to apply knowledge in the context of the scenario provided.

Part (a) tests your knowledge of considerations when relying on a management's expert. In order to gain a full mark for each point you need to make sure your answer is detailed enough.

Part (b) demonstrates your need to apply your financial reporting knowledge in the context of an audit. Anyone not up to date on IAS 16 *Property, plant and equipment* would have struggled with this question.

Easy marks. The easy marks can be found in (a) which is a largely knowledge based requirement.

                Marks

(a) Up to 1 mark per valid point
    ISA 500 provides guidance
    Consider if member of professional body or industry body association
    Assess whether relevant expertise
    Assess independence
    Evaluate assumptions
    Agree any further work required
    No reference in the audit report of Daffy & Co
    Maximum marks   4

(b) (i) Up to 1 mark per valid point
Disclosure
Revaluation surplus
Other assets
Maximum marks   2
(ii) Up to 1 mark per valid procedure
Maximum marks   <u>4</u>
<u>10</u>

(a) **Factors to consider when placing reliance on the work of the independent valuer**

The revaluation by the independent valuer took place during the year and has been used by Minnie to reach the property valuation included in the financial statements. Therefore the valuer is an example of **management's expert** as defined by ISA 500 *Audit evidence* (and ISA 620 *Using the work of an auditor's expert*) rather than an auditor's expert who is engaged directly by the auditor to help gain audit evidence.

ISA 500 requires auditors to evaluate the competence and capabilities including expertise and objectivity of a management expert. The auditor will assess whether the valuer is suitably qualified and establish whether they are members of a relevant professional body or industry association.

Meeting with the expert and finding out if the expert has carried out similar valuations appropriate for valuating property in accordance with IAS 16 *Property, plant and equipment* will help establish the extent of the valuer's experience in this area.

The auditor will also need to evaluate the expert's independence, identifying any potential threats. For example enquiries should be made as to whether the valuer holds a direct or indirect interest in Minnie.

The valuation itself will need to be reviewed. Any assumptions made should be compared to those used previously when valuing property and to expectations formed from research carried out at planning. A misstatement has been made due to management providing incorrect assumptions so the methodology behind these will need to be discussed in detail with management and the valuer to establish why the assumptions were incorrect. It is possible the valuer may have to do more work to correct the identified misstatement.

The auditor must not refer to the work of an expert if the auditor's report contains an unmodified opinion (unless required by law or regulation). If the misstatement is uncorrected and warrants a modified opinion, so that the auditor makes reference to the expert's work in their report because it is relevant to the modification, the auditor must state in the auditor's report that this reference does not reduce the auditor's responsibility for the opinion.

Tutorial note: Only four valid points were needed to obtain full marks.

(b) (i) **Acceptability of revaluation**

The revaluation of property is acceptable, but the auditors will need to ensure that the company complies with a number of disclosure requirements. A note to the accounts should give details of the revaluation and the name of the valuer.

The surplus on revaluation should be transferred to a separate non-distributable reserve in the statement of financial position as part of shareholders' funds.

Furthermore, any other assets of a similar nature to this should also be revalued.

(ii) **Audit procedures**

(1) Inspect the building to confirm its existence and state of repair.

(2) Examine documents of title to confirm ownership.

(3) Enquire about any charges on the building and confirm that these have been properly recorded and disclosed.

(4) Assess the reasonableness of the valuation by comparison with any similar properties which may have recently changed hands on the open market.

(5)   Reperform the calculation of the revaluation adjustments and ensure the correct accounting treatment has been applied.

(6)   Inspect notes to the financial statements to ensure appropriate disclosures have been made in accordance with IFRSs.

Tutorial note: Only four procedures were required.

95 Panda

Text references. Assurance engagements are covered in Chapter 1 of the Study Text. Subsequent events are found in Chapter 18 and auditor's reports are discussed in Chapter 19.

Top tips. You first need to assess whether each of the issues is material or not so make sure you use the figures provided in the question for revenue and profit before taxation to make your assessment. Remember also to consider whether these are adjusting events or not. Each issue is worth six marks so assume there are three marks for explaining whether an amendment is required and three marks for the audit procedures.

Marks

Up to 1 mark per valid point, overall maximum of 6 marks per event

Event 1 – Defective chemicals
–   Provides evidence of conditions at the year end
–   Inventory to be adjusted to lower of cost and net realisable value
–   Calculation of materiality
–   Review board minutes/quality control reports
–   Discuss with the directors, adequate inventory to continue to trade
–   Obtain written representation re going concern
–   Obtain schedule of defective inventory, agree to supporting documentation
–   Discuss with directors basis of the scrap value

Maximum marks   5

Event 2 – Explosion
–   Provides evidence of conditions that arose subsequent to the year end
–   Non-adjusting event, requires disclosure if material
–   Calculation of materiality
–   Obtain schedule of damaged property, plant and equipment and
      agree values to asset register
–   Obtain latest inventory records to confirm damaged inventory levels
–   Discuss with the directors if they will make disclosures
–   Discuss with directors why no insurance claim will be made

Maximum marks   5
                                                                                                               10

Event 1: Defective chemicals

(i)   A batch of chemicals produced before the year-end, costing $0.85m to produce, has been found to be defective after the year-end. Its scrap value is £0.1m. Inventory should be valued at the lower of cost and net realisable value in accordance with IAS 2 *Inventories*. This is an adjusting event in accordance with IAS 10 *Events after the reporting period*. As it stands, the inventory is overstated by £0.75m. This represents 13.4% of profit before tax and 1.4% of revenue and is therefore material to the financial statements.

(ii)   **Audit procedures to be performed:**

        •   Obtain a schedule to confirm the cost value of the defective batch of £0.85m and documentary proof of the scrap value of $0.1m.

- Discuss with management whether this is the only defective batch or whether there are likely to be other batches affected.
- Review quality control reports to assess the likelihood of other batches being affected and discuss results of testing with technical team members at Panda.

Event 2: Explosion

(i) An explosion shortly after the year-end has resulted in damage to inventory and property, plant and equipment. The amount of inventory and property, plant and equipment damaged is estimated to be $0.9m. It has no scrap value. Inventory and property, plant and equipment are therefore overstated by $0.9m. This represents 16.1% of profit before tax and 1.6% of revenue, and is therefore material. The explosion represents a non-adjusting event in accordance with IAS 10 *Events after the reporting period*. It therefore does not require adjustment in the financial statements but should be disclosed as it is material.

(ii) **Audit procedures to be performed:**

- Obtain a schedule of the inventory and property, plant and equipment damaged in the explosion to verify the value of $0.9m.
- Visit the site where the explosion took place to assess damage.
- Discuss with directors the need to make disclosure in the financial statements and review any draft disclosure note drafted.
- Inspect insurance agreement to assess whether any claim can be made on the insurance.

96 Delphic

Text references. Chapters 11 and 14.

Top tips. This question tests your understanding of the implications of a computerised accounting system and in particular the use of audit software. In practice almost all accounting systems will be computerised to some degree so it is highly likely that computer issues will be examined regularly.

Part (a) asks you to explain the audit procedures that should be carried out using audit software on the receivables balance. The best approach to adopt is to try to think of the basic audit work that would be performed on receivables and then consider how audit software can used to assist. You are then asked to explain why that procedure is being performed. Make sure you understand this requirement. You are being asked to justify why you would perform the test eg to confirm the recoverability of receivables, not why you are using audit software.

Part (b) then asks you to explain the problems of using audit software and how they can be resolved. In general terms you should be familiar with the problems, however try to relate your answers to specific to the scenario.

Part (c) asks you to explain the concept of 'auditing around the computer' and to discuss why this approach increases audit risk. You may find this part of the question tricky but it is only worth 3 marks so don't panic.

Easy marks. This is a tough question so there are no easy marks as such. However, if you adopt a methodical approach and try to use the information in the scenario it is still possible to achieve a good mark.

Examiner's comments. In part (a), candidates had to explain audit procedures using audit software for receivables' balances and also explain the reason for each procedure. Weaknesses included focusing answers on test data rather than audit software, explaining points on the audit of sales, explaining procedures to test program controls, explaining tests using manual systems, and structuring answers around the different types of audit evidence.

Part (b) was on problems of using audit software at a specific client and how to overcome those problems. The overall standard was again inadequate, with weaknesses being to state general issues rather than client-specific ones and not including methods to overcome issues identified.

In part (c), candidates had to explain the concept of auditing 'around the computer'. Most candidates did not appear to understand this term. Common errors included explaining the audit risk model, explaining how CAATs could be used to audit computer systems, and suggesting that the term meant looking at computer controls only.

Marks

(a) Up to 2 marks for each procedure and explanation. 1 for the procedure and 1 for the explanation. Limit procedure to ½ if cannot be sustained from Delphic's systems.
- Cast sales ledger
- Compare ledger balance to credit limit
- Review balances, ensure not excessive
- Calculation of receivables days
- Stratification of balances/audit sample selection
- Verify items in ledger
- Aged receivables analysis
- Other valid tests

Maximum marks   9

Note to markers – no distinction is made between test of control and substantive procedures for this question. Marks can be obtained from either type of test or other relevant uses of audit software eg sample selection.

(b) 2 marks for each point. 1 for explaining the problem and 1 for showing how it can be resolved.
Tests ideally must be related to the scenario; allow half marks if not related.
- Cost
- Lack of software documentation
- Change in client's system
- Outputs obtained
- Use of copy files
- Other relevant points

Maximum marks   8

(c) Explanation of auditing around computer = 1 mark
1 mark for max two problems 1
- Actual computer files not tested
- Difficult to track errors
- Other relevant points

Maximum marks $\frac{3}{20}$

(a)

Procedure	Reason for procedure
Test casting of the sales ledger and comparison with the total on the sales ledger control account.	To verify the accuracy of the final receivables figure.
Stratification of receivables balances and selection of a sample for direct confirmation based on this stratification.	To ensure that the sample selected includes all material items and a sample of smaller balances.
Calculation of receivables days at each month end.	To monitor control over cash collection during the year. In addition a substantial increase in receivables days may indicate recoverability problems.
Checking of the ageing of receivables (or production of an aged receivables analysis if not produced by Delphic Co).	To ensure that the ageing is accurate before using the information to identify irrecoverable receivables as part of valuation testing.

Procedure	Reason for procedure
Tracing a sample of sales invoices to the sales day book and cash receipts to the cash receipts book.	To ensure that sales invoices and cash receipts have been accurately recorded in the accounting records.

Top tips. The following additional points would also be valid:

Comparison of the balance in a sample of individual receivables accounts with their credit limits.	To ensure that controls over credit limits are being applied effectively.
Review of sales ledger balances for unusual items, for example: – Journal entries – Accounts with significant adjustments or credit notes	To identify unusual transactions on the sales ledger so that they can be investigated.
Selection of a sample of credit notes over a certain value issued after the year end.	To determine the need to make adjustments against current period balances.

(b) **Use of audit software**

Potential problem	How it can be solved
(i) Cost As this is the first year that the auditor has used audit software there will be substantial set-up costs.	The auditor should reconsider whether the use of audit software is a cost-effective approach. A cost-benefit analysis should be performed to assist in this decision making process, to decide how much audit software can be effectively used this year.
(ii) Incomplete documentation The lack of software documentation makes the use of audit software more complex and time-consuming. The result may be an inefficient audit with disruption and added cost to the client.	The incompleteness of documentation should be a significant factor in the auditor's cost-benefit analysis.
(iii) Changes to the system The computer system is to be changed next year. This means that the set-up costs incurred this year will not be recouped in future.	Again this should be a factor in the auditor's cost-benefit analysis.
(iv) Reason for the change in audit approach The change in approach has been made to enable the auditor to fully understand the computer systems. There is the possibility that without careful planning the audit software will not produce the information which the auditor requires. Audit software generally produces very specific and detailed information which may not be suitable for obtaining knowledge of the system.	The audit manager should set clear objectives as to the purpose of tests performed using audit software and the output which he is expecting.
(v) Use of copy files As the audit software is to be applied to copy files there is no guarantee that they are genuine or that they will operate in the same way as the actual files.	The auditor should supervise and observe the copying of the files to ensure that they are genuine. Alternatively he could request the use of live files.

(c) **Auditing around the computer**

Auditing around the computer means that the auditor identifies the input into the computer system and then compares the expected output with the actual output. The processing performed 'in between' by the computer software is not directly audited by the auditor.

This increases audit risk because:

- Evidence regarding the accuracy of processing is obtained indirectly – the software itself is not audited

- Manual audit procedures may result in smaller samples being selected as compared to the use of audit software

- The audit opinion may need to be modified if the auditor is unable to obtain sufficient appropriate audit evidence regarding the processing of transactions.

97 Tam

Text references. Chapters 6, 7 and 11.

Top tips. This is a question on audit sampling and includes both knowledge-based and scenario-based aspects. In parts (a) and (c), don't just simply produce one line definitions for the terms in the question – you need to explain them fully in order to score well. In part (b), break the question down into three parts for each of the comments made by each of the audit team – this means you need to aim to write sufficiently to score three marks for each comment. Breaking the question down like this into smaller parts makes it more manageable and less daunting.

Easy marks. These are available in parts (a) and (c) of the question.

		Marks

(b) One mark per point
Audit manager comments

Explanation of sampling method	1
Small population	1
Transactions material	1

Audit senior points

Explanation of sampling method	1
Population homogenous – therefore use statistical sampling	1
Time to produce sample	1

Audit junior points

Explanation of sampling method	1
Sample selection not random	1
Can't draw valid statistical conclusion	1
Allow other relevant points	1
Maximum marks	**9**

(c) One mark per point
Definition

Materiality – omission or misstatement	1
Materiality – size of the item	1

Important because:

Financial statements incorrect	1
Directors/owners know of errors; auditor reporting to	1
Third parties rely on financial statements	1
Other relevant points	1
Maximum marks	**5**
	20

(a) (i) **'Sampling risk'** is the risk that the auditor's conclusion, based on a sample, may be different from the conclusion reached if the entire population were subject to the same audit procedure. There are two types of sampling risk. In the first type, the auditor concludes in a test of controls, that controls are more effective than they actually are, or in a test of details, that a material error does not exist when it actually does. In the second type, the auditor concludes in a test of controls, that controls are less effective than they actually are, or in a test of details, that a material error exists when it actually does not.

'Non-sampling risk' arises from factors that cause the auditor to reach an incorrect conclusion for any reason not related to the size of the sample. For example, the auditor may rely on audit evidence that is persuasive rather than conclusive, the auditor may use inappropriate audit procedures, or the auditor misinterprets audit evidence and fails to recognise an error.

(ii) Sampling risk can be controlled by the audit firm by **increasing sample size** for both tests of control and tests of detail.

Non-sampling risk can be controlled by the audit firm by **proper engagement planning**, **supervision and review**.

(b) The audit manager wants to check all the invoices in the year. This would ignore statistical sampling in favour of testing the entire population.

Although each transaction may not be material on its own in the context of revenue ($140,000 is 0.2% of revenue), each is significant and errors will quickly aggregate to a material amount. This may make it attractive to test the whole population.

It could be argued that the approach is feasible since the population is relatively small. However it would still involve checking around 500 invoices which may be impractical in terms of time and therefore cost. Although it is possible to test 500, it is unlikely that the firm would test 100% in practice.

The audit senior wants to select a sample using statistical sampling techniques. This would involve calculating a sample size appropriate to the auditor's assessment of factors such as risk, required confidence level, tolerable misstatement and expected error.

Such a sample can still produce valid conclusions and in this case, the population consists of items showing similar characteristics (it is homogeneous).

Where statistical sampling is used all the items in the population must have an equal chance of being selected, so the sample should be picked using a method such as random number tables or a systematic basis. Provided that the sales invoices are sequentially numbered, this should be easy to apply in the example.

The audit junior's suggestion is to use a 'random' method of selecting samples manually and choosing a few important ones.

This approach would not be appropriate because the auditor is not really choosing the sample randomly as there would be bias involved, which implies that 'haphazard' selection would be used

In addition valid conclusions would not be able to be drawn because statistical sampling had not been used to select the sample.

(c) Information is material if its omission or misstatement could **influence** the economic decisions of users taken on the basis of the financial statements. Materiality depends on the size of the item or error judged in the particular circumstances of its omission or misstatement. Materiality also has **qualitative**, as well as **quantitative**, aspects which must be considered. The auditor will determine materiality levels for the financial statements as a whole, but will also set lower levels of **performance materiality**:

- To reduce to an appropriately low level the risk that undetected or uncorrected aggregate misstatements exceed materiality for the financial statements as a whole.

- For particular classes of transactions, account balances or disclosures.

Materiality for the financial statements as a whole is often calculated as a percentage of different items in the financial statements, such as revenue, profit before tax or net assets. In the case of Tam Co, materiality is likely to be based on 0.5-1% of revenue, ie $350-700k.

The auditors of Tam Co must form an **opinion** on whether the financial statements are free from material misstatement because there is a requirement for an audit under local legislation for this company. Other users of the accounts may also be relying on the outcome of the audit, such as the bank since the company has recently taken out a five year bank loan to finance an expansion. The bank would be very interested in the accounts of Tam Co as a basis for assessing whether the company will be able to repay the loan. Users of the financial statements expect to receive reasonable assurance that the information is 'presented fairly in all material respects' or is 'true and fair'. This implies that there are no material misstatements or omissions.

98 BearsWorld

Text reference. Chapter 11.

Top tips. Part (a) should be reasonably straightforward for 10 marks. Each procedure is worth two marks, one for explaining it and one for an example. This should give you an idea of how much to write for each one. Part (b) is trickier but again you can split the question up as you are asked to consider each procedure in turn. Use the clues in the scenario to help you with your answer.

Easy marks. Part (a) contained the easiest marks. ISA 500 *Audit evidence* is a key standard so you should be able to explain the main techniques of gathering audit evidence. As long as you took care to avoid the traps, eg talking about procedures relating to receivables when the question states there are none, it should have been reasonably easy to think of relevant examples for most of them.

Marking scheme

Marks

Types of evidence

(a) (i) Types of audit evidence
Award one mark for each well explained point. Allow ½ for simply stating the appropriate area.

Analytical procedures	1
Inquiry	1
Inspection	1
Observation	1
Computation	1

(ii) Examples of evidence
Award one mark for each well explained point. Allow ½ for simply mentioning the appropriate test

Analytical procedures	1
Inquiry	1
Inspection	1
Observation	1
Computation	1
Maximum marks	**10**

Suitability of methods of gathering evidence

(b) Award one mark for explaining whether each technique is suitable for BearsWorld and one mark for explaining limitations in that technique to a maximum of

$$\frac{10}{20}$$

(a) **Analytical procedures**

(i) Analytical procedures mean the study of **trends and ratios** in financial and non-financial information. It is used within **audit planning** to identify risk areas and also as a means of gathering **substantive evidence**, for example by calculating an estimate of a particular figure based on knowledge of the business and comparing this to the actual figure.

(ii) A comparison of gross profit percentages month by month for BearsWorld could be performed and any unusual fluctuations investigated as these could indicate errors such as omission of sales, loss of inventory or other errors.

Inquiry

(i) Inquiry means requesting information. This could be from individuals within the company, either orally or in written representations, or in formal written requests to third parties.

(ii) In BearsWorld a relevant example would be to send a standard confirmation letter to the company's bank (could be illustrated with an example of enquiry to client staff).

Inspection

(i) Inspection means looking at documentation, books and records or assets. This could be done to confirm existence of an asset, to verify values or to provide evidence that a control has taken place.

(ii) The inventory of cuddly toys at the year-end could be inspected as part of the evidence relating to its value. The inspection would give evidence as to whether the inventory was in good saleable condition (could be illustrated with an example of inspection of documentation).

Observation

(i) Observation means watching a procedure being carried out. It is usually used as a means of gathering evidence about the internal controls in a company.

(ii) In BearsWorld it might be appropriate to observe the procedures that are carried out when the post is opened to assess whether controls exist to prevent the misappropriation of cash.

Recalculation

(i) Recalculation means the reperformance of an arithmetical process within the accounting system. This could involve re-checking a manual calculation or using a computer-assisted audit technique to reperform casts within the accounting records.

(ii) Depreciation is likely to be a significant expense within a manufacturing company such as BearsWorld. The auditor should recalculate this expense.

(b) The usefulness of **analytical procedures** depends on a number of factors including the reliability of the underlying information. It seems that, as a small business, BearsWorld has little segregation of duties and formal controls. This casts doubt on the reliability of the information and hence the conclusions that might be drawn from the analytical procedures.

Inquiry evidence from third parties will be essential in the audit of BearsWorld. As well as the bank confirmation it may be necessary to send confirmation letters to suppliers to obtain third party evidence of the liabilities at the year-end. Inquiry evidence from sources within BearsWorld will be obtained mainly from Mr Kyto and its reliability will be very dependent on how the auditors assess his integrity.

Inspection of documents will be a major part of the evidence gathered in the audit of BearsWorld. Supplier invoices will be inspected to verify values and to confirm that purchases and expenses are genuinely business items. There may be limits to the reliance that can be put on this as in a poor control environment it may be difficult to confirm whether documentation is complete.

Observation may be the only way to gather evidence about controls such as any that may exist over the opening of post. This type of evidence is limited in its usefulness for two reasons:

- It only provides evidence that the control operated at the point in time that the auditor carried out the test.

- Client staff are likely to perform their duties exactly according to the company's procedures manual when they are aware that the external auditor is observing them whereas this may not be the case on any other day of the year.

To place reliance on controls and reduce substantive testing the auditor needs evidence that controls operated effectively over the whole of the accounting period so the observation would be of limited usefulness. Observation of controls in operation over the year-end inventory count might be more useful as this is a one-off, rather than daily, procedure. If the auditor could see that the inventory count was being carried out in a well-controlled way then it may be possible to reduce substantive testing on the inventory sheets.

Re-calculation is a good check of the **accuracy** of invoices and control accounts. However it only covers figures that that have been recorded in the accounts, and will not identify omitted figures.

99 Wear Wraith

Text reference. Chapter 12.

Top tips. This is a fairly straightforward question on non-current assets. In part (a), think about the objectives when testing non-current assets, ie ownership, existence, valuation, completeness. You are asked to 'list' the audit work so make sure you are specific and succinct in your answers. In part (b), the best approach is to take each category of non-current assets in turn and deal with each separately. Note that the requirement specifically tells you to ignore the railway trucks.

The motor vehicles are a bit more complicated than the land and buildings and plant and machinery categories but you should, from the scenario, spot that the disposals in the year relate to vehicles that were five years old whereas the policy is to depreciate these over three years.

Easy marks. In part (b), easy marks are available for considering the land and buildings and plant and machinery categories first. You should remember from your financial reporting studies that land is normally not depreciated. From the plant and machinery figures, you should be able to identify fairly quickly from a quick scan of the figures that the depreciation on the disposals exceeds their cost value.

Examiner's comments. In part (a), many candidates obtained a good pass by stating six or seven clear audit tests on non-current assets. The tests were clearly related to the scenario. Some candidates, however, simply stated every possible test on non-current assets with no regard at all for the scenario. Spending a little time planning and thinking about the scenario is advisable prior to writing the answer. Overall, the standard was disappointing, with the average standard being a very marginal pass.

In part (b), candidates were required to identify any issues concerning the note that should be raised with management. The implication was that such issues would be unusual, not basic issues such as obtaining evidence of existence of the assets. It was therefore disappointing to see some candidates simply repeating all the audit tests again, having already done this in part (a). Weaknesses included a lack of knowledge of the information provided in a non-current asset note and suggesting that the note had arithmetical errors when the question explicitly stated that this was not the case.

Marking scheme

		Marks
(a)	One mark for each valid test	
	Board minutes	1
	Non-current asset ledger	1
	Non current asset note	1
	Inspect trucks	1
	Purchase invoices	1
	Depreciation policy OK?	1
	Depreciation disclosure amount	1
	Depreciation accurate calculation	1
	Treatment of any sales tax	1
	Confirm NBV using specialist or trade journal	1
	Other relevant points (each)	1
	Maximum marks	**10**
(b)	Key points up to 2 marks for explaining the problem and 1 mark for stating the solution	
	Land and buildings – depreciation of land	3
	Plant and machinery – depreciation eliminated > cost	3
	Motor vehicles – depreciation calculated not = disclosure note	3
	Motor vehicles – may be depreciating too quickly	3
	Maximum marks	**10**
		20

(a) **Audit work to perform on railway trucks**

- Reconcile the draft note figures for railway trucks to the non-current asset register and general ledger to ensure that the amount stated in the accounts is accurate.

- Cast the non-current assets note and verify that it agrees to the amount disclosed in the statement of financial position.

- Vouch a sample of additions in the year to supporting third party documentation such as invoices from suppliers to ensure that the amounts stated are correct and to confirm ownership.

- Review board minutes authorising purchase of the trucks in the year to confirm authorisation.

- Recalculate the depreciation charge for the year based on the total cost of the trucks and the stated depreciation policy.

- Verify that the proper depreciation charge has been posted to the statement of profit or loss and is stated correctly in the non-current assets note.

- Vouch the existence of a sample of railway trucks in the accounting records to the physical asset.

- Verify completeness of railway trucks by taking a sample of trucks by physical inspection and checking that they have been recorded in the accounting records and the non-current asset register.

- Verify that the depreciation policy for railway trucks is appropriate by reference to industry standards and the financial statements of other similar companies to Wear Wraith.

- Verify that the treatment of sales tax for a sample of assets is correct, eg capitalised where it is non-recoverable.

(b) **Non-current asset issues and how to resolve issues**

Land and buildings

The depreciation rate of 2% has been correctly applied however the charge for the year has been based on the total balance ie land and buildings. Per IAS 16, land is not generally depreciated as it is considered to have an unlimited life. Therefore the building element of the total should be separated out in order to calculate the charge for the year on the buildings element only.

Plant and machinery

The depreciation charge for additions and existing plant and machinery has been correctly calculated by applying 20% to the year-end balances (ie charging a full year's depreciation in the year of acquisition for new additions). Disposals costing $100,000 occurred in the year but the depreciation eliminated on these is $120,000, which is greater than the total cost, has been adjusted for which is incorrect. This must be discussed with management and any identified errors should be adjusted for accordingly.

Motor vehicles

The depreciation charge on the motor vehicles sold has correctly been adjusted for at $325,000 as they were fully depreciated assets at the time of disposal. However, the motor vehicles were 5 years old, whereas the policy for motor vehicles is to depreciate them over 3 years. This indicates that management should review the useful economic life of motor vehicles in order to assess whether the current policy is still appropriate.

The charge for the year appears to have been incorrectly calculated, as it seems to have been charged over 4 years rather than over 3 years. The charge for the year of $425,000 is less than it should be according to the rate per the depreciation policy for motor vehicles. Therefore either the policy has changed or the calculation has been performed incorrectly. This issue should be discussed with management to ascertain the reason and the appropriate amendment made, ie either to the policy note or to the charge for the year. This would not constitute a change in accounting policy (as it is a change in an accounting estimate, per IAS 18) so there would be no need to amend prior year figures.

100 Tracey Transporters

Text references. Chapters 12 and 14.

Top tips. In part (a), a good way of setting your answer out and giving it more structure would be to use a tabular format, ie 'Audit test' in one column and 'Reason for test' in the other column. Make sure that you do explain the reasons why you are carrying out each test – this is specifically requested in the question requirement. In part (b), think about the audit assertions first and make sure your audit work adequately covers them in your answer.

Easy marks. The marks in this question should be achievable fairly easily. Use the information in the scenario and give your answers as much structure as possible.

Examiner's comments. Answers to part (a) varied considerably. Well-prepared candidates provided excellent lists of tests, with appropriate explanations, which were relevant to the scenario. However the majority of candidates had difficulty explaining the tests.

Specific reasons for weak answers included:

- Including tests on the non-current assets register. Given that this was a sales audit, it was not clear why these tests were included here, and again in part (b)

- Providing comments such as 'check casting' without specifying which documents are to be cast, or why

- Explaining the audit of receivables without linking this to the objectives of completeness and accuracy of sales

- Explaining the systems and controls that should be in place rather than auditing the system. This did not meet the requirement of explaining audit tests.

The overall standard of answers to part (b) was much higher than for part (a). The majority of candidates managed to provide a sufficiently broad list of tests. Specific reasons for weaker answers included:

- Not fully explaining the points, eg saying, 'Obtain company records for ownership' but not actually stating which records needed to be obtained.

- Stating unclear or incorrect audit procedures, eg 'obtain non-current asset register, take sample of vehicles and see vehicle to check completeness of the register'. This is actually checking the accuracy of the register. Checking for completeness would normally involve seeing an asset then checking that it was included.

- A small minority of candidates mentioned tests on other areas of the statement of financial position. It was not clear whether the need to audit non-current assets had been identified. More focused answers are needed to obtain a pass standard.

Many candidates would benefit from taking a minute to jot down the assertions and then ensure that their answer covered all of them.

(a)

Audit test	Reason
Enquire about and observe the procedures used when bookings are received over the telephone.	The biggest risk of incomplete recording of orders relates to those received by telephone. Evidence is needed that checking and supervision occurs at this point.
With the client's permission, enter a sample of test data into the VMS booking system and review the details logged on the system.	This will confirm that there are no flaws in the system causing omission or error at the input stage.
For a sample of e-mail orders, agree details to the VMS booking system.	This will identify errors arising when the e-mail details are input to the VMS system.
For a sample of booking records within the VMS system, agree the details to the corresponding invoice produced by the receivables ledger programme.	This will identify whether information is transferred completely and accurately between the two modules of the system.
For a sample of invoices, agree the hire prices charged to the master file record of approved prices.	This will identify whether the full approved prices are being charged to customers.
For a sample of credit notes issued in the year, agree to supporting documentation and check for evidence of authorisation by the appropriate level of management.	This will check that credit notes are only issued and sales entries reversed when there is a valid reason.
Cast the list of invoices issued in one month (or other appropriate period) and agree the total to the entry made to the nominal ledger.	This will identify whether the journals posted to the nominal ledger are complete and accurate.
Cast the sales account in the nominal ledger and agree the total to the sales figure in the draft statement of profit or loss.	This will identify whether any arithmetical errors have arisen in the accounting system and whether any errors have arisen in the transfer of information from the accounting system to the financial statements.
Perform analytical procedures, comparing the following ratios to prior years (or month by month if the information is available): – Turnover per vehicle – Gross profit margin Obtain explanations and corroborate evidence for any unexpected variations.	If material amounts have been omitted from sales it would be likely to have a significant effect on these ratios.
Review the results of audit procedures on receivables, such as the results of any direct confirmation of balances, and consider whether any errors identified also have an effect on the sales figure.	The double entry effect of errors needs to be considered and if, say, a confirmation reply from a customer reveals that an amount has been incorrectly posted to the receivables account, this will have a corresponding effect on sales.

(b)   **Audit work on vehicles**

   (i)   Obtain a schedule reconciling the movement on the vehicles cost account and vehicles depreciation account over the year and agree:

- Opening balances to prior year audit files
- Closing balances to non-current asset register and nominal ledger

   (ii)   Cast the columns for costs, depreciation and carrying amount in the non-current asset register.

(iii) Select a sample of additions in the year from the non-current asset register and:

- Agree to the purchase invoice to confirm ownership *(rights and obligations assertion)* and that the correct amount has been capitalised, excluding any revenue items such as petrol or road tax *(valuation and allocation assertion)*.

- From the date on the purchase invoice confirm that the purchase has been recorded in the correct accounting period *(occurrence assertion)*.

- Physically inspect the vehicle to confirm existence (or alternatively, if the vehicle is out on hire at the time inspect the hire documentation, insurance policy and vehicle registration document) *(existence assertion)*.

(iv) From the company's insurance policy, agree a sample of vehicles currently owned (and hence insured by TT) to the non-current asset register *(completeness assertion)*.

(v) Review the repairs and maintenance expense account and agree any unusually large amounts to invoices to check that no purchases of a capital nature have been misclassified *(completeness assertion)*.

(vi) Obtain a list of disposals in the year and:

- Inspect to confirm that the vehicle has been removed from the non-current assets register
- Agree sales proceeds to the cash book

(vii) Perform a proof in total of the depreciation charge for the year, applying the depreciation rate as disclosed in the financial statements to the opening balance *(valuation assertion)*.

(viii) For a sample of individual vehicles from the non-current asset register, reperform the depreciation calculation *(valuation assertion)*.

(ix) Review the depreciation policy for reasonableness *(valuation assertion)* by:

- Reviewing for consistency with prior years

- Comparing it with that used by other companies in the industry

- Considering whether significant gains or losses have arisen on disposals during the year

- Comparing the useful life applied in the depreciation calculation to the age of the lorries that were sold during the year

(x) Review the notes to the accounts to check that:

- The depreciation policy has been disclosed.

- The movements on the vehicles cost and depreciation have been appropriately disclosed in the non-current assets note *(disclosure assertion)*.

(**Note.** The audit testing assertions are included in the answer as candidates are likely to structure their answer around these headings but there are no specific marks for mentioning them.)

101 Duckworth Computers

Text reference. Chapter 15.

Top tips. The question specifically tells you to assume the recipient has no knowledge in part (a). You should ensure that you write your answer so that someone who knows nothing about auditing could audit the bank reconciliation.

Easy marks. Parts (b) and (c) should represent reasonably straightforward marks.

(a)   (i)   Audit procedures to verify bank reconciliation

Tests of details of balances

(1)   Confirm the bank balances per the client's working papers and general ledger to the bank letter on the file and the bank statements.

(2)   Compare the receipts on the list of receipts with those on the bank statement for October, to ascertain if the outstanding deposits on the bank reconciliation are the only ones that are outstanding. Ensure that any deposits on the bank statement which are not on the list of receipts for October were listed as reconciling items on the September bank reconciliation.

(3)   Compare the payments on the list of payments with those on the bank statement for October, to ascertain if the unpresented cheques on the bank reconciliation are the only ones that are outstanding. Ensure any cheques on the bank statement which are not on the list of payments for October were listed as reconciling items on the September bank reconciliation.

(4)   Compare the October bank reconciliation with the September reconciliation to ensure that any reconciling items on the September bank reconciliation that remain outstanding have also been included on the October bank reconciliation.

(5)   Verify reconciling items on the October bank reconciliation.

- Trace the outstanding deposits and cheques on the reconciliation to November bank statements to ensure that they clear the bank in reasonable time.

- Agree the returned cheque to the entries on the bank statement for correctness.

- Agree that the bank charges on the reconciliation statement agree to the bank statement and that they are the only such charge that has not been included in the cashbook.

(6)   List all the items that are still outstanding from the bank reconciliation at the end of the audit and put the list on the report to partner section of the file, for his attention.

(ii)   **Audit objectives**

(Numbers in this answer refer to the number of the points in part (i).)

(1)   Confirmation of the bank general ledger balance to the bank letter is carried out to verify the accuracy of the bank balance recorded in the general ledger.

(2)   The comparison of the bank statements with the list of receipts and deposits on the bank reconciliation is carried out to test the completeness of deposits outstanding on the bank reconciliation.

(3)   The comparison of the bank statements with the list of payments and unpresented cheques on the bank reconciliation is carried out to test the completeness of unpresented cheques in the bank reconciliation.

(4)   The comparison of the October and September bank reconciliations is done to test the completeness of reconciling items on the bank reconciliation.

(5)   Tracing through and agreeing items on the October bank reconciliation is carried out in order to verify the existence of the reconciling items on the reconciliation.

(6)   The outstanding items list is compiled to highlight items where there may be doubt as to their existence.

(b)   **Reliability of bank statements**

Bank statements are **third party evidence** as they are issued by the bank.

However, the bank sends them to the client so they are **not third party evidence received directly from the third party.** This means that there is scope for the client to adjust them in some way if the client wants to deceive the auditor.

It is rare for such a fraud to occur but the auditor should be **aware of the possibility of such evidence tampering** and treat the evidence accordingly.

Should the auditor have grounds to fear that the evidence will be tampered with, the auditor **could request bank statements directly from the bank**. The auditor would have to obtain the client's permission for this.

(c)   (i)   **Auditing around the computer**

This is where the auditor audits the information input to a computer and audits the output of the computer but does not audit the computer processing of the information.

Auditing through the computer

This is where as well as auditing input and output, the auditor checks the processing routines and program controls of the computer as well.

(ii)   **Situations where it is inappropriate to audit around the computer**

In general terms the inappropriateness of auditing around the computer increases with the **complexity of the computer program.**

Specifically, it is inappropriate to audit around the computer when the **computer generates totals for which no detailed analysis can be obtained.** It is also inappropriate in the absence of control totals and audit trails.

It is also inappropriate to audit around the computer where the **use of CAATs could reduce control risk and the level of substantive procedures significantly,** or substantive procedures could be done more efficiently by the use of CAATs. This is likely to be the case where a significant amount of use is made of the computer by the business and valuable information is contained within it.

102 Metcalf

Text references. Chapters 8 and 16.

Top tips. This is a question on audit evidence. The majority of the marks are available in part (b) for 16 marks but don't be daunted by this – this part of the question is then split down into three separate parts so deal with each one in turn and it won't seem so overwhelming. To score well in this part of the question, you need to be specific in your description of the substantive procedures you would carry out, as well as explain why you are doing them. Our answer gives more points than are needed to score full marks but you should have stuck to your time allocation for each part before moving on.

Easy marks. Easy marks are available in part (a) of this question on the factors to consider when evaluating the sufficiency of audit evidence. However, you should also be able to score reasonably in part (b) on substantive audit procedures provided that you explain why you are carrying out those procedures.

Examiner's comments. In part (a) many candidates simply omitted answering this question, indicating a lack of knowledge, or possibly not being able to think of general factors affecting sufficiency of evidence. The overall average standard of answer in part (b), especially in part (i), was unsatisfactory. Common errors in this part included:

- Focusing answers on the audit of purchases, rather than payables

- Omitting standard procedures on payables such as cut-off testing or casting and agreeing the list of payables to the financial statements

- Not explaining the purpose of procedures

- Too much 'checking'; in other words, not stating the audit procedure. For example, 'check the supplier statement' is not an audit procedure because it is unclear what the statement is being checked for. The actual procedure must be stated, for example ' obtain supplier statements and reconcile to the purchase ledger account to identify invoices omitted from the ledger'.

The standard for parts (b) (ii) and (iii) was better overall.

Marks

(a) 1 mark per well explained point
Assessment of inherent risk
Materiality of the item
Nature of the accounting and control systems
Control risk
Experience from previous audits
Result of audit procedures
Source and reliability of information available
Other relevant points

Maximum marks 4

(b) (i) Trade payables (1 for test and 1 for explanation)
List of payables – cast and agree to general ledger
Agree list to payables ledger and ledger to list
Analytical procedures
Select sample for testing – rationale for sample
Supplier statement reconciliation – agree balances
Treatment of non-reconciling items
Cut-off – prior year end – invoice to GRN
GRN to invoice prior year end
Cut-off – post year end
Debit balances treatment

Maximum marks 8

(ii) Accruals (1 for test and 1 for explanation)
Obtain list cast and agree general ledger
Analytical procedures
Payments made post year end
Supporting documentation

Maximum marks 4

(iii) Legal provision (1 for test and 1 for explanation)
Discuss with directors
Lawyer letter
Correspondence with customer
Letter of representation
Post year end payment (if possible)

Maximum marks 4
—
20

(a) **Factors concerning the sufficiency of audit evidence**

Source of evidence

The auditor will be concerned about the **source** of the evidence, that is, whether it is generated by the entity being audited or by a third party or if it is auditor-generated evidence.

Materiality of the amount

More audit evidence would be required when examining more **material balances**, and the lower the level of materiality set.

Inherent and control risks

The **higher** these risks are, the more audit evidence will be required in order to provide assurance over figures in the financial statements.

Accounting and control systems

Depending on whether the systems in place are **reliable** or not, this will influence the amount of audit evidence required to support various audit assertions.

(b) **Substantive procedures in the audit of current liabilities**

Substantive procedure	Reason for test
(i) Trade payables	
Undertake an analytical review on a breakdown of the trade payables figure, comparing this year's closing balance to the previous year's closing balance. Investigate further if the difference is significant.	To confirm the reasonableness of the figure in the current year's financial statements.
Select a sample of trade payables for further testing, agreeing the amounts to supporting documentation such as invoices and purchase orders and post year-end payments. Focus the sample on material balances, but include other smaller items too.	To confirm the accuracy of amounts recognised in the financial statements and their correct inclusion as liabilities in the year-end accounts.
Match a sample of items on the trade payables listing to the ledger and vice versa.	To confirm the completeness and existence of trade payables.
Cast the trade payables listing and agree the total figure to the figures recorded in the accounting system.	To confirm the completeness of the amount.
Obtain the supplier statements for a sample of suppliers and reconcile the year-end balances to the amounts recorded in the ledger.	To confirm the valuation, completeness and existence of amounts outstanding at the year-end.
For a sample of purchase invoices recorded just before the year-end, match these to the relevant goods received notes to confirm that the goods were received prior to the year-end.	To confirm the accurate application of cut-off of purchases (ie that invoices recorded in the period related to goods genuinely received in the period), therefore also gaining evidence over the existence of payables.*
For a sample of goods received notes received just before the year-end, trace these to the appropriate purchase invoice and ensure they were recorded pre year end.	To confirm accurate application of cut-off of purchase transactions, therefore providing evidence that goods received pre year end have been recorded and payables are complete.*
For a sample of goods received notes received just after the year end, trace to purchase invoices and make sure they were recorded post year end.	To confirm accurate application of cut-off of purchase transactions, therefore providing evidence that goods received post year end have been not been recorded and payables are not overstated.*
For a sample of debits on the payables listing, seek explanations from appropriate client staff to establish why these have arisen and whether they have been correctly recorded.	To confirm correct disclosure of amounts within payables.

Substantive procedure	Reason for test
(ii) Accruals	
Undertake an analytical review on the accruals figure, comparing this year's closing balance to the previous year's and to the current year's budget. Investigate further if the difference is significant.	To confirm the reasonableness of the figure in the current year's financial statements.
Perform cut-off tests for a sample of invoices received just before and just after the year-end.	To ensure that invoices received before the year-end but unpaid at the year-end and relating to goods and services received in the year are included as trade payables and that invoices received after the year-end that relate to goods and services received in the year are included within the accruals balance.
Review a sample of payments made after the year-end.	To verify the completeness of accruals by identifying any amounts that relate to goods and services received in the year and which should therefore be included within the accruals listing.
For a sample of accruals from the accruals listing, match back to supporting documentation such as invoices and purchase orders.	To confirm the accuracy of amounts recognised as accruals in the year-end figure.
(iii) Provision for legal action	
Inspect correspondence relating to the provision for legal action.	To obtain further information and evidence to support the recognition of the provision in the financial statements.
Inspect calculations to support the $60,000 provision figure.	To confirm the accuracy of the amount recognised in the financial statements.
Discuss with directors how the figure has been arrived at.	To confirm that the amount recognised in the statement of financial position and statement of profit or loss of $60,000 is reasonable.
Discuss with legal advisers of Metcalf what their assessment of the case is and the likely costs involved.	To confirm that the conditions for recognising a provision have been met.
Review board minutes and other correspondence relating to this incident to ascertain when it happened.	To confirm that the conditions for recognising a provision in accordance with IAS 37 have been achieved.

*Tutorial note:** More procedures and reasons are given in our answer than are needed to obtain full marks. For illustrative purposes the answer to (b)(i) contains three cut-off procedures to show the different ways cut-off procedures can be carried out and how they relate to the account balance assertions. However, when answering a question like this in the exam you should aim to cover a range of common procedures up to the full mark allocation.

103 Have A Bite

Text references. Chapters 10 and 16.

Top tips. Three of the four requirements clearly state the number of items you need to state and/or explain (whether it be assertions, controls etc). This should help you to keep to time and give you an idea of how the marks are allocated; therefore helping you decide how much detail to go into for each aspect you need to explain.

Easy marks. A basic understanding of assertions will gain you full marks in part (a) as long as you 'explain' and don't just 'identify' assertions relevant to payables.

Marking scheme

Marks

(a) **Accounts payable assertions**
½ mark for identification of assertion and up to 1 mark
for each explanation of assertion, maximum 6.
Rights and obligation
Valuation and allocation
Existence
Completeness
Maximum marks   6

(b) **Control risk and audit procedures**
Up to 1 mark for each control identified, but maximum 2. Up to 1 mark
for each audit procedure, but maximum 2.
Overall authority
Approved suppliers
Inspection on receipt
Storage of food
Use-by dates
Maximum marks   4

(c) **Evidence on claim**
Up to 1 mark for identification of each item of evidence
and up to a further 1 mark for explanation.
Written claim
Review controls
Inspection reports
View of lawyer
Representations
Maximum marks   6

(d) **Substantive procedures re revenue**
Up to 1 mark for each procedure
Profit margin
Average spend per customer
Seasonal fluctuations
Variance analysis

4
20

(a) **Assertions relevant to accounts payable**

The assertions relevant to accounts payable at the year end date include:

- **Existence** – Trade payables are valid liabilities and exist.

- **Rights and obligations** – Trade payables are the obligations of the entity (services or goods have been provided resulting in an obligation to transfer economic benefits in the future).

- **Completeness** – All liabilities in respect of trade payables have been recorded in the accounting records.

- **Valuation and allocation** – All trade payables are included in the accounts at appropriate amounts.

(b) **Food purchase and preparation – controls and procedures**

Controls that the company should have in place to reduce the risk associated with purchases of food and its preparation are set out in the table below along with related procedures to be carried out during controls testing.

(i) Control	(ii) Procedure
Only pre-approved suppliers should be used and a list of these suppliers should be provided to purchasing staff along with instructions prohibiting the use of other suppliers.	Inspect the approved supplier list and ensure only these are used by interrogating purchases data for evidence of use of other suppliers.
Food purchases should be inspected or tested where necessary on arrival. Staff inspecting should evidence this by signing the goods received note or a formal inspection document.	Examine a sample of the document used to evidence inspection/testing and ensure they are all signed.

Top tips. There are other valid controls (including keeping the food stored in a refrigerated and clean place and adherence to use-by dates) and related procedures (examination of the storage area and confirming no food is past its use-by date), but only two of each were required in order to gain full marks.

(c) **Evidence and conclusion in respect of potential claim**

Evidence should be collected which will enable a conclusion to be formed on the likelihood of the claim being successful. Once this has been established, it is possible to apply IAS 37 *Provisions, contingent liabilities and contingent assets* to determine whether any provision is necessary. Evidence obtained should include the following:

- Obtain and inspect the written claim by the customer. This should give details of the claim including

  - The reason for the claim
  - Which food is involved and where it was consumed
  - When the incident took place

- Request and obtain written representations from management on their view of how likely it is the claim will succeed. Although this is internal evidence and not as good as third party evidence, it can be used together with other evidence in forming an overall conclusion on the claim.

- Communicate with the company's legal advisers using a specific letter of enquiry which includes:

  - Management's assessment of the outcome of the identified claim and its estimate of the financial implications

  - A request that the entity's external legal advisers confirm the reasonableness of management's assessments and provide the auditor with further information if they consider the list to be incomplete or incorrect

This will provide third party evidence from professional legal advisers on the likelihood of the claim being successful.

(d) **Substantive analytical procedures in respect of revenue**

   (i) Calculate the current year **gross profit margin** for food and drink sales, and compare the margin with the previous year. If the current year gross profit is not consistent with the previous year, discuss the reasons why with management.

   (ii) Compare the **revenue each month** with month with the corresponding month's revenue in prior years. Determine whether seasonal fluctuations in revenue are consistent from year to year. Where the trend is inconsistent with prior years, make inquiries of management as to the reasons why.

   (iii) Based on revenue and the number of meals sold, calculate the **average spend** per customer per meal and evaluate whether this is in line with expectations based on past experience and pricing. In fast food restaurants, average spend should be fairly constant.

   (iv) Perform **variance analysis** for each location. Compare the reported revenue arising in each location against budget. Where significant variances occur, make enquiries of management and local staff as to the possible reasons why.

104 FireFly Tennis Club

Marking scheme

		Marks
(a)	Income – one mark per relevant point	
	All income	
	Paying-in slips to bank statements	1
	Paying-in slips to cash book confirm amounts agree	1
	Analysis correct in cash book	1
	Cast cash book	1
	Agree totals per cash book to the financial statements	1
	Membership fees	
	Compare list of members to determine how many members 20X5	1
	Analytical review of subscriptions – overall process	1
	AR – calculating approximate fee income	1
	Agree subscriptions to FS accounting for differences	1
	Court hire fees	

	Marks
Obtain list of court hire fees/calculate for week hire fee	1
Confirm hire fee to paying-in slip – account for differences	1
Other relevant tests	1
Maximum marks	**10**

(b) Key points one for each point

Expenditure analysis back to cash book	1
Cast cash book	1
Cash book to purchase invoice – amounts and analysis in CB	1
Expenditure bona fide the club	1
Investigate any other expenditure	1
Other relevant points	1
Maximum marks	**5**

(c) Key points one for each point

Lack of segregation of duties	1
Lack of authorisation controls	1
Cost	1
Management override	1
Use of volunteers – lack of training	1
Lack of profit motivation	1
Other relevant points (each)	1
Maximum marks	**5**
	20

(a) **Audit work on completeness of income**

- **Compare** current year income for both membership fees and court hire to the prior year figures to confirm the reasonableness of the amounts. Investigate any large variances (eg greater than 10%) by enquiry of the treasurer.

- Carry out a **proof in total** on membership fees by taking the annual membership fees and the number of members in the year. Membership fees are $200 per year. New members joining during the year pay 50% of the total fees. There were 50 new members and 430 at the start of the year. Therefore, membership fee income should be (430 × 90% × 200) + (50 × 50% × 200) = $82,400.

- **Agree membership fee income** to the financial statements to ensure it has been disclosed correctly.

- **Agree court hire fee** income to the financial statements to ensure it has been disclosed correctly.

- Review the list of court hire in the club house for court hire during the year and calculate the expected income from court hire by multiplying this by $5. Compare this to the income from court hire in the cash book, bank paying-in slips and financial statements and seek explanations for any differences by enquiry of the treasurer.

- **Compare** the list of bankings for membership fees prepared by the secretary to the cash book and to the paying-in slips to ensure amounts reconcile.

- **Review** paying-in slips for the analysis between court hire fees and membership fees and agree these to the analysis in the financial statements.

- **Cast** the cash book to ensure all entries are included in the total and it is totalled correctly.

- For a sample of paying-in slips, **agree** amounts on the slips to the amounts banked on the bank statements.

- **Agree** amounts on paying-in slips to the amounts in the cash book to ensure accuracy and completeness of recording.

(b)   **Audit procedures on completeness and accuracy of expenditure**

- For a sample of expenditure invoices during the year, review the details to confirm that the expenditure is bona fide for the club, ie that it relates to court maintenance, power costs for floodlights, or tennis balls for championships.

- Reconcile the debit card statements to the cash book and receipts and to the financial statements. Investigate any discrepancies and seek explanations for them from the treasurer.

- Cast the expenditure columns in the cash book to ensure accuracy of the expenditure totals.

- Review the analysis in the accounts for each expenditure type, selecting a sample of payments from the cash book and tracing back to the invoice and to the financial statements to confirm that the analysis is correct.

- Perform an analytical procedure on expenditure by comparing the amounts for the current year to the prior year for each of the three types of expenditure to confirm whether it appears reasonable. For any large variances (say, greater than 10%), investigate further to obtain satisfactory explanations.

(c)   Internal control testing has limited value when auditing not-for-profit entities such as the FireFly Tennis Club because of the **lack of segregation of duties** due to the small number of staff, who may or may not be qualified. In the case of the tennis club, there appear to be two members of staff responsible for running the club and preparing the accounts – the treasurer and the club secretary.

Another issue is that the majority of the income may be in the form of **cash**. At FireFly Tennis Club, all income is cash-based and the controls over this appear to be weak, for example, non-members leave court hire fees in a cash box. This is open to theft and misappropriation by users or by staff.

There is also a **lack of authorisation controls** in place. For example, the treasurer pays for all expenditure items using the club's debit card but there is no system in place for another person to review and authorise the purpose of the expenditure.

In such a small organisation, it may not be possible to implement a **system of internal control** because of the very small number of staff and also because of the cost involved in setting up such a system.

Even when there is a system of internal control in place, senior officials are usually in position to override those controls. For example, suppose FireFly implemented a control whereby the cash book was reviewed periodically. The treasurer at FireFly could still pay for personal expenditure using the debit card and then ignore these items when carrying out a review of the cash book for unauthorised payments.

105 Walsh

Text references. Chapters 10 and 11.

Top tips. In part (a) you need to explain the two main types of CAATs (audit software and test data) and then you have to provide examples from the company in the question scenario to demonstrate the advantages of using CAATs in an audit. Part (b) should be very straightforward as the requirement is to list examples of audit tests to perform on the wages system. In part (c), you need to explain the benefits and drawbacks of using test data but also make sure you apply your knowledge to the company in the question scenario.

Easy marks. Easy marks are available in part (b) of this question where you are asked to list audit tests to perform on the wages system.

			Marks
(a)	**Explain two main categories of CAATs**		2
	Testing programmed controls		2
	Test larger number of items		2
	Test actual accounting records		2
	Cost		2
	Other relevant points		2
	Maximum marks		**8**
(b)	**Audit tests** – one mark per test		
	Recalculation of net pay		1
	Usual items – zero wages payments		1
	Unreasonable items – large payments		1
	Violation system rules – amendment of data		1
	New analysis – analytical review of wages		1
	Completeness checks – all employees clocked in and out		1
	Other relevant tests		1
	Maximum marks		**6**
(c)	**Use of audit test data** – one mark per point		
	Data submitted by auditor		1
	Live and dead testing		1
	Create dummy employee in Walsh		1
	Check accuracy of processing of wages		1
	Problem – damage client computer		1
	Problem – remove auditor data		1
	Problem – cost		1
	Other relevant tests		1
	Maximum marks		**6**
			20

(a) (i) There are two main types of computer assisted audit technique (CAAT) – **audit software** and **test data**. Audit software involves the use of computer programs by the auditor to process data of audit significance from the entity's accounting system. Test data is entering data into an entity's computer system and comparing the results with predetermined results.

(ii) The benefits of CAATs include the ability to **test program controls** as well as general internal controls associated with the system. For example, in the case of Walsh Co's wages system, one of the controls in the system is the generation of a report if overtime over 10% of standard hours is done.

CAATs allow auditors to test a **greater number of items** more quickly and accurately. In the case of Walsh Co, CAATs can be used to test a sample of wage and deduction calculations to provide evidence that these are being correctly calculated by the system.

CAATs enable the auditor to **test transactions electronically** rather than paper records of transactions.

CAATs can be **cost-effective** in the long-term, provided the client does not change its systems. In the case of Walsh Co, the wages system has just been implemented so this is likely to remain in place for a few years.

(b) Examples of audit tests to perform on Walsh Co's wages system using audit software.

- Analytical review of wages by carrying out a proof in total test of wages cost for the year.

- Looking for unusual amounts such as large payments or negative amounts by analysing the transaction data for wages in the year.

- Recalculation of pay and deductions for a sample of employees to confirm that the system is calculating amounts correctly.

- Selecting a sample from the data file for wages to perform detailed substantive testing.

- Verifying that access to the system is limited to authorised personnel, such as the financial accountant.

- Testing for completeness to confirm that an electronic record exists for all employees who have clocked in and out.

(c) Test data is a type of CAAT which involves entering data into the entity's computer system and comparing the results obtained with predetermined results.

The test data can be processed during a normal processing run or in a special run outside of the normal processing cycle.

Using test data should help in the audit of Walsh's wages system because it could be used to test specific controls in the system, such as password access to the system, which should be controlled so that only authorised personnel have access to it.

In addition, the auditor can create a test employee record on the wages master file, and then use a magnetic card to simulate that employee working a certain number of hours in the company over the course of, for example, a week.

By keeping a record of how many hours has been input into the wages system, the auditor can calculate the expected net pay and then compare this to the actual net pay produced by the computer system.

If no difference is found then this provides evidence of the accuracy of recording and processing of the wages software.

However, there are some problems with using test data in this way.

A significant problem with test data is that any resulting corruption of data files has to be corrected. This is difficult with modern real-time systems, which often have built-in (and highly desirable) controls to ensure that data entered cannot be easily removed without leaving a mark.

Test data only tests the operation of the system at the time of testing and therefore the results do not prove that the program was working throughout the period under review.

Initial computer time and costs can be high and Walsh may change its system in subsequent years.

106 Pineapple

Text references. Chapters 7, 8, 13, 14 and 16.

Top tips. In general terms this question tests your knowledge of assertions, substantive procedures and working papers.

Part (a) asks for an explanation of four financial statements assertions relevant to account balances and for each assertion a substantive procedure relevant to the audit of inventory. This part of the question is knowledge based so should be an opportunity to score well. Make sure that you are aware of which assertions relate to year end account balances and which relate to classes of transactions. Ensure that you explain the assertions asked for clearly rather than simply listing them. Check that the procedures you have suggested relate to inventory and provide evidence of the assertion described.

Part (b) requires substantive procedures for depreciation and a contingent liability. The key here is to ensure that your procedures are tailored so that they take in to account the information in the scenario.

Part (c) requires the identification and explanation of items that should be included on every working paper. Your answer must include a clear explanation (ie why the working paper includes that piece of information) to score well.

Easy marks. Part (c) represents easy marks provided adequate explanation is included.

Examiner's comments. Part (a) was unrelated to the scenario and was knowledge based, and candidates' performance was on the whole unsatisfactory.

Financial statement assertions are a key element of the F8 syllabus and so it was unsatisfactory to see that a significant minority of candidates do not know the assertions relevant to account balances; with many giving incorrect assertions of accuracy and cut-off which are relevant to classes of transactions rather than account balances. Where candidates did correctly identify the assertions they often failed to explain them adequately or did so with reference to transactions rather than assets and liabilities.

A significant minority did not even attempt part (b) of the question. On the depreciation many candidates did not focus their answer on the issue identified, which related to the depreciation method adopted for the capital expenditure incurred in the year. In the scenario the issue was headed up as depreciation and so this should have given candidates a clue that they needed to focus just on depreciation. However, a significant proportion of answers were on general PPE tests often without any reference at all to depreciation. In addition many felt that generic tests such as 'get an expert's advice' or 'obtain management representation' were appropriate tests; they are not. The food poisoning issue tended to be answered slightly better; however again tests tended to be too brief, 'read board minutes', 'discuss with management' or 'discuss with the lawyer' did not score any marks as they do not explain what is to be discussed or what we are looking for in the board minutes.

Part (c) was answered unsatisfactorily. Many candidates seemed completely confused by what was required and instead of focusing on contents of a working paper provided answers in relation to contents of an audit report, or contents of permanent and current audit files.

Marking scheme

Marks

(a) Up to 1 mark per assertion, ½ mark for stating assertion and ½ mark for explanation, max of 4 marks; up to 1 mark per relevant inventory substantive procedure, max of 4 marks.
Existence – explanation and relevant substantive procedure
Rights and obligations – explanation and relevant substantive procedure
Completeness – explanation and relevant substantive procedure
Valuation and allocation – explanation and relevant substantive procedure

8

(b) Up to 1 mark per relevant substantive procedure, max of 4 marks for each issue.
Depreciation
Review the reasonableness of the depreciation rates and compare to industry averages
Review the capital expenditure budgets
Review profits and losses on disposal for assets disposed of in year
Recalculate the depreciation charge for a sample of assets
Perform a proof in total calculation for the depreciation charged on the equipment
Review the disclosure of depreciation in the draft financial statements
Food poisoning
Review the correspondence from the customers
Send an enquiry to the lawyers as to the probability of the claim being successful
Review board minutes
Review the post year-end period to assess whether any payments have been made
Discuss with management as to whether they propose to include a contingent liability disclosure
Obtain a written management representation
Review any disclosures made in the financial statements

8

(c)   Up to 1 mark per well explained point, ½ mark only if just identifies item to be
      included, max of 4 points.
      Name of client
      Year-end date
      Subject
      Working paper reference
      Preparer
      Date prepared
      Reviewer
      Date of review
      Objective of work/test
      Details of work performed
      Results of work performed
      Conclusion

$$\frac{4}{\underline{\underline{20}}}$$

(a)   **Financial statement assertions and substantive procedures**

(i) Financial statement assertions	(ii) Substantive procedures relevant to inventory
Existence: assets, liabilities and equity interests exist	At the inventory count select a sample of items recorded on the count sheets and physically verify the corresponding inventory in the warehouse.
Rights and obligations: the entity holds or controls the rights to assets, and liabilities are the obligations of the entity.	For a sample of year end raw materials and finished goods agree inventory to a supplier invoice in the company name.
Completeness: all asses, liabilities and equity interests that should have been recorded have been recorded.	At the inventory count select a sample of physical inventory and trace back to the inventory records to ensure that they have been included.
Valuation and allocation: assets, liabilities and equity interests are included in the financial statements at appropriate amounts and any resulting valuation or allocation adjustments are appropriately recorded.	Follow up items identified at the inventory count as slow-moving and ensure that an adjustment has been made to these to reduce cost to net realisable value.

(b)   **Substantive procedures**

Depreciation

- Compare depreciation policy to that for other similar assets within the business and industry norms to determine whether it is reasonable

- Review capital expenditure budgets to determine whether assets recently purchased are likely to be replaced more frequently than every ten years

- For assets disposed of during the year review profit or loss on disposal calculations to determine whether these indicate that depreciation policies adopted to date have been reasonable

- For a sample of new assets recalculate the depreciation expense and verify that this agrees to the stated policy

- Perform analytical procedures on the depreciation expense eg proof in total and discuss any significant variations with management

- Check that disclosures agree to the accounting records and are in accordance with accounting standards

Food poisoning

- Review the details of the claim made by the customers to evaluate the likelihood of the claim being successful

- Review any correspondence from the company lawyer and consider any professional opinions contained in it

- Send a letter of enquiry to the lawyer and asking the lawyer to confirm their view of the likelihood of the outcome of the case

- Discuss the matter with management and confirm whether a contingent liability is to be disclosed, and if so, on what basis

- Review board minutes for details of any discussions including the board's assessment of the outcome of the case

- Obtain a written representation from management confirming that in their view they will successfully defend the case and that no provision is required

- Obtain details of any similar cases that the company has been involved in and consider whether the outcome was successfully predicted

- Perform a review in the post-year end period to determine whether any new information has come to light eg payments made to customers

- Assuming a contingent liability is disclosed, verify that the details accurately reflect the situation and comply with accounting standards

(c) **Purpose of items included on working papers**

Working papers should include:

Name of the client

To record which client the working paper relates to.

Period end date

To provide a record of the period which is being audited.

Subject

So that the area of the financial statements being audited can be identified.

Working paper reference

This ensures that all audit papers can be accounted for and allows cross referencing of the audit file.

Preparer

Identifies the person who performed the work so that any queries can be directed to the right person.

Date prepared

This puts the audit work into context in terms of information which was available at the time and information which may have come to light at a later date.

Objective of the work

So that the reviewer can assess whether the work performed is appropriate in relation to its aim.

Work performed

To provide a written record of the procedures performed by the auditor.

Results

This provides written evidence as to whether the outcome was as expected, whether there were any exceptions and whether any further work was required.

Conclusions

This is a summary of the key points culminating in whether the auditor can conclude that a true and fair view is given.

Reviewer

This provides evidence that a key quality control procedure has been performed and by whom.

Date of review

This should show that the evidence has been reviewed before the date of the signing of the audit report.

(**Note:** Only four items required to achieve full marks.)

107 Rose

Text references. Chapters 4, 11, 15 and 16.

Top tips. Part (a) on the fundamental principles is a straightforward requirement, but (b) requires application of knowledge to three issues.

In (b) it is important to note that you are being asked to 'describe' procedures rather than simply to identify them, so you need to include enough detail on each to obtain a full mark. Stay focused on the procedures and avoid being tempted to engage in a discussion of accounting issues, especially in relation to the reorganisation provision.

Easy marks. These were available in (a) for stating and explaining the fundamental principles.

Marking scheme

		Marks

(a)   Up to 1 mark per well explained point, being ½ mark for the principle and ½
        mark for the explanation
        Integrity
        Objectivity
        Professional competence and due care
        Confidentiality
        Professional behaviour   5

(b)   Up to 1 mark per well described procedure
        (i) Trade payables and accruals
             Calculate trade payable days
             Compare total trade payables and list of accruals against prior year
             Discuss with management process to quantify understatement of payables
             Discuss with management whether any correcting journal adjustment
             posted
             Sample invoices received between 25 October and year end and follow to
             inclusion in year-end accruals or trade payables correcting journal
             Review after date payments
             Review supplier statements reconciliations
             Perform a trade payables' circularisation
             Cut-off testing pre and post year-end GRN   6
        (ii) Receivables
             For non-responses arrange to send a follow up circularisation
             With the client's permission, telephone the customer and ask for a
             response
             For remaining non-responses, undertake alternative procedures to confirm
             receivables

For responses with differences, identify any disputed amounts, identify whether these relate to timing differences or whether there are possible errors in the records

Cash in transit should be vouched to post year-end cash receipts in the cash book

Review receivables ledger to identify any possible mispostings

Disputed balances, discuss with management whether a write down is necessary

5

(iii) Reorganisation

Review the board minutes where decision taken

Review the announcement to shareholders in late October

Obtain a breakdown and confirm that only direct expenditure from restructuring is included

Review expenditure to ensure retraining costs excluded

Cast the breakdown of the reorganisation provision

Agree costs included to supporting documentation

Obtain a written representation

Review the adequacy of the disclosures

$\frac{4}{20}$

(a) **Fundamental principles**

Principle	Explanation
Integrity	Members shall be straightforward and honest in all professional and business relationships.
Objectivity	Members shall not allow bias, conflicts of interest or undue influence of others to override professional or business judgements.
Professional competence and due care	Members have a continuing duty to maintain professional knowledge and skill at the level required to ensure that a client or employer receives competent professional services based on current developments in practice, legislation and techniques. Members shall act diligently and in accordance with applicable technical and professional standards.
Confidentiality	Members shall respect the confidentiality of information acquired as a result of professional and business relationships and, therefore, not disclose any such information to third parties without proper and specific authority, or unless there is a legal or professional right or duty to disclose. Confidential information acquired as a result of professional and business relationships must not be used for the personal advantage of members or third parties.
Professional behaviour	Members shall comply with relevant laws and regulations and avoid any action that discredits the profession.

(b) **Substantive procedures**

(i) **Trade payables and accruals**

- Ask management about the action they have taken to establish the value of the misstatement of trade payables. If they have ascertained the value of the error assess the materiality of it and the impact of it remaining uncorrected.

- Enquire whether any correcting journal entry has been calculated and whether it has been processed in relation to the misstatement.

- For a sample of purchase invoices received between 25 October and the end of 31 October 2012, verify that they are included within accruals or as part of trade payables via a journal adjustment.

- Reconcile supplier statements to purchase ledger balances, and investigate any reconciling items.

- Calculate and compare trade payables days to prior years. Significant differences should be investigated.

- Compare trade payables and accruals against the previous year and expectations. Investigate any significant differences and corroborate any explanations for differences to supporting evidence.

- Review the cash book payments and bank statements in the period immediately after the year end for evidence of payments relating to current year liabilities. Ensure any found are included in accruals, trade payables or the trade payables journal.

- For a sample of payable balances, perform a trade payables' circularisation. Any non-replies should be followed up and reconciling items between the balance confirmed and the trade payables' balance should be investigated.

- For a sample of goods received notes before the year end and after the year end, ensure the related invoices have been recorded in the period to which they relate.

(**Note:** Only six valid procedures were needed to gain full marks for (i))

(ii) **Receivables**

- For those receivables who don't respond, the team should arrange to send a follow up circularisation if agreed by the client.

- For non-responses to the follow up, and after obtaining client consent, the audit senior should telephone the customer and request the customer responds in writing to the circularisation request.

- Where all follow-ups are unsuccessful, alternative procedures must be carried out to confirm receivables, such as reviewing after date cash receipts for year end receivables.

- Where responses highlight differences, these should be investigated to establish if any amounts are disputed or require adjustment.

- Where it is found that differences are in relation to disputed invoices, they should be discussed with management and the need for an allowance or write off assessed.

- For timing differences identified on responses or otherwise (eg cash in transit), these should be agreed to post year-end cash receipts in the cash book and bank statement.

- For those responses highlighting an unresolved difference, the receivables ledger should be reviewed for unusual entries that could suggest errors made when posting transactions.

(**Note:** Only five valid procedures were needed to gain full marks for (i))

(iii) **Reorganisation**

- Verify the announcement to shareholders was actually made in late October by inspecting documentary evidence of the announcement.

- Board minutes should also be reviewed to confirm the decision to reorganise the business was taken pre year end.

- Obtain an analysis of the reorganisation provision and confirm that only expenditure attributable to the restructuring is included.

- Cast the breakdown of the reorganisation provision to ensure it has been correctly calculated.

- Review the expenditure and confirm retraining costs are not included.

- Agree costs included within the provision to supporting documentation to confirm the appropriateness and accuracy of items included.

- Review the related disclosures in the financial statements to assess whether they comply with the requirements of IAS 37 *Provisions, contingent liabilities and contingent assets*.

- Obtain a written representation confirming management discussions in relation to the announcement of the reorganisation.

(**Note:** Only four valid procedures were needed to gain full marks for (iii))

108 Textile Wholesalers

Text reference. Chapter 13.

Top tips. This question deals with the year-end inventory count and cut-off procedures. This is a popular exam topic. When considering the inventory count procedures try to think through the practical steps involved. This will help you to generate ideas and will provide a sensible structure for your answer. Cut-off is an important area of your studies. Management should ensure they have proper cut-off procedures to cover all stages of the movement of inventories (ie receipt of goods, internal transfers and final sales).

Easy marks. These are available in part (a). Notice how (ii) follows on from (i). Once you have identified the procedures that the company's staff should be carrying out you can then use these points as a basis for the audit procedures. For example, if the company procedure is to have full inventory count instructions the audit procedure would be to review these.

(a) (i) The procedures that the company's staff should carry out to ensure that inventories is counted accurately and cut-off details are recorded are as follows.

(1) Staff carrying out the inventory count should be issued with **full instructions** and so know how to proceed.

(2) Staff **counting inventories** should be **independent** of warehouse staff. They should count in **pairs**.

(3) A **senior member of staff** should **supervise the count**, carry out test counts and ensure at the end all inventories have been counted.

(4) All **inventory movements** should **stop** whilst the inventory counting is in progress.

(5) **Pre-numbered inventory sheets** should be used to record the counts and should be completed in ink signed by the counter. All sheets should be accounted for at the end of the inventory counting.

(6) The number of the **last Goods Received Note** and **Goods Dispatched Note** to be issued before the inventory counting should be recorded.

(7) Staff should **note the condition of inventories** where it is old or in poor condition.

(8) Staff should be designated **clearly defined areas** for counting to avoid double counting or inventory being missed. It may be possible to mark items in some way once they have been counted.

(ii) As auditor I would carry out the following procedures.

(1) **Review** the company's **inventory counting instructions** to ensure they were comprehensive and complete.

(2) **Observe** the client's **staff** during the count to ensure they were complying with issued instructions.

(3) **Carry out some test counts** and note the results in my working papers. My test counts will be in both directions (from the inventory sheets to the inventories, thus checking the inventories exists, and vice versa to ensure inventories has been completely recorded).

(4) **Note any items** considered to be **old** or in **poor condition**.

(5) **Note** the **sequence** of inventory sheets issued.

(6)   **Note down the last Goods Received Note and Goods Dispatched Note** numbers, also details of last returns to suppliers and from customers.

(7)   **Take copies of inventory sheets** and confirm during the final audit they remain unchanged and client's staff have not subsequently altered them.

(b)   Errors have been made in cut-off for items 2, 4, 5 and 6

(i)

GRN No	Goods received in October 20X6	Adjustment $
2	Invoice included in the purchase ledger and in accruals	5,164
4	Invoice not included in the purchase ledger and in accruals	(9,624)
	Goods received in November 20X6	
5	Receipt included in purchase ledger	8,243
6	Receipt included in accruals	6,389
	Increase in profit	10,172

Both purchases and payables will be decreased by this amount.

(ii)   The incidence of error in this test is very high – four out of the seven items tested had been incorrectly treated. I would therefore **extend my test** to cover a larger number of GRNs over a longer period, both before and after the year end.

I would also ensure purchases that were treated as accruals had been **accrued correctly**.

I would establish the treatment of goods on **invoices posted** early on the **following year** and confirm that invoices relating to following year deliveries had not been posted for this year.

I would also consider the results of the audit reconciliation of suppliers' statements to purchase ledger balances. This may highlight items which have been posted incorrectly (eg pre year-end invoices for goods received pre-year-end but not posted).

109 Multiple choice answers

1   B   The auditor has an active responsibility to perform procedures designed to obtain sufficient appropriate evidence that all events up to the date of the auditor's report that may require adjustment of, or disclosure in, the financial statements have been identified.

2   C   ISA 560 also requires the auditor to obtain an understanding of procedures put in place by management to ensure that subsequent events are identified and to read the entity's latest subsequent interim financial statements.

3   B   Not all subsequent events identified will need to be reflected in the financial statements. Some subsequent events may be non-adjusting in accordance with IAS 10 *Events after the reporting period*.

4   B   If a business is viewed as a going concern it is assumed that it will continue for the foreseeable future.

5   B   Management are responsible for the financial statements, so it is management's responsibility to determine whether the entity is a going concern. The auditor must evaluate management's assessment.

6   B   Where the period used by management to determine whether the entity is a going concern is less than 12 months from the period end, the auditor should request that management extends the assessment period to at least 12 months from the period end.

7   C   In accordance with ISA 570 *Going concern,* (1) and (4) are operating factors, not financial factors.

8   D   Other than inquiry of management the auditor is not required to perform any procedures regarding going concern issues after the period of assessment used by management.

9   D   The emphasis of matter paragraph is an explanatory paragraph detailing the uncertainty.

10   D   In accordance with ISA 570 *Going concern* where the going concern basis of preparation of the financial statements is adopted inappropriately the auditor issues an adverse opinion.

11	C	The date of the letter must be as near as practicable to the date of the auditor's report but not after.
12	B	In accordance with ISA 580 *Written representations*, written representations support other evidence relevant to financial statements, ie they are not sufficient appropriate evidence on their own.
13	A	In accordance with ISA 580 *Written representations*, written representations from management must be sought regarding the preparation of financial statements and information provided and completeness of transactions. Other representations **may** be sought to support other audit evidence where the auditor judges this to be necessary. In normal circumstances, alternative sufficient appropriate evidence regarding the recoverability of accounts receivable and valuation of inventory should be available.
14	A	Analytical procedures **must** be used as risk assessment procedures as part of the overall review of the financial statements at the end of the audit. They **may** also be used as substantive procedures.
15	C	This is in accordance with ISA 450 *Evaluation of misstatements identified during the audit*.
16	D	The basic elements of the auditor's report are title, addressee, introductory paragraph, management's responsibility for financial statements, auditor's responsibility, opinion paragraph, other reporting responsibilities, auditor's signature, date of the report and auditor's address.
17	C	An unmodified opinion is expressed when the auditor concludes that the financial statements are prepared, in all material respects, in accordance with the applicable financial reporting framework.
18	D	In A and C a qualified opinion would be issued. In B an adverse opinion would be issued.
19	C	The auditor issues a qualified opinion as the issue is material but not pervasive. The grounds for the modification are that the financial statements are misstated rather than due to insufficient evidence.
20	B	Although the receivables balance is overstated, the amount involved is not material.
21	B	An emphasis of matter paragraph is used to draw the readers attention to matters which are referred to in the financial statements but which are fundamental to the users' understanding of the financial statements.
22	B	This is in accordance with ISA 706 *Emphasis of matter paragraphs and other matter paragraphs in the independent auditor's report*.
23	B	The impact of the lack of evidence is both material and pervasive due to the extent of the loss of books and records.
24	C	Both statements are materially misstated as the asset must be written off reducing the profit for the year. An unmodified opinion can only be issued if both statements are adjusted.

110 Evaluating misstatements and responsibilities

Text references. Chapters 18 and 19.

Top tips. As with all the 10 mark questions, make sure you do not spend too long on this question overall and stick to the time allocations for each part.

Easy marks. This question should present you with no real problems.

Marking scheme

		Marks
(a)	Up to 1 mark per well explained point	
	Definition	
	Consider aggregate of uncorrected misstatements	
	Communicate to management	
	Written representation	4

(b)   Representation letter contents
       ½ mark per valid point   3

(c)   Up to 1 mark per well explained point
       Qualified opinion – misstatements which are material but not pervasive
       Qualified opinion – cannot obtain sufficient evidence, possible
       misstatements which are material but not pervasive
       Adverse opinion
       Disclaimer of opinion $\frac{3}{\underline{\underline{10}}}$

(a)   **Uncorrected misstatements**

       An uncorrected misstatement is a misstatement accumulated during the audit by the auditor which has not
       been corrected.

       As part of the completion procedures, the auditor must consider whether the aggregate of uncorrected
       misstatements in the financial statements is material, having first reassessed materiality to confirm that it is
       still appropriate. When determining whether uncorrected misstatements are material (individually or in
       aggregate), the auditor must consider the size and nature of the misstatements and the effect of uncorrected
       misstatements related to prior periods on the financial statements as a whole.

       The auditor must communicate uncorrected misstatements and their effect to those charged with
       governance, with material uncorrected misstatements being identified individually.

       The auditor must also request a written representation from management and those charged with
       governance whether they believe the effects of uncorrected misstatements are immaterial.

(b)   **Items to include in a written representation letter**

       - Acknowledgement from management that it has fulfilled its responsibility for the preparation and
         presentation of the financial statements as set out in the terms of the audit engagement and in
         particular, whether the financial statements are prepared and presented in accordance with the
         applicable financial reporting framework.

       - Acknowledgement from management that it has provided the auditor with all relevant information
         agreed in the terms of the audit engagement.

       - All transactions have been recorded and are reflected in the financial statements.

       - Appropriateness of selection and application of accounting policies.

       - Whether matters such as the following have been recognised, measured, presented or disclosed in
         accordance with the applicable financial reporting framework:

         - Plans or intentions that may affect the carrying value or classification of assets and liabilities.

         - Liabilities (actual and contingent).

         - Title to, or control over, assets, liens or encumbrances on assets, and assets pledged as
           collateral.

         - Aspects of laws, regulations and contractual agreements that may affect the financial
           statements, including non-compliance.

       - No irregularities involving management or employees with a significant role in the accounting and
         internal control systems or that could have a material effect on the financial statements.

       - Communication to the auditor of all deficiencies in internal control of which management is aware.

       - Representations about specific assertions in the financial statements.

       - Significant assumptions used by management in making accounting estimates are reasonable.

       - Related party relationships and transactions have been appropriately accounted for and disclosed.

- All subsequent events requiring adjustment or disclosure have been adjusted or disclosed.

- The effects of uncorrected misstatements are immaterial, both individually and in aggregate, and a list of these is attached with this letter.

Tutorial note: Only six were required.

(c) **Modified audit opinions**

ISA 705 *Modifications to the opinion in the independent auditor's report* sets out three types of modified opinion:

Qualified opinion

A qualified opinion must be expressed in the auditor's report in the following two situations.

(1) The auditor concludes that misstatements are material, but not pervasive, to the financial statements.

(2) The auditor cannot obtain sufficient appropriate audit evidence on which to base the opinion but concludes that the possible effects of undetected misstatements, if any, could be material but not pervasive.

Adverse opinion

An adverse opinion is expressed when the auditor, having obtained sufficient appropriate audit evidence, concludes that misstatements are both material and pervasive to the financial statements.

Disclaimer of opinion

An opinion must be disclaimed when the auditor cannot obtain sufficient appropriate audit evidence on which to base the opinion and concludes that the possible effects on the financial statements of undetected misstatements, if any, could be both material and pervasive.

111 Written representation and going concern

Text references. Chapters 4 and 18.

Top tips. This is a knowledge-based question covering ethical principles and going concern, both topics you should feel reasonably comfortable with. Make sure that you do not run over time on this question – be specific and answer the question set.

Note the requirement in part (a)(i) to 'explain why' – this means that your answer should not just consist of a list of bullet points but that you must develop each point more fully. This question assumes a good knowledge of ISA 580 *Written representations* so make sure you are familiar with this area of the syllabus as it could come up in scenario-based questions about audit evidence or in a knowledge-based context, as in this case.

Part (b) requires an explanation of the actions the auditors should carry out when assessing whether an entity is a going concern. This tests your knowledge of quite a specific part of ISA 570 *Going Concern* although a reasonable answer can be produced if you apply some common sense and have a good understanding of the principles of ISA 570. Think carefully about the requirement – you are not being asked to list the factors which might indicate that the company is not a going concern, but the actions the auditor would perform.

Easy marks. You should be able to pick up good marks in part (a) provided that you ensure that you explain the fundamental principles rather than simply listing them.

Marks

(a) Written representations
Up to 1 mark per point to maximum of 2
Common categories of matter included in the letter of representation

½ mark per point to maximum of 3
Total marks

5

(b) 1 mark per action
   -   Review management plans
   -   Additional audit procedures
   -   Written representations
   -   Loans from bank
   -   Receivables ageing
   -   Other relevant points – Allow ½ marks where candidate lists audit procedures such as review cash flow forecasts, review management accounts post year end, etc.

Maximum marks

$\dfrac{5}{10}$

(a) (i) **Written representations**

During an audit many representations are made to the auditor, usually in response to specific queries. Where the auditor considers that other **sufficient appropriate evidence is not expected to exist,** written confirmation is sought. This might include instances for example where knowledge of the facts is confined to management or where the matter is principally one of judgement. This reduces the possibility of misunderstandings arising.

Written representations should not however, be a substitute for other independent evidence.

Written representations may also be used to obtain confirmations regarding more general matters. These are listed in points (1) – (3) below.

(ii) **Matters commonly included**

(1) Acknowledgement of directors' responsibility for the preparation and presentation of the financial statements

(2) Confirmation that the transactions of the company have been recorded in the books and records and that all of these have been made available to the auditor

(3) Opinion as to the expected outcome of any legal claims

(4) Assumptions used in respect of tax treatments

(5) Confirmation as to the existence or otherwise of related party transactions

(6) That there have been no events since the end of the reporting period which require revision of the accounts

(b) **Audit actions to ascertain whether an entity is a going concern**

When planning the audit the auditor must:

•   Consider in particular whether there are any events, conditions and business risks which might cast doubt on the entity's ability to continue as a going concern

•   Evaluate management's assessment of the entity's ability to continue as a going concern

When events or conditions have been identified which cast significant doubt on the viability of the business the following additional actions should be taken:

•   Review management's plans for future actions based on its going concern assessment and ensure that these are feasible and that the outcome of these plans will improve the situation. (Specific procedures might include analysing and discussing cash flow, reviewing the terms of debentures and loan agreements)

- Gather sufficient appropriate audit evidence to confirm or dispel whether or not a material uncertainty exists regarding going concern. This will involve considering any additional facts or information which has become available since management's going concern assessment.

- Seek written representations from management regarding its plans for future actions and the feasibility of these plans

- Obtain information regarding the continuance of loan facilities from the company's bankers

- Identify indications of cash flow problems eg determine whether there has been an increase in receivables days by reviewing the receivables ageing analysis

112 Corsco

Text references. Chapters 18 and 19.

Top tips. This question considers the issue of going concern and the potential impact on the auditor's report. This is primarily a technical question so the key will be to use your knowledge of ISA 570 and ISA 700/705/706.

For part (a) do not jump to conclusions but make sure you read all the information and weigh it up. Also remember that modified opinions are issued relatively infrequently. In part (b) you need to think as practically as possible. Notice that you are asked to consider the difficulties which would be faced by both Corsco and the auditors.

Easy marks. If you have a good knowledge of ISA 570, all the marks available are equally achievable.

Examiner's comments. In part (a) too many candidates assumed that a modified audit opinion would be required.

Marking scheme

		Marks
(a)	Report issued to Corsco Up to 2 marks per point to a maximum of	4
(b)	Difficulties associated with reporting on going concern Up to 1½ marks per point to a maximum of	6 **10**

(a) **Report issued to Corsco**

Although the company is obviously experiencing some difficulties, the evidence provided does not suggest that the business will cease to trade in the near future. The company has net assets and still appears to have options available to it in order to resolve its problems. The fact that the company has taken steps to restructure its finance and has been able to do so is also a positive sign.

On the basis that the situation is no worse than in previous years and that no reference has been made to going concern in the past it would not seem appropriate to refer to it this year. An auditor's report with an unmodified audit opinion would be issued.

(b) **Difficulties**

If the auditor's report mentions a going concern problem, it is likely that Corsco will find it difficult to raise finance from banks or investors. It is often said that it becomes a 'self-fulfilling prophecy' although this should not dissuade the auditor from modifying the audit opinion if the auditor feels there is genuine need.

In addition, customers and suppliers may notice the reference in the auditor's report and subsequently be more cautious in doing business with Corsco. This is likely to further worsen the position and liquidity of the business. For example, Corso's suppliers may decrease the number of days credit they allow Corsco or their credit limit.

The relationship between the auditor and the management of Corsco could become very strained, particularly where the management of Corsco genuinely believe that no reference is required. This is particularly difficult as the matter is essentially one of judgement and will rarely be clear-cut. In extreme circumstances, the auditors may lose the audit and fees from associated work.

In this particular case, as there has been no reference to going concern in the past, referring to it this year would imply that the situation has deteriorated further, or that previous reports were not correct. This is a particularly contentious issue as there is ongoing public concern about the role of the auditor in warning shareholders about matters which will affect the value of their investment.

113 Going concern and auditor's reports

Marking scheme

		Marks
(a)	External auditor responsibilities – going concern Up to 1 mark per point to a maximum of	5
(b)	Possible audit reports and circumstances Up to 1½ marks per point to a maximum of	5 10

(a) **External auditor's responsibilities and the work that the auditor should perform in relation to going concern**

(i) *Responsibilities*

According to ISA 570 the auditor must:

- Evaluate **management's assessment** of the entity's ability to continue as a going concern

- Consider whether there are, and remain alert throughout the audit for, events or conditions that may cast significant doubt on the entity's ability to continue as a going concern

- Enquire of management its knowledge of events or conditions beyond the period of the assessment that may cast significant doubt on the entity's ability to continue as a going concern

- Obtain sufficient appropriate audit evidence to determine whether a material uncertainty exists if events or conditions are identified that may cast significant doubt on the entity's ability to continue as a going concern

(ii) *Audit work*

- As part of the overall risk assessment the auditor must consider whether there are any events or conditions and related business risks which may cast significant doubt on the company's ability to continue.

- The auditor should evaluate the process by which management has assessed the viability of the company. The auditor should make enquiries of those charged with governance and examine supporting documentation such as cash flow forecasts and budgets.

- The auditor must consider whether the period used by management to assess the viability of the company is sufficient. If the period covers less than twelve months from the reporting date the auditor should ask management to extend the period to twelve months from the reporting date.

- The auditor should evaluate the assumptions used by management and determine whether they seem reasonable in the light of other known facts.

- Where events or conditions have been identified which may cast significant doubt on the entity's ability to continue as a going concern the auditor must review management's plans for future actions and gather sufficient appropriate audit evidence to confirm whether a material uncertainty exists. This will include:

    - Analysing and discussing the cash flow and interim financial statements

    - Reviewing the terms of debentures and loan agreements

    - Reading minutes of the meetings of shareholders and directors for reference to financing difficulties

    - Inquiring of the company's lawyers regarding litigation and claims

    - Assessing the possibility of raising additional funds

    - Reviewing events after the period end

- The auditor must seek written representations from management regarding its plans for future action.

(b) **Auditor's reports**

(i) Where the use of the going concern assumption is appropriate but a material uncertainty exists, provided that the auditor agrees with the basis of preparation of the accounts and the situation is adequately disclosed, an **unmodified opinion** is issued. The audit report will however include an **emphasis of matter paragraph** highlighting the uncertainty to the user and referring them to the details in the disclosure note.

(ii) Where the material uncertainty exists but the situation is not adequately disclosed the opinion should be **modified on the grounds that there is** insufficient disclosure and the financial statements are materially misstated. Depending on the specific circumstances this may be a qualified 'except for' or adverse opinion.

(iii) If in the auditor's judgement the company will not be able to continue as a going concern and the financial statements have been prepared on a going concern basis the auditor shall express **an adverse opinion**.

(iv) If the auditors are unable to form an opinion because they were not able to obtain sufficient appropriate audit evidence they shall issue **an 'except for' qualified opinion or a disclaimer**.

(v) If management is unwilling to extend its assessment where the period considered is less than twelve months from the reporting date the auditor shall consider **the need to modify** the opinion as a result of not obtaining this evidence.

114 Greenfields

Text reference. Chapters 11, 18 and 19.

Top tips. This question requires a **discussion** in (i). Make sure you do present a discussion on questions like this. In terms of written representations it is very important that you realise they are used to support other evidence (not as stand alone evidence), particularly in areas of judgement such as accounting estimates. You should have weighed up the appropriateness of written representations using the relevant rules for evidence – written evidence is better than verbal, but internal evidence is not as good as external. However you should have taken care to apply

those rules to the specific situation described in the scenario, as just stating general rules without applying them is not sufficient for a exam at this level. For both (i) and (ii), hopefully you took note of the first line of the requirement – 'for each of the two issues above'. This is telling you to make sure you keep your answer focused on the issues described.

Examiner's comments. In the first part on written representations, many candidates wrote at length about written representations in general but the question asked specifically about two situations and these needed to be addressed. In addition many candidates did not seem to understand the difference between the two situations in that for the receivable balance alternative evidence should exist, for example, through a receivables circularisation, but because of the nature of the warranty provision alternative evidence was not generally available.

The second part of the question considered additional procedures that should now be performed for these two issues. Again performance was unsatisfactory, it was clear from the scenario that the audit fieldwork had already been performed as it was stated that the manager was performing a final review of the audit. Therefore procedures needed to reflect that the main work on testing receivables and provisions had already been undertaken and at this stage it was just a case of updating this knowledge.

Marking scheme

		Marks
(i)	Up to 2 marks for each discussion of reliability of representations	
	Receivable balance	
	Warranty provision	4
(ii)	Up to 1 mark per procedure, max of 3 marks per issue	
	Receivables balance:	
	Discuss with management why circularisation not allowed	
	Review post year end receipts	
	Review customer correspondence	
	Board minutes and legal correspondence	
	Discuss with management need for provision or write down	
	Consider impact on audit opinion	3
	Warranty provision:	
	Review post year end claims	
	Compare prior year end provisions to claims made	
	Review board minutes	3
		10

Yellowmix receivable balance

(i) *Written representation*

Management have offered a written representation over the recoverability of the balance but have not allowed circularisation of the receivable. This suggests they believe the written representation is an adequate substitute for the evidence gained from a circularisation.

However, this is not the case. The circularisation would provide evidence is on existence, valuation and rights/obligations on the receivable balance. The written representation proposed by management is focused on the recoverability and gives only weak evidence over the relevant assertions. Despite being in writing and more reliable than a verbal representation, the internally generated representation is not as good as evidence from an external source (such as any potential response from Yellowmix to the circularisation).

With the other evidence available being limited due to the lack of payment activity over the last six months, without further more compelling evidence, the representation alone would appear insufficient to conclude that receivables are free from material misstatement.

(ii) *Additional procedures*

In order to conclude on the receivables balance the auditor should perform additional procedures including the following:

- Enquire of management why they did not permit the circularisation

- Review any correspondence with Yellomix to see if there is any reason for the delay in payment or for any disputes of invoices outstanding at the year end

- Review post year end cash receipts to see if any related to Yellowmix and give evidence of existence and recoverability of the year end balance.

> **Top tips.** Only three procedures were needed for each issue. However in respect of the receivables balance, here are some others you may have come up with:
>
> - Review board minutes and legal correspondence for evidence of legal action in respect of recovering the debt.
> - Discuss with management whether a provision is needed.
> - It the balance is considered materially misstated, consider the effect on the auditor's opinion in the auditor's report.

Warranty provision

(i) *Written representation*

The audit team has already carried out some procedures in testing the calculations and assumptions and found them to be in accordance with prior years (and presumably in accordance with expectations). All of the evidence to date is from internal sources, but there is unlikely to be readily available reliable external sources.

It will be difficult for anyone to predict how many warranty claims there will be in the future and the value of any future claims, and written representation on this matter will be one of the few sources of evidence available. It will be a useful piece of evidence as a written confirmation that management believe the assumptions and the provision are reasonable, and more reliable than verbal representations, despite being from an internal source.

(ii) *Additional procedures*

In order to conclude on the warranty provision the auditor should perform additional procedures including the following:

- Assess the adequacy of the provision having established the level of warranty claims occurring after the year end.

- Compare the amounts provided for warranties in previous years with amounts claimed to see how accurate management's provisions have proved in the past.

- Review minutes of board meetings for evidence that equipment manufactured by Greenfields might contain defects and result in more claims, necessitating an increase in the provision.

115 Tye

> **Text references.** Chapters 4, 6, 13, 18 and 19.
>
> **Top tips.** Part (a) highlights an inventory valuation issue arising at the finalisation stage. The requirement is to list actions and procedures in response to the directors wanting to adopt a policy which will result in a material misstatement (based on the draft profit for the year). The audit work is complete apart from this matter and the procedures should be confined to this matter. Procedures at this stage of the audit will focus on the relevant accounting standard, discussions with the directors and the impact on the audit report.
>
> **Easy marks.** Part (b) on accounting estimates should not cause you too many problems, if you are familiar with this part of the syllabus.

Marking scheme

		Marks
(a)	**Aviation fuel inventory**	

1 mark each for each valid procedure or action:
- Any alternative treatments in GAAP
- Materiality calculation
- Review prior year working papers
- Discuss with directors
- Warn directors possible qualification
- Quantify amount
- Management representation
- Draft audit report
- Other relevant points

Maximum marks   6

(b)   **Audit procedures for accounting estimates**

1 mark for each procedure $\underline{4}$

$\underline{\underline{10}}$

(a)   **Proposed valuation of inventory – procedures and actions**

1   Identify the relevant section of IAS 2 which prohibits the valuation of the inventory at market value (IAS 2 requires that inventory should be valued at the lower of cost and net realisable value) and ensure there are no exceptions permitted by the standard.

2   Calculate the magnitude of the misstatement which is clearly material in the context of the results for the year of $500,000. The maximum misstatement is ($120 – 15) × 6000 = $630,000.

3   Ask the directors their reasons for wanting to value the inventory in this way.

4   Point out to the directors that the treatment is incorrect, the misstatement is material and any opinion on financial statements where inventory is valued in this way will be qualified.

5   Review findings last year to establish treatment in the past and, if this has occurred before, how it has been dealt with.

6   If the directors refuse to change the treatment, draft a suitable qualification.

(b)   **Audit procedures in respect of accounting estimates**

- Enquire of management how the estimate has been arrived at and evaluate whether the assumptions used are reasonable.

- Review the judgements and decisions of management in making the accounting estimates to identify if there are indications of possible management bias.

- Develop a point estimate or range with which to evaluate the reasonableness of the accounting estimate made by management.

- Test whether controls over development of management estimates are operating effectively.

116 EastVale

Text references. Chapters 18 and 19.

Top tips. This question tests your knowledge and application of audit reviews and reports. It's also important that you remember your financial reporting studies to apply to the two events that occur after the end of the reporting period. The best way to present your answer is to take each event in turn and answer the two requirements. This allows you to break the question down into more manageable chunks and gives more structure to your answers. Make sure that in (i), you support your answer with good explanations. In (ii), you must justify your answer in order to score well.

Easy marks. There aren't easy marks as such in this question but if you take each situation in turn, and answer each of the requirements, you should be able to score reasonably well.

Marking scheme

		Marks
(a)	**Fire at warehouse**	
(i)	Amendment to financial statements 2 marks – 1 per well-explained point	
	Disclosure in FS – unlikely with reason	1
	No amendment to statement of financial position	1
	Other relevant points	1
	Maximum marks	**2**
(ii)	Modification of audit report 3 marks – 1 per well-explained point	
	Modification of report	
	Going concern status?	1
	Inadequate disclosure by directors	1
	Other relevant points (each)	1
	Maximum marks	**2**
		Marks
(b)	**Batch of cheese**	
(i)	Disclosure of event 2 marks – 1 per well-explained point	
	Disclosure event – because significant impact	1
	No adjustment	1
	Going concern issue – reputation	1
	May result in amendment to FS	1
	Other relevant points (each)	1
	Maximum marks	**3**

		Marks
(ii)	Impact on audit report – 3 marks – 1 per well-explained point	
	Preparation of FS breakup basis	1
	Prepared going concern basis – emphasis of matter to note this	1
	Prepared going concern – but in doubt – emphasis of matter to note this	1
	Prepared going concern and disagree – adverse opinion	1
	Maximum marks	**3**
		10

(a) **Fire in warehouse**

(i) *Impact on financial statements*

As the fire is a non-adjusting event after the reporting period, providing the going concern basis is still appropriate no amendments are required to the financial statements for the financial year being audited. However, disclosure of the event is required by IAS 10 *Events after the reporting period* as the event is likely to be material. This disclosure should include the nature of the event and an estimate of its financial effect.

(ii) *Impact on auditor's report*

Providing the directors have properly disclosed the event the audit opinion would not be modified as this is a non-adjusting event after the period-end date and does not provide evidence of conditions that existed at the period-end date. However, an emphasis of matter paragraph could be included in the audit report to highlight the matter and draw it to the attention of users of the financial statements.

(b) **Cheese**

(i) *Impact on financial statements*

This is a non-adjusting event after the reporting period. However, given its nature it should be disclosed in a note to the financial statements. If it impacts on the going concern status of the company, then the accounts would have to be prepared on a different basis and disclosures in accordance with IAS 8 *Accounting policies, changes in accounting estimates and errors* would be required.

(ii) *Impact on auditor's report*

If the directors consider that as a result of the food poisoning reports the company cannot continue as a going concern and they produce the accounts on a break-up basis, then the audit opinion would not be modified but the audit report would include an emphasis of matter paragraph to draw attention to users of this matter.

If the accounts are prepared on the assumption that the company is a going concern but the auditors do not agree with this then the audit report would include an adverse opinion on the financial statements.

117 ZeeDiem

Text references. Chapters 18 and 19.

Top tips. This question for 20 marks is about subsequent events. You need to be familiar with ISA 560 *Subsequent events* to score well in this question. There are several dates to bear in mind with this question so you might find it helpful to draw a timeline with the key dates on it while you are planning your answer, to help you get things into context.

Easy marks. Easy marks are available in part (a) (i) for four marks to explain whether the two events are adjusting or non-adjusting.

Marking scheme

			Marks
(a)		1 mark for each point regarding auditor responsibility	
		Maximum marks	3
(b)	(i)	1 mark for each valid audit procedure	
		Maximum 6 marks for each event	
		Destruction of inventory	
		Audit must identify material events post reporting period	
		Need to check value of $225,000 is receivable	
		Documentation from insurers	
		Payment from third party	
		Disclosure in financial statements	
		Total inventory value end of year	
		Other inventory affected?	
		Representation point	
		Maximum marks	4
	(ii)	1 mark for each valid audit procedure	
		Release of dye	
		Ensure that material events is disclosed appropriately in financial statements	
		Documentation of event	
		Extent of disclosure in financial statements	
		Action if disagree with amount of disclosure	
		Possibility of modified audit opinion	
		Written representation letter	
		Maximum marks	<u>3</u>
		Total marks	<u>**10**</u>

(a) Auditor's responsibilities

ISA 560 *Subsequent events* requires that auditors perform audit procedures to obtain sufficient, appropriate audit evidence that all events up to the date of the auditor's report that may require adjustment or disclosure in the financial statements have been identified. In this case, since the auditor's report will not be signed until the following week, the auditors must perform additional audit procedures for this event.

When the auditors identify events that require adjustment of, or disclosure in, the financial statements, they need to determine whether these events are appropriately reflected in the financial statements.

The auditors are required to request management to provide a written representation that all events occurring subsequent to the date of the financial statements and for which the applicable financial reporting framework requires adjustment or disclosure have been adjusted or disclosed.

(b)   **Audit procedures**

    (i)   *Event 1*

        The following audit procedures should be carried out:

- Inspect the insurers' report to confirm the value of inventory that is affected and to confirm the valuation of this inventory as a result.

- If any of the defective mattresses have subsequently been sold, agree the amounts to supporting documentation and to the bank.

- Discuss the issue with the directors and inform them that the financial statements should be adjusted to reduce the value of year-end inventory by $525k.

- Obtain a written representation from management as to the value of inventory at the year-end.

- Review the amended financial statements to confirm that the inventory write-down has indeed been made.

- If the directors refuse to make the necessary amendments, the audit report may need to include a qualified 'except for' opinion on the grounds that the financial statements are materially misstated if this issue is material.

    (ii)   *Event 2*

        The following audit procedures should be carried out:

- Inspect any reports from the Environmental Agency as to whether the release of dye was in breach of legislation and the outcome of this.

- Discuss the issue with the directors and inform them that the financial statements will need additional disclosure for this event.

- Obtain a written representation point from management about this event.

- Review the amended financial statements to confirm that the disclosure has been made satisfactorily.

- If the directors refuse to make the necessary disclosure, consider whether the audit report will need to contain a qualified 'except for' opinion.

118 Green

Text reference. Chapter 18.

Top tips. In this question, the scenario is quite long so spend a bit of time going through it carefully and noting down potential issues arising. In part (b), you have to list the audit procedures you would undertake to determine whether the going concern basis is appropriate. Make sure the tests you describe are specific and sensible – vague answers won't score well.

Easy marks. You should be able to score well in part (b) on going concern.

Examiner's comments. Answers to part (a) varied considerably. Many candidates still seemed to be confused by the concept of going concern. The main confusion related to describing going concern as a situation where the company would not be continuing in business rather than one where it would continue in business. In part (a)(ii) poorer answers provided long lists of directors' and auditors' responsibilities, which were not related to going concern.

Part (b) produced the best answers although only a minority of candidates related their comments to the scenario. Common errors included:

- Stating going concern indicators rather than work on the going concern concept
- Re-auditing historical information. Procedures needed to relate to going concern, which implied trying to determine how the company would perform in the future.

		Marks
(a)	Key points, 1 for each point	
(i)	State going concern (enterprise operational existence)	1
(ii)	Directors responsibilities – prepare FS	1
	Evidence produce	1
	Auditor responsibilities – check GC concept	1
	Collect audit evidence	1
	Disclosure of going concern concept if necessary	1
	Maximum marks	5

		Marks
(b)	Key points 1 for each point	
	Profit and cash flow forecasts	1
	Review order books	1
	Contact lawyers	1
	Review financial status – other GC indicators	1
	Correspondence organic certification	1
	Contact bank	1
	Representation letter	1
	Other good relevant points	1
	Maximum marks	5
		10

(a) **Going concern**

(i) Going concern relates to a company's ability to continue operating for the foreseeable future – this period is not defined but is generally assumed to be at least 12 months from the reporting date. It should not be applied to the preparation of financial statements when the company intends to cease trading or when it has intentions to file for bankruptcy.

(ii) Directors have a responsibility to make a specific assessment of the entity's ability to continue as a going concern. They must also satisfy themselves when preparing the financial statements that the going concern assumption is still appropriate. This applies even if there is no explicit requirement to do so in the financial reporting framework.

The auditors have a responsibility to consider the appropriateness of management's use of the going concern assumption in the preparation of the financial statements and to consider whether there are any material uncertainties about the entity's ability to continue as a going concern that need to be disclosed in the financial statements.

They must also remain alert for evidence of events that may cast doubt on the entity's ability to continue as a going concern and must consider whether there are adequate disclosures in the financial statements regarding the going concern basis, so that the accounts give a true and fair view.

(b) **Audit procedures regarding going concern**

- Discuss with the managers of Green how they have concluded that the company can continue as a going concern

- Review profit forecasts and budgets of Green to assess whether the going concern assumption is relevant

- Review correspondence from legal advisers of Green concerning the potential court case against Black

- Discuss with legal advisers of Green the chances of Green being successful if this case is brought to court and potential costs involved

BPP
LEARNING MEDIA

- Inspect relevant lending documentation issued by Green's bank to establish level of any borrowings/overdraft facilities and discuss with Green's bank manager

- Obtain a written representation point from the managers of Green to confirm that the company can continue as a going concern

119 Minnie

Text references. Chapters 18 and 19.

Top tips. This question contains a mixture of knowledge based requirements and requirements which need you to apply knowledge in the context of the scenario provided.

Part (a) is unrelated to the scenario. Remember to provide a balanced answer which addresses both parts of the requirement. In other words don't just focus on what a misstatement is and forget about addressing the auditor's responsibilities.

In part (b) you are given figures relating to each audit issue along with the profit before tax figure. This is a very big clue that you need to use these to assess whether the misstatements arising from the issues are material.

ISA 320 *Materiality in planning and performing an audit* includes a materiality benchmark guideline of 5% of profit before tax. Note that you need to initially discuss the issue before describing the impact on the auditor's report. If you have remembered the criteria for issuing each type of modified opinion and made a judgement as to how material each issue is, you will not have a problem identifying the impact on the auditor's report. You are told audit report extracts are not needed so don't provide them! Also don't waste time talking about what would happen if the issue is resolved because you are told in the question to assume this will not happen.

Note that this question demonstrates your need to apply your financial reporting knowledge in the context of an audit. Anyone not up to date on IAS 37 *Provisions, contingent liabilities and contingent assets* would have struggled with this question.

Easy marks. The easy marks can be found in (a), which is a largely knowledge based requirement.

Examiner's comments. Part (a) was unrelated to the scenario, and was not answered well by many candidates. Most candidates were able to gain 1 mark by explaining that a misstatement was an error, however they could not then explain the auditor's responsibility.

ISA 450 *Evaluation of misstatements identified during the audit* provides guidance on this area. This is a relatively new ISA and was issued as part of the clarity project. As this ISA had not yet been tested then this is an area which should have been prioritised by candidates.

However, many candidates clearly had not studied this area at all. They therefore provided answers which focused on the auditor's responsibilities to provide an opinion on the truth and fairness of the financial statements or to detect material misstatements. In addition a minority of candidates produced answers which focused on materiality.

In Part (b), candidates' performance was unsatisfactory. Each of the two issues had a maximum of 4 marks available and in order to score well, candidates needed to consider the following in their answer:

- A description of the audit issue; such as incorrectly depreciating land, or lack of evidence to support wages or contingent liability disclosure.

- A calculation of whether the issue was material or not, using the financial information provided in the scenario.

- An explanation of the type of auditor's report required.

- A description of the impact on the auditor's report.

In relation to the materiality calculation, some candidates stated the issue was material but without using the financial information provided.

Many candidates used terms such as "except for", "modified" or "qualified" but the accompanying sentences demonstrated that candidates did not actually understand what these terms meant. In addition, a significant proportion of candidates do not understand when an "emphasis of matter" paragraph is relevant, and seemed to think that it was an alternative to an "except for" qualification. In relation to the impact on the auditor's report, many candidates were unable to describe how the opinion paragraph would change and that a basis for qualified opinion paragraph was necessary for issue (i). Future candidates are once again reminded that auditor's reports are the only output of a statutory audit and hence an understanding of how an auditor's report can be modified and in which circumstances, is considered very important for this exam.

Marks

(a) Up to 1 mark per well explained point
Definition of misstatements
Definition of uncorrected misstatements
Factual misstatements
Judgemental misstatements
Projected misstatements
Auditor should accumulate misstatements
Consider if audit strategy/plan should be revised
Assess if uncorrected misstatements material
Communicate to those charged with governance, request changes
If refused then assess impact on audit report
Request written representation
Maximum marks   4

(b) Up to 1 mark per valid point, overall maximum of 3 marks **per issue**
Discussion of issue
Calculation of materiality
Impact on auditor's report
Maximum marks $\frac{6}{10}$

(a) **Misstatements and the auditor's responsibilities in relation to them**

A **misstatement** is a difference between the amount, classification, presentation, or disclosure of a reported financial statement item and the amount, classification, presentation, or disclosure that is required for the item to be in accordance with the applicable financial reporting framework. It can arise from error or fraud.

ISA 450 *Evaluation of misstatements identified during the audit* provides guidance and distinguishes between **factual misstatements** (misstatements about which there is no doubt), **judgemental misstatements** (misstatements arising from management's judgement concerning accounting estimates or accounting policies) and **projected misstatements** (the auditor's best estimate of misstatements arising from sampling populations).

A misstatement accumulated during the audit by the auditor which has not been corrected is referred to as an **uncorrected misstatement**. The auditor must accumulate misstatements over the course of the audit unless they are clearly trivial.

As part of their completion procedures, auditors must consider whether the **aggregate of uncorrected misstatements** in the financial statements is **material** having considered the size and nature of the misstatements. Uncorrected misstatements and their effect must be communicated to those charged with governance, with material uncorrected misstatements being identified individually.

The auditor shall request uncorrected misstatements to be corrected. If they are not adjusted and are considered material then the auditor will have to consider the impact on the auditor' report.

The auditor must also request a **written representation** from management and those charged with governance stating whether they believe the effects of uncorrected misstatements are immaterial (individually and in aggregate) and a summary of these items has to be attached to the representation.

(**Note:** Only four well explained points were needed to obtain full marks)

(b) (i) **Corrupted wages records**

The corruption of Minnie's wages program has resulted in two months of wages data being lost.

If Daffy & Co are unable to verify the wages data for these months using alternative procedures then insufficient evidence is available for the two month period. This represents 11% of profit before tax ($1.1m/$10m) and is a material amount.

The effects of the possible misstatement of wages would be material, but not pervasive. As a result a qualified opinion should be expressed on the grounds that the auditor is unable to obtain sufficient appropriate audit evidence over a material area.

Daffy and Co's report will contain a basis for qualified opinion paragraph explaining they were unable to obtain sufficient appropriate audit evidence over the wages expense included in the financial statements due to the corrupted payroll records. The qualified opinion paragraph would state that, except for possible effects of the matter described in the basis for opinion paragraph, the financial statements are presented fairly in all material respects (or show a true and fair view).

(ii) **Lawsuit for breach of copyright**

Although legal action is being taken against the company for breach of copyright, the matter has been correctly disclosed in accordance with IAS 37 *Provisions, contingent liabilities and contingent assets.*

The $5m lawsuit represents 50% of profit before tax ($5.0m/$10m) and there is no doubt this is clearly a material matter.

No modification of the audit opinion is required because the matter is appropriately disclosed. However the uncertainty relating to the future outcome of this exceptional litigation is of such importance that it is fundamental to users' understanding of the financial statements. Therefore an emphasis of matter paragraph should be included in the auditor's report.

The emphasis of matter paragraph will appear after the opinion paragraph and should state there is an uncertainty over the outcome of the lawsuit and cross refer to the contingent liability disclosure note. The paragraph will state that the opinion is not qualified in respect of this matter.

120 Medimade

Text references. Chapters 18 and 19.

Top tips. Remember in (a) that assessing going concern is a forward looking exercise and audit procedures should focus on prospective financial information rather than historical financial information.

A common scenario is one where a company's future is uncertain but the going concern basis is still appropriate. Sometimes students rush into suggesting no modification to the audit opinion is necessary simply because the company is a going concern and see an emphasis of matter paragraph as the answer to all problems. However do not neglect to consider whether management's disclosures are adequate before you write off a potential modification of the opinion. In part (b) you have been told management will make disclosures, but the auditor must still check that they are adequate. If they are not, the financial statements may be materially misstated and a qualified or adverse opinion may be warranted.

Examiner's comments. Many had a reasonable attempt at part (a) and generated some satisfactory tests, however there were also a number of unsatisfactory tests provided.

Common errors included:

- Providing procedures which were based upon the year that had passed rather than the coming 12 months

- Requesting a written confirmation or a meeting with the bank to ascertain whether they would renew the overdraft facility, this is unrealistic.

- Lack of detail in the going concern procedure, such as "review board minutes" without an explanation of what to look for.

- Lack of variety of procedures, many tests started with "discuss with management".

Part (b) for 4 marks required a description of the impact on the audit report if the auditor believed Medimade Co was a going concern but a material uncertainty existed. In addition the scenario stated that the directors had now agreed to make going concern disclosures. This question was unsatisfactorily answered by many candidates. As the auditors believed that the going concern basis was appropriate, and the directors had made disclosures then the impact on the audit report was dependent on the adequacy of the disclosures made. If adequate then an emphasis of matter paragraph would be needed, if the disclosures were not adequate then a material misstatement modification would be required. Unfortunately, not many candidates understood the point about the adequacy of disclosures; they did suggest an emphasis of matter paragraph or material misstatement modifications, but this was without any reference to disclosures and so demonstrated a lack of understanding. In addition a number of

candidates wasted time on a discussion of whether the company was a going concern and therefore whether the break up basis should instead be used, this was despite the scenario stating that the auditor believed the company was a going concern. Candidates must take the time to read the scenario and requirements carefully.

Marks

(a)   Up to 1 mark per well explained point – If the procedure does not clearly
        explain how this will help the auditor to consider going concern then a
        ½ mark only should be awarded:
        – Review cash flow forecasts
        – Sensitivity analysis
        – Review bank agreements, breach of key ratios
        – Review bank correspondence
        – Discuss if alternative finance obtained
        – Review post year end sales and order book
        – Review suppliers correspondence
        – Inquire lawyers any litigation
        – Subsequent events
        – Board minutes
        – Management accounts
        – Consider additional disclosures under IAS 1
        – Written representation

6

(b)   Up to 1 mark per point
        – Depends on adequacy of disclosures
        – Adequately disclosed – unmodified
        – Emphasis of matter para – after opinion
        – Not adequately disclosed – modified
        – Material misstatement
        – Add paragraph before opinion and impact on opinion paragraph

$\frac{4}{10}$

(a)   **Audit procedures to assess whether the company is a going concern**

- Review correspondence with the bank for indications of the likelihood of renewal of the overdraft facility.

- Obtain the cash flow forecasts and assess whether the cash inflows and outflows appear realistic and consistent with knowledge built up during the audit. Consider the reasonableness of the assumptions on which the forecasts are based and discuss any findings with management.

- Review any post year end management accounts and compare the cash position they show with that forecast to help assess the reliability of the forecasts.

- Review any available post year end correspondence with suppliers to see if the trend of withdrawal of credit terms has continued, or eased, since the year end date.

- Review board minutes for meetings held after the year end for issues which indicate further financial difficulties or issues/funding which will alleviate cash flow problems to some degree.

- Obtain written representations from directors/management that they consider the company to be a going concern.

- Perform a sensitivity analysis on the cash flows to establish the margin of safety the company has in relation to its net cash inflow/outflow.

- Review current agreements with the bank to determine whether any key covenants have been breached.

- Consider whether all the disclosures required by IAS 1 *Presentation of financial statements* have been made in relation to material uncertainties over going concern.

> **Top tips**. Only six well explained procedures were required to gain full marks.

(b) **Impact on auditor's report: going concern appropriate but material uncertainty exists**

The auditor agrees with the directors that the company is a going concern and this is the basis on which the accounts are drawn up. However, the directors have agreed to include going concern disclosures and these disclosures will need to be assessed to see if they adequately describe the material uncertainty over going concern.

If the disclosure is inadequate the audit opinion will be modified on the grounds that the financial statements are material misstated.

If the inadequate disclosure is deemed a pervasive material misstatement, then an adverse opinion will be expressed stating the accounts are not presented fairly, in all material respects. The reason for the adverse opinion will be stated in a 'basis for adverse opinion' paragraph immediately before the opinion paragraph.

If the misstatement is not deemed pervasive, a qualified opinion will be expressed stating that except for the disclosure over going concern, the financial statements are presented fairly. The reason for the qualified opinion will be stated in a 'basis for qualified opinion' paragraph immediately before the opinion paragraph.

If the disclosure is adequate, then the accounts will be fairly presented in all material respects and an unmodified opinion will be issued, but as a material uncertainty exists, an emphasis of matter paragraph will be included after the opinion paragraph and will highlight this and refer to the disclosure provided by management.

121 Reporting

> **Text reference**. Chapter 19.
>
> **Top tips.** In part (a) you are asked for three types of audit opinion modification. Giving more than the required number is a waste of your time and giving less than the required number will ensure you lose the straightforward marks available in this question.
>
> In part (b) it was not enough to simply list five elements – you needed to 'describe' them for five marks.
>
> **Easy marks.** Describing the elements of the auditor's report should not have presented you with many problems.

Marking scheme

		Marks
(a)	Modification of audit opinion. 3 marks. ½ for the type of opinion and ½ for explanation.	
	Maximum marks	3
(b)	Up to 1 mark per well described element	
	Title	
	Addressee	
	Introductory paragraph	
	Management responsibility	
	Auditor's responsibility	
	Opinion paragraph	
	Other reporting responsibilities	
	Signature of the auditor	
	Date of the auditor's report	
	Auditor's address	5
(c)	Up to 1 mark per well described point	2
		10

(a) **Modified audit opinions**

There are three types of modified opinion:

Qualified opinion

A qualified opinion will be issued due to either the auditor being unable to obtain sufficient appropriate audit evidence in respect of a material matter or because the auditor concludes the financial statements contain material misstatements. The opinion will be expressed as being '**except for** the effects' (or possible effects) of the matter that the qualification relates to. The misstatements (or possible misstatements) will be material but not pervasive.

Disclaimer of opinion

Where the auditor is unable to obtain sufficient appropriate audit evidence and the possible effects are both material and **pervasive**, the auditor is unable to express an opinion on the financial statements and a **disclaimer of opinion** will be expressed.

Adverse opinion

Where the auditor concludes the accounts are materially misstated and the misstatements are both **material and pervasive,** the financial statements are misleading, and an **adverse opinion** will be expressed.

(b) The elements of an unmodified audit report include the following:

Element	Explanation
Title	The auditor's report must have a title that clearly indicates that it is the report of the independent auditor. This distinguishes the auditor's report from other reports.
Addressee	The addressee will be determined by law or regulation, but is likely to be the shareholders or those charged with governance.
Introductory paragraph	This will identify the entity being audited, state that the financial statements have been audited, identify the title of each statement that comprises the financial statements being audited, refer to the summary of significant accounting policies and other explanatory notes, and specify the date or period covered by each statement comprising the financial statements.
Management's responsibility for the financial statements	This part of the report describes the responsibilities of those who are responsible for the preparation of the financial statements. It will explain management is responsible for the preparation of the financial statements in accordance with the applicable financial reporting framework and for the related internal controls.
Auditor's responsibility	The section will state that the auditor is responsible for expressing an opinion on the financial statements based on the audit, that the audit was conducted in accordance with International Standards on Auditing and ethical requirements, and that the auditor planned and performed the audit so as to obtain reasonable assurance that the financial statements are free from material misstatement.
Opinion paragraph	If the auditor expresses an unmodified opinion on financial statements prepared in accordance with a fair presentation framework, the opinion will state the financial statements are presented fairly (or give a true and fair view).
Other reporting responsibilities	If the auditor is required by law to report on any other matters, this must be done in an additional paragraph below the opinion paragraph which is titled 'Report on other legal and regulatory requirements' or otherwise as appropriate.

Element	Explanation
Auditor's signature	The report must contain the auditor's signature, whether this is the auditor's own name or the audit firm's name or both.
Date of the report	The report must be dated no earlier than the date on which the auditor has obtained sufficient appropriate audit evidence on which to base the auditor's opinion on the financial statements.
Auditor's address	The location where the auditor practises must be included.

(**Note:** Only five elements needed to be explained to gain full marks.)

(c) **Purpose of the emphasis of matter paragraph**

An emphasis of matter paragraph is a paragraph included in the auditor's report that refers to a matter appropriately presented or disclosed in the financial statements that, in the auditor's judgement, is of such importance that it is **fundamental to users' understanding** of the financial statements.

Emphasis of matter paragraphs are used to draw readers' attention to a matter already presented or disclosed in the financial statements that the auditor feels is fundamental to their understanding, provided that the auditor has obtained sufficient appropriate audit evidence that the matter is **not materially misstated**.

122 Hood Enterprises

Text reference. Chapter 19.

Top tips. Take a methodical approach and look at each sentence in turn.

Easy marks. There should have been a few easy marks for spotting some of the more obvious differences from what you will have seen in standard audit reports in your study material.

Examiner's comments. The overall standard in this question was unsatisfactory. The main reason for this appeared to be the requirement word 'explain'. Most candidates managed to identify some of the errors in the report but answers contained very little explanation of why the point was an error. A minority of answers simply stated the contents of a normal unmodified report, which did not meet the question heading.

	Marks
Auditors' reports	
Up to 2 marks per relevant point	
Use of term Auditing Standards	2
Limitation on use of judgements and estimates	2
Time limitation	2
FS free from material error	2
Directors' responsibilities	2
Reference to annual report	2
Allow other relevant points	2
Maximum marks	**10**

Errors in the report extract

'Presentation of information in the company's annual report'

The auditor's legal responsibilities relate to the financial statements, which comprise the primary statements plus the supporting notes. They do not extend to any other information, for example a chairman's statement, or 5-year summary. To make this clear, this section should refer only to the financial statements.

Under ISA 720 *The auditor's responsibilities relating to other information in documents containing audited financial statements* the auditor has a responsibility to read the other information to identify whether there are any inconsistencies with the financial statements or anything that is misleading, but the primary opinion is given on the financial statements only.

'In accordance with Auditing Standards'

The report should specify exactly which auditing standards have been used so that there is no risk that readers misunderstand how the audit has been done. It should specify that the audit has been performed in accordance with **International Standards on Auditing.**

'Evaluating ....the reasonableness of all accounting estimates'

It is inappropriate to imply that the auditor has considered every estimate made by management. This is unlikely to be true because auditors do not look at every single transaction and item in the financial statements; it is the duty of the auditor to give assurance only on whether the financial statements are free from material misstatement.

'As much audit evidence as possible in the time available'

This phrase is inappropriate because it implies that the auditor has not had time to obtain all the evidence that is needed. The auditor is expected to obtain sufficient evidence on which to base conclusions. The auditor should have planned the audit so as to obtain sufficient evidence in the time available.

'Confirm'

This word should not be used because it implies a greater degree of certainty than is possible based on normal audit procedures. The certainty implied by the word *'confirm'* may expose the auditor to negligence claims if it turns out that there are any material errors in the financial statements. A more accurate description of the level of assurance given by an audit is 'reasonable assurance'.

'No liability for errors can be accepted by the auditor'

This disclaimer at first might appear to be useful in protecting the auditor against liability. However, the view of the ACCA is that general disclaimers should not be included in audit reports, as their use would tend to devalue the audit opinion.

'The directors are wholly responsible for the accuracy of the financial statements'

This statement should not appear in the auditor's responsibility section of the report. Details of management's responsibilities is differently worded and should appear in an earlier separate section of the report outlining the responsibility of management for the preparation of the financial statements.

123 Galartha

Text references. Chapters 18 and 19.

Top tips. This question examines your understanding of the review stage of the audit and the auditor's report. It is important that you have a sound knowledge of the basic audit report and the circumstances in which the opinion will be modified. However, as with the majority of questions on this paper you also need to be able to apply this knowledge.

In part (b) you are provided with extracts from an auditor's report and are asked to explain the meaning and purpose of each of the extracts. Think about what each extract tells the reader and why you think it is important that this information is provided. The suggested answer below is presented in a columnar format but dealing with the meaning and purpose together would be equally acceptable.

Part (c) examines your knowledge of modified audit opinions. When stating the effect on the auditor's report, remember to consider both the grounds for modification and the degree of seriousness ('except for' or disclaimer/adverse). Make sure you justify the decision you have made.

Easy marks. Part (b) is the most straightforward part of the question. You should also score well in part (c).

Marking scheme

                                                                                                  Marks

(a) 1 mark per point
     Para 1
     Shows auditor disagrees with directors
     Shows auditor view based on standards
     Para 2
     Quantifies effect of non-compliance
     Shows what depreciation policy normally is
     Para 3
     Confirms quantification of effect on financial statements
     Para 4
     'Except for' = material qualification
     Everything else OK in FS
     Other relevant points
     Maximum marks   8

(b) 1 mark per point
     (i)   Still disagree – modify (+ reason)
            Qualification = 'fundamental' $\dfrac{2}{10}$

(a) **Meaning and purpose of extracts**

Extract 1	
Meaning	**Purpose**
This explains that the accounting treatment of non-depreciation adopted by the company is not conducted in accordance with recognised practice as contained within the IFRSs.	The basis of the auditor's conclusion that the accounts contain a misstatement is highlighted ie the non-depreciation of buildings. The reference to the IFRSs gives authority to the auditor's opinion that the non-depreciation is incorrect.
Extract 2	
Meaning	**Purpose**
The depreciation provision in the financial statements is understated by $420,000.	This explains the adjustment which should have been made in the financial statements and quantifies the effect of the non-depreciation so that the reader can assess the impact. It also indicates the depreciation policy so that the reader can understand the basis of the adjustment.

Extract 3	
Meaning	**Purpose**
Non-current assets, profit for the year and accumulated reserves are all materially misstated.	This quantifies more specifically the effect of the adjustment on both the position statement balances and statement of profit or loss.

Extract 4	
Meaning	**Purpose**
Based on the professional judgement of the auditors the financial statements are factual, are free from bias and reflect the commercial substance of the business's transactions with the exception of the treatment of depreciation. This misstatement does materially affect the financial statements but does not render them meaningless overall.	This highlights that the audit report is modified due on the basis the financial statements are not free from material misstatement. The phrase 'except for' indicates that the misstatement relates to one specific issue but that in other respects the financial statements give a true and fair view.

(b) **Effect of alternative situation on the auditor's report**

- The auditor would issue a modified audit opinion on the grounds that the accounts contain a material misstatement due to the continued non-depreciation of non-current assets.

- Due to the significant impact of the adjustment (a profit to a significant loss) the auditor may conclude that the effect is both material and pervasive, and so express an adverse opinion. Otherwise a qualified opinion will be expressed.

124 Humphries

Text references. Chapters 18 and 19.

Top tips. For the lawsuit, you needed to apply your knowledge of IAS 10 *Events after the Reporting Period* and your knowledge of when to set up a provision as opposed to disclosing a contingent liability. The figures are there so you can assess the materiality of each issue and then use this to assess the impact on the audit opinion in the auditor's report once you have decided whether an amendment is needed. Remember to cover all three requirements for both issues and take note that equal weighting is given to each issue. This means the maximum you can score is five marks on each issue and you should therefore spread you time equally between each.

Marking scheme

	Marks
Up to 1 mark per valid point, overall maximum of 5 marks per event	
Lawsuit	
Provides evidence of present obligation at the year end	
Provision required and not contingent liability disclosures	
Discuss with company lawyer	
Review correspondence with supplier	
Discuss with management and obtain written representation	
Calculation of materiality	
Type of auditor's report modification required	
Impact on auditor's report	5

Warehouse

Provides evidence of conditions that arose subsequent to the year end

No adjustment required, possible disclosure of any uninsured sums

Discuss with management whether sufficient levels of inventory to continue operating

Obtain written representation that going concern status appropriate

Obtain schedule of damaged inventory and review reasonableness

Review correspondence with insurance firm to assess levels of uninsured goods

Calculation of materiality

Type of auditor's report modification required

Impact on auditor's report

$\underline{5}$

$\underline{\underline{10}}$

Lawsuit for $1m

(i) *Financial statement implications*

A key supplier is suing Humphries for $1 million. However, post-year end correspondence shows the supplier has agreed to settle for $0.6 million and it is likely Humphries will agree to this. The agreed settlement after the year end provides evidence that the company had a present obligation at the year end and the probable transfer of funds means under IAS 37 *Provisions, Contingent Liabilities and Contingent Assets* a provision for $0.6m should be included in the accounts to 30 September 20X1. Instead management has only included a contingent liability disclosure.

If confirmed $0.6m is to be the settlement, the financial statements should be adjusted to show the provision for this amount and the existing disclosure should be removed.

(ii) *Further audit procedures*

Audit procedures to be applied to confirm the level of the adjustment required include:

- Confirming with management that they are likely to pay the $0.6m and asking them to provide a written representation confirming this.

- Seeking Humphries' lawyers opinion on the probability of the settlement and ask if they can confirm that $0.6 million is the likely amount.

- Reviewing the correspondence with the supplier to confirm that the amount they are willing to accept is $0.6 million.

(iii) *Impact on auditor's opinion if unresolved*

The probable payment and anticipated adjustment needed of $0.6 million represents 8% of profit ($0.6m/$7.5m × 100%). This is material and if management refuse to adjust for the provision then the audit opinion will need to be modified on the basis management has not complied with IAS 37.

The misstatement is material but not pervasive, so a qualified opinion would be expressed.

A basis for qualified opinion paragraph would explain the material misstatement in relation to the $0.6m not provided and will describe the effect on the financial statements. The opinion paragraph would state that 'except for' this issue the financial statements are presented fairly.

Warehouse flood

(i) *Financial statement implications*

The warehouse in Bass was flooded post year end, the entire inventory has been disposed of and the company has insurance in place. However, it is unclear as to how much inventory is insured. The inventory in the warehouse in November is unlikely to have been in the warehouse on 30 September given that the company is a food wholesaler.

Under IAS 10 this is a non-adjusting event as the flood did not exist at the year end date.

No adjustment to the financial statements is necessary but if uninsured losses are material, disclosure of the event and an estimate of the financial impact may be necessary. If the amount is immaterial then disclosure is not required.

Consideration should also be given as to whether If the impact of the uninsured level of inventory is such that the company's going concern status is impacted. If it is, disclosure of any uncertainty will be needed in the financial statements.

(ii)   *Further audit procedures*

Audit procedures to be applied to form a conclusion as to the extent of any disclosures include:

- Discussing the matter with the directors including enquiring whether the company has sufficient inventory to continue trading in the short term.

- Obtaining written representation confirming that the going concern status is not affected.

- Obtaining an analysis of the inventory destroyed and comparing this to the average inventory in the other warehouses to see if the amount claimed to be damaged is reasonable.

- Reviewing correspondence from the insurers to confirm the amount of the insurance claim and the extent of any uninsured amounts.

(iii)   *Impact on auditor's opinion if unresolved*

Although the inventory damaged is likely to be material, only the uninsured level of inventory will need to be disclosed. If uninsured amounts are also material, disclosure of this subsequent event is required and if management don't make these disclosures, then the audit opinion should be modified. A qualified opinion would be appropriate on the grounds the amounts involved are unlikely to result in the effects of the misstatement being pervasive.

The reason for the qualified opinion would be explained in the basis for qualified opinion paragraph and the opinion paragraph would state that 'except for' this issue of non-disclosure, the financial statements are presented fairly (or show a true and fair view).

If disclosures are not required then there will be no impact on the auditor's report.

If the level of the uninsured inventory means that the company's going concern status is threatened, and management has not included sufficient disclosure or prepared the accounts on the wrong basis, the audit opinion should be appropriately modified.

If necessary disclosure over uncertainty is included and the going concern status is appropriate, the auditor will not modify the opinion but will include an emphasis of matter paragraph drawing attention to the uncertainty.

125 Boggart

Text references. Chapters 18 and 19.

Top tips. Part (a) should not have presented you with too many problems and you should make sure you know the auditor's responsibilities for subsequent events before the real exam.

For part (b) you needed to apply your knowledge of IAS 10 *Events after the reporting period*.

Easy marks. Part (a) was knowledge based and you should have found this straightforward.

Examiner's comments. Part (a) required a description of the auditor's responsibility in relation to subsequent events occurring between the year-end and the date the auditor's report is signed, and then from this point to the date the financial statements are issued. Performance was on the whole unsatisfactory. The question focused on responsibilities as opposed to audit procedures; however a significant proportion of candidates provided a list of audit procedures to be performed during a subsequent events review. This suggests that these candidates did not read the question carefully, saw the words subsequent events and proceeded to just list any procedures they had knowledge of.

Marks

(a)   Up to 1 mark per valid point

Auditor shall perform audit procedures to identify subsequent events requiring adjustment or disclosure

No need to perform additional procedures for areas already tested

No obligation to perform audit procedures on financial statements after auditor's report signed

Discuss with management if fact known which may have changed audit report

Determine if adjustments required, if so discuss with management

If amended then audit adjustment, extend subsequent events testing, provide new auditor's report

If financial statements are not amended, take steps to prevent reliance   5

(b)   Up to 1 mark per valid point, overall maximum of 5 marks

Provides evidence of conditions at the year end

Receivable to be adjusted via write down or allowance

Review correspondence with customer

Discuss with management

Review post year-end period for cash receipts

Calculation of materiality

No audit report modification required   5
                                                                                                          10

(a)   (i)   **Events after the year end occurring up to the date of the auditor's report**

The auditor must perform procedures designed to obtain sufficient appropriate audit evidence that all events up to the date of the auditor's report that may require adjustment of, or disclosure in, the financial statements have been identified.

These procedures should be applied to any matters examined during the audit which may be susceptible to change after the year-end. They are in addition to tests on specific transactions after the period end, eg cut-off tests.

(ii) **Facts discovered after the date of the auditor's report but before the financial statements are issued**

The auditor does not have any obligation to perform procedures, or make enquires regarding the financial statements, after the date of the auditor's report.

However if the auditor becomes aware of a fact that, had it been known to the auditor at the date of signature of the auditor's report, may have caused the auditor to amend the auditor's report, the auditor must:

- Discuss the matter with management and those charged with governance

- Determine whether the financial statements need amendment

- If amendment is required, inquire how management intends to address the matter in the financial statements.

If amendment is required to the financial statements and management makes the necessary changes, the auditor must undertake any necessary audit procedures on the changes made, extend audit procedures for identifying subsequent events that may require adjustment of or disclosure in the financial statements to the date of the new auditor's report, and provide a new auditor's report on the amended financial statements.

If management refuse to amend the financial statements and the auditor's report has already been provided to the entity, and if management intend to issue the financial statements with this report, the auditor should take steps to prevent reliance on the report. This might include speaking at the AGM or resigning.

(b) (i) *Financial statement implications*

A customer, owing $0.2 million at the year end, is experiencing significant going concern difficulties. The fact that a customer owing $0.2m has had going concern problems, although only discovered after the year end, provides further evidence about the recoverability of the year end customer balance.

Under IAS 10 *Events after the reporting period*, the evidence about the condition in existence at the year end date should be adjusted for, if material, by management as it seems at least part of the balance is not recoverable and no allowance has been made.

(ii) *Further audit procedures*

Audit procedures to be applied to establish the adjustment required include:

- Discussing with management why they consider no adjustment is needed.

- Reviewing the post year-end period for payments received from the customer in respect of the year end debt.

- Reviewing any correspondence with the customer to assess the likelihood of recovery of the $0.2m.

(iii) *Impact on audit opinion if unresolved*

The receivable of $0.2 million represents 3.7% of profit ($0.2m/$5.3m × 100%) and 0.3% of revenue ($0.2m/$54.6m × 100%) and is not material. If the full amount is deemed not recoverable and remains unadjusted, then the $0.2m should be noted in the summary of uncorrected misstatements. However, in itself this misstatement is immaterial and no modification is required to the audit opinion solely in respect of this issue.

126 Strawberry

Text references. Chapters 18 and 19.

Top tips. Part (a) asks for a description of the audit procedures which would be performed to assess whether the company is a going concern. The key here is to describe procedures which address the particular issues faced by the company. Think about the indicators you have identified in part in part (b) to help you.

Part (b) requires an explanation of the auditor's responsibility for reporting on going concern and the impact on the audit report if the directors inappropriately adopt the going concern basis. Note the question is asking for the auditor's responsibilities, not those of management. Also make sure that you describe the impact on the audit report rather than just identifying the type of opinion which will be expressed.

Examiner's comments. In part (a) performance was mixed. Candidates failed to maximise their marks here by providing too brief tests such as 'check cash flow forecasts' and 'obtain management rep' or unrealistic tests such as 'write to the bank and ask if they will require the loan to be repaid', the bank will not answer such a request.

Part (b)(i) required Kiwi's responsibility for reporting going concern to the directors. This question was answered unsatisfactorily. Many candidates were unable to correctly identify any of the auditors' responsibilities on reporting going concern to the directors.

Part (b)(ii) required the impact on the audit report if the directors refused to amend the financial statements. This was answered unsatisfactorily. Many candidates were unable to provide the correct audit opinion and so adopted a scatter gun approach of listing every audit report modification available. Also many candidates correctly identified that the opinion needed to be modified; however they then suggested an emphasis of matter paragraph. This demonstrates that candidates do not understand when an 'emphasis of matter' paragraph is relevant, and seem to think that it is an acceptable alternative to modifying the opinion. This demonstrates candidates' fundamental lack of understanding of auditor's reports.

Marks

(a) Up to 1 mark per well explained point.
Review cash flow forecasts
Sensitivity analysis
Discuss if sales director replaced and new customers obtained
Review post year-end sales and order book
Review the loan agreement and recalculate the covenant breached to confirm
timing and amount of the loan repayment
Review bank agreements, breach of covenants
Review bank correspondence
Discuss if alternative finance obtained
Review shareholders' correspondence
Review suppliers' correspondence
Enquire of lawyers any further litigation by suppliers
Subsequent events
Board minutes
Management accounts
Consider going concern basis appropriate
Written representation   5

(b) (i) Up to 1 mark per well explained point
Events or conditions constitute a material uncertainty
Use of the going concern assumption is appropriate
Adequacy of disclosures in the financial statements   2

(ii) Up to 1 mark per well explained point
Not going concern therefore modified opinion
Adverse opinion
Basis for adverse opinion paragraph, going concern basis not
appropriate
Opinion paragraph, financial statements not true and fair $\frac{3}{10}$

(a) **Audit procedures to assess whether the company is a going concern**

- Discuss with management any further attempts that might be made to recover the cash owed by the major customer and steps taken to win major new customers.

- Discuss with management whether steps are being taken to replace the sales director, and if not future plans for generating new sales.

- Review the post year end sales order book to determine the likely levels of trade and the impact this will have on future revenues.

- Obtain a copy of the cash flow forecast and review the nature of the cash flows and the reasonableness of any assumptions made. Discuss the findings with the finance director.

- Perform a sensitivity analysis on the cash flow forecast to assess the amount of head-room which exists.

- Review legal correspondence and make enquiries of the company's lawyers to determine whether any suppliers have commenced legal action and the amounts for which the company might be liable.

- Review correspondence with suppliers post year-end to determine whether any additional suppliers are to take legal action or are refusing to supply Strawberry.

- Obtain a copy of the loan agreement and confirm that the covenant has been breached. Check the terms of the loan and confirm that the amount and timing of the repayment are accurate.

- Review correspondence with the bank to determine whether any other covenants exist and whether these have been breached.

- Discuss with the directors any alternative sources of finance/any future plans that they have to generate the cash required to repay the loan.

- Assess the likelihood of new shareholder investment by reviewing any correspondence between the company and the shareholders.

- Perform a subsequent events review, including a review of board minutes, to determine whether any further information is relevant that would suggest that the company is or is not a going concern.

- Review post-year end management accounts and assess whether the results are in line with the draft accounts and the cash flow forecast. Discuss any discrepancies with the finance director.

- Obtain a written representation from management confirming the management's opinion that the business is a going concern.

- Evaluate the evidence obtained and come to a conclusion as to whether the company is a going concern and that the going concern basis should be used for the preparation of the financial statements.

(b) **Reporting**

(i) **Kiwi & Co's responsibility to report on going concern to the directors**

Kiwi & Co must report to the directors any information which casts doubt on the ability of the company to continue as a going concern. In accordance with ISA 570 *Going concern* Kiwi & Co will report the following:

- Whether the events or conditions constitute a material uncertainty
- Whether the use of the going concern assumption is appropriate in the preparation of the financial statements
- The adequacy of related disclosures in the financial statements

(ii) **Impact on the auditor's report**

If the directors refuse to amend the financial statements and we believe that the company is not a going concern, the audit opinion will be modified. An adverse opinion will be issued as the matter is both material and pervasive.

The basis for adverse opinion paragraph will provide an explanation of the inappropriate use of the going concern assumption by the directors.

The adverse opinion paragraph will state that the financial statements do not present fairly or do not give a true and fair view.

Mock exams

ACCA
Paper F8
Audit and Assurance

Mock Examination 1

Question Paper	
Time allowed	
Reading and Planning Writing	**15 minutes** **3 hours**
ALL questions are compulsory and MUST be attempted	
During reading and planning time only the question paper may be annotated	

DO NOT OPEN THIS PAPER UNTIL YOU ARE READY TO START UNDER EXAMINATION CONDITIONS

Section A

Multiple choice questions

1　What level of assurance is provided by a review engagement?

    A　Absolute assurance
    B　Reasonable assurance
    C　No assurance
    D　Limited assurance　　　　　　　　　　　　　　　　　　　　　　**(2 marks)**

2　What is the main objective of the statutory audit?

    A　To detect fraud and misstatements
    B　To assess the performance of the company
    C　To express an independent opinion on the financial statements
    D　To evaluate the system of internal control　　　　　　　　　　**(2 marks)**

3　Is the following statement true or false?

International Standards on Auditing issued by the International Auditing and Assurance Standards Board override national requirements.

    A　True
    B　False　　　　　　　　　　　　　　　　　　　　　　　　　　**(1 mark)**

4　Which of the following is **not** part of the overall audit objectives as set out in ISA 200 *Overall objectives of the independent auditor and the conduct of an audit in accordance with International Standards on Auditing*?

    A　To obtain reasonable assurance that the financial statements are free from material misstatement

    B　To express an opinion on whether the financial statements are prepared in accordance with the applicable financial reporting framework

    C　To report on the financial statements

    D　To report to management on the effectiveness of internal controls　　　　**(2 marks)**

5　Which of the following procedures would normally be performed during an interim audit?

    A　Subsequent events review
    B　Inherent risk assessment
    C　Agreeing of financial statements to accounting records
    D　Assessment of going concern status of the company　　　　　　**(2 marks)**

6　The auditor of Z Co has identified that there is a risk of overstatement of inventory as net realisable value may be lower than cost.

Which of the following would be a valid response to this risk by the auditor?

(1)　Increase emphasis on the review of aged inventory analysis to identify slow-moving or obsolete items

(2)　Increase test counts performed at the year-end inventory count

(3)　Extend the post year end review of sales of inventory held at the year end and compare selling price with cost

    A　(2) only
    B　(3) only
    C　(1) and (2)
    D　(1) and (3)　　　　　　　　　　　　　　　　　　　　　　**(2 marks)**

7   Which of the following is **not** a component of internal control as described in ISA 315 *Identifying and assessing the risks of material misstatement through understanding the entity and its environment*?

A   Monitoring of controls
B   Control environment
C   Control risk
D   Control activities   **(2 marks)**

8   As a result of audit work performed the auditor may identify deficiencies in internal control.

Which of the following correctly describes the auditor's responsibilities with respect to reporting these deficiencies in accordance with ISA 265 *Communicating deficiencies in internal control to those charged with governance and management* ?

A   The auditor must report all deficiencies identified in writing to those charged with governance.

B   The auditor must report all deficiencies identified in writing to management at an appropriate level of responsibility.

C   The auditor must report all significant deficiencies identified in writing to those charged with governance.   **(1 mark)**

9   The auditor of R Co has performed a number of audit procedures on payroll.

Which of the following is an example of analytical procedures used as a substantive procedure?

A   Reperformance of tax deduction calculations for a sample of employees
B   Checking of pay rate details to personnel files
C   Performance of a proof in total of the wages and salaries expense
D   Tracing of payroll payments to entries on the bank statement   **(2 marks)**

10   Which of the following statements is true with respect to sample sizes?

(1) The lower the risk the auditor is willing to accept, the greater the sample size will need to be.
(2) The lower the risk the auditor is willing to accept, the smaller the sample size will need to be.
(3) The higher the risk the auditor is willing to accept, the smaller the sample size will need to be.
(4) The higher the risk the auditor is willing to accept, the greater the sample size will need to be.

A   (1) and (3)
B   (2) and (4)
C   None of the statement is true as there is no connection between sample size and risk.   **(1 mark)**

11   The auditor has conducted a subsequent events review and has identified a number of material issues.

For which of the following would the auditor require an adjustment to the figures in the financial statements?

A   Dividends declared after the period end
B   A flood causing substantial damage to a warehouse
C   Announcement of plans of a major restructuring of the business
D   Settlement of a court case resulting in the payment of damages to a former employee   **(2 marks)**

12   Is the following statement regarding the misstatement of disclosures in the financial statements true or false?

A misstatement of disclosures that are fundamental to the users' understanding of the financial statements would be judged by the auditor to have a pervasive effect on the financial statements.

A   True
B   False   **(1 mark)**

Question 1

You are the audit manager of Violet & Co and you are currently reviewing the audit files for several of your clients for which the audit fieldwork is complete. The audit seniors have raised the following issues:

Daisy Designs Co (Daisy)

Daisy's year end is 30 September, however, subsequent to the year end the company's sales ledger has been corrupted by a computer virus. Daisy's finance director was able to produce the financial statements prior to this occurring; however, the audit team has been unable to access the sales ledger to undertake detailed testing of revenue or year-end receivables. All other accounting records are unaffected and there are no backups available for the sales ledger. Daisy's revenue is $15.6m, its receivables are $3.4m and profit before tax is $2m.

Fuchsia Enterprises Co (Fuchsia)

Fuchsia has experienced difficult trading conditions and as a result it has lost significant market share. The cash flow forecast has been reviewed during the audit fieldwork and it shows a significant net cash outflow. Management are confident that further funding can be obtained and so have prepared the financial statements on a going concern basis with no additional disclosures; the audit senior is highly sceptical about this. The prior year financial statements showed a profit before tax of $1.2m; however, the current year loss before tax is $4.4m and the forecast net cash outflow for the next 12 months is $3.2m.

Required

For each of the two issues:

(i)   Discuss the issue, including an assessment of whether it is material.
(ii)   Describe the impact on the auditor's report if the issue remains unresolved.

Notes: (1)   The total marks will be split equally between each issue.
         (2)   Auditor's report extracts are **not** required.   **(10 marks)**

Question 2

(a)   Describe **five** types of procedures for obtaining audit evidence.   **(5 marks)**

(b)   For each procedure, describe an example relevant to the audit of property, plant and equipment.   **(5 marks)**

(Total = 10 marks)

Question 3

Bush-Baby Hotels Co operates a chain of 18 hotels located across the country. Each hotel has bedrooms, a restaurant and leisure club facilities. Most visitors to the restaurant and leisure club are hotel guests; however, these facilities are open to the public as well. Hotel guests generally charge any costs to their room but other visitors must make payment directly to the hotel staff.

During the year, senior management noticed an increased level of cash discrepancies and inventory discrepancies, and they suspect that some employees have been stealing cash and goods from the hotels. They are keen to prevent this from reoccurring and are considering establishing an internal audit department to undertake a fraud investigation.

Required

(a) Explain how the new internal audit department of Bush-Baby Hotels Co could assist the directors in preventing and detecting fraud and error. **(3 marks)**

(b) Describe the limitations of Bush-Baby Hotels Co establishing and maintaining an internal audit department. **(2 marks)**

The directors would like the internal audit department to have as broad a role as possible, as this will make the decision to recruit an internal audit department more cost effective.

Required

(c) Describe additional functions, other than fraud investigations, the directors of Bush-Baby Hotels Co could ask the internal audit department to undertake. **(5 marks)**

(Total = 10 marks)

Question 4

(a) Describe substantive procedures the auditor should perform to confirm the bank and cash balance of Green Co at the year end. **(6 marks)**

(b) You are asked to replace an audit senior, who is unable to work due to illness, on the ongoing audit of Green Co. Reviewing the audit files, you find the following comment:

'In order to confirm raw material inventory quantities, we relied on the work undertaken by an independent expert.'

Required

Describe **four** factors to consider and steps the audit team should take, prior to placing reliance on the work of the independent expert, in order to confirm raw material quantities. **(4 marks)**

(Total = 10 marks)

Question 5

(a) Explain the concepts of materiality and performance materiality in accordance with ISA 320 *Materiality in Planning and Performing an Audit*. **(5 marks)**

(b) You are the audit senior of Rhino & Co and you are planning the audit of Kangaroo Construction Co (Kangaroo) for the year ended 31 March 20X3. Kangaroo specialises in building houses and provides a five-year building warranty to its customers. Your audit manager has held a planning meeting with the finance director. He has provided you with the following notes of his meeting and financial statement extracts:

Kangaroo has had a difficult year; house prices have fallen and, as a result, revenue has dropped. In order to address this, management has offered significantly extended credit terms to their customers. However, demand has fallen such that there are still some completed houses in inventory where the selling price may be below cost. During the year, whilst calculating depreciation, the directors extended the useful lives of plant and machinery from three years to five years. This reduced the annual depreciation charge.

The directors need to meet a target profit before interest and taxation of $0.5 million in order to be paid their annual bonus. In addition, to try and improve profits, Kangaroo changed their main material supplier to a cheaper alternative. This has resulted in some customers claiming on their building warranties for extensive repairs. To help with operating cash flow, the directors borrowed $1 million from the bank during the year. This is due for repayment at the end of 20X3.

Financial statement extracts for year ended 31 March

	DRAFT 20X3 $m	ACTUAL 20X2 $m
Revenue	12.5	15.0
Cost of sales	(7.0)	(8.0)
Gross profit	5.5	7.0
Operating expenses	(5.0)	(5.1)
Profit before interest and taxation	0.5	1.9
Inventory	1.9	1.4
Receivables	3.1	2.0
Cash	0.8	1.9
Trade payables	1.6	1.2
Loan	1.0	–

Required

Using the information above:

(i) Calculate **five** ratios, for **both** years, which would assist the audit senior in planning the audit.

(5 marks)

(ii) Using the information provided and the ratios calculated, identify and describe **five** audit risks and explain the auditor's response to each risk in planning the audit of Kangaroo Construction Co.

(10 marks)

(Total = 20 marks)

Question 6

(a) ISA 260 *Communication with Those Charged with Governance* provides guidance to auditors in relation to communicating with those charged with governance on matters arising from the audit of an entity's financial statements.

Required

(i) Explain why it is important that auditors communicate throughout the audit with those charged with governance. **(2 marks)**

(ii) Describe **four** examples of matters that the auditors may communicate to those charged with governance. **(4 marks)**

Fox Industries Co (Fox) manufactures engineering parts. It has one operating site and a customer base spread across Europe. The company's year end was 30 April 20X3. Below is a description of the purchasing and payments system.

Whenever production materials are required, the relevant department sends a requisition form to the ordering department. An order clerk raises a purchase order and contacts a number of suppliers to see which can despatch the goods first. This supplier is then chosen. The order clerk sends out the purchase order. This is not sequentially numbered and only orders above $5,000 require authorisation.

Purchase invoices are input daily by the purchase ledger clerk, who has been in the role for many years and, as an experienced team member, he does not apply any application controls over the input process. Every week the purchase day book automatically updates the purchase ledger, the purchase ledger is then posted manually to the general ledger by the purchase ledger clerk.

Required

(b) As the external auditor of Fox Industries Co, write a report to management in respect of the purchasing and payments system described above which:

(i) Identifies and explains **four** deficiencies in the system
(ii) Explains the possible implication of each deficiency
(iii) Provides a recommendation to address each deficiency

A covering letter **is** required.

Note: Up to two marks will be awarded within this requirement for presentation and the remaining marks will be split equally between each part. **(14 marks)**

(Total = 20 marks)

Answers

DO NOT TURN THIS PAGE UNTIL YOU HAVE
COMPLETED THE MOCK EXAM

A plan of attack

If this were the real Audit and Assurance exam and you had been told to turn over and begin, what would be going through your mind?

An important thing to say (while there is still time) is that it is vital to have a good breadth of knowledge of the syllabus because all the questions are compulsory. However, don't panic. Below we provide guidance on how to approach the exam.

Approaching the paper

Part A is a good place to start with. The short multiple choice questions will help to settle you in, before you tackle **Part B**.

In Part B, use your 15 minutes of reading time usefully to look through the questions, particularly Question 1, to get a feel for what is required and to become familiar with the question scenarios.

Since all the questions in this paper are compulsory, it is vital that you attempt them all to increase your chances of passing. For example, don't run over time on Question 2 and then find you don't have enough time for the remaining questions.

Question 1 is a knowledge-based 10-mark question, consisting of three mini-requirements examining ethical threats, going concern and the emphasis of matter paragraph. You should be able to score well on this one. Spend just nine minutes on each part (worth 5 marks each) so you don't eat into your time available for the other questions.

Question 2 is a knowledge-based 10-mark question, which you should find relatively easy if you have revised your knowledge of audit evidence. Note the verb 'describe' in both parts of the question – this indicates that it is not enough for you to simply 'list' the procedures. Make sure that the audit procedures you suggest in part (b) relates to plant and machinery. Again, keep to the time allocation of 18 minutes for this question and move on at the end of the allocated time.

Question 3 is a 10-mark question that incorporates a scenario. Read the requirement first: you will see that in fact parts (a) and (c) are essentially knowledge-based questions. Then scan the scenario for pieces of pertinent information. Part (c) is probably the easiest, so if you are short for time, it may be an idea to do this part first and obtain your five marks here.

Question 4 is a 10-mark question that is essentially knowledge-based. Part (a), focussing on communication with those charged with governance, should be relatively easy. In part (b), a mini-scenario focuses on reliance on experts. Note the number of marks available and keep within your time allocation.

Question 5 is a longer 20-mark scenario-based question. Part (a), for 5 marks, is knowledge-based and focuses on the concepts of materiality **and** performance materiality. Part (b), for 15 marks, requires you to perform analytical procedures using ratios. Don't just blindly calculate a lot of ratios. You should let the scenario guide you in terms of the five ratios you are asked to calculate: reducing revenue prompts you to consider profit-related ratios and ratios related to going concern (current ratio and quick ratio); extended customer credit terms should hint towards a receivables-related ratio and unsold houses in inventory should suggest an inventory-related ratio. A three-column table format is useful here: one for the ratios, one for the audit risks and one for the auditor's response to the risks.

Question 5 is a 20-mark scenario-based question. Fourteen of these marks focus on internal controls – the deficiency, implication and recommendation structure should be one you have seen already. A table format may be appropriate, but note the comment that a covering letter is required: your language and the presentation of you answer needs to be tailored accordingly. This is the last question in the exam, but watch the amount of time you spend in part (a) to ensure you have enough time to get the marks in part (b), which tests your knowledge of substantive procedures.

Forget about it

And don't worry if you found the paper difficult. More than likely other candidates will too. If this were the real thing you would need to forget the exam the minute you left the exam hall and think about the next one. Or, if it is the last one, celebrate!

Section A

Multiple choice answers

1   D   A lower level of assurance is given in a review engagement as compared to an audit where reasonable assurance is given.

2   C   Although the auditor may achieve the objectives in A, B and D as part of the audit process the main objective which is set out in law in most jurisdictions is to express an audit opinion.

3   B   ISAs do not override national requirements, however increasingly national and international requirements are being brought in to line.

4   D   Reporting on control effectiveness is normally a by-product of the audit but does not form part of the overall objective as expressed in ISA 200.

5   B   Procedures listed in A, C and D would be performed during the final audit.

6   D   Increasing test counts will provide additional evidence regarding the amount of inventory but will not provide evidence of valuation.

7   C   The five components of internal control are: the control environment, the entity's risk assessment process, the information system, control activities and monitoring of controls.

8   C   ISA 265 makes a distinction between significant deficiencies and other deficiencies. The auditor also communicates significant deficiencies in writing to management (unless it would be inappropriate in the circumstances) and other deficiencies which are of sufficient importance to merit management's attention.

9   C   This involves the calculation of an expected wages and salaries expense (ie by taking in to account staff numbers, pay rises etc) and comparing it to the actual wages and salaries expense.

10   A   There is an inverse relationship between risk and sample size. The lower the acceptable risk the bigger the sample size as this increases the chances of detecting misstatements.

11   D   In accordance with IAS 10 *Events after the reporting period* only adjusting events require adjustment in the financial statements. A, B and C are all examples of non-adjusting events.

12   A   The other instances where a misstatement would be judged to be pervasive are where the effect of the misstatement is not confined to specific elements, accounts or items in the financial statements and those which are confined to specific elements, accounts or items in the financial statements but represent a substantial portion of the financial statements.

Section B

Question 1

Marking scheme

	Marks
Up to 1 mark per valid point, overall maximum of 5 marks **per issue**	
Discussion of issue	
Calculation of materiality	
Procedures at completion stage	
Type of auditor's report modification required	
Impact on auditor's report	**10**

Daisy

(i) The company's sales ledger was corrupted by a computer virus so it has not been possible to carry out detailed procedures on receivables and the related revenue. Unless there is an alternative way of confirming revenue and receivables the auditor will have been unable to obtain sufficient appropriate evidence over two very material areas of the financial statements. Receivables of $3.4m are in excess of profit before tax (PBT) of $2m. Revenue, at $15.6m is nearly eight times PBT.

(ii) The auditor is unable to obtain sufficient appropriate evidence over the two highly material areas of receivables and revenue. More than one area is affected and this, together with the magnitude of the areas unable to be tested, means the possible effects of any misstatement could be pervasive. Therefore a disclaimer of opinion is necessary.

A basis for disclaimer of opinion paragraph explaining the inability to obtain evidence over revenue and receivables will be included before the opinion paragraph. The disclaimer of opinion in the opinion paragraph will state Violet & Co were unable to form an opinion on the financial statements.

Fuchsia

(i) The financial statements have been prepared on a going concern basis, even though there are indications that the company is not a going concern. Fuchsia has experienced difficult trading conditions, has lost market share and its cash flow forecast for the coming year shows a significant cash outflow of $3.2m. This anticipated outflow of $3.2m is 73% of the current year loss ($3.2/$4.4m) and is therefore a material issue. In any case, the basis of preparation of the accounts is a fundamental issue and material as it impacts on many financial statement areas.

(ii) If Violet & Co conclude the going concern basis is inappropriate then the financial statements have been prepared on the wrong basis and are misleading. The effects of this would be pervasive and an adverse opinion would be issued.

A basis for adverse opinion paragraph will be included before the opinion paragraph to explain that the going concern assumption has been applied when it should not have been. The adverse opinion in the opinion

paragraph will be an adverse opinion and will state that the financial statements are not presented fairly in all material respects (or do not give a true and fair view).

If management can demonstrate that the going concern basis is appropriate, they should still provide disclosures in light of the uncertainty over going concern. As there are no disclosures the financial statements will be materially misstated even if the going concern basis is appropriate and the audit opinion should be modified. A qualified or adverse opinion would be issued.

Question 2

Text references. Audit procedures are described in Chapters 8 and 11 of the Study Text. Tests of controls relating to non-current assets can be found in Chapter 10 and substantive audit procedures for non-current assets can be found in Chapter 12.

Top tips. This question is knowledge-based but make sure that you adequately describe the procedures and examples required. This part of the question would best be answered using a columnar format.

Easy marks. You can score ten marks here as long as your answer is sufficiently detailed. Vague example audit procedures will not score full marks.

Marking scheme

Marks

Up to 1 mark per well described procedure and up to 1 mark for a valid audit test, overall maximum of 2 marks per type of procedure and test, maximum of 5 marks for procedures and maximum of 5 marks for tests.

– Inspection
– Observation
– Analytical procedures
– Inquiry
– Recalculation
– External confirmation
– Reperformance

10

Audit procedures

(a) Audit procedure	(b) Example for property, plant and equipment
Inspection can relate to the examination of documents and records in paper, electronic or other forms, and it can also relate to the physical examination of an asset. Inspection provides audit evidence of existence and completeness.	Select a sample of non-current assets from the non-current asset register and physically inspect them to provide evidence that they actually exist. Select a sample of non-current assets from the client sites and trace back to the non-current asset register to provide evidence of completeness. Inspect purchase order requisitions for a sample of property, plant and equipment purchased in the year to confirm that they were properly authorised.
Observation involves watching a procedure or process being performed. This procedure is of limited use because it only confirms the procedure took place when the auditor was observing and because the process of being observed could affect how the procedure or process was performed.	Observe client staff updating the non-current asset register and ledger for additions/disposals of non-current assets.

(a) Audit procedure	(b) Example for property, plant and equipment
Inquiry involves seeking information from knowledgeable persons, both from client staff and external sources.	Discuss the useful economic lives for each category of non-current asset with the finance director to ensure they appear reasonable.
External confirmation involves obtaining a written representation of information or of an existing condition directly from a third party.	Obtain a valuation from an independent surveyor to verify the value assigned to property held by the client.
Recalculation is checking the mathematical accuracy of documents or records, either manually or using IT.	For a sample of assets from the non-current asset register, recalculate the depreciation charge for the year, based on the asset's life and the depreciation policy for the class of asset. Compare it to the amount recorded in the non-current asset register.
Reperformance is the auditor's independent execution of procedures or controls that were originally performed as part of the entity's internal control.	Reperform the reconciliation of the non-current asset register to the ledger.
Analytical procedures consist of evaluations of financial information through analysis of plausible relationships among both financial and non-financial data. They also encompass such investigation as is necessary of identified fluctuations or relationships that are inconsistent with other relevant information or that differ from expected values by a significant amount.	Perform a proof-in-total of the depreciation charge for the year to assess the reasonableness of the charge to the financial statements, by taking the opening figure, adjusting for additions and disposals and applying the depreciation policy in use by the client. Investigate the reasons for any large discrepancies.

(**Note**: Only five types of audit procedures and five examples for property, plant and equipment were required.)

Question 3

Text references. Chapters 5, 8, 10, 11 and 12 of the Study Text.

Top tips. This is a more challenging 10-mark question as you have to apply your knowledge to a scenario. Make sure your answers are relevant to the scenario in the question – think about the type of industry that Bush-Baby Hotels operates in and tailor your answer accordingly.

Marking scheme

Marks

(a)   Up to 1 mark per well explained point

- Internal audit (IA) can assess fraud risk and develop controls to mitigate fraud
- Regular reviews of compliance with these controls
- Where fraud suspected, IA can undertake detailed fraud investigation
- Existence of IA department acts as a fraud deterrent

3

(b)   Up to 1 mark per well described limitation

- Lack of independence as employees of the company
- No requirement to be professionally qualified
- Cost of establishing department
- Possible resistance from existing employees to idea of being audited

2

(c)   Up to 1 mark per well described point

-       Monitoring asset levels
-       Cash controls testing
-       Customer satisfaction levels
-       Financial/operational controls
-       IT system review
-       Value for money review
-       Regulatory compliance

$$\frac{5}{10}$$

(a)   **Internal audit department and preventing and detecting fraud and error**

The internal audit department could assist in preventing and detecting fraud and error by acting as a deterrent in the first instance.

They could first undertake a risk assessment to identify the risk areas over cash and inventory. They could then review the existing controls in place over inventory and cash handling and recommend improvements to those controls if deficiencies are identified. They also need to test that the controls are working by compliance testing. All findings from their work would be reported in writing to senior management for review and further action if necessary.

(b)   **Limitations of an internal audit department**

Bush-Baby Hotels have not had an internal audit department before so employees may not like the idea of being observed in their work and being reported on.

Setting up the department will cost a considerable amount and as there are 18 hotels in the company, the directors need to ensure they recruit an adequate number of internal audit staff to be able to achieve coverage across the company.

Unless the department will be set up from existing employees, it is unlikely that the staff recruited will have the knowledge and experience required to audit this type of industry. Furthermore, internal auditors are not required to be professionally qualified so staff may not be sufficiently knowledgeable in the industry or the work of internal audit initially.

Internal auditors can never be completely independent, unlike external auditors, as they are employees of the company. Independence is therefore impaired, especially if senior management are dominant. Internal auditors may be unwilling to report serious findings to senior management for fear of losing their jobs.

Internal auditors should report to both senior management and those charged with governance (dual reporting) but if this is not the case, management could unduly influence the internal audit plan, scope and reporting responsibilities.

(c)   **Additional functions**

The internal audit team could undertake value for money reviews, looking at the economy, effectiveness and efficiency of activities and processes within the company.

The internal auditors could perform IT audits, ie performing tests of controls on the computer systems of the company.

The internal auditors could carry out financial audits, using substantive procedures and tests of controls in different areas such as cash, inventory and purchasing for example.

The department could also do operational audits, looking at the operational processes in place.

The internal auditors could also examine compliance with laws and regulations. As the company operates in the hotel industry, this may be a key area to focus on.

Finally, the internal auditors could carry out customer service reviews. This would most likely be in the form of analysing the results of customer service surveys.

Question 4

Marking scheme

		Marks

(a) Up to 1 mark per substantive procedure

- Check additions of bank reconciliation
- Obtain bank confirmation letter
- Bank balance to statement/bank confirmation
- Cash book balance to cash book
- Outstanding lodgements
- Unpresented cheques review
- Old cheques write back
- Agree all balances on bank confirmation
- Unusual items/window dressing
- Security/legal right set-off
- Review reconciliations for saving (deposit) accounts
- Cash counts for significant cash balances
- Review disclosure of bank and cash in financial statements

6

(b) Up to 1 mark per valid point

- Consider if expert has necessary competence, capabilities and objectivity
- Consider the scope, nature and objective of their work
- Assess independence
- Assess whether relevant expertise
- Evaluate inventory assessment including assumptions and source data used
- No reference in the auditor's report

$\frac{4}{10}$

(a) **Substantive procedures on bank and cash balances**

- Send out a standard bank confirmation letter to each bank where the company holds bank accounts to confirm the year-end balance.

- Review the year-end reconciliation of the bank balance per the general ledger against the bank balance per the bank letter.

- Reperform the arithmetic of the bank reconciliation for each bank account held.

- Trace cheques shown as outstanding from the bank reconciliation to the cash book prior to the year-end and to the after-date bank statements and obtain explanations for any large or unusual items not cleared at the time of the audit.

- Compare cash book(s) and bank statements in detail for the last month of the year, and match items outstanding at the reconciliation date to bank statements.

- Review the bank reconciliation previous to the year-end bank reconciliation and test whether all items are cleared in the last period or taken forward to the year-end bank reconciliation.

- Obtain satisfactory explanations for all items in the cash book for which there are no corresponding entries in the bank statement and vice versa by discussion with finance staff.

- Verify contra items appearing in the cash books or bank statements with original entry.

- Verify by inspecting paying-in slips that uncleared bankings are paid in prior to the year-end.

- Examine all lodgements in respect of which payment has been refused by the bank; ensure that they are cleared on representation or that other appropriate steps have been taken to effect recovery of the amount due.

- Verify balances per the cash book according to the bank reconciliation by inspecting cash book, bank statements and general ledger.

- Verify the bank balances with the reply to standard bank letter and with the bank statements.

- Inspect the cash book and bank statements before and after the year-end for exceptional entries or transfers which have a material effect on the balance shown to be in-hand.

- Identify whether any accounts are secured on the assets of the company by discussion with management.

- Consider whether there is a legal right of set-off of overdrafts against positive bank balances.

- Determine whether the bank accounts are subject to any restrictions by inquiries with management.

- Count year-end cash balances and match to cash records such as the petty cash book.

- Obtain certificates of cash in hand from responsible officers.

- Review draft financial statements to confirm that all amounts and relevant disclosures relating to cash and bank have been correctly stated.

(**Note:** Assuming there is one mark per audit procedure, you would need to have six well-explained audit procedures in your answer to score the full six marks available.)

(b)   The independent expert who has undertaken work on raw material inventory quantities is an auditor's expert. ISA 620 *Using the Work of an Auditor's Expert* requires the auditor to evaluate whether their expert has the necessary competence, capabilities and objectivity before relying on the expert's work.

Evaluating the expert's competence will involve obtaining information about the expert's qualifications and professional memberships.

It will be relevant to obtain the expert's client portfolio, to understand whether it has performed similar services to comparable companies in the past. Other teams within our firm may previously have worked with the expert. If this is the case, a discussion with these team members will help to provide an understanding of the expert's level of technical competence and professional reputation.

We may wish to have a discussion with the expert in order to understand the scope of the work done on the raw material quantities, and the methodology used. The audit team will need to evaluate the adequacy of the work carried out by the expert, including the relevance and reasonableness of the assumptions and methods used and its consistency with other audit evidence (for example, records from previous inventory counts). The relevance, completeness and accuracy of any source data used should also be assessed.

In order to evaluate the expert's work, the audit team members will need to have a sufficient understanding of the audit of inventory quantities, so we must ensure that we have staff with the appropriate experience and knowledge on the team.

The expert's independence must also be assessed. We need to make enquiries of Paprika's management and the expert regarding any interests and relationships that could create a threat to independence (for example, whether a high proportion of the expert's income derives from its work for Paprika). If the expert's independence is impaired, its work should not be relied upon and it may be necessary for the audit team to use another, independent, expert to confirm the raw material inventory quantities.

Finally, reference should not be made to the expert in the auditor's report, as the responsibility for obtaining sufficient appropriate audit evidence always remains with the auditor.

Question 5

Marking scheme

			Marks

(a) Up to 1 mark per well explained point:

- Materiality for financial statements as a whole and also performance materiality levels
- Definition of materiality
- Amount or nature of misstatements, or both
- 5% profit before tax or 1% revenue or total expenses
- Judgement, needs of users and level of risk
- Small errors aggregated
- Performance materiality

5

(b) (i) ½ mark per ratio calculation per year.

- Gross margin
- Operating margin
- Inventory days
- Inventory turnover
- Receivable days
- Payable days
- Current ratio
- Quick ratio

5

(ii) Up to 1 mark per well described audit risk and up to 1 mark per well explained audit response

- Receivables valuation
- Inventory valuation
- Depreciation of plant and machinery
- Management manipulation of profit to reach bonus targets
- Completeness of warranty provision
- Disclosure of bank loan of £1 million
- Going concern risk

10
20

(a)   **Materiality and performance materiality**

Materiality is not specifically defined in ISA 320 *Materiality in planning and performing an audit* but it does state that misstatements are material if they could reasonably be expected to influence the economic decisions of users (either individually or in aggregate). ISA 320 also states that judgements about materiality are affected by the size and/or nature of a misstatement. Auditors set their own materiality levels, based on their judgement of risk. During audit planning, the auditor will set materiality for the financial statements as a whole and this involves the exercise of professional judgement. Benchmarks and percentages are often used to calculate a materiality level for the financial statements as a whole, eg 5% of profit before tax or 1-2% of total assets, but ultimately, the level of materiality set is down to the auditor's professional judgement, and may be revised during the course of the audit.

The auditor also has to set performance materiality, which is lower than materiality for the financial statements as a whole. Performance materiality is defined in ISA 320 as the amount or amounts set by the auditor at less than materiality for the financial statements as a whole to reduce to an appropriately low level the probability that the aggregate of uncorrected and undetected misstatements exceeds materiality for the financial statements as a whole.

(b)   (i)   **Ratios**

Ratio	20X3	20X2
Gross profit margin (gross profit/sales × 100)	5.5/12.5 × 100 = 44%	7.0/15.0 × 100 = 47%
Operating margin (profit before interest and taxation/sales × 100)	0.5/12.5 × 100 = 4%	1.9/15 × 100 = 13%
Inventory turnover (cost of sales/inventory)	7/1.9 = 3.7	8/1.4 = 5.7
Inventory days (inventory/cost of sales × 365)	1.9/7 × 365 = 99 days	1.4/8 × 365 = 64 days
Receivables days (receivables/sales × 365)	3.1/12.5 × 365 = 91 days	2/15 × 365 = 49 days
Payables days (payables/cost of sales × 365)	1.6/7 × 365 = 83 days	1.2/8 × 365 = 55 days
Current ratio (current assets/current liabilities)	(1.9 + 3.1 + 0.8)/(1.6 + 1.0) = 2.2	(1.4 + 2.0 + 1.9)/1.2 = 4.4
Quick ratio (current assets except inventory/current liabilities)	(3.1 + 0.8)/(1.6 + 1.0) = 1.5	(2.0 + 1.9)/1.2 = 3.3

(**Note:** only five ratios were required.)

(ii)   **Audit risk and responses**

Audit risk	Auditor's response
The company offers a five year building warranty on its houses. During the year, as a result of switching to a cheaper supplier, some customers have claimed on their guarantees. There is a risk that the warranty provision is understated in the financial statements.	As this is a judgemental area, the auditors need to discuss the basis of calculating the provision with the directors and assess the reasonableness of any assumptions made. They should also review a sample of guarantees claimed during the year and vouch amounts to repairs invoices. They should review the level of claims made in the year and assess whether the provision needs revising in light of this.
The company has had a difficult year due to a fall in house prices. Gross profit margin has fallen by 3% and operating margin has fallen significantly from 13% to 4%. In addition, the company has had to take out a loan of £1m during the year to help with operating cash flow. Payables days have also increased from 55 days to 83 days, indicating that the company is having problems paying suppliers. The current and quick ratios have also fallen significantly from the prior year. There is therefore a risk that the company may not be a going concern.	The auditors must discuss with directors whether they believe that the company is still a going concern in light of the results of the ratio analysis, and review cash flow forecasts and budgets for the forthcoming year.
Receivables days have increased from 49 days to 91 days as a result of the directors increasing the credit terms offered to customers. There is a risk that the receivables' balance at year-end is materially misstated as customers may not be able to pay.	The auditors should carry out post year-end testing and cut-off testing on receivables' balances to verify the accuracy of the year-end balance. The auditors should also review the aged receivables listing to identify any balances that need writing off.
There is a risk that inventory is overstated in the financial statements as there may be some houses whose selling price is less than cost. Inventory days have also increased from 64 days to 99 days, and inventory turnover has fallen from 5.7 to 3.7. Inventory should be valued at the lower of cost and net realisable value.	Detailed audit work on inventory should be carried out as this is likely to be a material balance. An auditor's expert may need to be used to independently verify the value of inventory at the year-end.
There is a risk that revenue and costs have been deliberately misstated in the financial statements in order for the directors to meet the target profit before interest and taxation figure of £0.5m so as to get their bonuses (window dressing). This is also indicated by the fact that the directors have changed the useful economic life of plant and machinery from three to five years to reduce the depreciation charge for the year and hence inflate the profit figure to attain the minimum target figure.	The auditors need to maintain professional scepticism throughout the audit and carry out detailed cut-off testing on revenue and expenses to confirm that the figures are correctly stated.

Audit risk	Auditor's response
There is a risk that the depreciation charge for the year is understated and non-current assets on the statement of financial position are overstated as the directors have amended the useful economic life of plant and machinery from three to five years.	The auditors should discuss the change and the reasons for it with the directors and assess whether it is reasonable or not. They should also examine a sample of plant and machinery assets to assess whether the change is appropriate.
The company has taken out a loan of £1m from the bank which is repayable within a year. There is a risk that this loan has been incorrectly disclosed in the financial statements. It should be disclosed as a current liability as it is repayable within a year.	The auditors should review the terms of the loan agreement to verify the repayment date and the amount borrowed. They should review the draft financial statements to confirm the correct disclosure of the loan.

(**Note:** only **five** audit risks were required.)

Question 6

Text references. Corporate governance is covered in Chapter 3. Controls over the purchasing system are discussed in Chapter 10. Reports to management are covered in Chapter 19.

Top tips. Part (b) should be presented in a tabular format for the deficiencies, impacts and recommendations but do note the requirement for a covering letter – this is relatively unusual for this type of question. Note also that there are two presentation marks available, so make sure your covering letter is addressed and dated appropriately and that you use a ruler for the table and headings. These two marks could be the difference between passing and failing. You must ensure that you identify deficiencies from both the purchases system and the payments system – go through the scenario line-by-line and make notes on areas where there are weaknesses. Your recommendations need to be sufficiently detailed and useful to the organisation. Imagine that you are drafting a real report to management to a real client. Saying things like 'Discuss with management' or 'Reconciliations' will not score many marks.

Easy marks. Part (a) on ISA 260 is straightforward and should not pose any problems.

			Marks
(a)	(i)	Up to 1 mark per well-explained point – Assists the auditor and those charged with governance in understanding matters related to the audit – Obtains information relevant to the audit – Helps those charged with governance in fulfilling their responsibility to oversee the financial reporting process	2
	(ii)	Up to 1 mark for each example matter to be communicated to those charged with governance	4
(b)		Up to 1 mark per well explained deficiency, implication and recommendation. If not well explained then just give ½ mark for each. Overall maximum of 4 marks each for deficiencies, implications and recommendations.	

2 marks for presentation: 1 for address and intro and 1 for conclusion.
– No approved suppliers list
– Purchase orders not sequentially numbered
– Orders below £5,000 are not authorised by a responsible official
– No application controls over input of purchase invoices

    –   Purchase ledger manually posted to general ledger
    –   Saving (deposit) bank accounts only reconciled every two months
    –   Payments to suppliers delayed
    –   Finance director only reviews the total of the payment list prior to
        payment authorising

14

20

(a)   **ISA 260 requirements**

    (i)   It is important that auditors communicate throughout the audit with those charged with governance for the following reasons.

- It assists the auditor and those charged with governance to understand audit-related matters in context and allows them to develop a constructive working relationship.

- It allows the auditor to obtain information relevant to the audit.

- It assists those charged with governance to fulfil their responsibility to oversee the financial reporting process, thus reducing the risks of material misstatement in the financial statements.

    (ii)   Examples of matters that the auditors may communicate with those charged with governance:

- The auditor's responsibilities in relation to the audit of the financial statements, including that the auditor is responsible for forming and expressing an opinion on the financial statements and that the audit does not relieve management or those charged with governance of their responsibilities

- The planned scope and timing of the audit

- Significant deficiencies in internal control

- The auditor's views about significant qualitative aspects of the entity's accounting practices, including accounting policies, accounting estimates and financial statement disclosures

- Significant difficulties encountered during the audit

- Significant matters arising from the audit that were discussed or subject to correspondence with management

- Written representations requested by the auditor

- Other matters that, in the auditor's professional judgement, are significant to the oversight of the financial reporting process

- For listed entities, a statement that the engagement team and others in the firm, the firm, and network firms have complied with relevant ethical requirements regarding independence, any relationships between the firm and entity that might affect independence, and safeguards applied to eliminate identified threats to independence or reduce them to an acceptable level.

(**Note:** Only four matters were required.)

(b)   **Purchasing and payments system**

ABC Auditors
Any Street
Any Town
AB1 2YZ
1 June 20X3

Board of Directors
Fox Industries Co
Trading Estate
Any Town
AB1 3DE

To the Board of Directors, Fox Industries Co,

Financial statements for the year ended 30 April 20X3

Please find enclosed in an Appendix to this letter the report to management detailing deficiencies in internal control found within the purchases and payments system during our recent external audit. This details only the significant deficiencies identified during our audit. If more extensive procedures on internal control had been carried out, we might have identified and reported more deficiencies.

This report to management is solely for the use of Fox Industries Co. It must not be disclosed to a third party, or quoted or referred to, without our consent. No responsibility is assumed by us to any other person.

Yours faithfully,

ABC Auditors

Appendix

(i) Deficiency	(ii) Implication	(iii) Recommendation
Purchase orders are not reviewed by a second person before the order is sent out unless the amount is greater than £5,000.	Orders can be made for unauthorised goods up to a value of £5,000.	All orders should be reviewed before the order is placed and signed off and dated as authorised by a more senior team member. Delegated levels of authority should be in place.
The purchase order clerk chooses the supplier based on the supplier who can deliver the goods fastest.	Goods of poor quality could be ordered or a higher price may be paid for goods from particular suppliers.	An approved suppliers list should be in place so that the company knows exactly who the supplier is and how much the goods cost.
Purchase orders are not sequentially numbered.	Purchase orders can be lost and there is no way of keeping track of unfulfilled orders.	Purchase orders should be sequentially numbered and multi-part. Order forms should be filed in sequential order and reviewed on a weekly basis to flag any unfulfilled orders for chasing up.
Purchase invoices are not matched back to the purchase order before being input onto the system.	Invoices for incorrect amounts and incorrect goods may be entered onto the system and paid for.	Purchase invoices should be matched back to the purchase order to ensure they tally up before being input onto the system. A copy of the order should be attached to the invoice and filed away.

(i) Deficiency	(ii) Implication	(iii) Recommendation
The purchase ledger clerk does not use any application controls over the input of purchase invoices to the ledger.	The lack of application controls increases the risk of errors being made during the input of invoices to the ledger. This could result in misstatements in the financial statements and also errors in amounts paid to suppliers and a consequent loss of goodwill.	There should be some application controls in place over the input of invoices to the system, such as control totals and document totals.
The purchase ledger clerk posts the purchase ledger to the general ledger manually.	Errors may be made during the posting process as it is done manually.	The system should be set up so that the purchase ledger is posted automatically to the general ledger. A reconciliation between the two should be performed each week by the purchase ledger clerk and this should be signed off and dated as reviewed by the finance director.
Deposit accounts are not reconciled on a timely basis, only every two months.	Unreconciled differences may go unnoticed for a long period of time. The length of time between reconciliations may also increase the risk of fraud being perpetrated by employees.	Deposit accounts should be reconciled at the same time as the current account. All reconciliations should be signed off and dated to evidence review by a more senior person, with all differences fully investigated and resolved on a timely basis.
Payment to suppliers is delayed for as long as possible.	Prompt payment discounts are not taken advantage of and suppliers may not look favourably on the company if it takes too long to pay and therefore may refuse credit later on, if the company is viewed as unreliable.	Suppliers should be paid as soon as possible to take advantage of early settlement discounts and to promote and maintain good relations with suppliers.
The finance director authorises the total amount of the payment list, without a review of the detail.	Unauthorised amounts may be missed as the finance director does not see the detail of the payments on the list. This opens the company up to the risk of fraud and error.	The finance director should review the detailed list of payments and query any amounts and supplier names that appear erroneous or suspicious. The review should be evidenced by the finance director's signature and date.

(**Note**: Only four deficiencies were required.)

ACCA

Paper F8

Audit and Assurance

Mock Examination 2

Question Paper	
Time allowed	
Reading and Planning Writing	15 minutes 3 hours
ALL questions are compulsory and MUST be attempted	
During reading and planning time only the question paper may be annotated	

DO NOT OPEN THIS PAPER UNTIL YOU ARE READY TO START UNDER EXAMINATION CONDITIONS

Section A

Multiple choice questions

1 Which of the following statements is true?

   A   Permission from the shareholders at the AGM must be obtained before auditors are given access to the books and records of the company.

   B   Auditors have a right to access the books and records of a company at all times.

   C   Auditors are allowed to access the books and records of the company with permission from the directors. **(1 mark)**

2 Which of the following would **not** be the responsibility of the audit committee?

   A   Review of significant financial reporting issues
   B   Monitoring effectiveness of the company's internal audit function
   C   Making decisions regarding the day-to-day operations of the company
   D   Reviewing external auditor independence **(2 marks)**

3 Which of the following is the correct definition of 'integrity' in accordance with ACCA's *Code of Ethics and Conduct*?

   A   To not allow bias, conflicts of interest or undue influence of others to override professional or business judgements.

   B   To maintain professional knowledge and skill at the level required to ensure that a client or employer receives competent professional services based on current developments in practice, legislation and techniques and act diligently and in accordance with applicable technical and professional standards.

   C   To comply with relevant laws and regulations and should avoid any action that discredits the profession.

   D   To be straightforward and honest in all business and professional relationships.

   (2 marks)

4 X Co is a contract catering company. Which of the following activities might the internal auditor be involved in?

   A   Implementing policies aimed to reduce food waste
   B   Making changes to controls in the purchase ledger system
   C   Performing the annual performance appraisal of site operations managers
   D   Reviewing the adequacy of controls over kitchen staff joiners and leavers in the payroll system
   (2 marks)

5 Which of the following is **not** a valid reason for producing audit documentation?

   A   It prevents the auditor from being sued for negligence
   B   It provides evidence for the basis of key conclusions
   C   It enables senior team members to direct, supervise and review the audit work
   D   It enables quality control reviews to be performed **(2 marks)**

6 The auditor of L Co is auditing the bank balance. Which of the following would be the most reliable source of evidence?

   A   A bank statement from the bank
   B   A bank reconciliation reperformed by the auditor
   C   A bank reconciliation performed by the client
   D   The bank balance on the general ledger **(2 marks)**

7   The auditor of A Co has identified that there is a risk that revenue expenditure incurred on the refurbishment of an item of plant has been incorrectly classified as capital expenditure.

Which of the following is a valid response to this risk?

A   Select a sample of entries included in revenue expenditure and agree to invoices to determine the nature of the work performed

B   Select a sample of entries in additions to plant and machinery and agree to invoices to determine the nature of the work performed

C   Select a sample of items of plant from the asset register and physically verify their existence

(1 mark)

8   Which of the following would be relevant when obtaining an understanding of the control environment?

(1)   Information system
(2)   Communication and enforcement of integrity and ethical values
(3)   Management's philosophy and operating style
(4)   Risk assessment process

A   (1) and (2)
B   (1) and (4)
C   (2) and (3)
D   (3) and (4)   (2 marks)

9   The auditor of G Co has identified that the gross profit margin for 20X8 has increased as compared with 20X7.

Which of the following could explain this change?

A   A management decision to reduce sales prices in 20X8
B   Increases in the costs of raw materials used by G Co
C   Sales cut-off errors
D   Lower interest payments   (2 marks)

10   An auditor adopts a sampling approach whereby all items in the population have an equal chance of being selected, sample size is calculated using a statistically based formula and probability theory is used to extrapolate the results.

What type of sampling method is the auditor using?

A   Judgement-based sampling
B   Non-statistical sampling
C   Statistical sampling   (1 mark)

11   Is the following statement regarding the auditor's responsibilities regarding subsequent events true or false?

The auditor does not have any obligation to perform procedures, or make enquiries regarding the financial statements after the date of the auditor's report.

A   True
B   False   (1 mark)

12   The auditor of C Co has identified a material inconsistency between the chairman's statement and the audited financial statements. The auditor has asked management to revise the chairman's statement but management has refused. This has been communicated to those charged with governance.

What further action could the auditor legitimately take in this situation?

(1)   Modify the audit opinion
(2)   Withhold the auditor's report
(3)   Withdraw from the engagement

A   (1) and (2)
B   (1) and (3)
C   (2) and (3)
D   (1), (2) and (3)   (2 marks)

Section B

Question 1

(a) (i) Define a 'test of control' and provide an example of a test of control in relation to the audit of wages and salaries.

    (ii) Define a 'substantive procedure' and provide an example of a substantive procedure in relation to the audit of wages and salaries.

Note: The total marks will be split equally between each part. **(4 marks)**

(b) ISA 500 *Audit evidence* requires auditors to obtain sufficient and appropriate audit evidence. Appropriateness is a measure of the quality of audit evidence; that is, its relevance and its reliability.

Required
Identify and explain **three** factors which influence the reliability of audit evidence. **(3 marks)**

(c) Auditors are required to perform an overall review of the financial statements before they provide their audit opinion.

Required
Explain **three** procedures an auditor should perform in conducting their overall review of the financial statements. **(3 marks)**

(Total = 10 marks)

Question 2

Salt & Pepper & Co (Salt & Pepper) is a firm of Chartered Certified Accountants which has seen its revenue decline steadily over the past few years. The firm is looking to increase its revenue and client base and so has developed a new advertising strategy where it has guaranteed that its audits will minimise disruption to companies as they will not last longer than two weeks. In addition, Salt & Pepper has offered all new audit clients a free accounts preparation service for the first year of the engagement, as it is believed that time spent on the audit will be reduced if the firm has produced the financial statements.

The firm is seeking to reduce audit costs and has therefore decided not to update the engagement letters of existing clients, on the basis that these letters do not tend to change much on a yearly basis. One of Salt & Pepper's existing clients has proposed that this year's audit fee should be based on a percentage of their final pre-tax profit. The partners are excited about this option as they believe it will increase the overall audit fee.

Required

(a) Identify and explain **five** ethical risks which arise from the above actions of Salt & Pepper & Co. **(5 marks)**

(b) For each ethical risk, explain the steps which Salt & Pepper & Co should adopt to reduce the risks arising. **(5 marks)**

(Total = 10 marks)

Question 3

(a) ISA 520 *Analytical procedures* provides guidance to auditors on the use of analytical procedures during the course of the external audit.

Required

When using analytical procedures as substantive audit procedures, list and briefly explain with examples three factors to consider when determining the extent of reliance that can be placed on the results of such procedures. **(3 marks)**

(b) Explain the meaning of the terms 'sampling risk' and 'non-sampling risk', including how these risks can be reduced. **(3 marks)**

(c) Computer-assisted audit techniques (CAATs) are the use of computers for audit work and comprise mainly audit software and test data.

Required

Explain the terms 'audit software' and 'test data' and list the advantages of using CAATs in an audit. **(4 marks)**

(Total = 10 marks)

Question 4

You are an audit manager in Brown & Co and you are nearing completion of the audit of Paprika & Co (Paprika). The audit senior has produced extracts below from the draft auditor's report for Paprika.

Auditor's responsibility

(1) Our responsibility is to express an opinion on all pages of the financial statements based on our audit. We conducted our audit in accordance with most of the International Standards on Auditing.

(2) Those standards require that we comply with ethical requirements and plan and perform the audit to obtain maximum assurance as to whether the financial statements are free from all misstatements whether caused by fraud or error.

(3) We have a responsibility to prevent and detect fraud and error and to prepare the financial statements in accordance with International Financial Reporting Standards.

(4) An audit involves performing procedures to obtain evidence about the amounts and disclosures in the financial statements. The procedures selected depend on the availability and experience of audit team members. We considered internal controls relevant to the entity; and express an opinion on the effectiveness of these internal controls.

(5) We did not evaluate the overall presentation of the financial statements, as this is management's responsibility. We considered the reasonableness of any new accounting estimates made by management. We did not review the appropriateness of accounting policies as these are the same as last year.

The extracts are numbered to help you refer to them in your answer.

Required

For the above auditor's report extracts, identify and explain **five** elements of this report which require amendment.

(10 marks)

Question 5

Minty Cola Co (Minty) manufactures fizzy drinks such as cola and lemonade as well as other soft drinks and its year end is 31 December 20X3. You are the audit manager of Parsley & Co and are currently planning the audit of Minty. You attended the planning meeting with the engagement partner and finance director last week and recorded the minutes from the meeting shown below. You are reviewing these as part of the process of preparing the audit strategy.

Minutes of planning meeting for Minty

Minty's trading results have been strong this year and the company is forecasting revenue of $85 million, which is an increase from the previous year. The company has invested significantly in the cola and fizzy drinks production process at the factory. This resulted in expenditure of $5 million on updating, repairing and replacing a significant amount of the machinery used in the production process.

As the level of production has increased, the company has expanded the number of warehouses it uses to store inventory. It now utilises 15 warehouses; some are owned by Minty and some are rented from third parties. There will be inventory counts taking place at all 15 of these sites at the year end.

A new accounting general ledger has been introduced at the beginning of the year, with the old and new systems being run in parallel for a period of two months.

As a result of the increase in revenue, Minty has recently recruited a new credit controller to chase outstanding receivables. The finance director thinks it is not necessary to continue to maintain an allowance for receivables and so has released the opening allowance of $1.5 million.

In addition, Minty has incurred expenditure of $4.5 million on developing a new brand of fizzy soft drinks. The company started this process in January 20X3 and is close to launching their new product into the market place. The finance director stated that there was a problem in November in the mixing of raw materials within the production process which resulted in a large batch of cola products tasting different. A number of these products were sold; however, due to complaints by customers about the flavour, no further sales of these goods have been made. No adjustment has been made to the valuation of the damaged inventory, which will still be held at cost of $1 million at the year end.

As in previous years, the management of Minty is due to be paid a significant annual bonus based on the value of year-end total assets.

Required

(a) Using the minutes provided, identify and describe **six** audit risks, and explain the auditor's response to each risk, in planning the audit of Minty Cola Co. **(12 marks)**

(b) Describe substantive procedures the audit team should perform to obtain sufficient and appropriate audit evidence in relation to the following three matters:

Required

(i) The treatment of the $5 million expenditure incurred on improving the factory production process

(3 marks)

(ii) The release of the $1.5 million allowance for receivables **(3 marks)**
(iii) The damaged inventory **(2 marks)**

(Total = 20 marks)

Question 6

You are a member of the recently formed internal audit department of Oregano Co (Oregano). The company manufactures tinned fruit and vegetables which are supplied to large and small food retailers. Management and those charged with governance of Oregano have concerns about the effectiveness of their sales and dispatch system and have asked internal audit to document and review the system.

Sales and dispatch system

Sales orders are mainly placed through Oregano's website but some are made via telephone. Online orders are automatically checked against inventory records for availability; telephone orders, however, are checked manually by order clerks after the call. A follow-up call is usually made to customers if there is insufficient inventory. When taking telephone orders, clerks note down the details on plain paper and afterwards they complete a three part pre-printed order form. These order forms are not sequentially numbered and are sent manually to both dispatch and the accounts department.

As the company is expanding, customers are able to place online orders which will exceed their agreed credit limit by 10%. Online orders are automatically forwarded to the dispatch and accounts department.

A daily pick list is printed by the dispatch department and this is used by the warehouse team to dispatch goods. The goods are accompanied by a dispatch note and all customers are required to sign a copy of this. On return, the signed dispatch notes are given to the warehouse team to file.

The sales quantities are entered from the dispatch notes and the authorised sales prices are generated by the invoicing system. If a discount has been given, this has to be manually entered by the sales clerk onto the invoice. Due to the expansion of the company, and as there is a large number of sale invoices, extra accounts staff have been asked to help out temporarily with producing the sales invoices. Normally it is only two sales clerks who produce the sales invoices.

Required

(a)   Describe **two** methods for documenting the sales and dispatch system; and for each explain an advantage and a disadvantage of using this method.   **(6 marks)**

(b)   List **two** control objectives of Oregano Co's sales and dispatch system.   **(2 marks)**

(c)   Identify and explain **six** deficiencies in Oregano Co's sales and dispatch system and provide a recommendation to address each of these deficiencies.   **(12 marks)**

(Total = 20 marks)

Answers

DO NOT TURN THIS PAGE UNTIL YOU HAVE
COMPLETED THE MOCK EXAM

A plan of attack

If this were the real Audit and Assurance exam and you had been told to turn over and begin, what would be going through your mind?

An important thing to say (while there is still time) is that it is vital to have a good breadth of knowledge of the syllabus because all the questions are compulsory. However, don't panic. Below we provide guidance on how to approach the exam.

Approaching the paper

Part A is a good place to start with. The short multiple choice questions will help to settle you in, before you tackle **Part B**.

In Part B, use your 15 minutes of reading time usefully, to look through the questions, particularly Question 1, to get a feel for what is required and to become familiar with the question scenarios.

Since all the questions in this paper are compulsory, it is vital that you attempt them all in order to increase your chances of passing. For example, don't run over time on Question 2 and then find that you don't have enough time for the remaining questions.

Question 1 is a 10-mark knowledge-based question, divided into three parts. You should be able to score fairly well here. For part (a), note that only one example each of substantive procedures and tests of control is requested, so don't spend too much time identifying more.

Question 2 is a 10-mark question, but it incorporates a scenario. Read the requirements first to identify what you need to focus on as you then read through the scenario. You may wish to present you answer in a two-column table format.

Question 3 is a 10-mark question that is knowledge-based. You should be able to score well here, if you make sure you answer all three parts of the question and respond to all the requirements.

Question 4 is a 10-mark question that is slightly unusual, in that it asks you to identify the errors in five extracts of an auditor's report. It should not be too difficult to gain marks here. Go through each paragraph in order to identify the errors. Don't waste time copying each sentence out – instead, use the numbering of the extracts to help you. Note also that you are not required to write out whole paragraphs of a standard auditor's report.

Question 5 is a 20-mark scenario-based question. You will find that both parts of the requirements relate to the scenario, so you should read the scenario quite carefully. Part (b) is divided into three sections. You can deduce from the marking scheme that three audit procedures are required for each section: don't spend time trying to identify more. Instead, use the time to ensure you clearly describe the audit procedures, rather than just listing them.

Question 6 is another 20-mark scenario-based question. Read the requirements first and you will see that part (a) is a stand-alone knowledge-based requirement which could be answered first. Parts (b) and (c) both relate directly to the scenario. Part (c) should take you to the end of your time allocation for the exam – remember that you are again asked not just to identify the deficiencies, but also to explain them. So, if you are using a table fomat, you may want to use three columns rather than two.

Forget about it!

And don't worry if you found the paper difficult. More than likely other candidates will too. If this were the real thing you would need to forget the exam the minute you left the exam hall and think about the next one. Or, if it is the last one, celebrate!

Section A

Multiple choice answers

1   B   In most jurisdictions this right is established in law.

2   C   Day-to-day operations are normally the responsibility of the executive directors and other management.

3   D   Statement A is the definition of objectivity. Statement B is the definition of professional competence and due care. Statement C is the definition of professional behaviour.

4   D   The internal auditor must ensure that policies are adequate and that they are operating effectively.

5   A   Audit documentation in itself does not prevent the auditor from being sued but would provide evidence in court to support the work which had been performed.

6   B   The bank reconciliation performed by the auditor would be more reliable than that performed by the client as it is produced directly by the auditor. The bank statement is a good source of evidence as it is external but would not take account of timing differences. The evidence provided by the general ledger is less reliable as it is internally generated.

7   B   The risk is that additions are overstated. The additions account therefore must be scrutinised to ensure that entries in this account are capital in nature.

8   C   The information system and risk assessment process are components of internal control. Other issues that may be considered are: commitment to competence, participation by those charged with governance, organisational structure, assignment of authority and responsibility and human resource policies and practices.

9   C   If some 20X9 sales have been included in 20X8 in error sales will be inflated with no corresponding amount in costs of sales. A and B would result in a decrease in gross profit margin. D does not have any effect as interest is not deducted in arriving at gross profit.

10 C   With statistical sampling risk can be measured and controlled.

11 A   The auditor does not have any obligation after the date of the auditor's report. However, if the auditor becomes aware of a fact which may have resulted in the auditor amending the auditor's report, he/she should discuss the matter with management and consider whether the financial statements should be amended.

12 C   As the problem is with the other information, not the financial statements, the audit opinion cannot be modified.

Question 1

Marking scheme

		Marks

(a)   Up to 1 mark each for definitions of test of control (TOC) and substantive procedure and up to 1 mark each for example test of controls and substantive procedures.
  –   Definition of TOC
  –   Example TOC
  –   Definition of substantive test
  –   Example substantive test   **4**

(b)   Up to 1 mark per well explained point, maximum of 3 points.
  –   Reliability increased when it is obtained from independent sources
  –   Internally generated evidence more reliable when the controls are effective
  –   Evidence obtained directly by the auditor is more reliable than evidence obtained indirectly or by inference
  –   Evidence in documentary form is more reliable than evidence obtained orally
  –   Evidence provided by original documents is more reliable than evidence provided by copies   **3**

(c)   Up to 1 mark per well explained point, maximum of 3 points.
  –   Review compliance with accounting standards and local legislation disclosure
  –   Review the disclosure of the accounting policies
  –   Review to ensure consistency with the auditor's knowledge of the business and the results of their audit work
  –   Review the financial statements to assess whether adequately reflect the information and explanations previously obtained and conclusions reached during the course of the audit
  –   Performing analytical procedures of the financial statements to form an overall conclusion
  –   Review aggregate of uncorrected misstatements to assess whether material in aggregate
  –   Assess whether the audit evidence gathered is sufficient and appropriate

$$\frac{3}{\underline{10}}$$

(a) (i) **Tests of control**

Testing of controls means obtaining sufficient appropriate audit evidence about the operating effectiveness of the controls in preventing or detecting and correcting material misstatements.

Examples of tests of control in relation to wages and salaries include:

- Observe whether there is segregation of duties between the HR and payroll departments

- Observe and test the existence of authorisation access controls to payroll data (ie by using test data)

- Review a sample of timesheets for overtime pay for evidence of authorisation by a responsible official.

(ii) **Substantive procedures**

Substantive procedures are audit procedures designed to detect material misstatements at the assertion level. Substantive procedures comprise:

(i) Tests of details (of classes of transactions, account balances, and disclosures)
(ii) Substantive analytical procedures

Examples of substantive procedures in relation to wages and salaries include:

- Carry out a sample recalculation of gross pay to net pay and agree to the payroll records

- Perform a proof in total for the expected total payroll costs and statutory deductions, taking into account joiners, leavers and changes in salary levels

- Agree accruals to post year end payments

- For a sample of joiners and leavers, agree the HR records to payroll to ensure that their pay relates to the correct period worked

(b) Reliability is influenced by the source and nature of the evidence. The following generalisations usually apply.

- Audit evidence is more reliable when it is obtained from independent sources outside the entity.

- Audit evidence that is generated internally is more reliable when the related controls imposed by the entity are effective.

- Audit evidence obtained directly by the auditor (for example, observation of the application of a control) is more reliable than audit evidence obtained indirectly or by inference (for example, inquiry about the application of a control).

- Documentary evidence is more reliable, whether paper, electronic or other medium (for example, a written record of a meeting is more reliable than a subsequent oral representation of the matters discussed).

- Original documents are more reliable than photocopies or faxes.

(c) **Overall review of financial statements**

The auditor should perform the following procedures.

- Reviewing the financial statements to determine whether they are prepared in accordance with national statutory requirements.

- Reviewing the disclosures in the financial statements to determine whether they comply with accounting standards, properly disclosed, consistently applied and appropriate to the entity.

- Reviewing the financial statements to determine whether they are consistent with their knowledge of the entity's business and with the results of other audit procedures.

- Considering the impact on the financial statements of the aggregate of uncorrected misstatements identified during the audit; if the impact is material, discuss the need for adjustment with management.

- Performing analytical procedures to corroborate the conclusions drawn during detailed testing.
- Reviewing the audit work papers to assess whether the audit evidence obtained is sufficient and appropriate.

Question 2

Text reference. Chapter 4.

Top tips. This is a slightly more challenging question for 10 marks, built around a short scenario. However, some ethical issues should be fairly easy to identify. Remember that you are asked to explain each ethical risk identified.

Keep your answer neat and structured: a two-column tabular format would work well.

Easy marks. Part (i) of the requirements is easier to answer, though you will need to ensure that you provide relevant explanations to gain good marks.

Marking scheme

Marks

Up to 1 mark per well explained ethical risk and up to 1 mark per well explained
step to reduce risk, max 5 marks for risks and 5 marks for steps to reduce

      Duration of audit no more than two weeks
      Free accounts preparation service
      Engagement letters not updated
      Contingent fees
      Timing of audit
      Contact previous auditor of Cinnamon Brothers Co

Maximum marks   <u>10</u>

Ethical risks and steps to mitigate the risks

(a) Ethical risks	(b) Steps to mitigate risks
Salt & Pepper guarantees that its audits will not last longer than two weeks.	Salt & Pepper should retract the 'two-week guarantee' immediately, and explain to its audit clients that the duration of audits will depend upon the level of complexity and risk associated with each business. The completion date of the audit will be agreed with each client at the planning stage, but this may need to change if any circumstances cause the auditor to re-evaluate the company's level of assessed risk.
The amount of time required to complete an audit depends upon the nature of each audit client's business and the level of associated risk. To restrict the duration of all audits to two weeks, regardless of the level of complexity and risks of the business, will result in sufficient and appropriate audit evidence not being obtained. Salt & Pepper would be at risk of giving incorrect audit opinions, leading to possible litigation. The firm would contravene the ACCA *Code of Ethics*.	

(a) Ethical risks	(b) Steps to mitigate risks
Salt & Pepper is offering a free accounts preparation service to new audit clients. The preparation of the accounts, which the firm will then audit, gives rise to a self-review threat. In addition, the fact that the accounts preparation service is offered for free may be considered low-balling.	Salt & Pepper should ensure that a separate team is allocated to the accounts preparation work. It must not offer the accounts preparation service to listed clients. It is important that the firm demonstrates that appropriate time and appropriately-qualified staff are assigned to its audit engagements, and that the ISAs are adhered to.
Salt & Pepper has decided not to update the engagement letters of existing clients. This goes against the requirements of ISA 210.	Salt & Pepper should review the need for updating engagement letters on an annual basis.
An existing client has suggested that their audit fee should be based on a percentage of their final pre-tax profit. This constitutes a contingent fee. Contingent fee structures create a self-interest threat which cannot be mitigated. They are therefore prohibited by the ACCA *Code of Ethics*.	Salt & Pepper should decline the client's proposal, and explain that audit fees would be based on the level work required to obtain sufficient appropriate audit evidence.
Salt & Pepper plans to rely on more junior staff to carry out the audit of a new client, Cinnamon, during a busy period for the firm. The risks associated with the Cinnamon audit are difficult to assess, as this is the first year that Salt & Pepper is performing the audit. Junior staff is unlikely to have sufficient knowledge and experience to determine the amount of audit work required, thus increasing the risk of giving an incorrect audit opinion.	Salt & Pepper needs to re-assess its resourcing plans, and allocate an appropriate number of experienced audit staff to the Cinnamon audit engagement. If this is not possible, Salt & Pepper should discuss with the client the possibility of changing the timing of the audit to a period when adequate staff resources are available.
Salt & Pepper has not contacted the outgoing auditor. It is important for the firm to communicate with the outgoing auditor, as it needs to understand whether there are any actions by the client which would preclude the firm from accepting the engagement on ethical grounds.	Salt & Pepper should contact the previous auditors, to confirm the reason behind the change of auditor and to ascertain that there are no ethical issues precluding the firm from acting as the auditor.

Question 3

Text reference. Chapter 4.

Top tips. This is a knowledge-based question. Make sure that you read the question carefully to answer the question asked in order to maximise your marks. For example, in (b), remember to explain ways to reduce sampling and non-sampling risk.

Easy marks. Provided you are familiar with the syllabus, you should find parts (b) and (c) easy.

		Marks
(a)	Up to 1 mark per well-described point.	
	– Materiality	
	– Other procedures	
	– Accuracy of predictions	
	– Frequency with which relationship is observed	
	– Assessment of risks	3
(b)	Up to 1 mark each for explanation of sampling and non-sampling risk	
	½ mark each for explanation how to reduce each risk	3
(c)	1 mark for explanation of audit software	
	1 mark for explanation of test data	
	½ mark each for each advantage of CAATs	4
		10

(a) **Factors to consider when assessing the reliance that can be placed on the results of analytical procedures**

Materiality of the items involved

If inventory balances are material, then auditors should not rely solely on analytical procedures.

Other audit procedures

In the audit of receivables, other audit procedures such as the review of subsequent cash receipts may confirm or dispel questions arising from the application of analytical procedures to an aged profile of customers' accounts.

Accuracy of predictions

Auditors would expect greater consistency in comparing the relationship between gross profit and sales from one period to the next than in comparing discretionary expenses such as research costs or advertising expenditure.

Frequency with which relationship is observed

A pattern repeated monthly as opposed to annually (for example, payroll costs).

Assessment of inherent and control risks

If internal controls over sales order processing are weak, and control risk is assessed as high, the auditors may rely more on tests of individual transactions or balances than on analytical procedures.

(**Note**: Only three were required.)

(b) 'Sampling risk' is the risk that the auditor's conclusion, based on a sample of a certain size, may be different from the conclusion that would be reached if the entire population was subjected to the same audit procedure. It can be reduced by increasing the sample size for both tests of controls and substantive procedures.

'Non-sampling risk' is the risk that the auditor reaches the wrong conclusion for any reason unrelated to the size of the sample, such as using inappropriate procedures or misinterpreting evidence and failing to recognise a misstatement or deviation. It can be reduced by proper engagement planning, supervision and review.

(c) 'Audit software' consists of computer programs used by auditors to process data of audit significance from the client's accounting system. It may comprise generalised audit software or custom audit software. It is used for substantive procedures.

'Test data' involves entering data such as a sample of transactions into the client's accounting system and comparing the results obtained with pre-determined results. Test data is used for tests of controls.

Advantages of CAATs

- Auditors can test program controls as well as general computer controls.
- A greater number of items can be tested more quickly and accurately.
- Transactions can be tested, rather than paper records that could be incorrect.
- CAATs are cost-effective in the long-term if the client does not change its systems.
- Results can be compared to results from traditional testing and if correlation exists, overall confidence is increased.

Question 4

Text references. Chapters 1, 2, 19.

Top tips. This question takes the rather unusual approach of asking candidates to identify and explain errors in an auditor's report. If you understand the principle of an audit, however, you should find it easy to gain marks here. Do not waste time redrafting auditor's report extracts. Instead, make sure that you explain why each error requires amendment.

Easy marks. If you are familiar with the basic principles of the ISAs and the form of the auditor's report, you should find plenty of easy marks here.

Marking scheme

Marks

Up to 1 mark for each element identified and up to 1 mark per explanation, overall maximum 5 marks for identification and 5 marks for explanation of elements.

Opinion on all pages
Audit in accordance with most ISAs
Maximum assurance, free from all misstatements
Responsibility to prevent and detect fraud and error
We prepare financial statements
Procedures depend upon availability and experience of team members
We express an opinion on the effectiveness of internal controls
Did not evaluate overall presentation of financial statements
Considered reasonableness of new accounting estimates
Did not review accounting policies

Maximum marks   <u>10</u>

Elements of the auditor's report which require amendment

- 'Our responsibility is to express an opinion on all pages of the financial statements': The auditor is only required to express an opinion on the statement of financial position, statement of profit or loss and comprehensive income, statement of cash flows, summary of significant accounting policies, and other information contained within the notes to the financial statements.

- 'We conducted our audit in accordance with most of the International Standards on Auditing': The auditor is required to comply with **all** of the ISAs. This fact must be stated in the auditor's report.

- 'The standards require that we [...] plan and perform the audit to obtain maximum assurance as to whether the financial statements are free from all misstatements': The auditor does not aim to obtain assurance that the financial statements are free from all misstatements, but only gives reasonable assurance that the financial statements are free from material misstatements. It is not practical for the auditor to test every

single transaction and account balance. Instead, the level of the audit procedures carried out, and the sample size tested, depends upon the auditor's assessment of audit risk and consequently, materiality.

- 'We have a responsibility to prevent and detect fraud and error and to prepare the financial statements in accordance with the International Financial Reporting Standards': Preventing and detecting fraud and error, and the preparation of the financial statements, are the responsibilities of the entity's management. The auditor's responsibility is to detect material misstatements, whether caused by fraud or error, and to express an opinion on the truth and fairness of the financial statements.

- 'The procedures selected depend on the availability and experience of the audit team members': The auditor is required to perform the necessary audit procedures to obtain sufficient and appropriate audit evidence. The audit team must be staffed adequately with appropriately experienced team members to ensure that the necessary audit procedures are performed.

- 'We express an opinion on the effectiveness of these internal controls': The auditor's report provides an opinion on the truth and fairness of the financial statements, but does not express an opinion on the effectiveness of internal controls. Any deficiencies identified by Brown & Co during the course of the audit will be reported to Paprika's management.

- 'We did not evaluate the overall presentation of the financial statements as this is management's responsibility': Although it is management's responsibility to prepare the financial statements, the auditor is required to review the overall presentation to determine whether it is in accordance with applicable accounting standards and consistent with the audit evidence obtained.

- 'We considered the reasonableness of any new accounting estimates': All accounting estimates must be considered by the auditor, whether they are brought forward or new. Accounting estimates carried forward from year to year, such as allowances and provisions, may need to be adjusted or reversed.

- 'We did not review the appropriateness of accounting policies as these are the same as last year': Accounting policies must be reviewed in each accounting period. A change in accounting policies may become necessary as a result of new accounting standards, or as the company's circumstances change.

Question 5

Text references. Chapters 6, 8, 12, 13 and 14.

Top tips. This scenario-based question tests your ability to identify and respond to audit risks, and then focuses on substantive procedures for three main accounts in the financial statements: non-current assets, receivables and inventory. Time-management is crucial here: keep an eye on the time you spend in part (a), and make sure you leave half of your allocated time for part (b).

In part (a), work through each paragraph of the scenario to identify the audit risks. A two-column tabular format will help you to keep track. There are plenty of issues at stake here, but remember that only six audit risks are required.

Part (b) consists of three sub-requirements. If you look at the mark allocation, you will see that only three substantive procedures are required for each sub-requirement. Make sure that your answer is related to the scenario.

Easy marks. This question is challenging, but it should be easy to identify a good number of audit risks in part (a).

Marks

(a) Up to 1 mark per well described risk and up to 1 mark for each well explained
response. Overall max of 6 marks for risks and 6 marks for responses.
- $5 million expenditure on production process
- Inventory counts at 15 warehouses at year end
- Treatment of owned v third party warehouses
- New general ledger system introduced at the beginning of the year
- Release of opening provision for allowance for receivables
- Research and development expenditure
- Damaged inventory
- Sales returns
- Management bonus based on asset values   12

(b) Up to 1 mark per well described substantive procedure, overall maximum of 3
marks per issue.

(i) **$5 million expenditure incurred on improving the factory production**
process
- Obtain a schedule of the $5 million expenditure and cast
- For capital items, agree to purchase invoices and ascertain if they are in
fact of a capital nature
- For capital items, agree to the non-current assets register to ensure that
they are correctly included
- For capital items, recalculate the depreciation charged to ensure it has
been appropriately time apportioned
- For items treated as repairs, vouch to invoices and that correctly
expensed to profit or loss

(ii) **Release of $1.5 million allowance for receivables**
- Discuss with the finance director rationale for not providing against any
receivables
- Review aged receivable ledger to identify any slow moving or old
receivable balances, discuss with the credit controller
- Review after date cash receipts for slow moving/old receivable balances
- Review customer correspondence to identify any balances in dispute or
unlikely to be paid
- Review board minutes to identify any significant concerns in relation to
payments by customers
- Calculate the potential level of receivables which are not recoverable and
assess if material or not

(iii) **Damaged inventory**
- Obtain a schedule of the $1 million damaged cola products and cast
- During the inventory count identify the damaged goods and agree to the
schedule
- Discuss with management whether these goods have a net realisable
value (NRV)
- If any goods sold post year end, agree to sales invoice to assess NRV
- Agree the cost of the inventory to supporting documentation to verify the
raw material cost, labour cost and any overheads attributed to the cost
- Quantify the level of adjustment required to value inventory at the lower
of cost and NRV and discuss with management   8
                                                                         ——
                                                                         20

(a)

Audit risk	Auditor's response
Significant investment in updating the cola and fizzy drinks production process: risk that capital and revenue expenditure is incorrectly classified, leading to over- or under-statement of non-current assets and profit or loss expense.	Review a breakdown of costs and carry out substantive testing on a sample of the expenditure.
Inventory being held at a larger number of different locations, some of which are not owned by Minty: risk that inventory is misstated. The spread of geographical location increases the risk that the inventory count procedures may be inconsistent.	Attend inventory counts at the locations where the greatest proportion of inventory is held, or where there have been a history of errors. Review supporting documentation from all warehouses to confirm ownership of the inventory, particularly inventory held by third parties.
A new general ledger being introduced: risk of records being incomplete and increased risk of errors as a result of staff being unaccustomed to the system.	Analytical procedures and comparisons with prior year trends, to identify any areas where figures in the financial statements appear to be inconsistent. Agree the opening balances to prior year closing balances, to confirm that they have been correctly recorded in the new system. Substantive testing of a sample of transactions and balances recorded over the transitional period and immediately after. Substantive testing of any accounts identified by analytical procedures as unexpected.
New general ledger: increased detection risk as the related system of internal controls has not been documented and tested by the auditor.	Document and test the new system. Review management reports produced over the transitional period to identify any issues with the recording of financial information.
Release of the allowance for receivables: risk that truly irrecoverable debts are no longer provided for, giving rise to the overstatement of profit and receivables.	Obtain documentation from management to support the release of the allowance. Make enquiries of the new credit controller to gain an understanding of the likelihood of recovering the $1.5m of receivables. Carry out extended testing of post year-end cash receipts and review the aged receivables ledger to determine the need for an allowance.
$4.5m expenditure on the development of a new fizzy drink product: risk that research costs (required to be expensed under IAS 38 *Intangible assets*) and development costs (to be capitalised) are incorrectly classified, giving rise to the overstatement of intangible assets and understatement of expenses.	Obtain a breakdown of development costs and research costs. Undertake detailed testing to determine the nature of the costs. Make enquiries of management regarding the basis on which the costs have been classified.
Defective cola products remain unsold and no adjustments have been made: risk that inventory is overstated.	Carry out detailed testing of the cost and NRV of the defective cola products to determine the level of inventory write-off required.

Audit risk	Auditor's response
There is a risk that customers would be unwilling to pay for the defective batch of cola products, causing receivables to be further overstated.	Obtain details of any credit notes issued and returns in relation to the cola products and agree them to revenue and receivables. Obtain correspondence with major retail customers to whom the cola products have been sold, and identify whether any discounts/credit notes have been agreed.
The management is paid a bonus based on the value of the company's assets: risk that the value of assets is overstated through inappropriate judgements applied in accounting estimates (such as the releasing of the allowance for receivables).	Apply professional scepticism throughout the audit. Review management assumptions in relation to accounting estimates. Work to a lower level of performance materiality to assets susceptible to judgement (for example, receivables, non-current assets and intangible assets).

(b)   **Substantive procedures**

(i) $5m expenditure on improving the factory production process

- Obtain a schedule of the $5m expenditure and check that it casts

- Agree items in the schedule to invoices to ascertain that items have been correctly classified

- Inspect the result of work done where necessary

- Agree items on the schedule to the non-current assets register and statement of profit or loss, respectively

(ii)   Release of $1.5m allowance for receivables

- Enquire of the finance director the rationale for releasing the allowance

- Review the aged receivables listing to identify old outstanding receivables balances, and discuss the likelihood of payment with the credit controller

- Obtain details of receipts after the year-end

- Review correspondence with customers to identify any balances in dispute

- Review board meeting minutes for evidence of doubts concerning the recovery of any receivable balances

- Based on the above procedures, calculate the potential level of unrecoverable receivables and assess whether this is material. Discuss the adjustment with management

(iii)   Damaged inventory

- Obtain a schedule of the $1m damaged inventory and cast

- Attend the inventory count. Inspect the damaged goods and agree the quantity to the schedule

- Discuss with management the company's plans for the damaged goods – whether they are to be scrapped or whether any net realisable value can still be assigned to them

- Obtain the sales invoices for any damaged goods sold post year-end to assess the net realisable value

- Determine the cost of the inventory by obtaining supporting documentation with regards to the raw material, labour and attributed overhead costs.

- Quantify the level of adjustment required to value the damaged inventory at the lower of cost and net realisable value and discuss with management

Question 6

Text references. Chapters 9 and 10.

Top tips. This scenario-based question tests your applied knowledge of internal controls.

Part (a) is knowledge-based so should be straightforward. Note that only two methods are required.

Part (b) asks for control objectives. This can be answered independently of the scenario, but your answer here should help to inform your answer for part (c).

In part (c), keep your answer in a tabular format and make sure your answer is related to the scenario.

Easy marks. Part (a) and (b) should both yield easy marks.

Marking scheme

		Marks
(a)	Up to 1 mark each for a description of a method, up to 1 mark each for an advantage, up to 1 mark each for a disadvantage. Overall max of 2 marks each for methods, advantages and disadvantages.	
	– Narrative notes	
	– Questionnaires	
	– Flowcharts	6
(b)	1 mark for each control objective, overall maximum of 2 points.	
	– To ensure orders are only accepted if goods are available to be processed for customers	
	– To ensure all orders are recorded completely and accurately	
	– To ensure goods are not supplied to poor credit risks	
	– To ensure goods are dispatched for all orders on a timely basis	
	– To ensure goods are dispatched correctly to customers and are of an adequate quality	
	– To ensure all goods dispatched are correctly invoiced	
	– To ensure completeness of income for goods dispatched	
	– To ensure sales discounts are only provided to valid customers	2
(c)	Up to 1 mark per well explained deficiency and up to 1 mark for each control. Overall max of 6 marks for deficiencies and 6 marks for controls.	
	– Inventory not checked when order taken	
	– Orders not completed on pre-printed order forms	
	– Order forms not sequentially numbered	
	– Credit limits being exceeded	
	– Goods dispatched not agreed to order to check quantity and quality	
	– Signed dispatch notes not being sent to accounts department	
	– Sales invoices being raised by inexperienced staff	
	– Sales discounts manually entered by sales clerks 12	$\frac{12}{\underline{\underline{20}}}$

(a) **Documenting the sales and dispatch system**

Narrative notes are written descriptions of the system, describing how the system processes each transaction, and the controls that operate at each stage.

Advantages

- Simple to record

- No training required to document and understand; easily understood by all members of the internal audit team

Disadvantages

- Cumbersome, especially if the sales and dispatch system is complex
- Not easily updated from year on year if it is not computerised
- More difficult for users to quickly identify internal control deficiencies

Flowcharts are graphical illustrations of the physical flow of information through the sales and dispatch system.

Advantages

- After some experience, they can be prepared quickly

- Information is prepared in standard form, so it is easy to follow. Deficiencies in internal control can also be quickly identified

- Ensures that the system is recorded in its entirety; any loose ends are easily identified

Disadvantages

- While appropriate for standard systems, unusual transactions cannot be captured without the use of additional narrative

- Time-consuming to amend as redrawing is required.

Questionnaires comprise a list of standard questions. Internal control questionnaires (ICQs) determine whether desirable controls are present, while internal control evaluation questionnaires (ICEQs) assess whether specific errors (or frauds) are possible at each stage of the sales and dispatch cycle.

Advantages

- If drafted thoroughly, they can ensure that all controls are considered
- Quick and easy to prepare
- Easy to use and control
- ICEQs are effective in identifying internal control deficiencies

Disadvantages

- Questionnaires are only as good as their author: drafted vaguely, the questions could be misunderstood, and if questions are incomplete, important controls could be missed

- Unusual controls may be missed

- It would be easy for staff members to overstate the level of controls

- Gives the false impression that all controls are of equal weight; in reality, certain controls may be more fundamental than others.

(b) **Control objectives**

Occurrence and existence

- To ensure that one person is not responsible for taking orders, recording sales and receiving payment
- To ensure that recorded sales transactions represent goods provided
- To ensure that goods are only supplied to customers with good credit ratings
- To ensure that goods are provided at authorised prices and on authorised terms
- To ensure that customers are encouraged to pay promptly

Completeness

- To ensure that all revenue relating to goods dispatched is recorded
- To ensure that all goods sold are correctly invoiced

Accuracy

- To ensure that all sales and adjustments are correctly journalised, summarised and posted to the correct accounts

Cut-off

- To ensure that transactions have been recorded in the correct period

Classification

- To ensure that all transactions are properly classified in accounts

(c) **Control deficiencies**

Deficiencies	Recommendations
Telephone orders are checked manually after an order has been placed. This creates a risk of goods for which orders have been placed being unavailable, leading to unfulfilled orders. This gives rise to dissatisfaction from customers and has a negative impact on the company's reputation.	Orders should not be confirmed before the availability of the product has been checked. To ensure that orders are fulfilled consistently, telephone orders and online orders should ideally be processed through the same system, with automatic notifications to the customer who has placed the order once product availability has been checked.
Order forms for telephone orders are completed after an order has been placed. This increases the risk that information on the order forms is incorrect or incomplete, leading to errors in fulfilling the order.	All order forms should be completed at the time the order is placed. For telephone orders, the order clerk should confirm with the customer that all details are correct.
The order forms used for telephone orders are not sequentially numbered. This increases the risk that order forms are lost in transit, leading to unfulfilled orders and reputational damage.	All order forms should be sequentially numbered.
The same order clerk takes the orders, checks the order forms and sends the order forms onto the accounts and dispatch departments. The lack of segregation of duties increases the risk of error and fraud.	Each telephone order taken should be cross-checked by another order clerk. The check should be evidenced by signature.
Customers are able to exceed their agreed credit limit by 10% when they place their orders online. This increases the risk that customers with bad credit histories are accepted, leading to slow-moving or bad debts.	The online ordering system should be modified to reject orders which would cause credit limits to be exceeded. Customers' credit limits should be assessed on a regular basis by a responsible official. Credit limits could be extended for customers with good credit histories.
Goods do not appear to be checked to the original order before dispatch. This increases the risk of errors in fulfilling the order.	Order forms for goods on the pick list should be printed on a daily basis. Goods should be checked to the order forms before being dispatched.

Deficiencies	Recommendations
The signed dispatch notes are not sent to the accounts department. This could result in delays in invoicing, leading to loss of revenue.	Copies of the signed dispatch notes should be forwarded to the accounts department once the goods have been delivered. Invoices should be raised based on the dispatch notes in a timely manner, and the dispatch notes filed by the accounts team along with evidence that the related invoices have been processed.
Discounts are manually entered by the sales clerk onto the invoice. This creates the risk of discounts being omitted by error. More importantly, the lack of authorisation process increases the risk of unauthorised discounts being given, leading to loss of revenue.	Discounts should be approved by a responsible official. The authorised discount levels should be recorded automatically in the customer master file, so that they appear on the invoices without manual input. The invoicing system should be modified to prevent the manual processing of discounts.
Extra accounts staff have been allocated to produce the sales invoices. The extra staff's lack of experience and training increases the risk of errors on the invoices, resulting in customers being over- or under-charged.	Only sales clerks with the appropriate experience should be allowed to produce sales invoices. Oregano could consider recruiting and training permanent staff with the appropriate experience.

ACCA
Paper F8
Audit and Assurance

Mock Examination 3

Specimen Paper

Question Paper	
Time allowed	
Reading and Planning Writing	**15 minutes** **3 hours**
ALL questions are compulsory and MUST be attempted	
During reading and planning time only the question paper may be annotated	

DO NOT OPEN THIS PAPER UNTIL YOU ARE READY TO START UNDER EXAMINATION CONDITIONS

Section A – ALL TWELVE questions are compulsory and MUST be attempted

Please use the space provided on the inside cover of the Candidate Answer Booklet to indicate your chosen answer to each multiple choice question.

1   Which of the following sampling methods correctly describes systematic sampling?

    A   A sampling method which is a type of value-weighted selection in which sample size, selection and evaluation results in a conclusion in monetary amounts

    B   A sampling method which involves having a constant sampling interval, the starting point for testing is determined randomly

    C   A sampling method in which the auditor selects a block(s) of contiguous items from within the population   **(1 mark)**

2   An audit junior has been assigned to the audit of bank and cash balances of Howard Co. He has obtained the following audit evidence:

    (1)   Bank reconciliation carried out by the cashier
    (2)   Bank confirmation report from Howard's bankers
    (3)   Verbal confirmation from the directors that the overdraft limit is to be increased
    (4)   Cash count carried out by the audit junior

    What is the order of reliability of the audit evidence starting with the most reliable first?

    A   (4), (2), (1) and (3)
    B   (2), (1), (4) and (3)
    C   (4), (3), (2) and (1)
    D   (2), (4), (1) and (3)   **(2 marks)**

3   Fellaini Co operates a large department store and has a large internal audit department in place. The management of Fellaini Co are keen to increase the range of assignments that internal audit undertake.

    Which of the following assignments could the internal audit department of Fellaini Co be asked to perform by management?

    A   Internal audit department members could undertake 'mystery shopper' reviews, where they enter the store as a customer, purchase goods and rate the overall shopping experience

    B   Internal audit could be asked to assist the external auditors by requesting bank confirmation letters

    C   Internal audit could be asked to implement a new payroll package for the payroll department

    D   Internal audit could be asked to assist the finance department with the preparation of the year end financial statements   **(2 marks)**

4   Application controls are manual or automated procedures that operate over accounting applications to ensure that all transactions are complete and accurate.

    Which **two** of the following are application controls?

    (1)   Password protection of programs
    (2)   Batch controls
    (3)   One for one checking
    (4)   Regular back up of programs

    A   (1) and (4)
    B   (3) and (4)
    C   (1) and (2)
    D   (2) and (3)   **(2 marks)**

5   Which **two** of the following are fundamental principles as stated in the ACCA's *Code of Ethics and Conduct*?

(1)   Objectivity
(2)   Independence
(3)   Confidentiality
(4)   Professional scepticism

A   (1) and (4)
B   (1) and (2)
C   (2) and (3)
D   (1) and (3)   **(2 marks)**

6   Auditors usually carry out their audit work at different stages known as the interim audit and the final audit.

Which of the following statements, if any, is/are correct?

(1)   Carrying out tests of control on the company's sales day books would normally be undertaken during an interim audit.
(2)   Review of aged receivables ledger to identify balances requiring write down or allowance would normally be undertaken during a final audit.

A   Neither (1) or (2)
B   Both (1) and (2)
C   (1) only
D   (2) only   **(2 marks)**

7   Which of the following statements relate to review engagements?

(1)   Subject matter is plausible
(2)   Reasonable assurance
(3)   Nothing has come to our attention which would indicate that the subject matter contains material misstatements
(4)   Positive assurance

A   (1) and (3)
B   (2) and (4)
C   (2) and (3)
D   (1) and (4)   **(2 marks)**

8   When placing reliance on the work of an expert is the following statement true or false?

In order to place reliance, the auditor is required to evaluate the work performed by the expert.

A   True
B   False   **(1 mark)**

9   An emphasis of matter paragraph is used in an audit report to draw attention to a matter affecting the financial statements.

Which **two** of the following are correct in relation to an Emphasis of Matter Paragraph in the Auditor's Report?

(1)   It is used when there is a significant uncertainty.
(2)   It constitutes a qualified audit opinion.
(3)   The audit report is referred to as an unmodified report.
(4)   The matter is deemed to be fundamental to the users understanding of the financial statements.

A   (1) and (2)
B   (1) and (4)
C   (1) and (3)
D   (2) and (4)   **(2 marks)**

10   During the planning stages of the final audit, the auditor believes that the probability of giving an inappropriate audit opinion is too high.

How should the auditor amend the audit plan to resolve this issue?

A   Increase the materiality level

B   Decrease the inherent risk

C   Decrease the detection risk   (1 mark)

11   The audit of Giggs Co's financial statements for the year ended 31 October 20X4 has been completed; the audit report and the financial statements have been signed but not yet issued.

The finance director of Giggs Co has just informed the audit team that he has received notification that a material receivable balance has become irrecoverable and Giggs Co will not receive any of the amounts owing.

What actions, if any, should the auditor now take to satisfy their responsibilities under ISA 560 *Subsequent Events*?

A   No actions required as the audit report and financial statements have already been signed

B   Request management to adjust the financial statements, verify the adjustment and provide a new audit report

C   Request management to make disclosure of this event in the financial statements

D   Request that management adjust for this event in the following year's financial statements as it occurred in year ending 31 October 20X5   (2 marks)

12   ISA 315 *Identifying and Assessing the Risks of Material Misstatement through Understanding the Entity and Its Environment* sets out the five components of internal control.

Which of the following is **not** set out as a component of internal control within ISA 315?

A   Control environment

B   The information system relevant to financial reporting

C   Human resource policies and practices   (1 mark)

Section B – ALL SIX questions are compulsory and MUST be attempted

Question 1

The audit engagement partner for Hazard Co (Hazard), a listed company, has been in place for approximately six years and her son has just accepted a job offer from Hazard as a sales manager. This role would entitle him to shares in Hazard as part of his remuneration package.

Hazard's directors are considering establishing an internal audit department, and the finance director has asked the audit firm, Remy & Co about the differences between internal audit and external audit.

If the internal audit department is established, and Remy & Co is appointed as internal as well as external auditors, then Hazard has suggested that the external audit fee should be renegotiated with at least 20% of the fee being based on the profit after tax of the company as they feel this will align the interests of Remy & Co and Hazard.

Required

(a) Using the information above:

    (i) Explain the ethical threats which may affect the independence of Remy & Co in respect of the audit of Hazard Co.   **(3 marks)**

    (ii) For each threat explain how it might be reduced to an acceptable level.   **(3 marks)**

(b) Distinguish between internal and external audit.   **(4 marks)**

                                                          (Total = 10 marks)

Question 2

(a) Auditors are required to obtain sufficient appropriate audit evidence. Tests of control and substantive procedures can be used to obtain such evidence.

    Required

    Define a 'test of control' and a 'substantive procedure'.   **(2 marks)**

(b) Balotelli Beach Hotel Co (Balotelli) operates a hotel providing accommodation, leisure facilities and restaurants. Its year end was 31 October 20X4. You are the audit senior of Mario & Co and are currently preparing the audit programmes for the year end audit of Balotelli. You are reviewing the notes of last week's meeting between the audit manager and finance director where two material issues were discussed.

Depreciation

Balotelli incurred significant capital expenditure during the year on updating the leisure facilities for the hotel. The finance director has proposed that the new leisure equipment should be depreciated over 10 years using the straight-line method.

Food poisoning

Balotelli's directors received correspondence in September from a group of customers who attended a wedding at the hotel. They have alleged that they suffered severe food poisoning from food eaten at the hotel and are claiming substantial damages. Balotelli's lawyers have received the claim and believe that the lawsuit against the company is unlikely to be successful.

Required

Describe substantive procedures to obtain sufficient and appropriate audit evidence in relation to the above two issues.   **(8 marks)**

Note: The total marks will be split equally between each issue.

                                                          (Total = 10 marks)

Question 3

(a)   You are the audit manager of Savage & Co and you are briefing your team on the approach to adopt in undertaking the review and finalisation stage of the audit. In particular, the audit senior is unsure about the steps to take in relation to uncorrected misstatements.

Required

Describe the auditor's responsibility in respect of misstatements.   **(2 marks)**

(b)   You are the audit manager of Villa & Co and you are currently reviewing the audit files for several of your clients for which the audit fieldwork is complete. The audit seniors have raised the following issues:

Czech Co

Czech Co is a pharmaceutical company and has incurred research expenditure of $2.1m and development expenditure of $3.2m during the year, this has all been capitalised as an intangible asset. Profit before tax is $26.3m.

Dawson Co

Dawson Co's computerised wages program is backed up daily, however for a period of two months the wages records and the back-ups have been corrupted, and therefore cannot be accessed. Wages and salaries for these two months are $1.1m. Profit before tax is $10m.

Required

For each of the clients above:

(i)   Discuss the issue, including an assessment of whether it is material.   **(4 marks)**

(ii)   Describe the impact on the auditor's report if the issue remains unresolved.   **(4 marks)**

(Total = 10 marks)

Question 4

(a)   Explain **four** financial statement assertions relevant to account balances at the period end.   **(4 marks)**

(b)   Torres Leisure Club Co (Torres) operates a chain of health and fitness clubs. Its year end was 31 October 20X4. You are the audit manager and the year-end audit is due to commence shortly. The following matter has been brought to your attention. Torres's trade receivables have historically been low as most members pay monthly in advance. However during the year a number of companies have taken up group memberships at Torres and hence the receivables balance is now material. The audit senior has undertaken a receivables circularisation for the balances at the year end; however, there are a number who have not responded and a number of responses with differences.

Required

Describe substantive procedures you would perform to obtain sufficient and appropriate audit evidence in relation to Torres's trade receivables.   **(6 marks)**

(Total = 10 marks)

Question 5

You are the audit senior of Holtby & Co and are planning the audit of Walters Co (Walters) for the year ended 31 December 20X4. The company produces printers and has been a client of your firm for two years; your audit manager has already had a planning meeting with the finance director. He has provided you with the following notes of his meeting and financial statement extracts.

Walters's management were disappointed with the 20X3 results and so in 20X4 undertook a number of strategies to improve the trading results. This included the introduction of a generous sales-related bonus scheme for their salesmen and a high profile advertising campaign. In addition, as market conditions are difficult for their customers, they have extended the credit period given to them.

The finance director of Walters has reviewed the inventory valuation policy and has included additional overheads incurred this year as he considers them to be production related.

The finance director has calculated a few key ratios for Walters; the gross profit margin has increased from 44.4% to52.2% and receivables days have increased from 61 days to 71 days. He is happy with the 20X4 results and feels that they are a good reflection of the improved trading levels.

Financial statement extracts for year ended 31 December

	DRAFT 20X4 $m	ACTUAL 20X3 $m
Revenue	23.0	18.0
Cost of sales	(11.0)	(10.0)
Gross profit	12.0	8.0
Operating expenses	(7.5)	(4.0)
Profit before interest and taxation	4.5	4.0
Inventory	2.1	1.6
Receivables	4.5	3.0
Cash	–	2.3
Trade payables	1.6	1.2
Overdraft	0.9	–

Required

(a)   Using the information above:

    (i)   Calculate an additional **three** ratios, for **both** years, which would assist the audit senior in planning the audit. **(3 marks)**

    (ii)   From a review of the above information and the ratios calculated, describe **six** audit risks and explain the auditor's response to each risk in planning the audit of Walters Co. **(12 marks)**

(b)   Describe the procedures that the auditor of Walters Co should perform in assessing whether or not the company is a going concern. **(5 marks)**

(Total = 20 marks)

Question 6

Garcia International Co (Garcia) is a manufacturer of electrical equipment. It has factories across the country and its customer base includes retailers as well as individuals, to whom direct sales are made through their website. The company's year end is 30 September 20X4. You are an audit supervisor of Suarez & Co and are currently reviewing documentation of Garcia's internal control in preparation for the interim audit.

Garcia's website allows individuals to order goods directly, and full payment is taken in advance. Currently the website is not integrated into the inventory system and inventory levels are not checked at the time when orders are placed. Inventory is valued at the lower of cost and net realisable value.

Goods are dispatched via local couriers; however, they do not always record customer signatures as proof that the customer has received the goods. Over the past 12 months there have been customer complaints about the delay between sales orders and receipt of goods. Garcia has investigated these and found that, in each case, the sales order had been entered into the sales system correctly but was not forwarded to the dispatch department for fulfilling.

Garcia's retail customers undergo credit checks prior to being accepted and credit limits are set accordingly by sales ledger clerks. These customers place their orders through one of the sales team, who decides on sales discount levels.

Raw materials used in the manufacturing process are purchased from a wide range of suppliers. As a result of staff changes in the purchase ledger department, supplier statement reconciliations are no longer performed. Additionally, changes to supplier details in the purchase ledger master file can be undertaken by purchase ledger clerks as well as supervisors.

In the past six months Garcia has changed part of its manufacturing process and as a result some new equipment has been purchased, however, there are considerable levels of plant and equipment which are now surplus to requirement. Purchase requisitions for all new equipment have been authorised by production supervisors and little has been done to reduce the surplus of old equipment.

Required

(a)   In respect of the internal control of Garcia International Co:

    (i)   Identify and explain **six** deficiencies.

    (ii)   Recommend a control to address each of these deficiencies.

    (iii)   Describe a test of control Suarez & Co would perform to assess if each of these controls is operating effectively.

    Note: The total marks will be split equally between each part   **(18 marks)**

(b)   Describe substantive procedures Suarez & Co should perform at the year end to confirm plant and equipment additions.   **(2 marks)**

(Total = 20 marks)

Answers

DO NOT TURN THIS PAGE UNTIL YOU HAVE COMPLETED THE MOCK EXAM

A plan of attack

If this were the real Audit and Assurance exam and you had been told to turn over and begin, what would be going through your mind?

An important thing to say (while there is still time) is that it is vital to have a good breadth of knowledge of the syllabus because all the questions are compulsory. However, don't panic. Below we provide guidance on how to approach the exam.

Approaching the paper

Part A is a good place to start with. The short multiple choice questions will help to settle you in, before you tackle **Part B**.

In Part B, use your 15 minutes of reading time usefully to look through the questions, particularly Question 1, to get a feel for what is required and to become familiar with the question scenarios.

Since all the questions in this paper are compulsory, it is vital that you attempt them all to increase your chances of passing. For example, don't run over time on Question 2 and then find you don't have enough time for the remaining questions.

Question 1 is a 10-mark question focused on ethics and internal audit. In part (a), you are required to apply your knowledge of independence threats and safeguards to a short scenario. Make sure that your answers are relevant to the scenario, and note the use of the word 'explain' in both parts (i) and (ii). Simply copying out phrases from the scenario as your response to part (i) will not get you marks: you must explain why each fact constitutes a threat to independence. Part (b) is purely knowledge-based, and should therefore be easy if you are familiar with the syllabus. Look at the mark allocation: you will need to identify four differences to score four marks.

Question 2 is a 10-mark question focused on audit procedures. Part (a) is knowledge-based, so you should be able to gain your two marks here quite quickly and move on. In part (b), there is again a short scenario. Read the scenario carefully and let the scenario inform your answer. Make sure that you 'describe' the procedures as specifically as possible.

Question 3 is a 10-mark question focused on the finalisation and reporting stage of the audit. Part (a), for two marks, is essentially knowledge-based. In part (b), make sure you answer both parts of the question, supporting your response in each case with reasons. It is important to read the scenario carefully – for each of the clients, you must consider the numbers provided in determining whether the issue is material.

Question 4 starts with a straightforward requirement on financial statement assertions for four marks, but note the word 'explain' again. Part (b) contains another short scenario where you are required to describe relevant substantive procedures. For six marks, you should be looking to describe, in specific detail, six audit procedures. Make sure you relate them to the scenario.

Question 5 requires you to apply your knowledge of analytical procedures and going concern for twenty marks in a more extended scenario. For part (a), gaining three marks are available for calculating ratios for both years should not be difficult, but the longer requirement in (a)(ii) obliges you to demonstrate that you understand the ratios, using the ratios available to discuss audit risks. This may seem daunting at first, but stay calm and remember the components of each ratio to help you answer this question. Make sure you leave sufficient time to answer part (b), which is easier.

Question 6 presents a typical approach to examining internal controls: identifying and explaining the deficiencies, providing recommendations and describing relevant tests of control. Read the scenario carefully, highlighting all the deficiencies you want to discuss: for eighteen marks at three marks each, you need six deficiencies. A three-column tabular format would be a good idea here, if you can keep it neat. In part (b), you need two substantive procedures – this should be fairly easy, but remember to 'describe.'

Forget about it

And don't worry if you found the paper difficult. More than likely other candidates will too. If this were the real thing you would need to forget the exam the minute you left the exam hall and think about the next one. Or, if it is the last one, celebrate!

Section A

1   B   Option A describes Monetary Unit Sampling. Option C is an example of block selection.

2   D   Third party evidence is the most reliable, followed by auditor-generated evidence. Client-generated evidence is deemed to be less reliable – more so when the evidence is verbal (not written).

3   A   Option B is incorrect, as only external auditors would request bank confirmation letters. Options C and D are both incorrect, because carrying out such assignments would impair the internal auditors' independence.

4   D   Password protection and batch controls both relate to many applications at the same time. Therefore, they are both examples of general IT controls, not application controls.

5   D   Independence is not a principle of the ACCA *Code of Ethics and Conduct*. It refers to the specific position of objectivity required of certain professional functions, such as that of an external auditor. Professional scepticism is a questioning attitude that auditors must maintain throughout the course of an audit. Again, it is not a principle of the ACCA *Code*.

6   B   Test of controls are typically carried out during interim audits. The review aged receivables is done on the year end balance, and is therefore normally performed during a final audit.

7   A   Reasonable, positive assurance are given in an external audit, not on review engagements.

8   A   ISA 620 requires the external auditor to evaluate the work performed by an expert before relying on it.

9   B   An emphasis of matter paragraph represents a modified auditor's report, but the audit opinion is not qualified.

10   C   Increasing the materiality level would increase the risk of giving an inappropriate audit opinion further. Inherent risk is not within the auditor's control.

11   B   A material receivable balance becoming irrecoverable is an adjusting event, as it provides evidence of conditions that existed at the year-end date. The current year's financial statements must therefore be adjusted and the auditor's report reissued.

12   C   Human resource policies and practices is not a component of internal control in itself; it is an element of the control environment.

Section B

Question 1

Text references. Chapters 4 and 5.

Top tips. For 10 marks, this question contains a short scenario. Work through the scenario to identify specific ethical threats for part (a). A tabular format will help here.

Part (b) is knowledge-based, and should be straightforward provided that you are familiar with the work of the internal audit function.

Easy marks. Easy marks are available in part (b).

ACCA examiner's answer. The ACCA examiner's answer to this question can be found at the back of this Kit.

Marking scheme

		Marks
(a)	Up to 1 mark per well explained threat and up to 1 mark for method of managing risk, overall maximum of 6 marks.	
	Familiarity threat – long association of partner	
	Self-interest threat – son gained employment at client company	
	Self-interest threat – financial interest (shares) in client company	
	Self-review threat – audit firm providing internal audit service	
	Contingent fees	6
(b)	Up to 1 mark per well explained point	
	Objective	
	Whom they report to	
	Reports – publicly available or not	
	Scope of work	
	Appointed by	
	Independence of company	4
		10

(a) **Ethical threats and managing these risks**

(i) Ethical threat	(ii) Managing risk
The audit engagement partner has been associated with Hazard for six years.	Remy & Co should must implement a policy of monitoring the relationship between audit staff and audit clients on a regular basis, and rotating engagement partners off the audits of listed clients after five years.
This gives rise to a familiarity threat, as her long association with the audit client may impair her independence and her ability to exercise professional scepticism.	
As Hazard is a listed client, the engagement partner's long association is in non-compliance with the FRC's Ethical Standard 3, in which recommends audit engagement partners on the audits of listed clients to be rotated every five years.	Unless Hazard's audit committee believes this is necessary to maintain audit quality and the extension is disclosed to shareholders, an alternative audit engagement partner should be appointed for the audit of Hazard.

(i) Ethical threat	(ii) Managing risk
The fact that the audit engagement partner's son has accepted a job as a sales manager at Hazard could give rise to a further familiarity threat. A self-review/self-interest threat would also arise if he is involved in the preparation of the financial statements.	While it is unlikely that a sales manager would influence the financial statements, the familiarity threat needs to be considered and safeguards should be put in place. The fact that the audit engagement partner's son now works for the client may be an additional reason for the firm to consider appointing an alternative audit partner.
The audit engagement partner's son is entitled to receive shares in Hazard. The son represents an immediate family member of the audit partner. As such, the ACCA's *Code of Ethics and Conduct* prohibits him to hold the shares.	The engagement partner's son should either refuse his entitlement to the shares, or the engagement partner should be removed from the audit. Given the independence issues already discussed above, the second option would be preferred.
Remy & Co has been asked by Hazard to provide an internal audit service. This can give rise to a self-review threat. Where the internal audit team is expected to make decisions on the behalf of Hazard's management, this gives rise to a further management threat.	Remy & Co must ensure that there is a Chinese wall between the internal audit and external audit teams. The external audit team must not be involved in the internal audit service. It is also important to ensure that Hazard's management retain responsibility for overseeing the internal audit activities, and is in a position to make informed decisions. This needs to be clearly set out in the engagement letter for internal audit services.
Hazard has proposed that the external audit fee be based on the company's profit after tax. The proposed fee structure is based on the outcome of work performed and therefore represents a contingent fee. As such, they are prohibited by ACCA's *Code of Ethics and Conduct*.	Remy & Co must refuse the proposal for contingent fees and should explain to Hazard that the external audit fee must be based on the time spent and the level of work performed.

(b) **Differences between internal and external audit**

The main differences between internal and external audit are as follows:

	External audit	Internal audit
Objective	The main objective of the external auditor is to express an opinion on the truth and fairness of the financial statements.	The main objective of internal audit is to add value and improve a company's operations.
Reporting	External auditors report to the shareholders or members of the company. Auditor's reports are published with the financial statements and hence are publicly available.	Internal auditors normally report to management or those charged with governance, such as the audit committee. Internal audit reports are not publicly available and are only intended to be seen by the addressee of the report within the company.
Scope of work	The external auditor's work relates to the financial statements.	The internal auditor's work relates to the company's operations. The scope of work is wide and is determined by the requirements of management or those charged with governance.

	External audit	Internal audit
Relationship with company	External auditors are independent of the company and its management. They are usually appointed by the company's shareholders.	Internal auditors are appointed by management. They are usually employees of the company, although the function can also be outsourced.
Planning and collection of evidence	Planning carried out to achieve objective regarding truth and fairness of financial statements. Materiality level set during planning (may be amended during course of audit). External audit work is risk-based. Evidence collected using a variety of procedures per ISAs to obtain sufficient appropriate audit evidence.	Strategic long term planning carried out, to achieve objective of assignments, with no materiality level being set. Some audits may be procedural, rather than risk-based. Evidence mainly from interviewing staff and inspecting documents (ie not external).

Question 2

Text references. Chapters 1, 2, and 9.

Top tips. Overall this is a relatively straightforward knowledge based question. In part (a) you only need three rights and you must be careful not to confuse auditors' rights with auditors' duties.

In part (b), as long as you are familiar with control activities there are a number of different ones to select from, apart from control accounts which you are specifically asked not to include.

The limitations of audit in part (c) all stem from the fact not everything in the financial statements is checked and confirmed (eg only a sample of inventory costs is traced to invoice cost) and the auditor has to use judgement to provide only reasonable (and not absolute) assurance. In addition some items in the financial statements are based on estimates and can not be conclusively proven to be correct or incorrect.

Easy marks. As a knowledge based question there is an opportunity to score well on all parts of this question, however part (a) on auditors' rights is probably the most straightforward.

ACCA examiner's answer. The ACCA examiner's answer to this question can be found at the back of this Kit.

Marking scheme

Marks

(a) 1 mark for each definition

  Definition of test of control
  Definition of substantive test   2

(b) Up to 1 mark per relevant substantive procedure, maximum of 4 marks for
  each issue.

  Depreciation
  Review the reasonableness of the depreciation rates and compare to industry
  averages
  Review the capital expenditure budgets
  Review profits and losses on disposal for assets disposed of in year
  Recalculate the depreciation charge for a sample of assets
  Perform a proof in total calculation for the depreciation charged on the
  equipment

Review the disclosure of depreciation in the draft financial statements

Food poisoning
Review the correspondence from the customers
Send an enquiry to the lawyers as to the probability of the claim being
successful
Review board minutes
Review the post year-end period to assess whether any payments have been
made
Discuss with management as to whether they propose to include a contingent
liability disclosure
Obtain a written management representation $\underline{8}$
Review any disclosures made in the financial statements $\underline{\underline{10}}$

(a)   **Tests of control** are designed to the operating effectiveness of controls in preventing, detecting or correcting material misstatements.

     Substantive procedures are designed to obtain audit evidence to detect material misstatements at the assertion level. They include analytical procedures, tests of detail of transactions, balances and disclosures.

(b)   **Substantive procedures**

     Depreciation

- Review the reasonableness of the depreciation rates applied to the new leisure equipment by comparing them to industry averages.

- For a sample of leisure equipment in the non-current asset register, recalculate the depreciation charge to ascertain its arithmetical accuracy.

- Make enquiries of management and review the capital expenditure forecasts to determine whether there are any plans to replace any of the new leisure equipment. Any plans to replace the equipment within 10 years would indicate a shorter useful life than has been assumed.

- Perform a proof in total calculation for the depreciation charged on the equipment and discuss any significant fluctuations with management.

- Review gains and losses on the disposal of assets during the year, to assess the reasonableness of the depreciation policies.

- Review the disclosure of the depreciation charges and policies in the draft financial statements.

     Food poisoning

- Assess whether Balotelli has a present obligation as a result of a past event by reviewing correspondence from the customers.

- With the client's permission, contact the company's lawyers to obtain their opinion on the probability of a successful lawsuit in writing.

- Make enquiries of Balotelli's management and review board minutes to determine whether the directors believe that the claim will be successful.

- Review the post year-end payments for evidence of any payments made to the claimants.

- Inquire of management whether a contingent liability will be disclosed in the financial statements, consider the reasonableness of this.

- Obtain a written representation confirming management's assessment of the likely outcome of the lawsuit, and the appropriateness of accounting treatment adopted for the damages.

- Review the adequacy of any disclosures made in the financial statements.

Question 3

Marking scheme

		Marks
(a)	Up to 1 mark per well described point	
	Auditor should accumulate misstatements	
	Consider if audit strategy/plan should be revised	
	Assess if uncorrected misstatements material	
	Communicate to those charged with governance, request changes	
	If refused then assess impact on audit report	
	Request written representation	2
(b)	Up to 1 mark for each issue and 1 mark for the impact on the auditor's report	
	Discussion of issue	
	Calculation of materiality	
	Type of auditor's report modification required	
	Impact on auditor's report	8
		10

(a)   **Misstatements**

ISA 450 *Evaluation of misstatements identified during the audit* states that the auditor has a responsibility to accumulate misstatements identified during the audit, other than those that are clearly trivial.

If the accumulated misstatements approach materiality, or if there are indications that other misstatements may exist that, when accumulated, could be material, the auditor must consider whether the overall audit strategy and audit plan need to be revised.

All the accumulated misstatements should be communicated to the appropriate level of management on a timely basis. The auditor must request management to correct the misstatements. If management refuses to correct some or all of the misstatements, the auditor must obtain an understanding of the reasons for not making the corrections, and take these into account when determining whether the financial statements are free from material misstatement.

The auditor should determine whether uncorrected misstatements are material, both individually and in aggregate.

A written representation should be requested from management to confirm whether they believe that the effects of the unadjusted misstatements are immaterial, both individually and in aggregate, to the financial statements as a whole.

(b)   **Auditor's reports**

Czech Co

Research expenditure of $2.1m has been capitalised within intangible assets. This is incorrect, as IAS 38 *Intangible Assets* requires research expenditure to be expensed to profit or loss.

The error is material as it represents 8% of profit before tax ($2.1m/$26.3m). Management should adjust the financial statements by reversing it from the research expenditure from intangibles and debiting the amount to profit or loss.

If management refuse to make the adjustment, the auditor's report will need to be modified. As the error is material but not pervasive, a qualified opinion would seem appropriate.

The basis of opinion section would need to include a paragraph explaining the misstatement and its effect on the financial statements. The opinion paragraph would be qualified 'except for'.

Dawson Co

Two months' worth of wages records have been lost. The auditors should seek alternative audit procedures to audit the wages and salaries account. If no alternative audit procedures are possible, the loss of data would constitute a limitation on scope.

Wages and salaries for the two month period represents 11% of profit before tax (£1.1m/£10m). Therefore, if alternative audit procedures are not possible, the limitation on scope would be material.

The auditors will need to modify the auditor's report on the basis that they are unable to obtain sufficient appropriate evidence in relation to a material amount in the financial statements. As the two months' salary and wages are not pervasive, a qualified opinion would seem appropriate.

The basis of opinion section would require an explanation of the limitation on scope in relation to the lack of sufficient appropriate evidence in relation to wages and salaries. The opinion paragraph would be qualified 'except for'.

Question 4

Text references. Chapters 8 and 14.

Top tips. Part (a), a knowledge-based requirement focusing on financial statement assertions, should be very straightforward if you are familiar with the topic.

In part (b), a short scenario has been provided. Your knowledge of the receivables circularisation process should ensure that you gain most of the marks in this question – just ensure that the procedures you suggest are appropriate to the scenario.

Easy marks. Part (a) provides easy marks.

ACCA examiner's answer. The ACCA examiner's answer to this question can be found at the back of this Kit.

Marking scheme

		Marks
(a)	Up to 1 mark per assertion, ½ mark for stating assertion and ½ mark for explanation.	
	Existence – explanation	
	Rights and obligations – explanation	
	Completeness – explanation	
	Valuation and allocation – explanation	4

For non-responses arrange to send a follow up circularisation
With the client's permission, telephone the customer and ask for a response
For remaining non-responses, undertake alternative procedures to confirm receivables
For responses with differences, identify any disputed amounts, identify whether these relate to timing differences or whether there are possible errors in the records
Cash in transit should be vouched to post year-end cash receipts in the cash book
Review receivables ledger to identify any possible mis-postings
Disputed balances, discuss with management whether a write down is necessary

$$\frac{6}{10}$$

(a) **Financial statement assertions relevant to account balances at the period end**

(i) **Existence**: Assets, liabilities and equity interests exist.

(ii) **Rights and obligations**: The entity holds or controls the rights to assets, and liabilities are the obligations of the entity.

(iii) **Completeness**: All assets, liabilities and equity interests that should have been recorded have been recorded.

(iv) **Valuation and allocation**: Assets, liabilities and equity interests are included in the financial statements at appropriate amounts and any resulting valuation or allocation adjustments are appropriately recorded.

(b) **Substantive procedures in relation to receivables**

- With the client's permission, the audit team should follow up the non-replies with a second request.

- If the customer does not respond to the follow-up within two or three weeks, then with the client's permission, we should phone the customer to request a written response.

- Alternative audit procedures should be carried out on any items still outstanding. These could include:

    (i) Checking receipt of cash after-date by reviewing post year-end bank statements

    (ii) Verifying valid purchase orders, if any

    (iii) Examining the account to see if the balance represents specific outstanding membership fees

    (iv) Make enquiries of relevant management in respect of fees remaining unpaid after subsequent ones have been paid

    (v) Observing whether the balance on the account is growing, and if so, find out why by discussions with management.

- All balance disagreements must be followed up to determine whether the disputed amounts relate to timing differences or whether there are possible errors in the records of Torres. We will need to assess their effect on total receivables evaluated.

- We should agree any differences due to timing, such as cash in transit, to the post year-end cash receipts in the cash book.

- Further substantive work should be performed on disputed amounts and potential errors by the client. The receivables ledger should be reviewed to identify any possible errors in posting.

- Where balances have been disputed by the customer, we should discuss with client management whether a write-down would be required.

- For balances agreed by the client, all that is required would be to ensure that the debt does appear to be collectable, by reviewing cash received after-date or considering the adequacy of any allowance made for a long outstanding amount.

Question 5

Text references. Chapters 7 and 18.

Top tips. In part (a), make sure you read the requirement carefully and calculate the required number of ratios. The risks and the auditor's response to each risk need to be clearly explained: the ratios must be linked to the audit risks, and specific audit procedures should be stated. Again, you will not be awarded marks for vague responses such as 'check cut-off is appropriate.'

Easy marks. Part (a)(i) should not pose a problem, and part (b) also contains easy marks.

ACCA examiner's answer. The ACCA examiner's answer to this question can be found at the back of this Kit.

Marking scheme

			Marks
(a)	(i)	½ mark per ratio calculation per year	
		Operating margin	
		Inventory days	
		Payable days	
		Current ratio	
		Quick ratio	3
	(ii)	Up to 1 mark per well explained audit risk, maximum of 6 marks for risks and up to 1 mark per audit response, maximum of 6 marks for responses	
		Management manipulation of results	
		Sales cut-off	
		Revenue growth	
		Misclassification of costs between cost of sales and operating	
		Inventory valuation	
		Receivables valuation	
		Going concern risk	12
(b)		1 mark per well explained point – If the procedure does not clearly explain how this will help the auditor to consider going concern then a ½ mark only should be awarded:	
		Review cash flow forecasts	
		Review bank agreements, breach of key ratios	
		Review post year-end sales and order book	
		Review suppliers correspondence	
		Inquire of lawyers for any litigation	
		Subsequent events	
		Board minutes	
		Management accounts	
		Consider additional disclosures under IAS 1	
		Written representation	5
			20

(a) (i) **Additional ratios**

		20X4	20X3
Operating margin	PBT/Revenue	4.5/23 = 19.6%	4/18 = 22.2%
Inventory days	Inventories/COS × 365 days	2.1/11 × 365 = 70 days	1.6/10 × 365 = 58 days
Payable days	Payables/COS × 365 days	1.6/11 × 365 = 53 days	1.2/10 × 365 = 44 days
Current ratio	Current assets/Current liabilities	6.6/2.5 = 2.6	6.9/1.2 = 5.8
Quick ratio	(Current assets – inventories)/Current liabilities	(6.6 – 2.1)/2.5 = 1.8	(6.9 – 1.6)/1.2 = 4.4

Note: Only three ratios were required.

(ii) **Audit risks and responses:**

Audit risk	Audit response
Management were disappointed with the 20X3 results and are under pressure to improve the trading results in 20X4. There is a risk that management have a greater incentive to manipulate the results by adopting a more aggressive approach in relation to accounting estimates (ie provisions).	The audit team will need to remain alert to the risk of creative accounting throughout the audit. It is important that they exercise professional scepticism and evaluate any assumptions made by management in auditing accounting estimates. Current year balances should be compared to the prior year to highlight any unusual trends.
A generous sales-related bonus scheme has been introduced for the company's salesmen. This increases the risk of misstatements arising from sales cut-off as the sales staff seek to maximise their bonus.	Increased sales cut-off testing will be required. Post year-end sales returns should be reviewed, as they may provide evidence of incorrect cut-off.
Revenue has grown by 28%, while cost of sales has only increased by 10%. The gross profit margin has increased significantly. Although the bonus scheme and the advertising campaign may explain the growth in revenue, the fact that the cost of sales has seen a corresponding increase need to be investigated.	Inquiries should be made of management regarding the reason why cost of sales has not increased in line with sales. Substantive procedures should be performed on an increased sample of costs, with an aim to identify any costs omitted or misclassified.

Audit risk	Audit response
Although the gross margin has increased from 44.4% to 52.2%, the operating margin has decreased from 22.2% to 19.6%. This trend is unusual. While the bonus scheme and advertising campaign could account for some of the increase in operating expenses, there is a possibility that costs may have been misclassified from cost of sales to operating expenses.	The classification of costs between cost of sales and operating expenses will be compared with the prior year to ensure consistency. A detailed breakdown of operating expenses and cost of sales should be reviewed for evidence of misclassification. The main components of costs of sales and operating expenses should be identified and compared to the prior year. Any unusual trends (for example, significant costs in the prior year not present in the current year, and vice versa) should be discussed with management.
The inventory valuation policy has been changed, with additional overheads to be included within inventory. Inventory days have increased from 58 to 70 days. There is a risk that inventory is overvalued.	The change in the inventory valuation policy should be discussed with management. The additional overheads included should be reviewed, to confirm that they are related to production. Detailed cost and net realisable value testing should be performed and the aged inventory report should be reviewed to assess whether a write-down is required.
Receivables days have increased from 61 to 71 days and management have extended the credit period given to customers. This leads to an increased risk of unrecoverable receivables.	Extended post year-end cash receipts testing and a review of the aged receivables ledger should be performed to assess the need for any write-offs or provision.
The current ratio and quick ratio have both decreased significantly. In addition, the company's positive cash balance of $2.3m in 20X3 has become an overdraft of $0.9m. Taken together with the growth in revenue and the increase in operating expenses, this may indicate overtrading. A going concern risk should be considered.	Detailed going concern testing to be performed during the audit. Cash flow forecasts covering at least twelve months from the year end should be reviewed, and the assumptions discussed with management.

(b)   **Going concern procedures**

- Obtain Walters' cash flow forecast and review the cash payments and receipts. Assess the assumptions for reasonableness and discuss the findings with management to understand if the company will have sufficient cash flows.

- Review any current agreements with the bank to determine whether any covenants in relation to the overdraft have been breached.

- Read minutes of the meetings of shareholders, the board of directors and important committees for reference to financing difficulties and for evidence of any future financing plans.

- Review the company's post year-end sales and order book to assess the levels of trade. Evaluate whether the revenue figures in the cash flow forecast are reasonable.

- Review post year-end correspondence with suppliers to identify any restriction in credit that may not be reflected in the cash flow forecasts.

- Inquire of the lawyers of Walters as to the existence of litigation and claims.

- Perform audit tests in relation to subsequent events to identify any items that might indicate or mitigate the risk of going concern not being appropriate.

- Review post year end management accounts to assess if it is in line with cash flow forecast.

- Consider whether any additional disclosures as required by IAS 1 *Presentation of Financial Statements* in relation to material uncertainties over going concern should be made in the financial statements.

- Confirm the existence, legality and enforceability of arrangements to provide or maintain financial support with related and third parties and assess the financial ability of such parties to provide additional funds.

- Consider Walter's position concerning any unfulfilled customer orders.

- Obtain a written representation confirming the director's view that Walters is a going concern.

Note: Only five procedures were required.

Question 6

> **Text references.** Chapters 9, 10 and 12.
>
> **Top tips.** The majority of marks in this question comes in part (a), requiring you to identify internal control deficiencies, recommend controls for the deficiencies and describe tests of controls. It is important that you answer the question in this order: notably, part (a)(ii) leads directly to part (a)(iii). Some of the deficiencies should be fairly obvious, but remember that it is not enough to simply identify them. You must explain what impact the deficiencies will have on the company's business and/or the financial statements.
>
> Part (b) should be straightforward in comparison – it is, effectively, a knowledge-based requirement. Make sure that you keep an eye on the time so you leave sufficient time to get the easy marks.
>
> **Easy marks.** Easy marks are available in part (b).
>
> **ACCA examiner's answer.** The ACCA examiner's answer to this question can be found at the back of this Kit.

Marking scheme

	Marks
(a) Up to 1 mark per deficiency, up to 1 mark per well explained control and up to 1 mark for each well described test of control, maximum of 6 marks for deficiencies, maximum of 6 marks for controls and maximum of 6 marks for tests of control.	
Website not integrated into inventory system	
Customer signatures	
Unfulfilled sales orders	
Customer credit limits	
Sales discounts	
Supplier statement reconciliations	
Purchase ledger master file	
Surplus plant and equipment	
Authorisation of capital expenditure	18

(b) Up to 1 mark per substantive procedure
Additions
Cast list of additions and agree to non-current asset register
Vouch cost to recent supplier invoice
Agree addition to a supplier invoice in the name of Garcia to confirm rights and obligations
Review additions and confirm capital expenditure items rather than repairs and maintenance
Review board minutes to ensure authorised by the board
Physically verify them on the factory floor to confirm existence

$\frac{2}{20}$

(a) **Internal control**

(i) Deficiency	(ii) Control	(iii) Test of control
The website is not integrated into inventory system and inventory levels are not checked when the order is placed. Customer orders may be accepted when the goods are not in inventory. This can then lead to loss of customer goodwill and consequently, sales.	The website should be updated to include an interface to the inventory system. Inventory levels should be checked and the order should only be processed if adequate inventory is held.	Test data could be used to attempt to place orders via the website for items which are not currently held in inventory. The order should be flagged as being out of stock.
For goods dispatched by local couriers, customer signatures are not always obtained. It would be possible for customers to claim that they have not received their goods, when it had in fact been delivered. Goods may thus be dispatched twice, resulting in duplicated costs.	Garcia should ensure that all local couriers obtain customer signatures as proof of delivery, possibly by stipulating that payment will not be made for any deliveries not evidenced by signatures.	Select a sample of dispatches by couriers and inspect the proof of delivery for customer signatures.
The fulfilment of orders have been delayed due to the sales order not being forwarded to the dispatch department. This can lead to a loss of customer goodwill, loss of revenue through unhappy customers refusing to pay, and ultimately damage Garcia's reputation.	The sales system should be updated, so that it automatically forwards each order placed to the dispatch department. Once goods are dispatched they should be matched to sales orders and flagged as fulfilled. Any sales orders not fulfilled within a predetermined period should be flagged for investigation by a responsible official.	Trace a sample of orders received to records within the dispatch department. Review a sample of goods dispatch notes for evidence that they have been matched to the relevant sales orders. Review the report of outstanding sales orders and discuss with the responsible official the actions he/she has taken with regards to them. Select a sample of sales orders and compare the date of order to the goods dispatch date to ascertain whether this is within the acceptable predetermined period.

(i) Deficiency	(ii) Control	(iii) Test of control
Customer credit limits are set by sales ledger clerks. It is unclear whether the sales ledger clerks have sufficient experience to determine the appropriate credit limits. They may set limits too high, leading to irrecoverable debts, or too low, leading to a loss of sales.	The credit limits should be set by a senior member of the sales ledger department. These limits should be regularly reviewed by a responsible official.	For a sample of new customers accepted in the year, review the authorisation of the credit limit for evidence that it has been approved by a responsible official. Using test data, attempt to set the credit limit for fictitious new customer from a sales ledger clerk's computer.
Sales discounts are set by the sales team. Sales staff may apply large discounts with an aim to maximise sales volume. This leads to loss of revenue.	A limit should be applied to the level of discounts sales staff are authorised to grant. Any sales discounts above these limits should be authorised by appropriate management. A regular review of sales discount levels should be undertaken by the management, and this review should be evidenced.	Discuss with members of the sales team the process for setting sales discounts. Review the sales discount report for evidence of review by the appropriate level of management.
Supplier statement reconciliations are no longer performed. This may result in errors in the recording of purchases and payables not being identified in a timely manner, leading to understated or overstated cost of sales.	Supplier statement reconciliations should be performed on a monthly basis. These should be reviewed by a responsible official.	Review the file of reconciliations to confirm whether they have been performed on a regular basis. Inspect the reconciliations for evidence that they have been reviewed by a responsible official.
Changes to supplier details in the purchase ledger master file can be undertaken by purchase ledger clerks. Key supplier data may be accidentally amended or fictitious suppliers may be set up fraudulently. This leads to potential interests and penalties for late payment, damage to the company's reputation, and loss of revenue through fraud.	Only purchase ledger supervisors should have the authority to amend master file data. This should be controlled via passwords. Any changes to master file data should be reviewed by a responsible official on a regular basis and the review should be evidenced.	Using test data, attempt to access the master file data and make an amendment in order to establish whether the attempt would be rejected by the system. Review a report of master data changes and review the authority of those making amendments.

(i) Deficiency	(ii) Control	(iii) Test of control
Garcia has considerable levels of surplus plant and equipment. This gives rise to the risk of theft. Surplus plant and equipment clutter the factory floors, leading to possible operational inefficiencies. From the perspective of the financial statements, there is also a risk that the value of the surplus plant and equipment have not been written off, leading to the overstatement of non-current assets.	Senior factory personnel should carry out regular reviews of the plant and equipment, to identify any surplus equipment. All surplus equipment identified should be flagged up to responsible management, to determine whether it is to be scrapped, disposed of or put to alternative use. Surplus plant and equipment should be reported to the Finance department, so that their value is written off or impaired as appropriate in the financial statements. The capital expenditure process should include determining and recording the treatment of the equipment being replaced, with the authorisation of a responsible official.	Observe the review process by senior factory personnel and identify the treatment of any old equipment. Inspect a report of surplus equipment for evidence that it has been reviewed by management. Inspect a list of surplus plant and equipment forwarded to the Finance department and review it against the non-current asset register for evidence that the appropriate write-off or impairment have been recorded. Review processed capital expenditure forms for evidence of the treatment of replaced equipment being determined and authorised.
Purchase requisitions are authorised by production supervisors. Production supervisors do not have the required experience or objectivity to authorise purchase requisitions. This may lead to unsuitable or poor quality equipment being purchased, leading to operational inefficiencies, or equipment being purchased at too high a price.	Capital expenditure authorisation levels should be established. Production supervisors should only be able to authorise low value items. High value items should require authorisation by the board.	Review a sample of authorised capital requisition forms for evidence that the appropriate level of management has authorised them.

Note: Only six deficiencies, with one control and one test of control each, is required.

(b) **Substantive procedures on plant and equipment additions**

- Obtain a breakdown of additions and cast to confirm arithmetical accuracy.

- Agree the items on the breakdown to the non-current asset register to confirm completeness.

- For a sample of additions, agree the cost to the supplier invoice to confirm valuation.

- Agree the addition of plant and equipment to supplier invoices to verify that they are in the name of the company, in order to confirm rights and obligations.

- Review the list of additions to identify any expenditure relating to repairs and maintenance rather than of a capital nature.

- Review the board minutes to for evidence of significant capital expenditure purchases being authorised by the board.

- For a sample of additions recorded in the non-current asset register, physically verify them on the factory floor to confirm existence.

ACCA examiner's answers:
Specimen paper

Section A

Question	Answer	See Note
1	B	1
2	D	2
3	A	3
4	D	4
5	D	5
6	B	6
7	A	7
8	A	8
9	B	9
10	C	10
11	B	11
12	C	12

Notes:

1   The descriptions are correct but relate to alternative sampling methods. A is monetary unit sampling and C is block selection method of sampling.

2   Audit evidence is often described in terms of the degree of reliability. Third party as most reliable followed by auditor generated, company documentation and least reliable verbal evidence.

3   B is incorrect as external auditors alone would request bank confirmation letters, this is not something they would expect internal audit to perform. C is incorrect since internal audit would not retain their independence if they implemented accounting packages; their role is to review how the package operates once implemented. D is incorrect as internal audit should not help prepare financial statements.

4   The controls given at 1 and 4 are incorrect as they are general IT controls that relate to many applications and support the overall IT system.

5   Professional skepticism refers to the state of mind the auditor should maintain whilst conducting the audit. With regards to independence there is an overriding requirement to be independent rather than it being a specific principle.

6   Tests of control are typically undertaken at the interim audit stage. Reviewing the aged receivables would be undertaken on the year end balances and hence at the final audit.

7   Statements 2 and 4 are incorrect as they relate to the level of assurance provided by an external audit rather than a review engagement.

8   The auditor can only rely on the work undertaken by an expert if this has been evaluated.

9   Statement 2 is incorrect since an emphasis of matter does not result in a qualified opinion. Statement 3 is incorrect as an emphasis of matter results in the report being modified but the opinion is unqualified.

10 It is inappropriate to adjust materiality levels to determine audit risk. Inherent risk is not under the auditor's control. Audit risk depends on inherent risk, control risk and detection risk. Only detection risk can be changed by the auditor to reduce audit risk.

11 A is incorrect as even though the financial statements have been signed the auditor has an on-going responsibility. C is incorrect as this is an adjusting event and so must be adjusted for as opposed to just disclosed. D is incorrect as the event requires adjustment in the current year financial statements even though it occurred in year ending 31 October 2015.

12 Human resource policies and practices is an element of a control environment which is itself a component of internal control.

1 (a) Ethical threats and managing these risks

Ethical threat	Managing risk
A familiarity threat arises where an engagement partner is associated with a client for a long period of time.	Remy & Co should monitor the relationship between engagement and client staff, and should consider rotating engagement partners when a long association has occurred.
Remy's partner has been involved in the audit of Hazard Co for six years and hence may not maintain her professional skepticism and objectivity.	In addition, ACCA's *Code of Ethics and Conduct* recommends that engagement partners rotate off an audit after five years for listed and public interest entities. Therefore consideration should be given to appointing an alternative audit partner.
The engagement partner's son has accepted a job as a sales manager at Hazard Co.	It is unlikely that as a sales manager the son would be in a position to influence the financial statements and hence additional safeguards would not be necessary.
This could represent a self-interest/familiarity threat if the son was involved in the financial statement process.	If it was believed that additional safeguards were required then consideration should be given to appointing an alternative audit partner.
A self-interest threat can arise when an audit firm has a financial interest in the company.	In this case as holding shares is prohibited by ACCA's *Code of Ethics and Conduct* then either the son should refuse the shares or more likely the engagement partner will need to be removed from the audit.
In this case the partner's son will receive shares as part of his remuneration. As the son is an immediate family member of the partner then if he holds the shares it will be as if the partner holds these shares, and this is prohibited.	
A self-review threat can arise when an audit firm provides an internal audit service to an audit client.	Remy & Co should have appropriate safeguards by ensuring the audit team is not involved in the internal audit service and also ensuring client staff remain responsible for the internal audit activities and approve all the work done.
Fees based on the outcome or results of work performed are known as contingent fees and are prohibited by ACCA's *Code of Ethics and Conduct*.	Remy & Co will not be able to accept contingent fees and should communicate to Hazard that the external audit fee needs to be based on the time spent and level of work performed
Hence Hazard's request that 20% of the external audit fee is based on profit after tax would represent a contingent fee.	

(b) Differences between internal and external audit

External Audit	Internal Audit
Objective	
The main objective of the external auditor is to express an opinion on the truth and fairness of the financial statements.	The main objective of internal audit is to improve a company's operations, by reviewing the efficiency and effectiveness of the company's internal controls.
Reporting	
External auditors report to the shareholders or members of the company. External audit reports are contained within the financial statements and hence are publicly available.	Internal auditors normally report to management or those charged with governance. Internal audit reports are not publicly available and are only intended to be seen by the addressee of the report. The reports are normally provided to the board of directors and those charged with governance such as the audit committee.
Scope of work	
The external auditor's work is limited to verifying the truth and fairness of the financial statements of the company.	The internal auditor can have a wide scope of work and it is determined by the requirements of management or those charged with governance. Commonly internal audit focus on the company's internal control environment, but any other area of a company's operations can be reviewed.
Relationship with company	
External auditors are appointed by the company's shareholders. They are independent of the company.	Internal auditors are appointed by management. As internal auditors are normally employees of the company they lack independence. However, the internal audit department can be outsourced and this can increase their independence.

2 (a) Tests of control and substantive procedures

Tests of control test the operating effectiveness of controls in preventing, detecting or correcting material misstatements.

Substantive procedures are aimed at detecting material misstatements at the assertion level. They include tests of detail of transactions, balances, disclosures and substantive analytical procedures

(b) Substantive procedures

Depreciation
- Review the reasonableness of the depreciation rates applied to the new leisure facilities and compare to industry averages.
- Review the capital expenditure budgets for the next few years to assess whether there are any plans to replace any of the new leisure equipment, as this would indicate that the useful life is less than 10 years.
- Review profits and losses on disposal of assets disposed of in the year, to assess the reasonableness of the depreciation policies.
- Select a sample of leisure equipment and recalculate the depreciation charge to ensure that the non-current asset register is correct.
- Perform a proof in total calculation for the depreciation charged on the equipment, discuss with management if significant fluctuations arise.
- Review the disclosure of the depreciation charges and policies in the draft financial statements.

Food poisoning
- Review the correspondence from the customers claiming food poisoning to assess whether Balotelli has a present obligation as a result of a past event.
- With the client's permission, send an enquiry letter to the lawyers of Balotelli to obtain their view as to the probability of the claim being successful.
- Review board minutes to understand whether the directors believe that the claim will be successful or not.
- Review the post year-end period to assess whether any payments have been made to any of the claimants.
- Discuss with management as to whether they propose to include a contingent liability disclosure or not, consider the reasonableness of this.
- Obtain a written management representation confirming management's view that the lawsuit is unlikely to be successful and hence no provision is required.
- Review the adequacy of any disclosures made in the financial statements

3 (a) Misstatements

As per ISA 450 *Evaluation of Misstatements Identified during the Audit* the auditor has a responsibility to accumulate misstatements which arise over the course of the audit unless they are very small amounts.

Identified misstatements should be considered during the course of the audit to assess whether the audit strategy and plan should be revised.

The auditor should determine whether uncorrected misstatements are material in aggregate or individually.

All misstatements should be communicated to those charged with governance on a timely basis and the auditor should request that they make necessary amendments. If this request is refused then the auditor should consider the potential impact on their audit report.

A written representation should be requested from management to confirm that unadjusted misstatements are immaterial.

(b) Audit reports

Czech Co
Czech Co has incurred research expenditure of $2·1m and development expenditure of $3·2m and this has all been capitalised within intangible assets. This is contrary to IAS 38 *Intangible Assets*, as research expenditure should be expensed to profit or loss account rather than capitalised.

The error is material as it represents 8% of profit before tax (2·1m/26·3m) and hence management should adjust the financial statements by removing the research expenditure from intangibles and charging it to profit or loss account instead.

If management refuse to amend this error then the audit report will need to be modified. As management has not complied with IAS 38 and the error is material but not pervasive then a qualified opinion would be necessary.

The basis of opinion paragraph would need to include a paragraph explaining the material misstatement in relation to the provision of depreciation on land and the effect on the financial statements. The opinion paragraph would be qualified 'except for'.

Dawson Co
Dawson Co's wages program has been corrupted leading to a loss of payroll data for a period of two months. The auditors should attempt to verify payroll in an alternative manner. If they are unable to do this then payroll for the whole year would not have been verified.

Wages and salaries for the two month period represents 11% of profit before tax (1·1m/10m) and therefore is a material balance for which audit evidence has not been available.

The auditors will need to modify the audit report as they are unable to obtain sufficient appropriate evidence in relation to a material, but not pervasive, element of wages and salaries and therefore a qualified opinion will be required.

The basis of opinion section will be amended to explain the limitation in relation to the lack of evidence over two months of payroll records. The opinion paragraph will be qualified 'except for'.

4 (a) Financial statement assertions for balances at the period end.

(i) Existence – Assets, liabilities and equity interests exist.
(ii) Rights and obligations – The entity holds or controls the rights to assets, and liabilities are the obligations of the entity.
(iii) Completeness – All assets, liabilities and equity interests that should have been recorded have been recorded.
(iv) Valuation and allocation – Assets, liabilities and equity interests are included in the financial statements at appropriate amounts and any resulting valuation or allocation adjustments are appropriately recorded.

(b) Substantive procedures receivables

- For non-responses, with the client's permission, the team should arrange to send a follow up circularisation.
- If the customer does not respond to the follow up, then with the client's permission, the senior should telephone and ask whether they are able to respond in writing to the circularisation request.
- If there are still non-responses, then the senior should undertake alternative procedures to confirm receivables.
- For responses with differences, the senior should identify any disputed amounts, and identify whether these relate to timing differences or whether there are possible errors in the records of Torres.
- Any differences due to timing, such as cash in transit, should be agreed to post year-end cash receipts in the cash book.
- The receivables ledger should be reviewed to identify any possible mis-postings as this could be a reason for a response with a difference.
- If any balances have been flagged as disputed by the receivable, then these should be discussed with management to identify whether a write down is necessary.

5 (a) (i) Ratios to assist the audit supervisor in planning the audit:

	2014	2013
Operating margin	4·5/23 = 19·6%	4/18 = 22·2%
Inventory days	2·1/11 * 365 = 70 days	1·6/10 * 365 = 58 days
Payable days	1·6/11 * 365 = 53 days	1·2/10 * 365 = 44 days
Current ratio	6·6/2·5 = 2·6	6·9/1·2 = 5·8
Quick ratio	(6·6 – 2·1)/2·5 = 1·8	(6·9 – 1·6)/1·2 = 4·4

(ii) Audit risks and responses:

Audit risk	Audit response
Management were disappointed with 2013 results and hence undertook strategies to improve the 2014 trading results. There is a risk that management might feel under pressure to manipulate the results through the judgements taken or through the use of provisions.	Throughout the audit the team will need to be alert to this risk. They will need to carefully review judgemental decisions and compare treatment against prior years.
A generous sales-related bonus scheme has been introduced in the year, this may lead to sales cut-off errors with employees aiming to maximise their current year bonus.	Increased sales cut-off testing will be performed along with a review of post year-end sales returns as they may indicate cut-off errors.
Revenue has grown by 28% in the year however, cost of sales has only increased by 10%. This increase in sales may be due to the bonus scheme and the advertising however, this does not explain the increase in gross margin. There is a risk that sales may be overstated.	During the audit a detailed breakdown of sales will be obtained, discussed with management and tested in order to understand the sales increase.
Gross margin has increased from 44·4% to 52·2%. Operating margin has decreased from 22·2% to 19·6%. This movement in gross margin is significant and there is a risk that costs may have been omitted or included in operating expenses rather than cost of sales. There has been a significant increase in operating expenses which may be due to the bonus and the advertising campaign but could be related to the misclassification of costs.	The classification of costs between cost of sales and operating expenses will be compared with the prior year to ensure consistency.

Audit risk	Audit response
The finance director has made a change to the inventory valuation in the year with additional overheads being included. In addition inventory days have increased from 58 to 70 days. There is a risk that inventory is overvalued.	The change in the inventory policy will be discussed with management and a review performed of the additional overheads included to ensure that these are of a production nature.
	Detailed cost and net realisable value testing to be performed and the aged inventory report to be reviewed to assess whether inventory requires writing down.
Receivables days have increased from 61 to 71 days and management have extended the credit period given to customers. This leads to an increased risk of recoverability of receivables.	Extended post year-end cash receipts testing and a review of the aged receivables ledger to be performed to assess valuation.
The current and quick ratios have decreased from 5·8 to 2·6 and 4·4 to 1·8 respectively. In addition, the cash balances have decreased significantly over the year.	Detailed going concern testing to be performed during the audit and discussed with management to ensure that the going concern basis is reasonable.
Although all ratios are above the minimum levels, this is still a significant decrease and along with the increase of sales could be evidence of overtrading which could result in going concern difficulties.	

(b)   Going concern procedures

- Obtain Walters' cash flow forecast and review the cash in and out flows. Assess the assumptions for reasonableness and discuss the findings with management to understand if the company will have sufficient cash flows.
- Review any current agreements with the bank to determine whether any key ratios have been breached with regards to the bank overdraft.
- Review the company's post year-end sales and order book to assess the levels of trade and if the revenue figures in the cash flow forecast are reasonable.
- Review post year end correspondence with suppliers to identify whether any restriction in credit have arisen, and if so ensure that the cash flow forecast reflects an immediate payment for trade payables.
- Inquire of the lawyers of Walters as to the existence of litigation and claims; if any exist then consider their materiality and impact on the going concern basis.
- Perform audit tests in relation to subsequent events to identify any items that might indicate or mitigate the risk of going concern not being appropriate.
- Review the post year end board minutes to identify any other issues that might indicate financial difficulties for the company.
- Review post year end management accounts to assess if in line with cash flow forecast.
- Consider whether any additional disclosures as required by IAS 1 *Presentation of Financial Statements* in relation to material uncertainties over going concern should be made in the financial statements.
- Obtain a written representation confirming the director's view that Walters is a going concern.

6   (a)   Garcia International's (Garcia) internal control

Deficiency	Control	Test of control
Currently the website is not integrated into inventory system. This can result in Garcia accepting customer orders when they do not have the goods in inventory. This can cause them to lose sales and customer goodwill.	The website should be updated to include an interface into the inventory system; this should check inventory levels and only process orders if adequate inventory is held. If inventory is out of stock, this should appear on the website with an approximate waiting time.	Test data could be used to attempt to process orders via the website for items which are not currently held in inventory. The orders should be flagged as being out of stock and indicate an approximate waiting time.
For goods despatched by local couriers, customer signatures are not always obtained. This can lead to customers falsely claiming that they have not received their goods. Garcia would not be able to prove that they had in fact despatched the goods and may result in goods being despatched twice.	Garcia should remind all local couriers that customer signatures must be obtained as proof of delivery and payment will not be made for any despatches with missing signatures.	Select a sample of despatches by couriers and ask Garcia for proof of delivery by viewing customer signatures.

Deficiency	Control	Test of control
There have been a number of situations where the sales orders have not been fulfilled in a timely manner. This can lead to a loss of customer goodwill and if it persists will damage the reputation of Garcia as a reliable supplier.	Once goods are despatched they should be matched to sales orders and flagged as fulfilled. The system should automatically flag any outstanding sales orders past a predetermined period, such as five days. This report should be reviewed by a responsible official.	Review the report of outstanding sales orders. If significant, discuss with a responsible official to understand why there is still a significant time period between sales order and despatch date. Select a sample of sales orders and compare the date of order to the goods despatch date to ascertain whether this is within the acceptable predetermined period.
Customer credit limits are set by sales ledger clerks. Sales ledger clerks are not sufficiently senior and so may set limits too high, leading to irrecoverable debts, or too low, leading to a loss of sales.	Credit limits should be set by a senior member of the sales ledger department and not by sales ledger clerks. These limits should be regularly reviewed by a responsible official.	For a sample of new customers accepted in the year, review the authorisation of the credit limit, and ensure that this was performed by a responsible official. Enquire of sales ledger clerks as to who can set credit limits.
Sales discounts are set by Garcia's sales team. In order to boost their sales, members of the sales team may set the discounts too high, leading to a loss of revenue.	All members of the sales team should be given authority to grant sales discounts up to a set limit. Any sales discounts above these limits should be authorised by sales area managers or the sales director. Regular review of sales discount levels should be undertaken by the sales director, and this review should be evidenced.	Discuss with members of the sales team the process for setting sales discounts. Review the sales discount report for evidence of review by the sales director.
Supplier statement reconciliations are no longer performed. This may result in errors in the recording of purchases and payables not being identified in a timely manner.	Supplier statement reconciliations should be performed on a monthly basis for all suppliers and these should be reviewed by a responsible official.	Review the file of reconciliations to ensure that they are being performed on a regular basis and that they have been reviewed by a responsible official
Changes to supplier details in the purchase ledger master file can be undertaken by purchase ledger clerks. This could lead to key supplier data being accidently amended or fictious suppliers being set up, which can increase the risk of fraud.	Only purchase ledger supervisors should have the authority to make changes to master file data. This should be controlled via passwords. Regular review of any changes to master file data by a responsible official and this review should be evidenced.	Request a purchase ledger clerk to attempt to access the master file and to make an amendment, the system should not allow this. Review a report of master data changes and review the authority of those making amendments.
Garcia has considerable levels of surplus plant and equipment. Surplus unused plant is at risk of theft. In addition, if the surplus plant is not disposed of then the company could lose sundry income.	Regular review of the plant and equipment on the factory floor by senior factory personnel to identify any old or surplus equipment. As part of the capital expenditure process there should be a requirement to confirm the treatment of the equipment being replaced.	Observe the review process by senior factory personnel, identifying the treatment of any old equipment. Review processed capital expenditure forms to ascertain if the treatment of replaced equipment is stated.
Purchase requisitions are authorised by production supervisors. Production supervisors are not sufficiently independent or senior to authorise capital expenditure.	Capital expenditure authorisation levels to be established. Production supervisors should only be able to authorise low value items, any high value items should be authorised by the board.	Review a sample of authorised capital expenditure forms and identify if the correct signatory has authorised them.

(b) **Substantive procedures additions**

- Obtain a breakdown of additions, cast the list and agree to the non-current asset register to confirm completeness of plant and equipment (P&E).
- Select a sample of additions and agree cost to supplier invoice to confirm valuation.
- Verify rights and obligations by agreeing the addition of plant and equipment to a supplier invoice in the name of Garcia.
- Review the list of additions and confirm that they relate to capital expenditure items rather than repairs and maintenance.
- Review board minutes to ensure that significant capital expenditure purchases have been authorised by the board.
- For a sample of additions recorded in P&E, physically verify them on the factory floor to confirm existence.

Marks

Section A

Questions 1–12 multiple choice 20

Total marks 20

Section B

1 **(a)** Up to 1 mark per well explained threat and up to 1 mark for method of managing risk, overall maximum of 6 marks.

Familiarity threat – long association of partner
Self-interest threat – son gained employment at client company
Self-interest threat – financial interest (shares) in client company
Self-review threat – audit firm providing internal audit service
Contingent fees 6

(b) Up to 1 mark per well explained point

Objective
Whom they report to
Reports – publicly available or not
Scope of work
Appointed by
Independence of company 4

 10

2 **(a)** 1 mark for each definition

Definition of test of control
Definition of substantive test 2

(b) Up to 1 mark per relevant substantive procedure, maximum of 4 marks for each issue.

Depreciation
Review the reasonableness of the depreciation rates and compare to industry averages
Review the capital expenditure budgets
Review profits and losses on disposal for assets disposed of in year
Recalculate the depreciation charge for a sample of assets
Perform a proof in total calculation for the depreciation charged on the equipment
Review the disclosure of depreciation in the draft financial statements

Food poisoning
Review the correspondence from the customers
Send an enquiry to the lawyers as to the probability of the claim being successful
Review board minutes
Review the post year-end period to assess whether any payments have been made
Discuss with management as to whether they propose to include a contingent liability disclosure
Obtain a written management representation
Review any disclosures made in the financial statements 8

 10

3 **(a)** Up to 1 mark per well described point

Auditor should accumulate misstatements
Consider if audit strategy/plan should be revised
Assess if uncorrected misstatements material
Communicate to those charged with governance, request changes
If refused then assess impact on audit report
Request written representation

2

(b) Up to 1 mark per valid point, overall maximum of 4 marks per client issue.

Discussion of issue
Calculation of materiality
Type of audit report modification required
Impact on audit report

$$\frac{8}{\underline{\underline{10}}}$$

4 **(a)** Up to 1 mark per assertion, ½ mark for stating assertion and ½ mark for explanation.

Existence – explanation
Rights and obligations – explanation
Completeness – explanation
Valuation and allocation – explanation

4

(b) Up to 1 mark per relevant substantive procedure

For non-responses arrange to send a follow up circularisation
With the client's permission, telephone the customer and ask for a response
For remaining non-responses, undertake alternative procedures to confirm receivables
For responses with differences, identify any disputed amounts, identify whether these relate to timing differences or whether there are possible errors in the records
Cash in transit should be vouched to post year-end cash receipts in the cash book
Review receivables ledger to identify any possible mis-postings
Disputed balances, discuss with management whether a write down is necessary

$$\frac{6}{\underline{\underline{10}}}$$

5 **(a)** **(i)** ½ mark per ratio calculation per year

Operating margin
Inventory days
Payable days
Current ratio
Quick ratio   3

(ii) Up to 1 mark per well explained audit risk, maximum of 6 marks for risks and up to 1 mark
per audit response, maximum of 6 marks for responses

Management manipulation of results
Sales cut-off
Revenue growth
Misclassification of costs between cost of sales and operating
Inventory valuation
Receivables valuation
Going concern risk   12

(b) 1 mark per well explained point – If the procedure does not clearly explain how this will help
the auditor to consider going concern then a ½ mark only should be awarded:

Review cash flow forecasts
Review bank agreements, breach of key ratios
Review post year-end sales and order book
Review suppliers correspondence
Inquire of lawyers for any litigation
Subsequent events
Board minutes
Management accounts
Consider additional disclosures under IAS 1
Written representation   5
                                                                                   ___
                                                                                   20
                                                                                   ═══

6 **(a)** Up to 1 mark per deficiency, up to 1 mark per well explained control and up to 1 mark
for each well described test of control, maximum of 6 marks for deficiencies, maximum of 6 marks
for controls and maximum of 6 marks for tests of control.

Website not integrated into inventory system
Customer signatures
Unfulfilled sales orders
Customer credit limits
Sales discounts
Supplier statement reconciliations
Purchase ledger master file
Surplus plant and equipment
Authorisation of capital expenditure   18

(b) Up to 1 mark per substantive procedure

Additions
Cast list of additions and agree to non-current asset register
Vouch cost to recent supplier invoice
Agree addition to a supplier invoice in the name of Garcia to confirm rights and obligations
Review additions and confirm capital expenditure items rather than repairs and maintenance
Review board minutes to ensure authorised by the board
Physically verify them on the factory floor to confirm existence   2
                                                                                   ___
                                                                                   20
                                                                                   ═══

Review Form – Paper F8 Audit and Assurance (06/14)

Name: _____   Address: _____

_____

_____

How have you used this Kit?
(Tick one box only)

☐ Home study (book only)

☐ On a course: college _____

☐ With 'correspondence' package

☐ Other _____

Why did you decide to purchase this Kit?
(Tick one box only)

☐ Have used the complementary Study text

☐ Have used other BPP products in the past

☐ Recommendation by friend/colleague

☐ Recommendation by a lecturer at college

☐ Saw advertising

☐ Other _____

During the past six months do you recall seeing/receiving any of the following?
(Tick as many boxes as are relevant)

☐ Our advertisement in *Student Accountant*

☐ Our advertisement in *Pass*

☐ Our advertisement in *PQ*

☐ Our brochure with a letter through the post

☐ Our website www.bpp.com

Which (if any) aspects of our advertising do you find useful?
(Tick as many boxes as are relevant)

☐ Prices and publication dates of new editions

☐ Information on product content

☐ Facility to order books off-the-page

☐ None of the above

Which BPP products have you used?

Text	☐	Passcards	☐	Home Study Package	☐
Kit	☑	i-Pass	☐		

Your ratings, comments and suggestions would be appreciated on the following areas.

	Very useful	Useful	Not useful
Passing F8	☐	☐	☐
Questions	☐	☐	☐
Top Tips etc in answers	☐	☐	☐
Content and structure of answers	☐	☐	☐
Mock exam answers	☐	☐	☐

Overall opinion of this Kit   Excellent ☐   Good ☐   Adequate ☐   Poor ☐

Do you intend to continue using BPP products?   Yes ☐   No ☐

The BPP author of this edition can be e-mailed at: Yen-peiChen@bpp.com

Please return this form to: Pippa Riley, ACCA Publishing Manager, BPP Learning Media Ltd, FREEPOST, London, W12 8AA

Review Form (continued)

TELL US WHAT YOU THINK

Please note any further comments and suggestions/errors below.